THE COMPANION TO THE
BOOK OF COMMON WORSHIP

THE COMPANION TO THE
BOOK OF COMMON WORSHIP

PETER C. BOWER

EDITOR

Geneva Press
Louisville, Kentucky

Office of Theology and Worship
Presbyterian Church (U.S.A.)

Book design by Sharon Adams
Cover design by Night & Day Design

First edition
Published by Geneva Press
Louisville, Kentucky

This book is printed on acid-free paper that meets the American National Standards Institute Z39.48 standard. ♾

PRINTED IN THE UNITED STATES OF AMERICA

05 06 07 08 09 10 11 12 — 10 9 8 7 6 5 4 3 2

Library of Congress Cataloging-in-Publication Data

The companion to the Book of common worship / Peter C. Bower, editor.— 1st ed.
    p. cm.
    Includes bibliographical references and index.
    ISBN 0-664-50232-6 (alk. paper)
        1. Presbyterian Church (U.S.A.). Book of common worship (1993) 2. Presbyterian Church (U.S.A.)—Liturgy. I. Bower, Peter C. II. Presbyterian Church (U.S.A.). Book of common worship (1993)

    BX8969.5 .C66 2003
    264'.05137—dc21
                                                                    2002192711

In memory of *Virginia Maud*
an undaunted leader

Remember *"the words of King Lemuel.*
An oracle that his mother taught him:
Speak out for those who cannot speak,
for the rights of all the destitute.
Speak out, judge righteously,
defend the rights of the poor and needy."
PROVERBS 31:1, 8–9

Contents

Preface

Purpose

In general, this *Companion* presents a variety of possibilities for enacting services in the *Book of Common Worship* (BCW) and, thereby, stimulates the imagination of worship planners and leaders in accomplishing their various tasks. In particular, this *Companion* provides background information regarding the services, comments on the rubrics accompanying texts, and suggests some ways to use the texts and, occasionally, abridge or augment them for particular situations.

Role of the Directory for Worship

To accomplish the above undertakings, this *Companion* necessarily alludes to standards and emphases of the Directory for Worship which, since its inception in 1644, has highly influenced worship of English-speaking, Reformed churches. Moreover, since 1788, the Directory has served as American Presbyterians' constitutional basis for worship. The Directory is far more than suggestive; it is part of and, therefore, on a par with the rest of the *Book of Order*. From a practical standpoint, the Directory functions as an applied theology handbook that prescribes and describes how things "shall, should, can, or may" be done in worship. The Directory, therefore, though void of liturgical text, serves as a primary planning resource for Presbyterians.

Rather than quote "chapter and verse" from what is, in effect, a *semper reformanda* ("always being reformed") Directory, this *Companion* draws on the Directory's ongoing standards that

> present norms for the ordering and conduct of worship
> call for authentic and appropriate language

invite expression of the faith through music and other arts
encourage experiences of the fullness of psalmody through singing
rejoice in the diversity of Presbyterian congregations particularly in
    enculturating various elements of worship
mandate appraisal of the fruit of worship in a congregation's life and work
encourage continuing reform of worship
charge people to enact their ministries in their daily life

In short, a constant question before Presbyterian congregations is, In what ways does our corporate worship embody the directives set forth in the Directory for Worship?

The *Book of Common Worship* (1993)

A manifestation of the Directory for Worship is the *Book of Common Worship* (1993), which is the basic liturgical resource on which many worship planners draw and to which congregations are referred. Worship celebrations of the church's long tradition, therefore, appropriate the BCW's time-honored fourfold structure or *ordo*:

Gathering—The Word—The Eucharist or Thanksgiving—Sending

These encompass a sequence of elements: call to worship, hymn of praise, confession and pardon, prayer for illumination, reading and preaching of the Word of God, affirmation of faith, prayers of the people, Lord's Supper or prayer of thanksgiving, hymn, charge and blessing. Every service is basically the same (in structure), yet every service is different (in mood, focus, content, and so on), because critical to every congregation's worship is *how* such elements are celebrated for each service. Moreover, the elements of worship vary in texture according to occasion and time and place, both "in season and out of season" (for example, Christmas, Epiphany, Ash Wednesday, Good Friday, Easter, Pentecost, Sundays in Ordinary Time).

Resources for Planning Worship

To plan a service, one needs a Bible, Directory for Worship, *Book of Common Worship*, and a hymnal such as *The Presbyterian Hymnal: Hymns, Psalms, and Spiritual Songs*; *Come, Let Us Worship: The Korean-English Presbyterian Hymnal and Service Book*; or *El Himnario Presbiteriano*. Other valuable resources include the *Book of Occasional Services*, *Handbook to the Revised Common Lectionary*, *Holy Is the Lord: Music for Lord's Day Worship*, and *The Psalter: Psalms and Canticles for Singing*.

Those Who Shared in the Creation of This Book

Given that this *Companion* has drawn on all of the Supplemental Liturgical Resources (SLRs) published by the denomination during the years 1984–92, this present work represents the labor of a multitude of saints. To produce those resources, servants of Christ's church met in seven different task forces for several years shaping the form and substance of the church's liturgies which, several years later, developed into the actual services in the *Book of Common Worship*. The names of these devoted contributors who paved the way for the *Book of Common Worship* are printed in that work (pp. 10–11).

The task of appropriating those past Resources and blending them with current scholarship and practice so as to create this *Companion* was embraced by four persons who served as principal writers for the following areas:

> Mary Beth Anton, Chaplain of Trinity School, Midland, Texas—Pastoral Liturgies and Book of Occasional Services
>
> Peter C. Bower, Interim Pastor of Appleby Manor Memorial Presbyterian Church, Ford City, Pennsylvania—Resources for the Liturgical Year, Daily Prayer, Singing the Psalms, Study Guide, Glossary of Terms, For Further Reading, and Index
>
> Ron Byars, Professor of Preaching and Worship, Union Theological Seminary–Presbyterian School of Christian Education, Richmond, Virginia—The Service for the Lord's Day and Prayers for Various Occasions
>
> Brant S. Copeland, Pastor of First Presbyterian Church, Tallahassee, Florida—Baptism and the Reaffirmation of the Baptismal Covenant, Christian Marriage, and The Funeral: A Service of Witness to the Resurrection

These four persons were ably assisted by denominational staff whose oversight of the project as well as personal commitment to its realization was constant from start to finish. Their insights and encouragement are especially treasured:

> Alan Barthel, Executive Director of the Presbyterian Association of Musicians (PAM), Presbyterian Church (U.S.A.), Louisville, Kentucky

Martha Moore-Keish, Associate for Worship, Office of Theology and
Worship, Presbyterian Church (U.S.A.), Louisville, Kentucky

Joseph D. Small, III, Associate Director of Theology, Worship, and Discipleship, and Coordinator of the Office of Theology and Worship,
Presbyterian Church (U.S.A.), Louisville, Kentucky

Special gratitude is due to Horace T. Allen Jr. and Harold M. Daniels, both
former leaders of the Office of Worship in the Presbyterian Church (U.S.A.),
who painstakingly examined every page and paragraph and sentence, offering numerous helpful suggestions. Their singular gifts and experiences have
greatly enhanced this resource for the church's use. Words cannot express the
depth of appreciation for both of these saints, but all of us are blessed by their
dedication.

Many, many thanks are extended to reviewers who freely gave of themselves to critique portions or even entire drafts of the text. Their additions,
corrections, and deletions were both *needed* and *welcomed*. Reviewers
include: John E. Ambrose, Rubén P. Armendáriz, David B. Batchelder, Donald A. Busarow, Carole J. Carter, Melva Wilson Costen, Carol Doran, Donald
P. Ely, Arlo D. Duba, Patricia M. Fort, Paul H. Galbreath, Jane Parker Huber,
W. Ben Lane, Cynthia Weeks Logan, Adele Dieckmann McKee, John W.
Neely Jr., David C. Partington, Richard M. Peek, David H. Pfleiderer, Jane
Rogers Vann, John Weaver, Mina Belle Packer Wichmann (also proofreader
par excellence), Janet Wolfe, Helen Wright, and the Worship Committee of
Pebble Hill Presbyterian Church, Dewitt, New York.

All of the above saints spiritedly embrace the following words written
nearly a century ago in the *Book of Common Worship*, 1906:

Concerning the Use of This Book: None of the Forms of Service in this
Book are intended to be in any sense obligatory; but where a given Order
is voluntarily used it will promote unity. (BCW 1906 vii)

Amen!

Soli Deo gloria ("To God alone be glory!")

—PETER C. BOWER

Abbreviations

BCW	*Book of Common Worship.* Louisville, Ky.: Westminster/John Knox Press, 1993.
BCW-DP	*Book of Common Worship: Daily Prayer.* Louisville, Ky.: Westminster/John Knox Press, 1993 (pocket-sized edition of the *Daily Prayer* section of BCW 489–837, 1049–1097).
BOS	*Book of Occasional Services.* Louisville, Ky.: Westminster John Knox Press, 1999.
HB	*The Hymnbook.* Philadelphia: Presbyterian Church in the U.S.A., 1955.
HBRCL	Peter C. Bower. *Handbook to the Revised Common Lectionary.* Louisville, Ky.: Westminster John Knox Press, 1996.
HL	*Holy Is the Lord: Music for Lord's Day Worship.* Louisville, Ky.: Geneva Press, 2002.
HP	*El Himnario Presbiteriano.* Louisville, Ky.: Westminster John Knox Press, 1999.
K-E	*Come, Let Us Worship: The Korean-English Presbyterian Hymnal and Service Book.* Louisville, Ky.: Geneva Press, 2001.
PH	*The Presbyterian Hymnal: Hymns, Psalms, and Spiritual Songs.* Louisville, Ky.: Westminster/John Knox Press, 1990.
PS	*The Psalter: Psalms and Canticles for Singing.* Louisville, Ky.: Westminster/John Knox Press, 1993.
RCL	Consultation on Common Texts. *The Revised Common Lectionary: Includes Complete List of Lectures for Years A, B, and*

C. Nashville: Abingdon Press, 1992 [included in BCW, 1035–1048].

WB   *The Worshipbook—Services and Hymns.* Philadelphia: Westminster Press, 1972.

Preparation for Worship

(BCW 15)

Prayers for Use before Worship (BCW 17–30)

Nearly a century ago, the *Book of Common Worship*, 1906, succinctly yet profoundly described the essence of not only this section but the entire book:

> We have searched the Holy Scriptures, the usage of the Reformed Churches, and the devotional treasures of early Christianity, for the most noble, clear, and loving expressions of the Spirit of Praise and Prayer; and we have added to these ancient and venerable forms and models, such others as might serve, under the guidance of the Spirit, to give a voice to the present needs, the urgent desires, and the vital hopes of the Church living in these latter days and in the freedom of this Republic. (BCW, 1906, iv–v)

The same can be affirmed regarding liturgical texts throughout the *Book of Common Worship*, 1993. Prayers for Illumination (BCW 60, 90–91), Prayers of the People (BCW 99–124), Great Thanksgivings (BCW 126–156), Prayers for Various Occasions (BCW 785–837; BCW-DP 391–455), and other prayers represent ancient and venerable forms and models and also give voice to the present needs, urgent desires, and vital hopes of the church.

The Service for the Lord's Day

(BCW 31–161)

Convictions about Worship

Worship: Why? Who? What? When? Where? How?

Building Up the Church

An elderly woman, having lost her hearing and most of her sight, continued to request a ride to church every Sunday morning. A friend asked her why she bothered, since she could not hear the sermon, the prayers, or the music. She replied, "I go to show whose side I'm on." Sometimes it is as simple as that. In a society that is home to people of both no faith and faith in every sort of deity, we stand to be counted, at least once a week, among the congregation of Jesus Christ.

Sometimes we go to church in search of something. We hope for a word of encouragement, a word of healing, some support for our flagging hope. Or we go because our faith is at high tide, and we are brimful of the need to celebrate that faith. We go to be supported by others, or to be a support—and, then, in another week or two, when things have shifted, we trade roles. A case can be made for going to worship to support and encourage one another and to "build up" the church (1 Cor. 14:4).

Some of us learned why we worship from the answer we recited in the Shorter Catechism: the very purpose of human life is "to glorify God," and "enjoy" God, forever (First Question and Answer, Westminster Shorter Catechism, *The Book of Confessions*; Louisville, Ky: Office of the General Assembly, Presbyterian Church (U.S.A.)). There is something about glorifying and enjoying God that makes it require company, a community, sharing an act. According to the witness of the New Testament, to be a Christian is to be part of a people: "For in the one Spirit we were all baptized into one body" (1 Cor. 12:13). Christianity simply is not a solitary affair. And, "because there is one bread, we who are many are one body" (1 Cor. 10:17).

2

Royal Priesthood

Whatever personal reasons lead us to church, another reason, whether we are aware of it or not, invites our attention. God has called the church to assemble and offer its service as a corporate priesthood. Scripture puts it like this: "But you are a chosen race, a royal priesthood, a holy nation, God's own people." Chosen for what? God's own people for what? "In order that you may proclaim the mighty acts of him who called you out of darkness into his marvelous light" (1 Pet. 2:9).

As a "royal priesthood," we gather weekly to worship God and to pray not only for ourselves but for this entire broken world. We pray for those who believe and for those who do not believe; for those who pray for themselves and for those who do not or cannot pray; for those who love God and for those who are indifferent or even hostile to God. We pray for our enemies, for those who have set themselves against us and against Christ's church (Matt. 5:43–48). That is our priesthood, in which the Christian church persists in the mission first given to the descendants of Abraham and Sarah: to be a blessing to "all the families of the earth" (Gen. 12:3).

Forming Worship

Whenever and wherever a people gather for worship, the service has some form. Even a silent Quaker meeting has a form. The most informal prayer meeting has a form. The question is not whether there ought to be some form to a gathering for worship, but how to shape that form. The worship of the earliest Christian churches formed around two poles: the reading and preaching of Scripture, *and* the covenant meal, the Lord's Supper.

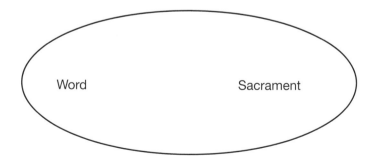

Luke's story of the travelers on the road to Emmaus displays both foci of Word and Meal when it says that, as Jesus sat at table with the travelers, "their eyes were opened, and they recognized him" (Luke 24:31); and, as they reflected on their conversation with him on the road, they asked each other, "Were not our hearts burning within us while he was talking to us on the road, while he was opening the scriptures to us?" (Luke 24:32). However much gatherings for worship may have varied from place to place, it seems evident that they were shaped by a form that embraced both Word and Meal. For instance, all four Gospels, notes liturgical scholar Gordon Lathrop, "follow exactly the same shape: baptism, narratives, meal and passion, resurrection, and sending. Such a list is, in exactly this order, recognizable to us as the emerging shape of the Christian Sunday meeting."[1]

Gospel-Shaped Worship

Twentieth-century scholarship undertaken by representatives from all branches of the church has led us to rediscover how Christian worship began to form a relatively consistent shape at least as early as the second century. That shape resembles that of the Gospels, as Lathrop has noted: Scripture and preaching, Lord's Supper with its commemoration of Jesus Christ crucified and risen, and sending out the congregation with a charge and a blessing. As a result of these scholarly investigations, a remarkable ecumenical consensus has formed among students of worship in many denominations and confessional bodies. Whereas some Roman Catholics have complained that their services are becoming "too Protestant," and some Protestants have complained that their services are becoming "too Catholic," the truth is that both have been influenced more by the results of twentieth-century research than by directly imitating one another. Both the current Directory for Worship of the Presbyterian Church (U.S.A.) and "The Service for the Lord's Day" are fruits of the ecumenical consensus. While they exhibit some of the characteristic marks of the Reformed tradition, they also recover a heritage from a time before a Catholic/Protestant divide could even be conceived. This heritage is rightfully ours just as it is also the legacy of other Christians.

Our Prayer and the Prayer of the Whole Church

An instructive paragraph in the Preface to the *Book of Common Worship* states:

Local pastoral concerns will determine the appropriate way to use the texts and services.

Some will find strength and a sense of unity in the prayers shared in common with the whole church and so will use the liturgical texts as they appear in this book.

> Others will find it more appropriate to adapt the prayers for use in a particular setting.
>
> Others will be prompted to follow the structure of the services as they are outlined and use the texts as models for a free and spontaneous style of prayer.

> Each of these styles is appropriate within the provisions of the directories for worship, and it is the intent of the *Book of Common Worship* to provide the necessary resources (BCW 6–7).

That is to say, employ the *Book of Common Worship* in the way most appropriate to a particular congregation. In shaping the liturgy, however, take seriously the *Book of Common Worship*'s *ordo* (Latin, "order," "structure," "shape," "pattern") concerning the overall structure of services as well as the form and function of specific texts, such as the eucharistic prayer. The *Book of Common Worship* does not provide liturgical recipes among a smorgasbord of worship cookbooks from which to select a morsel or two for a service, but it presents a resource of texts that fit within and give expression to a certain shape or *ordo*. Texts drawn from a worship resource pressing a particular agenda or from well-intentioned but inconsistent "homemade" materials may lead to confusing, tenuous, or contradictory content or tone. A well-crafted, poetic eucharistic prayer may miss the mark of a eucharistic prayer's form and function. In short, in planning liturgy, take care both to know and to give expression to the *ordo* that the *Book of Common Worship* embraces. Knowing the *ordo* (both the ordering and the nature of particular prayers) of the liturgy both precedes and permits freedom. In this manner, the *Book of Common Worship* can offer an instrument to help plan a liturgy in which worshipers can recognize the prayer of the whole ecumenical church while at the same time know themselves to be worshipers in and of a particular time and place.

No congregation is expected to conform slavishly to the *Book of Common Worship*, indifferent to the local context, as though the purpose of the liturgy is to speak and sing all the right words in the proper order. On the other hand, attempts to reinvent the liturgy every week almost certainly will lead to failure and disappointment. What is critical is the shape of the liturgy, both its order and its texts. Grounded in this liturgical bedrock, the *Book of Common Worship* invites each of the above styles: using the texts and services "as is," adapting the liturgical texts for use in a particular setting, or following the structure of the services and using the texts as models.

Convictions about the Service for the Lord's Day

"The Service for the Lord's Day," reflecting both the ecumenical consensus and the experience of the Reformed churches, is based on several convictions.

1. Liturgy and Life

Use-less Worship

From a certain point of view, worship is use-less. It may be, of course, that people have found worship to be useful. It may have been useful in reducing stress; in developing closer ties to family members, friends, and even strangers; in introducing us to a deeper appreciation for Scripture and to the doctrines of the church; in making contacts that proved to be fruitful personally or professionally. However useful worship may have proved to be, the church does not gather to worship as a strategy to achieve some useful end.

Worship is, first and foremost, a people's meeting with the God who has taken the initiative to gather that people. It is a gathering intended for no other purpose than to offer our praise, our thanksgiving, and our lament, while trusting the Spirit to bring us into the presence of the risen Christ. It is not adult education. It is not socializing. It is not therapy. It is not networking. It is not a rally to support programs or causes. For all practical purposes, it is and ought to be use-less. (See Marva J. Dawn, *A Royal "Waste" of Time: The Splendor of Worshiping God and Being Church for the World*; Grand Rapids: Wm. B. Eerdmans Publishing Co., 1999.)

Worship Shapes Particular Kinds of Communities

Nevertheless, to be use-less does not mean to be divorced from life. The consistent discipline of the church's worship shapes a particular kind of community. The Word of grace read and preached shapes graciousness in a congregation. Praying for others shapes people's sensibilities and can also shape the ways a congregation orients itself to each other and to the world. Offering praise and thanksgiving shapes the living of a thanks-filled life. Invited to gather at the Lord's Table, we glimpse the reconciled humanity that God intends, where people come from all points of the compass in peace (Luke 13:29), none dominating the others, all made strong in the same nourishing Spirit. If this image of a reconciled humanity is to be made clear, our worship will be at its best when it includes children—particularly baptized children, who become members of the church at baptism, as the Reformed tradition has affirmed, and American Directories for Worship have testified. Moreover, "membership in the faithful assembly knows no criteria of age, weight, education, or intelligence quotient—only those of faithful initiation into Christ in his Church."[2]

The Directory for Worship realizes this conviction underlying "The Service for the Lord's Day" when it links worship with God's call to the church to respond to God's grace by joining Christ's mission in the world. As Jesus washed the disciples' feet in the upper room, in worship he also equips us with towel and basin to extend our ministry to those weary from their journey. When we leave worship, we leave with both a charge and a blessing. The last words of the liturgy send us out to where we will once again find "all the families of the earth," whatever their description or condition (for example, "fainthearted," "weak," "suffering," "all people," BCW 78). With them, for them, and among them, we continue to exercise the "royal priesthood" expressed in our worship.

2. Word and Sacrament

Calvin said it: "A Defect"

A second conviction is that Word and Sacrament form the normative pattern for the weekly assembly. The New Testament strongly suggests that the church's worship as early as the first generation centered on the Word and the Meal (for example, Acts 2:42; 20:7, and Luke 24), and it was certainly true in the postapostolic age immediately following. For several centuries, church congregations enjoyed a vigorous worship life centered in the weekly assembly around the Word read and preached, and the Lord's Supper. In the medieval period, for all practical purposes, Word and Sacrament became separated. During Sunday mass, congregations seldom heard a sermon; in fact, they devolved into silent onlookers as the priest took for his own even that part of the service—eucharist—which had belonged to the people. In due time, the typical layperson actually received Communion only once a year, at Easter, in order to meet the requirement of church law and, then, received it reluctantly and often anxiously.

Against this background, John Calvin, the Protestant reformer who, more than anyone else, influenced the evolution of Reformed theology, advocated a return to the practice of the early church. Calvin believed that the normative form of the weekly Christian service included both the Word read and preached *and* the Lord's Supper. He propounded, therefore, that the whole gathered church community join actively in the service and receive Communion every Sunday.

The City Council of Geneva overruled Calvin for various reasons. Perhaps they feared that it would be too traumatic to increase the frequency of communing from once a year to fifty-two times a year. Or, possibly, the Council was motivated by the fact that at that time both Roman Catholics and the new Protestants conceived the Lord's Supper in rather somber terms, centering on Jesus' death, while minimizing the resurrection. Whatever the Council's rationale or fears, though the scholarship of the Protestant reformers was formidable, it had not led them to see beyond medieval prejudices to discover the powerful sense of the presence of the risen Lord in the eucharists of the early centuries, which had made every Lord's Day a celebratory occasion. The City Council, as a result, limited observance of the Lord's Supper to only four times a year. Calvin described this as "a defect" because it failed to follow "the example of the apostles."[3]

Why Should We Try to Mend This Defect?

As early as 1961, Directories for Worship began to affirm the appropriateness of celebrating the Lord's Supper as often as each Lord's Day, and celebrating regularly and frequently enough to recognize the Lord's Supper as integral to "The Service for the Lord's Day." The *Book of Common Worship* comments that "the Eucharist is increasingly recognized as central to the liturgy on the Lord's Day, and there is a steady movement toward weekly celebration" (BCW 7). Word and Sacrament are interdependent. The Word amplifies the Sacrament, and the Sacrament magnifies the Word. Word and Sacrament become more fully themselves when each stands next to the other. Recovery of Word and Sacrament as the normative weekly service is not simply a matter of imitating early Christian practice or trying to mend a "defect" for Calvin's sake. Word and Sacrament each contribute to the integrity of the other. The Word reduces the possibility that the Sacrament will turn into superstition or an empty observance; and the Sacrament reduces the possibility that the Word will mutate into moralizing or unenacted words.

3. Freedom and Form

The Superstructure of the Service: the Ordo

The basic structure of the service is crucial. The ancient form of Lord's Day worship (sometimes called the *ordo* of worship) includes

1. actions of gathering the congregation, followed by
2. the ministry of the Word—the reading and preaching of Scripture, then
3. the actions around the Communion Table, followed by
4. sending out the people into the world with a blessing.

The *Book of Common Worship* represents that fourfold *ordo* (Latin, "order," "structure," "shape," "pattern") in its outline of "The Service for the Lord's Day" as Gathering, The Word, The Eucharist, Sending (BCW 46–47).

The movement of the *ordo*, echoing the structure of the four Gospels (see p. 14), rehearses in word *and* action the very substance of the Christian faith. Because worship is the church's basic faith-forming experience, it shapes our theology and molds our discipleship. Given such import, it is wise to take the *ordo*—the structure of the liturgy—with great seriousness. The *ordo* is a gift to be received.

A Dependable Superstructure Does Not Require Uniformity

To structure worship within the framework of the *ordo* does not require or imply uniformity. Within that framework exists a great deal of room for variation. Churches familiar with and committed to the fourfold *ordo* have discovered that its structure provides them a framework that keeps their liturgical innovation from straying too far off-track. In actual practice, "The Service for the Lord's Day" is an enacted event that makes use of words, although it is more than words. The printed text serves as a sort of schematic from which the event itself will be created. Form and freedom complement each other.

Freedom within the basic architectural form of the service not only involves a variety of texts but also permits considerable variation in the action of the liturgy. Two services, each structured according to the fourfold *ordo*, may look and feel very different depending on the arrangement or dressing of the liturgical space, the instrumental and vocal music, the ratio of silence to speech, and the physical movements of both the assembly and worship leaders. Within the *ordo* resides great freedom to contextualize the liturgy to local, ethnic, and generational cultures.

4. People and Participation

An Active Role

Another conviction, both Reformed and ecumenical, affirms the people's role as active participants in the liturgy. (See especially Craig Douglas Erickson, *Participating in Worship: History, Theory, and Practice*; Louisville, Ky.: Westminster/John Knox Press, 1989.) Though the actions of hearing and seeing are integral to worship, a congregation is not merely an audience. Worship leaders have been compared to choreographers, choral conductors, or prompters who lead the assembly in the exercise of their corporate priesthood.

Danish writer Søren Kierkegaard (1813–1855), for example, has described worship using the analogy of the theater. In Kierkegaard's analogy, the assembled congregation are the players, the leaders are the prompters, and God is the audience. This model serves to remind us that the role of the congregation is not a passive one. This model, however, may obscure the fact that God is also a primary actor in an ongoing dialogue between God and the people of God. The assembly confesses its sin and hears God's word of pardon. We pray for the illumination of the Spirit, and we wait to hear in readings from Scripture a Word from the Lord. "The Service for the Lord's Day" has been designed to guarantee to the congregation their rightful role in this dialogue between God and the assembly.

The language of the service is contemporary, but not colloquial. It is not the casual language of the street, but language appropriate to a people gathered before the triune God. The order presumes a wide variety of musical, graphic, and ceremonial expressions, as well as providing a variety of spoken and enacted parts for leader(s) and people, unison prayers and affirmations, and multiple leaders. The Protestant reformers, particularly those in the Reformed cities of Geneva, Strasbourg, Zurich, and Edinburgh, were the first to make available to the people printed service books. Resources such as the *Book of Common Worship* testify that the liturgy is not the special property of ministers and church officers alone, but belongs in an essential way to the whole church.

5. The Formative Role of Scripture

Shaping a Biblical Consciousness Requires—Scripture

Another conviction underlying "The Service for the Lord's Day" is that liturgical language is rooted in Scripture. Not only is the liturgy saturated with Scripture, but it begins and ends with words of Scripture. Many branches of Christ's church, including our own, claim to honor Scripture and to rely on its authority. Yet it is not uncommon to hear little of Scripture in worship. Not so in "The Service for the Lord's Day." From the Call to Worship through the final Blessing, the texts in this service either come directly from Scripture or have been formed by scriptural language and allusions. The direct use of Scripture, a calling by God to worship, and a blessing from God as ending the liturgy redirects humans from calling themselves to worship or blessing themselves. The Call to Worship and the Blessing in words of Scripture provide the opening and closing parentheses to the service.

This practice differs from some contemporary ones in which those responsible for creating an order of service shy away from scriptural language as though it may be too obscure or too remote for people today. In hearing or reading aloud words of Scripture, one senses that in, under, and behind the words there is God. When hearing or reading aloud words composed for the occasion, it is difficult to escape the sense that in, under, and behind the words there is a human writer whose sensibilities may or may not match the depths and heights of Scripture. The principle, however, that the best way to shape a biblical consciousness is by immersion in Scripture directs selection and creation of texts throughout the *Book of Common Worship*. Such reliance on Scripture also should guide worship leaders who modify these liturgical texts, write their own texts for various elements (for example, Call to Worship, Confession of Sin, Prayer for Illumination), or draw from publications containing freely composed examples.

The Bible in "The Service for the Lord's Day"

In the right-hand margin, look for the specific biblical texts (identified in *italics*) that are incorporated into elements such as the Call to Worship (BCW 48), Call to Confession (BCW 52), Declaration of Forgiveness (BCW 56), Exhortation (BCW 57), the Peace (BCW 57), Ascription of Praise (BCW 62), Invitation to Discipleship (BCW 92), Offering (BCW 67), Invitation to the Lord's Table (BCW 68), Lord's Prayer (BCW 73), Charge and Blessing (BCW 78). In addition, the prayers frequently employ biblical language or make use of biblical images or allusions to Scripture. For example, Prayer of the Day 2 (BCW 51): "God of all glory, on this first day you began creation, bringing light out of darkness . . ." (Gen. 1); or Prayer for Illumination 4 (BCW 60): "O Lord our God, your Word is a lamp to our feet . . ." (Ps. 119:105). The responses (BCW 55) sung or said after the Confession of Sin make use of scriptural language or allusions; for example, "Lord, have mercy" (Kyrie Eleison) and "Lamb of God, you take away the sin of the world . . ." (Agnus Dei). The Apostles' Creed (BCW 65) derives almost line by line from specific passages of Scripture, and the Great (Prayers of) Thanksgiving (BCW 69, and elsewhere) draw heavily on biblical language and metaphor.

The Holy Spirit and the Service of the Word

Most notably, perhaps, this order integrates Prayer for Illumination, Scripture readings, Psalms, Sermon, Invitation, Affirmation of Faith, and Prayers of the People in that section of the *ordo* described in this service as The Word. These elements, which Presbyterians have always respected and cherished, have often been scattered throughout the service, thus obscuring their interrelatedness. The sequence is important.

The Prayer for Illumination is one of three crucial places in the liturgy in which we pray for the Holy Spirit to be at work in and among us. (*The other two are in the prayer over the water in the baptismal rite, and the Great (Prayer of) Thanksgiving used in celebrating the Lord's Supper.*) The Prayer for Illumination derives specifically from John Calvin, who believed that apart from the Holy Spirit, neither Scripture nor proclamation could be for the hearers more than an accumulation of words, words, words. This prayer precedes the first reading from Scripture and is sufficient for all readings. It does not need to be followed by a second prayer between Scripture and sermon.

The Lectionary

The *Book of Common Worship* includes the three-year Revised Common Lectionary (RCL) for use in "The Service for the Lord's Day" (BCW 1033). An advantage of a lectionary is that it walks the church through most of the Old and New Testaments in a systematic way. This is particularly important in the period from Advent to Pentecost, in which Jesus Christ is the chief focal point and the lens through whom Scripture is read and understood. The Directory for Worship points to Jesus' birth, life, death, resurrection, ascension, and promised return as points of reference that give meaning to the seasons of the church year, and guide the selection of Scriptures read and proclaimed (see also HBRCL).

The RCL readings in Ordinary Time provide for extended reading of narratives from Old Testament books and from New Testament epistles, adapting the method of *lectio continua* (continuous readings). Each of the lectionary Years A, B, and C, highlights one Gospel—Matthew in Year A, Mark in Year B, and Luke in Year C. The RCL highlights the Gospel of John every year, particularly during the seven Sundays of the Easter season, culminating in Pentecost. If a preacher who keeps the discipline of a lectionary should choose to depart from it for a time to highlight texts not included in the lectionary, it is preferable to do so in Ordinary Time.

6. Contemporary and Traditional Language

Treasures Old and New

Finally, "The Service for the Lord's Day" appropriates both time-honored and contemporary resources. After all, writes C. S. Lewis, "If you have a vernacular liturgy you must have a changing liturgy; otherwise it will finally be vernacular only in name. The ideal of 'timeless English' is sheer nonsense. No living language can be timeless. You might as well ask for a motionless river."[4] The rich heritage of the past, therefore, has been neither cherished simply because it is old, nor rejected in an effort to speak relevantly to our time.

The editing of the Great (Prayers of) Thanksgiving illustrates this point. Great Thanksgiving F (BCW 146) has been adapted from the Alexandrine Liturgy of St. Basil (fourth century), and Great Thanksgiving G (BCW 150) originated even earlier, deriving from Hippolytus of Rome, dating about A.D. 215. The rubric indicates "it is the earliest known text of a eucharistic prayer." On the other hand, Great Thanksgiving C (BCW 130) comes from *The Worshipbook* of 1970 (p. 35). Great Thanksgiving B (BCW 126) appeared first in *Service for the Lord's Day, Supplemental Liturgical Resource 1*, published in 1984 (p. 98). Great Thanksgiving D (BCW 138), which has been adapted from the 1946 *Book of Common Worship*, falls between the earliest and the latest.

Liturgical texts that belong to our common ecumenical heritage, such as the Lord's Prayer, the Apostles' Creed, and the *Sursum Corda,* have been made available in the most recent versions prepared by the International Consultation on English Texts (ICET). The Consultation consisted of Protestant and Roman Catholic representatives from twenty countries where English is the primary language. ICET's work is a remarkable achievement in Christian unity. The result is that the service books of most churches in English-speaking countries are using common texts. In 1974, ICET completed its work, and was succeeded at the international and ecumenical level by the English Language Liturgical Consultation (ELLC).

The *Book of Common Worship* has taken care, as far as possible, to use inclusive language in reference to human beings and expansive biblical images of God. "Guidelines for inclusive language adopted by the General Assembly in 1975, 1979, 1980, and 1985 were implicitly followed in the preparation of the texts" (BCW 10). For example, inclusive language regarding humans:

> Keep us one in faith and service, . . .
> and proclaiming the good news to the world,
> that all may believe you are love . . .
> (BCW 100)

or

> Bless the leaders of our land,
> that we may be a people at peace among ourselves
> and a blessing to other nations of the earth . . .
> (BCW 822)

and expansive biblical images of God:

> Merciful God,
> since Jesus longed to protect Jerusalem
> as a hen gathers her young under her wings,
> we ask you to guard and strengthen all who live and work here.
> (Matt. 23:37; Luke 13:34) (BCW 105)

Origin and Development of the Fourfold *Ordo* of the Service for the Lord's Day

The order for "The Service for the Lord's Day" consists of four successive actions:

1. **Gathering:** The people assemble in the name of the Lord. Called to worship by the presiding minister, they offer praise in words of Scripture, prayer, and song. The people acknowledge before God their sinfulness, and the brokenness of the world and the church, and receive the declaration of God's forgiveness.
2. **The Word:** The congregation hears the Scriptures read and their messages proclaimed. Between the readings, they may sing psalms, hymns, spirituals, or anthems. In response to the reading and proclamation of God's Word, they may make acts of commitment and professions of faith. They may offer concerns and prayers for local and worldwide needs, and bring their gifts.
3. **The Eucharist ("Thanksgiving"):** The presiding minister and/or representatives of the people prepare the Lord's table for the Lord's Supper. The presiding minister offers prayer in a Trinitarian format, praising God for creation and providence; remembering (*anamnesis*) with thanksgiving Christ's work of redemption; and invoking (*epiclesis*) the Holy Spirit to bless the church and the eucharistic action, that the body of Christ may truly be manifest. The presiding minister breaks bread, and persons assisting then deliver bread and cup to the assembly.
4. **Sending:** A liturgical leader charges all assembled to go out into the world, and the presiding minister offers God's blessing.

At the heart of the order is the classic juxtaposition of Word and Sacrament. Surrounding these two central actions are briefer rites for meeting and parting. These outer rites of the fourfold order provide transitions between the community's involvement in the secular order and its own assembly as God's people gathered for Word and Sacrament. When planning the Lord's Day service, it is well to embrace this structure, which links our assembly with those of other Christians, past and present. Once again, the keeping of the fourfold structure is a gift to be received.

Our Bibles translate the Greek word *ecclesia* (root of words such as "ecclesiastical") with the English word "church." *Kaleo* is the Greek word for "call," and *ek* means "out." *Ek-klesia* unites the preposition and the verb to form a new word, which the biblical writers used to identify those whom God has "called out" of the world—the church. God has called us out to be God's people, corporately exercising a "royal priesthood" (1 Pet. 2:9). God has commissioned us to serve Jesus Christ in the world. The Gathering portion of the service reminds us of God's call which gathered the church and included us in it, and the Sending reiterates the commission God has given us to love and serve our neighbors in the world.

The First Christians

The very first Christians, primarily Jews, continued to worship for a time in the temple and in the synagogue. In addition, they met together as believers in Jesus to eat a full meal together during which they took bread, blessed, broke, and gave it to those assembled, as Jesus had commanded his disciples to do. Although, for a time, they continued to worship in the synagogue on the Sabbath day, the Jewish Christians also met for the meal on Sunday, which they called the Lord's Day—the day on which Jesus was resurrected. Since Sunday was an ordinary workday, they probably met in the evening.

After a time, Christians were no longer welcome to worship in the synagogue. The two separate services—Saturday/Sunday, synagogue/Meal—then began to be combined. The Jewish Christians began to incorporate into their Lord's Day assembly many of the features of synagogue worship. These certainly included the reading of Scripture (what we call the Old Testament) and the preaching of the Word, as well as prayer and song. These they added to their celebration of the Meal.

Word and Meal

While the New Testament gives no detailed description of their worship, it seems that a service incorporating synagogue service and meal became the typical practice of Christian churches in mission situations as well as in Judea, extending the practice of Jewish Christians to Gentile Christians. Early in the second century, at least in Asia Minor, the Roman Empire outlawed evening meetings of "clubs" and "associations," probably fearing subversion.

When the church could no longer assemble in the evening for a common meal, they probably incorporated an abbreviated meal into a morning gathering on the Lord's Day. The full meal eaten in common had to be sacrificed, and only those parts of the meal specifically related to the Lord's Supper remained.[5] The resulting form of worship was a morning service uniting worship practices from the synagogue with the blessing and sharing of the bread and cup: Word and Sacrament. This is the service described by Justin Martyr in his report to Emperor Antoninus Pius and the Senate of Rome in his *First Apology*, about A.D. 150.

On the day which is called Sunday, all who live in the cities or in the countryside gather together in one place. And the memoirs of the apostles or the writings of the prophets are read as long as there is time. Then, when the reader has finished, the president, in a discourse, admonishes and invites the people to practice these examples of virtue. Then we all stand up together and offer prayers. And, as we mentioned before, when we have finished the prayer, bread is presented, and wine with water; the president likewise offers up prayers and thanksgivings according to his ability, and the people assent by saying, Amen. The elements which have been "eucharistized" are distributed and received by each one; and they are sent to the absent by the deacons.[6]

Actions centered on the Word—including the reading of materials which later became New Testament books as well as reading Hebrew Scriptures—and around the Meal have served from very early on as the heart and core of the weekly assembly of the church. Around these two actions there developed rites related to calling the assembly to order at the beginning and dismissing them at the end. Thus emerged the fourfold order which the *Book of Common Worship* designates quite clearly and plainly as Gathering, The Word, The Eucharist, and Sending (BCW 33). This *ordo* is the legacy of the whole church.

Reform

The Agenda of the Protestant Reformers

The Protestant reformers of the sixteenth century, especially in Geneva, drew on Scripture and their knowledge of the tradition of the early centuries in forming their reformed service for the Lord's Day. Calvin's prayer books carried in their title, "according to the custom of the ancient church."[7] Both Martin Luther and Calvin understood the "custom of the ancient church" to place both Word and Sacrament squarely in the center of the weekly assembly for worship.

Calvin's agenda for reform of the medieval mass was to restore preaching to the position of prominence it had held in early centuries, and to recover the Lord's Supper alongside it, each strengthening the other. In his intention for the Reformed church, the whole company of the faithful would commune together in one common weekly celebration. As noted earlier, authorities of the City of Geneva frustrated this plan and left to Calvin's heirs an ambiguous legacy.

The order of service as formed by the Reformers had four movements:

1. assembly in praise and confession;
2. the reading and preaching of the Word, followed by a creed;
3. prayer and Communion; and
4. post-Communion prayer, praise, and blessing.

One can recognize the classical *ordo* which "The Service for the Lord's Day" has called Gathering, The Word, The Eucharist, and Sending. When the Lord's Supper was not included in the order, the fourfold order retained its integrity as nearly as possible, altering only those elements directly pertaining to the Eucharist. The intention was, despite the Genevan authorities, to exhibit the fundamental structure of the Word/Sacrament service even when the Sacrament was not permitted to be celebrated, in order that it be clear that Word and Sacrament were the norm rather than the exception.

Early Scottish Practice

This fourfold pattern continued to be followed in the Church of Scotland, whose worship was at first guided by John Knox's *Book of Common Order*. Worship in Scotland, however, unfortunately became deeply mired in both national and ecclesiastical politics. The Scots resisted attempts by a London-based monarch to impose English worship practices on the Scottish kirk by decree. This resistance also inclined to make the Scots sympathetic to the Puritan party in England, represented by ministers within the Church of England who harbored Presbyterian as well as Congregational and Baptist sympathies.

The various Puritan parties, motivated in different degrees by dissatisfaction with some practices of the Church of England at the time, and by political grievances as well, staked out a reforming agenda of their own which took a radical form. Puritanism not only put on the defensive those who appreciated the English prayer book, but also those who had followed Knox's *Common Order*. The Westminster Assembly, in which a handful of Scottish ministers participated alongside the mainly English Puritan body, drew up a Directory for Worship (1644), which is the mother directory of all subsequent Presbyterian Directories for Worship.

The Westminster Directory

The Westminster Directory was not a service book, but a set of guidelines for use by ministers who chose to make use of it. A strength of the Westminster Directory is its strong statement about the importance of including an *epiclesis* (prayer seeking the blessing of the Holy Spirit) in the Great (Prayer of) Thanksgiving at the Lord's Supper, even offering a suggested wording. The directory, however, displaced the fourfold order inherited from the ancient church and honored by Calvin and Knox.

Inspired by Puritan innovations, the directory described a service in which the sermon was the climax, to be followed only by a prayer, psalm, or hymn, and benediction. It relocated the prayers of the church (intercession, supplication, thanksgiving) from their classical position after the sermon to a place preceding it. Thus, the historic structure was set aside except on those Sundays when the Lord's Supper was celebrated.

American Presbyterians adopted the Westminster Directory in 1788; thus, the directory's recommended structure of a service in which the sermon was the climax became the accepted pattern for American Presbyterianism. Thus a structural difference between Sundays with both sermon and Lord's Supper and Sundays with only a sermon came to characterize Presbyterian worship in this country, and the pattern of Sundays with a sermon but no Eucharist became the norm.

By such historical accidents we who claim to be heirs of Calvin's Reformation have inherited a tradition shaped not by Calvin or Knox, but in large part by the sixteenth-century City Council of Geneva, English Puritans with grievances indigenous to seventeenth-century England, and Scottish Presbyterians who had an ax to grind with a London-based monarch. Such are the ironies of history!

Why Change?

In 1961, harvesting the fruits of a century of historical, theological, and liturgical scholarship, a new Directory for Worship adopted by the former United Presbyterian Church in the U.S.A. reclaimed the heritage of the Genevan Reformation and of the early centuries of the church. *The Worshipbook: Services*, published in 1970 by the UPCUSA, followed the lead of the 1961 directory in presuming that the normative form of Sunday worship has at its heart both Word and Sacrament, and preserving as far as possible that structure even when the Lord's Supper is not celebrated. Since 1961, subsequent directories have affirmed this model, as does "The Service for the Lord's Day."

In no way does this recovery of Reformation and ecumenical tradition intend to diminish the importance of the sermon. The intention, rather, is to complement the sermon and to strengthen it by restoring it to its historic context in juxtaposition to the Sacrament of Holy Communion. On Sundays when the congregation does not celebrate the Lord's Supper, the sermon leads to prayers of the people, the Offering (historically always linked to the Lord's Supper), and an act of thanksgiving, followed by the rites of dismissal.

Purposes of the *Ordo* of the Service for the Lord's Day

Each part of the fourfold pattern of "The Service for the Lord's Day" fulfills a separate and distinctive purpose. At the same time, the four movements of the *ordo* each serve one another in such a way as to form an integrated whole.

I. Gathering (BCW 48)

Thresholds

Worship begins with God. God takes the initiative, calling us together. Our first act of public worship, therefore, is to heed God's call and to join with others in praising God. We adore God best when we live as people who belong to this holy, righteous, gracious, and merciful God.

The portions of the service described as Gathering and Sending serve similar purposes. Because they are transitions into and out of the heart of the service (Word and Sacrament), it is appropriate to describe them as "threshold" or "transition" moments. The entry rite, or Gathering, provides a means of moving the congregation with its liturgical leaders *from* the ordinary, structured context that characterizes daily life *toward* a kind of anti-structure, in which the worshipers stand on equal ground in the presence of the triune God. (See Victor Turner, *The Ritual Process: Structure and Anti-Structure*; Ithaca, N.Y.: Cornell University Press, 1969.) Laying aside the various ways that society categorizes people and assigns status (for example, occupation, education, physical traits, age, capital worth, power), the assembly awaits God's gifts. The first gift is God's own self. The second is the gift of community.

That portion of the service designated as Gathering begins whenever someone turns on the lights and prepares to welcome the first worshipers, and moves through a sequence that builds in intensity until it reaches its conclusion in Confession and Pardon. Note that "the gathering rite" is deliberately brief. The operative word is "gathering." The rite's purpose is to get us to the Word.

As worshipers gather for corporate worship, they greet one another, talking together as neighbors in faith. Then, cued by some scriptural greeting (BCW 48) from the presiding minister, the worshipers begin to center themselves with prayer, meditation, hymn-reading, prayerful corporate song, or common silence as music is played or sung by others.

The placement of the prelude (or voluntary) varies. By definition, a "prelude" is "an introductory action," "offered beforehand," "a preface" indicating that it precedes something (for example, Greeting or Sentences of

Scripture). Congregations who embrace the concept that the prelude constitutes the first act of worship have been known to print at the top of their bulletin something akin to the following rubric: "The service begins with the first note of the prelude. If you must whisper, let it be a prayer." A discipline of silence thus evolves, allowing for short, medium, or long musical compositions to be offered prior to the Call to Worship. Others place the prelude *after* the Greeting or parish announcements or brief instructions about the day's liturgy, so that a worshipful mood established *during* the prelude is not interrupted *after* it.

If the placement of the prelude varies, then the placement of announcements varies even more. Worship planners need to choose among a number of options regarding sequence of these elements, recognizing that whatever is chosen communicates a theological statement about worship:

1. Prelude, Greeting, Sentences of Scripture (the pattern displayed on BCW 48–50)
2. Prelude, Greeting, Programmatic Announcements, Sentences of Scripture
3. Prelude, Greeting, Programmatic Announcements and Pastoral Concerns, Sentences of Scripture
4. Prelude, Programmatic Announcements, Greeting, Sentences of Scripture
5. Prelude, Programmatic Announcements and Pastoral Concerns, Greeting, Sentences of Scripture
6. Greeting, Programmatic Announcements, Prelude, Sentences of Scripture
7. Greeting, Programmatic Announcements and Pastoral Concerns, Prelude, Sentences of Scripture
8. Some other locally adopted custom that incorporates the above words and actions in a well-conceived, thoughtful, and consistent sequence within the *Ordo*

The above patterns are generated by the question regarding where to locate programmatic announcements and pastoral concerns. Note that no sequence, particularly no "correct sequence," is indicated by the *Book of Common Worship*.

"Programmatic announcements" include church activities, mission opportunities, liturgical instructions, and so forth. "Pastoral concerns" include joys and sorrows and special needs of the world, nation, local communities, church universal, and the congregation's own life and ministry. Some congregations intermingle programmatic announcements and pastoral concerns into one element. Some take care to maintain each as sequential halves of one element. And, some maintain each element's separate identity and function by locating them at different points in the service.

Though theological and practical concerns overlap regarding programmatic announcements and pastoral concerns, each element needs to be identified and located within a consistent rationale about the mood and sequence of the service.

The various placements of these elements reflect existent rationales. For some, the presiding minister or other leader makes brief, necessary programmatic announcements and pastoral concerns during the Gathering, and invites others to add theirs. Those who prefer this placement of announcements say that throughout the service they may keep prayerfully in mind the persons and service opportunities mentioned at the outset. Some place brief announcements during the transition from the Gathering to the service of the Word as the least intrusive spot within the whole service; this seems to be more a practical than a theological rationale. Others say the Word evokes our prayers and mission. Thus, the service opportunities and pastoral concerns, in response to the Word, provide focus for the Prayers of the People (intercessions and supplications). Still other congregations place their announcements and service opportunities prior to the Charge and Blessing, in effect communicating, "Here is 'going out' information for this gathered community as it now scatters throughout the world." Whatever the pattern adopted for "announcements," the operative watchwords are "brief" and "necessary." And, most important, recognize that whichever sequence of elements is chosen communicates a theological statement about worship.

Call to Worship (BCW 48)

Note that the words used to "call us to worship" are scriptural, and remind us that "our worship centers in God and not in ourselves" (BCW 35). Thus, adoration is central at the beginning of worship.

> We acknowledge God's holiness and offer our love and devotion.
> We praise God and affirm the good news of the divine saving activity among us.
> We worship precisely because of what God has done for us in Christ.

In addition to these verses which recite God's work in Christ, sometimes we employ the familiar words "Our help is in the name of the Lord, **who made heaven and earth**" (Ps. 124:8) (BCW 49) used by worshipers in Geneva and, subsequently, by Presbyterian congregations in Scotland and in this country.

The versicle, "Praise the Lord. **The Lord's name be praised**" (BCW 50) serves as a bridge between the announcement of God's work in Christ, and our joyful response.

From the time of preparation, the Gathering portion of the service moves toward acts of praise: Call to Worship, Prayer of the Day or Opening Prayer (offering praise to God), then a Hymn of Praise, Psalm or Spiritual. Since it is God who calls us to worship, there is no need for a prayer of "invocation," as though it were our responsibility to summon God to our assembly. Similar to Isaiah's vision (Isaiah 6), the congregation focuses on the magnificence of the holy God. With attention fixed on the God of majesty and grace, the congregation then joins in confession of sin.

Confession and Pardon (BCW 52)

Why Confession? The Call to Confession (BCW 52–53) serves as the opening movement of an integrally related triadic (threefold) form: Call to Confession, Confession of Sin, and Declaration of Forgiveness. The Call to Confession both lays the ground of confessing and provides, in Reformed fashion, a note of grace, for forgiveness precedes repentance. God's grace is prior to our confession. True repentance is not a cause of grace, for grace is already and always at work. In announcing God's mercy, the call to confession invites us to confess the brokenness in our lives.

Why offer a prayer of confession? To remember all that God has done for us in Christ is to be confronted with the fact of God's astonishing love and our own unworthiness. Who can deserve Christ's sacrifice? All we can do is to respond to God's merciful goodness by confessing our sin together in true repentance.

Although all Christian liturgy makes provision for some sort of confession of sin, the form it has taken in the Reformed tradition is original and a contribution to the church universal. The Reformers expected that personal, face-to-face confession would be a function of pastoral care, which they understood to be an important facet of the church's ministry. Nevertheless, in the absence of a required Sacrament of Penance, which they had abolished, the Reformers needed to provide a regular opportunity for congregations to bow in humility before the God of grace. Penance as a sacrament was abolished, but reformers preserved the availability of private confession and forgiveness.

It is likely that the Reformers were following an available precedent in the Roman Catholic mass, in which the priest, at the foot of the altar at the beginning of the mass, prayed the *confiteor* (from the Latin, "I confess"), a personal confession of sin. By transferring the prayer of the priest to the whole congregation, the Reformers made the statement that it was the congregation as a whole who celebrated the liturgy, and not the priest alone with the congregation as an audience. John Calvin, in fact, is credited with the introduction of "corporate confession of sin" into Christian worship, for he changed the pronoun from the first person singular ("I") to the first person plural ("we"), and asked that pastors lead their people in such prayer as the first act of worship each Lord's Day.[8] The *confiteor* (I confess), thus, became a confession of the community of faith.

Protestant Reformers may have understood such confession to be a continual renewal of the baptismal covenant, recalling the link between penitence and baptism in the preaching of John the Baptist, who called out to those who came to be baptized in the Jordan, "Repent, for the kingdom of heaven has come near" (Matt. 3:1).[9]

Frequently, people misunderstand the Prayer of Confession, as though its intention were to enumerate sins specific to individuals. However, in the Prayer of Confession, we trust God's mercy enough to lay before God not only those sins which may belong to us individually and personally, but also the sins and brokenness of the congregation, the church universal, and the world. We do not confess primarily specific acts of omission or commission, but rather the tragic brokenness of our human condition, in which, even without intending to, we are constantly running away from God and our neighbors (for example, Rom. 7:19).

"The Service for the Lord's Day" permits the Prayer of Confession to be offered here, as part of the Gathering rite, where it has usually appeared in Reformed services, or "following the prayers of the people, and before the peace" (BCW 84). Either way, the confession is prayed only once in each service.

Lord, Have Mercy (Kyrie Eleison). Many congregations sing a Kyrie Eleison (BCW 55, PH 565, 572, 573, 574; HL 157–169) immediately following the Prayer of Confession. Framed in the Greek language with early roots in the liturgy, preceding even the use of Latin, it means, "Lord, have mercy," possibly based on Psalm 51:1 or Matthew 15:25. The Kyrie was used by both Martin Luther and John Calvin as an act of contrition. Actually, the Kyrie is both an act of contrition and an affirmation, an affirmation that the Lord *has* mercy! Other possibilities for responses to the Confession of Sin are also suggested (BCW 55).

Declaration of Forgiveness (BCW 56)

Forgiveness and Reconciliation. After the Confession of Sin, a worship leader offers, in the words of Scripture, the gospel promises of God's redemption: Jesus Christ is the pledge of God's mercy and help for sinners (BCW 56). The Declaration of Forgiveness proclaims God's faithfulness. Our lives are redeemed by the saving grace of God—the Gospel in miniature. God does for us what we cannot do for ourselves. Leaders do not say so because their words procure forgiveness, but because they are declaring to all assembled the reality of the divine mercy. The power to forgive sin does not rest within the church, particularly with its leaders. Rather, forgiveness is the gospel we preach, the good news of the cross. An important principle to remember about the declaration of pardon: The leader can declare it, but God gives it. The astoundingly good news of our reconciliation to God through Jesus Christ frees our tongues to sing mighty praise to God.

"The Service for the Lord's Day" offers at this point an option of including an exhortation (BCW 57) or a reading of the summary of the law (Matt. 22:37–40) (BCW 29) or the Ten Commandments (Ex. 20:1–17) (BCW 28), each of which functions as an ethical charge to the congregation, thus purging any notion of cheap grace. The use of the commandments in this place represents what has been called Calvin's "Third Use" of the Law. In early Reformed liturgies, ministers read the commandments *after* the assurance of God's pardon as a sign that God's forgiven people, who have been set free to live the Christian life, may turn to God's law as a guide and resource for their lives. This has regularly been practiced among churches in Dutch Reformed tradition.

The Peace (BCW 57)

Those who have received the promise of reconciliation with God may now offer signs of reconciliation with one another as they exchange signs of Peace. The Peace originated in the practice of the early Christians, who were accustomed to exchanging a "holy kiss" during the liturgy (for example, Rom. 16:16). In ancient traditions, it was most likely placed either before the Offering (for example, Matt. 5:23f.) or at the beginning of the Communion liturgy. Presbyterians have recovered use of the Peace only since the first edition of the "Service for the Lord's Day" in 1964—an abbreviated version that did not involve an exchange among worshipers appeared immediately after the invitation to the Lord's Table.[10] In *The Worshipbook: Services* (1970) it appeared in a fuller form after the prayers of the people, just before the Offering.[11] The significance of its placement after the confession and pardon is that it completes the theme of reconciliation by moving toward the exchange of reconciling words and gestures among the people of God. Suggested alternative placements for the Peace are following the prayers of the people (before the Offering), or following the Lord's Prayer, preceding the breaking of the bread (BCW 36, 57, 84).

Canticle, Psalm, Hymn, or Spiritual (BCW 58)

Many congregations sing the Gloria Patri ("Glory to the Father") (BCW 59) as a response to the promise of God's mercy and reconciliation. The Gloria Patri is a shortened version of the more traditional Gloria in Excelsis ("Glory to God") (BCW 58) sung during the twelve-day Christmas and fifty-day Easter seasons. As trinitarian acclamations, the "Glorias" are an appropriate way to acknowledge with thanks and joy that we are the beneficiaries of the unmerited gift of God's mercy. The Gathering concludes at this point, as the assembly prepares to listen for God's Word.

II. The Word (BCW 60)

Prayer for Illumination (BCW 60)

Before the Scriptures are read, and before a sermon is preached, we offer a Prayer for Illumination (BCW 60, 90–91). Why? This prayer asks that the Holy Spirit open our minds and our hearts to the Word so that we may not only hear but understand and believe.

Reformed worship, at its heart, is what one might describe as epicletic, in that it calls upon the Holy Spirit to animate our worship. It was John Calvin who first introduced the Prayer for Illumination preceding the reading of Scripture and the preaching of the Word. The Directory for Worship calls for prayer to be offered seeking the illumination of the Holy Spirit. In this prayer, we acknowledge our dependence on the action of the Spirit to transfigure the language of Scripture and preaching from ordinary words into the Living Word which has the power to open hearts and minds, in order to transform God's people in heart, mind, and soul. That part of "The Service for the Lord's Day" described as The Word appropriately begins with a Prayer for Illumination (BCW 60, 90–91), a tradition cherished by the Reformed churches, expressing the conviction that the words of Scripture of themselves have no power apart from God's power.

Scripture Readings and Songs (BCW 61)

Why More than One Scripture Reading? At services in the ancient Jewish synagogue, a series of biblical lessons were read. This practice was imitated in Christian worship from early times. In "The Service for the Lord's Day," it is intended that there be more than one Scripture reading, and that the readings follow one another closely, interspersed with silence for reflection between Scripture passages, the singing of a psalm and, perhaps, hymns or spiritual songs. Presbyterian directories have called for the choosing of Scriptures appropriate to the liturgical year, and specifically suggest the use of a lectionary.

Why a Lectionary? The use of a lectionary is particularly helpful in opening up the calendar of the church year as it unfolds the mystery of Jesus Christ in his incarnation, life and ministry, death, resurrection, ascension, and promised return. The 1932 *Book of Common Worship* included a rudimentary lectionary. The 1946 *Book of Common Worship* introduced a two-year lectionary with Sunday-by-Sunday readings of Old Testament, Epistle, and Gospel, with a psalm for the day.

Many denominations and confessions use the Revised Common Lectionary (RCL), which is included in the 1993 *Book of Common Worship* (1035–1048). In the RCL, the Gospel is the key reading during the seasons of the church year from Advent to the Day of Pentecost, and readings from the Old Testament and the epistles have been chosen to stand in juxtaposition to it. The Gospel reading offers a perspective on the Old Testament and epistle readings, and vice versa. The readings designated by a lectionary are not the only possible juxtapositions, of course, but they have been chosen (in some cases, centuries ago) for the ways that each helps to open up the others.

A lectionary belongs not just to those who preach, but to the whole church. Some church members have come to rely on a lectionary as they read, reflect on, and pray from the texts scheduled to be heard on the next Lord's Day. A lectionary can help Christians to discover the principle that the Lord's Day liturgy, rooted in an engagement with Holy Scripture, does not belong exclusively to those ordained to the ministry of Word and Sacrament, but belongs to the whole church.

Use of a lectionary offers advantages in planning services well ahead of time. Where musicians can rely on it, they can plan for choral as well as instrumental music that relates to the Scripture for the day, and have adequate time for securing the music and rehearsing it. Lectionary use offers excellent opportunities for ministers, musicians, worship committees, and others sharing leadership responsibility for services to reflect on upcoming texts together and engage in cooperative planning.

Use of a lectionary also serves as a discipline to keep preaching close to Scripture. Echoing historic Reformed conviction, the directory states quite clearly that preaching is meant to find its foundation in the written Word— Holy Scripture. This is a basic principle of the Reformation. Preaching is not independent of Scripture, nor is it sufficient under ordinary circumstances that preaching be "scriptural" in some sort of general way without accountability to a particular text. At least from a Reformed point of view, preaching is peculiar speech, defined by its intimate dependence on Holy Scripture.

Because of the critical relationship of Scripture and sermon, it is important that preaching find its beginnings in Scripture rather than Scripture being chosen as an afterthought to support a sermon already formed. Keeping the discipline of a lectionary is one way for a preacher to make a commitment to beginning with Scripture, particularly if she or he does not abandon a lectionary when none of the readings for the day seem to yield easily to a sermon! Often, the texts that seem impossible require the greatest struggle, and can be the most rewarding both for preacher and for congregation. Note also that as part of the call of ministers to hear when the Holy Spirit is calling for a word to be spoken at a time of crisis, preachers are free to respond to crisis situations in a congregation, community, nation, or world by reading and preaching on other appropriate passages of Scripture.

An added bonus accompanying the discipline of a lectionary is that it is widely used ecumenically. Churches of several denominations or confessions are likely to hear the same Scriptures any given Sunday, and often hear sermons on the same texts. This can be a stimulus to ecumenical discussion and reflection for church people in the same community, and can offer opportunities for preachers to form lectionary-based ecumenical study groups.

That segment of the church year after the Day of Pentecost and through Christ the King, denominated as Ordinary Time, provides for the systematic reading of some of the major narrative portions of the Old Testament. Year A turns our attention to the Genesis narratives beginning with Abraham and Sarah and their successor-generations who inherit the promises of God, then turning to the story of Moses and the exodus from Egypt. Year B focuses primarily on the story of King David, and Year C on the Elijah/Elisha stories, followed by readings from the prophets.

During this part of the church year, the RCL leads us sequentially through various epistles as well. Sometimes called "the church's half year," because it focuses on teachings rather than on the shape of Christ's life, death, and resurrection, Ordinary Time can be adapted quite easily to other ways of organizing biblical preaching should the preacher choose to adopt a *lectio continua* project with other biblical books than those on which the lectionary focuses, or to preach from texts not provided for in the lectionary.

Lectio continua. Other methods for selecting texts for preaching do exist. One widely used at the time of the Reformation was *lectio continua*, which involves a commitment to preach sequentially through entire books of Scripture. A serious disadvantage of this method is that it takes no account of the church year with its sequence of unfolding christological themes from incarnation to passion and resurrection. Of course, a preacher may interrupt *lectio continua* to read and preach from passages out of sequence but appropriate to Christmas, for example, or Easter.

Lectio continua with interruptions for major Christian festivals is, however, quite similar to the pattern of the Revised Common Lectionary (RCL) itself. (See especially Horace T. Allen Jr., "Common Lectionary: Origins,

Assumptions, and Issues." *Studia Liturgica* 21, no. 1 [1991].) Year A features nearly sequential readings from Matthew; Year B from Mark; and Year C from Luke. Where sequential readings are interrupted, it is for the purpose of turning to scriptural texts appropriate to the movement of the church year. Moreover, the RCL takes account of the fact that the church year includes important themes and events surrounding Christmas and Easter.

For example, the church year always begins the first Sunday of Advent with sayings of Jesus related to the *eschaton*—the coming reign of God, or kingdom of heaven. In subsequent Sundays of Advent, the lectionary turns the church's attention to John the Baptist and to his message, and to the messages delivered by angels to Mary (Luke's Gospel) or to Joseph (Matthew's Gospel) anticipating Jesus' birth. While these themes will surface sooner or later in a system of *lectio continua*, a lectionary ensures that they appear in their proper place in the sequence of narratives that form the church year (see HBRCL).

The Psalter. That portion of "The Service for the Lord's Day" identified under the name of The Word also includes the use of the Psalter. For Jews and Christians, this ancient songbook of prayers is one of the primary resources for worship. They were also Jesus' prayer book. Recall his allusions to various psalms throughout the Gospel narratives (for example, "My God, my God, why have you forsaken me?" Ps. 22:1; Matt. 27:46; Mark 15:34; "My soul is very sorrowful (troubled, cast down)," Pss. 42:5, 11; 43:5; Matt. 26:38; John 12:27). The psalms are emotive, repetitious, contradictory, earthy, angry, and full of wonder at simple things. Like life itself, the psalms are salty, sad, haunting, dancing, and worth preserving. In song, they come to their full expression.

The psalms are both the church's songbook and the church's prayer book. Psalms are for singing, and psalms are for praying. The psalms are the prayer-songs that accompany the people of God on their journey of faith from birth to death. Every psalm, whatever its type—hymn, lament, thanksgiving, song of trust, wisdom meditation, or others—is, at heart, a prayer-song that extols and glorifies God. As with most poetry, we should pay close attention to the images portrayed as well as the emotions expressed in seeking to discern the essence of these sung prayers, which John Calvin called the "anatomy of the soul."

In the centuries preceding the Middle Ages, the most common custom for psalm-singing was for a cantor to sing or chant lines of the psalm, while the people joined their voices periodically by singing an antiphon, or refrain. A cantor is someone with a strong voice and musical sensibility who has the skill both to sing alone and to encourage the singing of others. The practice of responding to a cantor's singing of the psalm with the congregation singing a refrain was particularly helpful in an era in which scant printed texts were available for use by congregations, and in which many people would not have been able to read them in any case. A cantor can also lead another method of singing the psalms by "lining them out." That is to say, the cantor sings a line which the congregation then repeats. Scottish congregations followed this practice for generations.

A major aspect of John Calvin's agenda for the reform of worship was to recover congregational psalm-singing. Thus, Reformed communities became known for their singing of psalms, usually in metrical versions in which the psalm texts had been paraphrased to fit a regular meter (a pattern, consistent in each stanza, involving the number of syllables in the lines), unlike Hebrew poetry, which has no meter. In fact, in France, where at various times professing the Reformed faith became a punishable offense, psalm-singing was outlawed. Inadvertently whistling Psalm 100 or humming Psalm 150 could result in arrest. The Scottish Psalter continued the psalm-singing tradition of Geneva. Through Scottish and Puritan practice, congregational singing of metrical psalms became familiar to American congregations.

Psalm-singing long has characterized Reformed worship. Over the centuries, in fact, a commonly used nickname for Calvinists/Presbyterians has been "psalm-singers." The reason psalm-singing was considered an essential part of the prayer of the church is that the Reformers understood psalms as prayers of the Holy Spirit. Since prayer is not human response to God, but the work of the Holy Spirit in the body of Christ to the glory of God, then worshipers could both *learn how to pray* from the psalms and *use* the psalms as their prayers.

Though the people's singing of Scripture was not exclusive to the Reformed tradition, it made such singing a priority. When Isaac Watts and his successors began to write psalm-like hymns, Presbyterians broadened their musical repertoire. Unfortunately, this apparent broadening frequently led to a narrowing of the repertoire as Presbyterians forgot their heritage of psalm-singing. The Directory for Worship urges the singing of psalms. Like other neglected pieces of our liturgical heritage, psalm-singing is worthy of recovery. Latino congregations that sing psalms to Latin rhythms today offer us one model for such recovery.

While Psalms may serve as the texts for sermons, more commonly they serve as a kind of biblical hymnbook. In the Revised Common Lectionary, the psalm reflects on the first Scripture reading. *The Presbyterian Hymnal* provides a whole section devoted to 70 of the 150 Psalms, in numerical order, some to be sung in metrical form, and others to be sung in prose style by a cantor with a congregational refrain (PH 158–258). Likewise for both *El*

Himnario Presbiteriano (HP 405–441) and *Come, Let Us Worship: The Korean-English Presbyterian Hymnal and Service Book* (K-E 394–535).

The *Book of Common Worship* contains all psalms (132 out of 150) designated for use in the Revised Common Lectionary for Sundays and Festivals, and all designated for use in the daily prayer lectionary (BCW 611–783). Also included are instructions on how to sing the psalms in the ancient way, with cantor and congregational refrain (PH 599–600). This collection is a faithful and unobtrusive rendering of the psalms in inclusive language for singing, or, when singing is impossible, for reading responsively or in unison. Other sources for both metrical and prose psalms include *The Psalter: Psalms and Canticles for Singing* (Louisville, Ky.: Westminster/John Knox Press, 1993), and Michael Morgan, *Psalter for Christian Worship* (Louisville, Ky.: Witherspoon Press, 1999).

Canticles: Biblical Songs. Canticles are portions of Scripture written to be sung. The *Book of Common Worship* contains 29 canticles (BCW 573–591). Some of them replicate the three canticles available in *The Presbyterian Hymnal* and *The Hymnbook* ("Canticle/Song of Mary" or Magnificat (BCW 575; PH 600; HB 596), "Canticle/Song of Zechariah" or Benedictus (BCW 573; PH 601, 602; HB 592), and "Canticle/Song of Simeon" or Nunc Dimittis (BCW 576; PH 603–605; HB 597–600). Canticles can also be sung in the same style as prose psalms (though not as a substitute for the psalm), in the ancient way, with a cantor singing the main text and the congregation responding with a refrain. The congregation can easily and quickly memorize the refrain so that they need neither hold a text nor know how to read music. Many congregations have found a good deal of satisfaction in singing scriptural paraphrases. Introduction of appropriate canticles along with psalms can reinforce the hearing and absorption of Scripture, but will become a delight for their own sake.

Sermon (BCW 62)

Why the Reformers Restored Preaching. It is hard to imagine a Lord's Day service in a Reformed church without a sermon. Throughout all the historical fluctuations that have at times disfigured the Reformed service, one constant remains: the reading of Scripture and the proclamation of the gospel in a sermon. "The Service for the Lord's Day" affirms the importance of the ministry of the Word. Scripture and proclamation lay at the heart of worship in the apostolic and patristic ages (first few centuries of the Christian era), becoming diminished only in medieval times. The Reformers sought to recover ecumenical practice from the early centuries in which a service of both Word and Sacrament was the norm for worship every Lord's Day—a norm that had become obscured in the pre-Reformation church.

Both in its *Book of Confessions* and in its Directory for Worship, the Presbyterian Church (U.S.A.) lifts up the majesty of the Word read and preached. All editions of the Directory over recent decades consistently say that the Scriptures read and preached witness to God's self-revelation. Where the Scriptures are read and preached, the Holy Spirit is at work to manifest Jesus Christ, the Living Word, in the midst of the assembly. However edifying it may be to use the sermon time for teaching, therapy, Bible study, or advocacy of good causes, these are not the purpose of preaching. The sermon may teach; it may prove to be therapeutic; it may offer a more profound knowledge of the biblical text; and it may stir commitment to a good cause, but these are all side effects, not the main point of preaching. The Reformed tradition believes that, though the reading and preaching of the Word is not a sacrament, it is sacramental. That is to say, by the reading and preaching of the Word, Jesus Christ does indeed become present to the congregation (as opposed to a Christ whose words are simply being recalled from a historical distance) to the congregation, just as we believe Christ becomes present among us in the celebration of Baptism and the Lord's Supper. This presence is not ours to command, but is a gift of God by means of the Holy Spirit. Gordon Lathrop writes,

> Indeed, the juxtaposition of this sermon to the celebration of the Lord's Supper makes it most clear that this is a Word which is to be eaten and drunk in faith, just as the Eucharist is a meal which preaches (I Corinthians 11:26). The sermon says in words from the texts the same thing the bread and cup say in sign; "The body and blood of Christ, given and shed for you. Take. Eat. Drink. Believe. Live." As well, the sermon should bring to expression what "Church" is at all—an open assembly, with the word of forgiveness and the bread of Christ's presence at the center, available for the world, turned toward the outsiders and the poor.[12]

Therefore, preach so that hearers taste the words.

Children's Sermons? In a number of Presbyterian congregations, a custom has evolved over recent decades of inviting children to hear a "children's sermon" or "words for children" or "children's time." Perhaps congregations would feel less pressed to resort to this practice if the whole service were more inviting to children and others who need to engage all the senses in worship rather than only the sense of hearing. Conversely, and more boldly, some reject children's sermons as liturgically unnecessary and pedagogically inappropriate. "Children learn much by vigorous ritual engagement, as Eric Erickson has pointed out. They learn perhaps even more by observing what ritual and liturgy do or do not do to adults, especially their parents, and to their peers and siblings."[13]

In situations where the children's sermon is firmly rooted, there are ways to reduce the likelihood that the children will be exploited for the entertainment of the adults in the congregation. It is possible, for example, to give a children's sermon without asking the children to leave their places. This protects those children who are reluctant to be exposed to the whole assembly, while also protecting the children from exposure to the laughter of the congregation, and it minimizes the danger of tempting children to show off. The children's sermon is not to be used as a means to communicate with adults, nor is it a time to entertain adults with humorous things children may say. Children's sermons that resort to object lessons and abstractions are almost always developmentally inappropriate to the ages of the children. It is best simply to tell or retell a biblical story appropriate to the day, leaving it open-ended, without providing a moral at the end. Children can relate especially to the people in the stories, and work on their own interpretations without having them prematurely interpreted by an adult. Whatever congregations opt for with children, it is wisest to keep them present with the worshiping assembly so they may fully experience the whole liturgy. Children can *participate* and *enter into* the worship. A Word and Sacrament service, for example, can offer much more accessibility to children and others who feel excluded by an excessively intellectual and verbal form of worship.

Response to the Word Read and Preached. In response to the preached Word, there may follow an Invitation to Discipleship (BCW 63, 92–93), a hymn, canticle, psalm, or spiritual, and an Affirmation of Faith (BCW 63). Here is also the most appropriate point for celebration of the Sacrament of Baptism (BCW 401) or a Pastoral Rite of the Church (BCW 65), such as confirmation/commissioning, reception of new members, reaffirmation of the baptismal covenant, ordination and/or installation, a marriage service, or other services of commissioning. Other acts of response may include a Moment for Mission or announcements (see p. 21). While the *Book of Common Worship* makes no mention of announcements at this point in the service, a case can be made for including them here. It offers the opportunity to name the sick, the bereaved, and those with special needs *immediately prior* to the Prayers of the People, or to identify issues before the congregation or community to be included in the prayers that follow. Wherever the announcements are offered—before or after the service, or following the Word—they should be kept to a minimum and avoid repeating what has already been printed in the bulletin. If there is to be a Moment for Mission, this also could be an appropriate place for announcements. Care should be taken that it is in fact a Moment for *Mission*, which follows from the preaching of the Word.

Prayers of the People (BCW 65)

The service of The Word concludes with the Prayers of the People (BCW 65–66). The BCW includes numerous models of these prayers that address a variety of persons, situations, and institutions (for example, BCW 99–124, 787–837). In the Prayers of the People (or the Church), care needs to be taken to avoid parochialism, a common temptation to focus on local interests. When people are invited to offer concerns, often they tend to center on the sick and bereaved of their own number which, though important to lift up in prayer, can narrow and even insulate a congregation's focus. "The crisis of the present moment, like the nearest telegraph post, will always loom largest."[14] The inclusiveness of the rubric, "The congregation prays for worldwide and local concerns, offering intercessions for: . . ." (BCW 99), as displayed in the prayers themselves, is of fundamental import. These prayers need to be as inclusive as the headlines of the current newspaper. Of all places in the liturgy, the church must resist the temptation to be provincial so that it can open out in broad embrace to the world. "Our prayers should be as wide as God's love and as specific as God's tender compassion for the least ones among us" (BCW 40).

Also, regarding sequence of elements, if either the Prayer of Confession or the Peace was not included earlier in the service, it is appropriate to include them, in that order, following the Prayers of the People (BCW 65).

III. The Eucharist (BCW 67)

Offering (BCW 67)

Why an Offering? The third movement of "The Service for the Lord's Day" begins with the Offering. It forms a bridge between The Word and the Eucharist, since it is an appropriate response to the hearing of the Word read and preached. Nevertheless, the Offering has an intimate relation to the Lord's Supper. The Offering did not originate as a way of raising revenue or exerting monetary pressure on people to give when they supposedly were in a heightened state of spiritual sensitivity.

In early centuries, Christians brought to the Lord's Day assembly gifts of bread and wine from their own tables. A place to receive such gifts was designated near the entrance to the room where the congregation assembled for worship. During the service, deacons would set apart the amount of bread and wine needed for the Lord's Supper, and after the service of the Word, bring them forward to the Holy Table.

The gifts of bread and wine represented the people's offering of their own lives in the service of Jesus Christ (cf. Rom. 12:1). First Chronicles 29:14, for example, proclaims to God: "of your own we give you." At the completion of the service, church officers distributed whatever bread and wine had not been blessed at the Table to poor people in the community who needed them for sustenance. Frequently, worshipers would also bring alms for the poor, which were collected after the service for distribution among the needy. Apparently in the early church, each individual brought a portion of food to the table, more than was necessary for the Supper, in order to be able to share bread with the hungry. Intercessory concern was linked with sacramental action.

Reformed churches of the 1500s scheduled the "collection" at the *end* of the service, as the people *departed*. As a visual reminder of the importance of giving alms to the poor, a great chest was put at the church door to receive contributions. The money was then used by the deacons to support the church's ministry to those in distress. The alms chest was placed at the door because they believed *their meeting with Christ at the Table* was to be *continued in the world* where Christ awaited discovery in the guise of the neighbor in need. The weekly discipline of almsgiving ("the collection"), therefore, is related to prayer. Prayer and social concern are inseparable. The *worship* of the congregation is to be reflected in the *work* of the congregation.

Our Offering, then, has deep historical and theological roots. It is closely tied to the church's calling to serve the poor and to reach out to those outside it. Because it is rooted in the people's offerings of bread and wine, it has a profound relation to the church's Eucharist, and for that reason is the first action of the third movement of "The Service for the Lord's Day."

Invitation to the Lord's Table (BCW 68)

Why do we do what we do at the Lord's Table? Following the Offering, and after briefly thanking God for the gifts which may include bread and wine, the presiding minister offers an Invitation to the Lord's Table using words of Scripture (BCW 68). Some may prefer to offer the Invitation *before* the Offering, as in the *Book of Occasional Services* (BOS 32). The rationale for such a placement is that the Offering is historically an offering of bread and wine, to be brought to the table in response to the invitation. However, *if* the bread and wine are already in place on the table, with the accent falling entirely on God's gift of the Sacrament with no suggestion of any human role, *then* the invitation will more appropriately follow the Offering.

Great Thanksgiving (BCW 69)

Eucharist; Lord's Supper; Holy Communion. The word "thanksgiving," in its Greek-derived form, "Eucharist," has become perhaps the most widely known designation in ecumenical use for the Sacrament of the Meal. Other ways of describing the Meal are "Lord's Supper" or "Holy Communion." The name "Lord's Supper" evokes the sense of *koinōnia* (fellowship), enjoyed by the people of God with one another as they gather at Table with Christ, their host. The words "Holy Communion" accent the congregation's intimate spiritual relation with the Christ whose presence is given in the Sacrament.

The specific origin of the Eucharist is the meal which Jesus ate with his disciples in the upper room on the night of his betrayal, commonly called the Last Supper. However, the church's Eucharist has also been shaped by other meals Jesus shared with his disciples and others, including, for example, the feeding of the five thousand, and meals eaten with persons publicly identified as sinners (Matt. 9:10).

Why Rejoicing at the Lord's Table? The biblical stories of the feeding of the multitudes can be understood as a foretaste of a messianic banquet, a glorious reunion meal at which the table is set in heaven for the whole human race. "Then people will come from east and west, from north and south, and will eat in the kingdom of God" (Luke 13:29). The Lord's Supper has also been shaped by meals eaten in Jesus' presence *after* the resurrection. The meal plays a key role in Jesus' postresurrection appearances on the road to Emmaus (Luke 24) and on the shore of the Sea of Galilee (John 21) (see p. 36). The Eucharist is, in a sense, a feast that enables us to recognize the risen Lord and celebrate his presence in our midst.

It is too restricting to understand the Lord's Supper simply in terms of the Last Supper, immediately preceding Jesus' arrest and crucifixion, and yet churches have often framed their Eucharists in this very narrow way. The pre-Reformation church had distorted its Eucharist, conceiving it as a kind of representation of Jesus' suffering and death. In such a context, the appropriate way of approaching Holy Communion was in an atmosphere of sorrow, regret, and penitence.

Unfortunately, this very somber pattern survived the Reformation and continued unchallenged in the various Protestant churches, and has persisted to the present day, so that in many congregations, the Lord's Supper resembles nothing quite so much as a funeral for Jesus.

And, yet, in early centuries, this was not the case. Those who gathered for Word and Sacrament on the Lord's Day expected that in their Eucharist they would meet their friend, the risen Savior, and this expectation made their Holy Communion a celebrative banquet—a solemnly joyful feast. While the Lord's Supper lifted up the memory of Jesus Christ, crucified, it also celebrated Jesus Christ, risen.

Twentieth-century studies rediscovered the joyful tenor of the early church's Eucharists, and our own church has drawn attention to this note of joy in directories for worship for decades, declaring that in our celebrations at Table, we eat and drink sacramentally with the risen Lord, and enjoy communion with him. At the same time, we anticipate the great reunion Table spread for all in God's eternal realm.

A Joyful Thanksgiving. The Sacrament of Holy Communion embodies a richness and theological breadth that "The Service for the Lord's Day" seeks to recover. Celebrations of the Lord's Supper are truest to New Testament and early Christian precedents when the emphasis falls on praise and thanksgiving. When Jesus said, "Do this in remembrance of me," he was not calling on us to visualize him abandoned on the cross as though the story ended at that point.

The words for "remember" in both Hebrew and Greek include a sense of joyful and grateful participation in the present reality of the events recalled. The events recalled, for which we give thanks in the Eucharist (the Great Thanksgiving), include not only the Last Supper and death of Jesus, but also his resurrection and his promise of reunion at Table in the kingdom of God (Luke 22:18). As some have put it, at the Table we remember ourselves into the future.

Remembrance is not a matter of mental gymnastics, but of doing ("*Do this in remembrance of me*"). The verbs used in the stories of the feeding of the multitudes, the story of the Last Supper, and the story of Jesus' meeting with disciples on the road to Emmaus are all similar: taking, thanking, breaking, and giving (Luke 9:16; 22:19; 24:30; see also Mark 6:41, Matt. 26:26, and John 21:13). It is in the *doing* of these things—taking, thanking, breaking, giving—that the church remembers Jesus crucified, risen, and coming again. This is why medieval Latin documents such as the Tridentine Missal and the Canon of the Mass (*Canon Missae*) speak of the eucharistic sequence as an "action," a doing of these things. Likewise, the Scottish Presbyterians also called the eucharistic service "The Action."

The name "Eucharist" comes from that part of the meal which specifically involves giving thanks over the bread and cup. (In the Gospels, the Greek word used to describe this action is sometimes "bless.") Whether giving thanks or blessing the bread and wine, the practice is rooted in prayer at Jewish meals. Blessing, or praise, is a basic form of Jewish prayer.

The most familiar of Jewish blessings is addressed to God at the time of the meal: "Blessed are you, O Lord our God, ruler of the universe, who brings forth bread from the earth." The Gospel accounts of the institution of the Lord's Supper, and references to other meals Jesus ate with his disciples, refer to this practice of giving thanks or blessing. When Jesus said, "Do this . . . ," we must presume that the *doing* to which he referred includes this important and basic element of thanking and blessing.

Eucharist is not an object revered or adored but an action. That is to say, Eucharist is not a noun but a verb; therefore, to shift the Eucharist from verb to noun disfigures the Eucharist. "To remember [at the Table] was to do something not to think about something."[15]

"The Lord be with you" (Sursum Corda) (BCW 69). Following the Invitation (or following the Offering), the minister begins the Great Thanksgiving by greeting the congregation with the ancient words, "The Lord be with you." The people answer, "**And also with you**." The minister then calls on the people: "Lift up your hearts." ("So if you have been raised with Christ, seek the things that are above, where Christ is, seated at the right hand of God" [Col. 3:1].)

Called in Latin the *Sursum Corda* (upwards the hearts), this exhortation is important to the Reformed tradition as exemplified in the thought of John Calvin, who taught that in the Lord's Supper, it is not so much that Christ comes down to us, but that we are lifted by the Holy Spirit into the presence of the ascended Christ (also an Eastern Orthodox concept). After the people's response, "**We lift them to the Lord**," the minister moves to the heart of the matter: "Let us give thanks to the Lord our God." The people answer, "**It is right to give our thanks and praise**."

Early Models of Thanking and Blessing. The earliest references we have of the church's eucharistic practice (for example, the *Didache*, or *Teaching of the Twelve Apostles*, about A.D. 115) include prayers of thanksgiving or blessing of the bread and cup. In early centuries, eucharistic prayers were generally framed by the officer presiding at the Lord's Table, but the officers followed common patterns that began to develop within various geographic regions. One early example is exhibited in the eucharistic prayer of Hippolytus of Rome, dating from about A.D. 215 (Great Thanksgiving G, BCW 150).

The Trinitarian Pattern. In our time, churches of many confessions have affirmed the value of eucharistic prayer in a Trinitarian pattern, of the sort that began to be the norm in many churches from at least as early as the third century. The *Book of Common Worship* calls the eucharistic prayer the Great Thanksgiving, and all of its Great Thanksgivings follow the Trinitarian pattern.

Thanks to God for Creating the World and . . . Ordinarily, the first part of the prayer begins its thanksgiving with praise to God for the creation of the universe (for example, Great Thanksgiving A, BCW 69: "In your wisdom, you made all things and sustain them by your power"). Thanksgiving for the goodness of the created world was typical of eucharistic prayer in the Eastern churches from very early. It takes on particular importance for us in these times when there is concern for a proper stewardship of the environment.

This first part of the Trinitarian prayer continues to recite some of the mighty acts of God, climaxing with the congregation's acclamation of praise: "Holy, holy, holy Lord, God of power and might . . ." (for example, BCW 70). This acclamation, called the Sanctus (from the Latin word for "holy") derives from Isaiah 6, and from Psalm 118 ("Blessed is the one who comes in the name of the Lord . . .").

Acts of Redemption in Jesus Christ . . . The second part of the Trinitarian prayer offers thanks specifically for God's work of redemption in Jesus Christ. Typically, it recalls Jesus' birth, his life and ministry, death and resurrection, his ascension, and it thanks God for the promise of his coming again (for example, "We praise you that Christ now reigns with you in glory, and will come again to make all things new," Great Thanksgiving A, BCW 70). This second part of the Great Thanksgiving climaxes with the recollection of Jesus' words instituting the Lord's Supper, which are quoted in the prayer. This is the ecumenical practice, as it was also the practice in the early centuries.

Reformed practice has usually departed from the more ancient pattern and relocated the Words of Institution to either before the Great Thanksgiving, or afterward, at the distribution of the bread and cup. When placed before the prayer, the Words of Institution serve as a biblical "warrant"—a statement declaring the dominical authority for the continuing celebration of this sacrament. "The Service for the Lord's Day" provides for either including the Words of Institution within the prayer or using them outside the prayer. Note, for example, the brackets that mark this part of the prayer on BCW 70 and 71. In either case, the Words of Institution are used only once. The second part of the Great Thanksgiving ends with a second acclamation by the people, the Memorial Acclamation (for example, BCW 71). A venerable eucharistic prayer from the Roman tradition inserted the words "Mystery of faith" following the Words of Institution related to the cup. Many service books, including the *Book of Common Worship*, now invite the people's acclamation when the presiding minister says, "Great is the mystery of faith," or "Praise to you, Lord Jesus," or something similar.

. . . *and Prayer for the Holy Spirit*. The third part of the Great Thanksgiving is an *epiclesis*–prayer for the presence and action of the Holy Spirit (for example, "Gracious God, pour out your Holy Spirit upon us and upon these your gifts of bread and wine . . . ," Great Thanksgiving A, BCW 72). No part of this Trinitarian eucharistic prayer is more Calvinist than this. The Reformed theology of the Lord's Supper, taught with such care by John

Calvin, grounds the Sacrament entirely in the action of the Holy Spirit, just as Calvin also grounded the effectiveness of reading Scripture and preaching it in the action of the Holy Spirit. "The bond of this connection [between Christ and the church] is therefore the Spirit of Christ, with whom we are joined in unity, and is like a channel through which all that Christ himself is and has is conveyed to us."[16]

This third part of the Great Thanksgiving ends with an ascription of praise to the triune God, to which the people add their "Amen," said or sung, and the entire eucharistic prayer ends with the Lord's Prayer, which serves in the words of Tertullian as "a summary of the whole."

Both a Statement of Faith and an Act of Praise. The *Book of Common Worship* describes this Trinitarian pattern of blessing or giving thanks in some detail in Great Thanksgivings I and J, (BCW 153, 156), in order to provide guidance for those who prefer to pray it in a free style rather than using one of the texts provided in the *Book of Common Worship.* The Directory for Worship likewise describes the Trinitarian pattern. Both Great Prayers I and J draw their description of the prayer from the Directory for Worship. Prayer I takes care to preserve the important texts in the *Book of Common Worship* that are finely tuned, with free prayer following the guidelines. Prayer J gives assurance that free prayer is appropriate, but needs to be faithful to the *ordo.*

The Great Thanksgiving is both a recital of God's mighty acts, with thanksgiving for what God has done and will do, and it is doxological. It resembles a creed and it resembles a hymn of praise. In fact, in the early church, it served as the assembly's creed. Eucharistic prayer calls on biblical precedents such as Joshua's recital of the mighty acts of God (Josh. 24) or Stephen's rehearsal of God's redemptive work when he testified before the Council (Acts 7), just as it also draws on the tradition of psalms of praise and thanksgiving, such as Psalm 111.

Going Forward to Receive Communion. The earliest Reformed method for Communion was for the people to approach the Lord's Table to receive the bread and cup. "With Calvin, the people came forward as they had always done . . . one by one, receiving the bread from one Minister at one end of the table, and the Wine from another Minister at the other end."[17] In the English congregation in Geneva, John Knox had the people leave their places to sit at tables set up in the church. This practice continued in both Scotland and the Netherlands. Under the influence of the English Puritans, the Scottish church slowly and reluctantly moved toward receiving Communion in the pews, beginning in the mid-seventeenth century. Pew Communion provides an opportunity for Christians to serve one another; it also tends to reinforce the individualism and passivity that characterize many sacramental occasions.

At a minimum, congregations should try other serving methods than their present one as a way to add to the richness of receiving the Sacrament. As the *Book of Common Worship* indicates: "The people may gather around the table . . . the people may go to persons serving the elements . . . or the bread and wine may be served to the people where they are" (BCW 44).

Bread, Wine? Many churches provide broken loaves from which either the server or the communicant breaks off a smaller piece. The loaf more nearly resembles the bread to which we are accustomed and, therefore, functions as a stronger symbol for the meal. In order that the symbolism of the loaf broken at the table be authentic, it is best that the loaf broken actually be served to the people rather than being set aside after breaking.

More frequently, congregations have returned to the ecumenical and Reformed practice of providing wine for the Lord's Supper rather than grape juice exclusively. The General Assemblies of both the northern and southern churches resisted the use of grape juice even into the early twentieth century. Churches that have returned to the use of wine also need to provide grape juice or a nonalcoholic wine as an option.

While a nonalcoholic fruit of the vine must be available to those who cannot or should not drink wine, there are sound reasons for restoring the use of wine as well. Wine is not only the biblical drink but, in many cultures, it is a festive drink, as grape juice is not. It is well to take care that wine used in the Lord's Supper is of good, palatable quality.

In some congregations, those serving the bread and cup call persons by their given or first names, saying something such as, "N., the body of Christ, given for you" or, "N., the blood of Christ, shed for you" (BCW 75). Some have argued against this practice. William Seth Adams, for one, writes: "Naming the recipient of the sacramental bread or wine risks injustice to the stranger."[18] Therefore, if some are named as they are served elements, then all are named, which means congregations and worship leaders in particular will need to contemplate graceful and genuine ways to accomplish this. For example, prior to serving the elements, a server can ask the communicant for her or his name in order to name the recipient.

"The Service for the Lord's Day" provides, after all have received the Sacrament, for either singing or saying Psalm 103:1, 2 (BCW 76; PH 222, 223; PS 102), or a Prayer After Communion, which links God's feeding or nourishing us *with* God's sending us (BCW 76–77, 157–158). A prayer of thanksgiving has origins in at least the fourth or fifth centuries, and Calvin's liturgy called for a Thanksgiving after the Supper.[19] The thanksgiving after Communion has typically summed up many of the themes of the Lord's Supper.

A Reformed Goal: Weekly Reunion of Word and Sacrament. The fourfold *ordo* of "The Service for the Lord's Day" presumes that the normal pattern of every Lord's Day service includes a weekly celebration of the Lord's Supper. That does not describe the actual practice of the majority of congregations in the Presbyterian Church (U.S.A.) today. "The Service for the Lord's Day" recognizes that and makes provision for thanksgiving even when omitting Holy Communion.

For example, the *Book of Common Worship* provides substitute texts and actions for this part of the service by skipping from the bottom of page 66 to the top of page 79. The substituted texts and actions include the Offering and a Prayer of Thanksgiving, not to be understood as a prayer to bless the Offering, but purely as a giving of thanks that concludes The Word portion of the service. One may initiate this prayer with part of the same opening dialogue that introduces the Great Thanksgiving ("Let us give thanks to the Lord our God . . .") (BCW 80) thereby reminding people that ordinarily we pray here the eucharistic prayer, and conclude, as does the eucharistic prayer, with the Lord's Prayer (BCW 81). In this way, the service, with or without the Sacrament, bears witness to the fact that our worship is meant to be eucharistic in every sense of the word.

One could make the case that the divorce of Lord's Supper and Lord's Day has contributed to the Supper becoming more of a Good Friday event than an Easter event, and the Lord's Day losing its character as a celebration of the resurrection, the first day of the new creation. Presbyterians witness to the roots of their tradition in seeking to mend what Calvin understood to be a defect, to find ways to recover a weekly Eucharist on the Lord's Day, so that Word and Sacrament reinforce each other, and the feast of the risen Lord becomes a regular part of worship on each Day of the risen Lord.

The reunion of Lord's Supper and Lord's Day will help to correct the rationalism that has threatened to turn worship in the direction of a sterile didacticism; it will strengthen the church's profession of the Lord's resurrection; and it will help the church to trust God's promise, implicit in the resurrection, of a new heaven and earth (2 Pet. 3:13; Rev. 21:1).

The Challenge. It is, admittedly, difficult for many congregations to find an unencumbered path leading to celebration of the Lord's Supper weekly. Part of that difficulty may stem from the fact that many Presbyterians have been conditioned to think of the Lord's Supper in the same penitential terms inherited from the medieval church and persisting after the Reformation, and associated primarily with Jesus' death. Another difficulty may be a perception that the Eucharist seems to be a superfluous gesture meant to stimulate memories from ancient times.

"The Service for the Lord's Day," carefully attended to, leads us toward a deeper and more joyful eucharistic piety. It celebrates that the crucified One is also the risen One, in whose resurrection God promises a new creation, and who, by the power of the Holy Spirit, becomes present to the assembly in Word and Sacrament. It is not only about the past, but also about the present and about the ultimate future. The Great Thanksgiving, prayed at every celebration of Holy Communion, is a profession of faith in doxological fashion.

Adding a Service? Consider Word and Sacrament. Many congregations have been considering adding a service to one already in place. Sometimes it is easier to introduce changes by adding a service than by making significant changes to existing ones. Some congregations have experienced problems when adding a service with a different format from an existing one. Whenever adding a service, even when it is identical to existing services, there is a risk that a congregation may feel that its unity has been compromised. When considering adding a service, it is important to engage in a process of theological reflection so that the project may be undertaken with eyes open, weighing both the risks and the opportunities. The form and style of worship is not just a matter of taste. Services reflect theological commitments and, also, have the power to shape or misshape faith according to these commitments.

Very often, churches adding a service have adopted a worship model enjoying current popularity. An alternative, consistent with the *Book of Common Worship*, is a service that realizes the unity of Word and Sacrament on a weekly basis.

Most people learn a eucharistic piety from experiencing it rather than from being cognitively persuaded, much less argued, into it. A congregation can move toward experiencing weekly Eucharist by celebrating the Lord's Supper during a season of the church year, such as the Sundays from Easter Day through the Day of Pentecost (the fifty-day season celebrating resurrection), or the First Sunday of Advent through Christmas Eve/Day (the Word made flesh in the first coming undergirds this season's anticipation of the second coming when Word and Sacrament will be realized) or Epiphany (celebrating the spreading out of the True Light to all corners of creation), or throughout the summer months. Another way to step toward weekly Eucharist is by celebrating the Lord's Supper on the first Sunday of each new season (Advent, Christmas, Lent, and Easter) as well as "feast days," such as Christmas Eve/Day, Epiphany, Baptism of the Lord, Transfiguration of the Lord, Maundy Thursday, Easter Day, Day of Pentecost, Trinity Sunday, All Saints' Day (or the Sunday after), and Christ the King (or Reign of Christ) (see pp. 89–90). Either of the above paths or any combination thereof leads to increased experience of the Lord's Supper and, one hopes, increased eucharistic piety.

What Shall We Do in the Meantime? The fourfold *ordo* of "The Service for the Lord's Day" maintains the long tradition of Word and Sacrament, utilizing the same structure every Lord's Day even when circumstances prevent celebrating the Lord's Supper, until such time as we may be able to realize a weekly Eucharist. Even if the Lord's Supper is not celebrated (BCW 79–83), the service remains virtually the same except for the specifically eucharistic portions. In that case, as a step toward (not a substitute for) realizing weekly Eucharist, part of the opening dialogue:

> Let us give thanks to the Lord our God.
> **It is right to give our thanks and praise.**

that usually introduces the Great (Prayer of) Thanksgiving (BCW 69) precedes a Prayer of Thanksgiving (BCW 80) which leads into the Lord's Prayer (BCW 81), immediately prior to the final hymn of the service (BCW 82).

IV. Sending (BCW 77)

Thresholds, Again

Like the opening rite, or Gathering, the concluding movement of the *ordo* is a threshold movement, this time preparing the congregation to disperse into the world. Having assembled in God's name, they now prepare to go out in God's name. All that has happened in the assembly by way of praise, confession, proclamation, prayer, and thanksgiving becomes directed in the final moments of worship toward daily praise and dedicated service in those places in which we live out our lives. This fourth movement typically moves from congregational song to Charge and Blessing, to a musical postlude.

Although as we worship we step outside the ordinary structures and boundaries of daily life, this period of stepping outside, paradoxically, more adequately forms and strengthens us to be Christ's body in the world. In Word and Sacrament, we rehearse what it means to be God's people: recipients of mercy and agents of mercy, heirs of the kingdom and its agents in the world.

Having been fed by Word and Sacrament, we go out to share that nourishment in the ordinary intersections of our daily lives. The Lord's Day service is the indispensable event that identifies the church with its Lord and equips it to identify with those whom the Lord has called us to serve.

Charge and Blessing (BCW 78)

To underscore this relation between worship and service, the concluding movement of the service, the act of Sending, includes both a Charge and a Blessing. "Go out into the world in peace . . . love and serve the Lord" is a charge drawn from Scripture and addressed to the congregation (BCW 78). Historically, the charge was given by a deacon, as the final words of the liturgy.

The Blessing (or Benediction) ordinarily follows, although sometimes these may be reversed, with the Charge following the Blessing (see instructions, BCW 85). The Blessing is not a closing prayer, but God's blessing pronounced by the minister on the people who are about to make their departure, and it also uses the words of Holy Scripture. We go out to meet joys and obligations, pleasures and troubles, secure in the shelter of God's trustworthy Word, and strong in its power.

Some place the announcements and Moments for Mission here, at the very end of the service, with the understanding that the causes, concerns, and opportunities made public here form part of the agenda for mission as the people go out into the world. A postlude or closing voluntary may follow. (See p. 46 regarding "background music.")

Commentary on the Service for the Lord's Day

"The Service for the Lord's Day," true to the Directory for Worship, suggests a number of variations possible within the fourfold structure of the service. It provides a variety of texts for nearly every element of the service, including twenty-four texts of the Great Thanksgiving for use on the Lord's Day (for general use, BCW 126–152; for variations keyed to liturgical days or seasons, BCW 163–400, "Resources for the Liturgical Year"), as well as other Great Thanksgivings for use at weddings (BCW 869), funerals (BCW 929), or with those unable to attend public worship (for example, homebound, in a hospital or nursing home) (BCW 998). Two of the settings for general use (Great Thanksgivings I and J, BCW 153 and 156) offer forms for praying the Great Thanksgiving in a free and spontaneous style.

Not only does "The Service for the Lord's Day" provide several models for the Prayers of the People (BCW 99–124), but it describes in several places those persons, situations, and institutions which the church has taken care to include in its prayers (for example, BCW 787–837). Using such models, it is relatively simple to produce an inclusive, but homegrown, prayer adapted to the local context. Even the texts provided are meant to be suggestive rather than limiting. They serve as patterns that can guide users in discovering similar texts in Scripture or other sources, or in creating their own.

Gathering (BCW 48)

The Ministry of Hospitality

The first movement of the *ordo*, the Gathering, begins quite informally with the arrival of the first worshipers, and concludes with the service of confession and forgiveness, and exchanging the Peace. Greeters and ushers play a key role, as they are in fact ministers of hospitality.

What may on the surface seem like perfunctory duties are actually holy tasks, sacred duties, unlikely functions of welcoming, ushering people into a communal experience of the awesome mystery of what God has done, is doing, and will do, ushering people into the community of faith where they will hear, see, taste, and touch mysteries God offers us, particularly in the life, death, and resurrection of Christ.

In the life of the church, therefore, the ministry of hospitality is one of critical importance as well as one held in great respect, because in our ministry of hospitality, we can continue to meet the risen Christ by welcoming all those whom Christ loves. In the words of St. Benedict, "Let all guests be received as Christ." Thus, our meeting with Christ at the Table can be continued in our daily lives by "hosting people unable to host us in return" (see Luke 14:12–14) and, therefore, seeing the face of Christ. Those responsible for planning worship will provide opportunities for those who exercise this ministry of hospitality to understand it both biblically and practically, in order that they serve as effectively as possible.

Some churches provide a ministry of hospitality outside the building, directing newcomers to parking spaces reserved for them and to the usual entrances for those coming to worship, or to the entrances appropriate to those looking for the nursery or church school facilities. Greeters stationed inside the building should be trained to be alert to newcomers and to make them feel welcome by providing whatever direction is helpful in reducing the anxiety that usually accompanies a new place, new situation, and new people.

Ushers need to arrive well ahead of the start of the service to verify that the worship space has been properly prepared, and to help those who arrive early. Ushers' primary task is to lead, escort, guide—"usher"—worshipers to a seat or pew and, usually, to distribute to each person (adults and children) a copy of the service and announcements. Sometimes, ushers also serve in other ways such as the "official counters" of the number of people (of all ages) present, *including* choirs, lectors, acolytes, musicians, and pastors.

When worshipers begin to enter the worship space, they typically greet one another. Some pastors prefer to join in this period of greeting, either welcoming people at the door, or ambling about the sanctuary to speak to them. This period of greeting is part of gathering for worship, but it should not continue indefinitely. It is appropriate for there to be a time when those who have gathered turn to preparing themselves for worship, free from the sound of conversation.

On entry into the space for worship—a place of prayer—there is also a long tradition for a few moments of prayer: praise to God, acknowledging the One in whose name we gather, and invoking the Spirit on all who lead and all who this day gather to worship God in this place. The longer tradition is to stand silently in one's place or to bow down. Worshipers in the Eastern Orthodox tradition, for instance, stand silently for a few moments in preservice prayer. This is a practice that some Presbyterians feel comfortable engaging. On entering the pew they stand in silent prayer for a few moments. No kneelers needed. Standing is a posture of respect and giving of honor. It also reminds others that they, too, might properly engage in silent prayer for a few moments as the first act of worship in this place.

Music

The presiding minister can signal that the time for greeting has come to an end by addressing the assembly from a visible position before the congregation, greeting the people with words such as, "The grace of the Lord Jesus Christ be with you all" (2 Thess. 3:18) to which they can respond, "**And also with you**" (BCW 48). In some churches, this is the time when the presiding minister also extends a welcome to visitors, makes announcements appropriate to the life of the congregation (see some options, p. 20), or introduces a new hymn or liturgical response to be learned (see various patterns described on p. 80). Then, if there is to be an instrumental prelude, it begins immediately afterward, introduced, perhaps, by that simplest and most elegant invitation, as old as the Christian liturgy itself, "Let us worship God."

Some congregations sing the gathering music rather than hearing it played. If so, either the presiding minister, or another designated worship leader, such as a cantor, should introduce the first piece of music to be sung (for example, something from the Taizé or Iona communities), or a refrain from a hymn, a spiritual, or a spiritual song.

Our society has become accustomed to music playing a background role. Whether in an elevator, waiting for a phone to be answered, at a wedding reception, in a restaurant, or in a dentist's office, there is a great deal of music to which no one really listens. This is not the way we use music in the church.

When the congregation is not itself singing, any music in worship is offered to God on behalf of the congregation, and it is a part of worship, not meant as background for conversation.

Ideally, the musician has chosen the music because it anticipates in some way the biblical texts and liturgical emphases of the day. Even if this is not the case, the music intends to help worshipers gather themselves and begin to focus on the God for whose sake we have gathered. The music is not something that happens before worship, but something that marks the beginning of our worship. For that reason, if announcements are made at the outset of the service, then the music should follow announcements rather than precede them, since announcements following the prelude or gathering music will seem like an interruption.

Call to Worship (BCW 48)

At the conclusion of the prelude or gathering music, the congregation begins to move more deeply into the entrance rite. The first words of the liturgy are spoken by the minister—the one who has accepted the leadership role—accepted as a privilege given and accepted, not a position of honor taken. The presiding minister calls the people to worship in God's name, using words of Scripture.

A casual greeting such as "Good morning" is entirely inappropriate, even though it has become commonplace. If the pastor or other worship leaders wish to extend personal greetings, then that should be done either at the door as people enter, or while circulating for a time among worshipers as they gather. When the presiding minister calls the congregation to worship, he or she assumes a different role—the called, chosen, elected servant of God (who preaches, presides, and proclaims on behalf of the congregation). The presiding minister "presides not over the assembly but within it; . . . does not lead it but serves it; . . . is the speaker of its house of worship."[20] Moreover, both leaders and congregation alike stand before the holy God. It is a time for holy words.

Ministers or other leaders who feel uncomfortable using scriptural language, as though formal language may make them appear to take themselves too seriously, should rest assured that the assembly for worship is not about them. It is not an occasion for projecting their personality or establishing that they, too, are human. It is not an occasion to be embarrassed by holy words, as though to use them involves some sort of pretense. Worship is a series of actions and, at this point, the action requires the kind of language appropriate to the majesty of the God whom we are about to praise. To deflate the language deliberately, as though the point of leading worship is to "be oneself" rather than to take on the leadership role assigned and expected, serves to sabotage the liturgy as well as to self-deprecate and subvert one's ordination as a minister of Word and Sacrament. Those who lead worship well make themselves almost invisible, present only to facilitate. They fulfill the roles for which they are responsible and fade from the center. Worship leaders should use their gifts so that they become transparent to the divine, not pretenders of the divine.

Strive also to eliminate all the "Now is the time for . . . " introductions and instructions as they both waste time and clutter up the liturgy. Provide such instructions through gestures and let the liturgical action speak for itself.

For example, a worship leader indicates by an upward lifting of the hands or by a verbal cue that the people should stand.

Numerous examples of scriptural calls to worship are modeled in the *Book of Common Worship* (48–50, 165–400) and, of course, many other possibilities in Scripture also may be used, including verses from the appointed psalm of the day. The Sentences of Scripture can be spoken by one person, or read alternately with the people responding to the leader, or one side of the congregation reading one line and the other side the next (in antiphonal fashion), or alternating treble and bass clef voices, or any number of other possibilities, including creative though sometimes risky three-part versions.

To minimize dependence on a printed order of service, it is also possible for the congregation to offer the same response after every line said by the leader. For example, the worship leader may say, "O sing to the Lord a new song," prompting the response, "**Sing to the Lord!**" The leader's next line would be "Sing to the Lord, all the earth," to which the people respond again, "**Sing to the Lord!**" Then, "Sing, and give praise to God's name, **Sing to the Lord!**" "Tell the glad news of salvation from day to day, **Sing to the Lord!**" (BCW 49, modified version). Before beginning, the leader should indicate the appropriate response.

The Call to Worship can be offered from a position behind the Communion table (or next to it), or it can be offered from next to the baptismal font, presuming that the font is in the front of the sanctuary and clearly visible to the congregation.

Prayer of the Day or Opening Prayer (BCW 50)

An act or acts of praise appropriately follow the Call to Worship. "The Service for the Lord's Day" offers examples of prayers of adoration, described as Prayer of the Day or Opening Prayer (BCW 50–52), and also provides texts for each day of the church year (BCW 172–400, selected pages). Since the Prayer of Confession will follow soon, an option is to omit the Prayer of the Day or to use it at the beginning of or as the concluding collect to the Prayers of the People, later in the service (BCW 66). With or without the use of the Prayer of the Day or Opening Prayer, a hymn of praise, a psalm, or a spiritual song follows. Planners should choose the hymn carefully, keeping clearly in mind the idea of praise.

In some church buildings, the most natural and efficient way of moving the choir and worship leaders into their places is by use of a procession. Processions have a long history, and because they involve movement and a certain drama, they can serve the sense of gathering quite effectively. Some Presbyterian congregations use processions led by a processional cross. Following typical Scottish practice, someone may also carry the large Bible to the pulpit and place it there with great dignity, opening it with care and deliberateness.

In most instances, the choir precedes the worship leaders, with the presiding minister coming last. Some choirs enter an aisle during the instrumental introduction to the hymn, and remain in the midst of the congregation during the hymn, supporting the singing. During the final stanza, they then proceed to their places. If a congregation begins worship with a procession, then the procession needs to precede the Call to Worship, either in silence or accompanied by music, in order that the person leading the Call to Worship may lead from a position in full view of the people. Another option is for that leader to take such a position prior to the procession and, thereupon, lead the Call to Worship.

Confession and Pardon (BCW 52)

While standing at the table or the font, the worship leader opens the triadic pattern of Confession and Pardon (Call to Confession, Confession of Sin, and Declaration of Forgiveness) by calling the people to confession using words of Scripture (BCW 52–53). The Call to Confession both leads into confession and provides, in Reformed fashion, a note of grace, for forgiveness precedes repentance.

Since even our postures affect the ways we experience and perceive things, sitting is probably not the optimal posture for an act of humility before the God of grace. The congregation could be invited to stand. In some places, it may be possible and acceptable to kneel, which is the most humbling posture. In other settings, the people may raise a hand or simply open a hand, palm up, as they pray.

The people can pray the Prayer of Confession by reading one printed from "The Service for the Lord's Day" (BCW 53, 54, and seasonal prayers, BCW 172–400). Preparers of the service should lay out the prayer in the bulletin in such a way that a group of people can easily pray it aloud in unison. That means setting it in "phrase-lines" (that is, resembling more nearly a poem on the page than a paragraph from a textbook) as in the *Book of Common Worship*. Some lines will be shorter and others longer, governed by the phrasing appropriate for unison speech.

For those who prefer to limit dependence on a printed order of service, an option is to use the same brief Prayer of Confession for a period of time, in expectation that after a few Sundays the congregation may learn it by heart, or at least pray it with minimal reliance on the printed text. Familiarity can develop also by using the same prayer seasonally, throughout, for example, Advent or Lent. Weekly novelty can be overrated, particularly when weighed against the value of limiting reliance on the printed page. It is also possible for a worship leader, perhaps someone who comes forth from the congregation, to offer the prayer alone on behalf of the people, who affirm and make it their own with their vocal "Amen."

The Prayer of Confession also can be sung. Many hymns and psalms are, in fact, sung prayer. The Directory for Worship says what the whole of Christian tradition has said, that prayer may be sung or enacted as well as spoken. Psalm 51, for example, is a psalm of confession. Musical settings of Psalm 51 are available in *The Presbyterian Hymnal* (PH 195, 196) as well as a pointed psalm text in the *Book of Common Worship* (669) that enables Psalm 51 to be sung to simple psalm tones located in "The Psalm Refrains and Tones" (BCW 607) and those provided in *The Psalter: Psalms and Canticles for Singing* (PS 47–49). A spiritual song or a hymn also can serve as a sung Prayer of Confession.

The Confession and Pardon may provide for a period of silence, (a) after the Call to Confession and before the Prayer, (b) during the Prayer, or (c) after the Prayer of Confession and before the Declaration of Forgiveness. The worship leader invites the people to keep silence at the appropriate time. How long should the silence be? Longer than a mere pause, at least fifteen seconds. John Cassian, a fourth-century monk, said long enough to pray in silence but not too long to allow the Devil to steal into a worshiper's heart. "Liturgical silence is purposeful, pregnant, and controlled—the thunderous quiet of people communicating that which escapes being put into mere words."[21]

"The Service for the Lord's Day" indicates that the Confession of Sin be followed by singing the Kyrie Eleison ("Lord, have mercy"), or the Trisagion ("Holy God . . . have mercy upon us," from the Orthodox tradition), or the Agnus Dei ("Lamb of God, you take away the sin of the world") (BCW 55).

Declaration of Forgiveness (BCW 56)

The Declaration of Forgiveness follows. The worship leader declares forgiveness; God gives forgiveness! Calvin certainly called for a strong absolution, which the title "Declaration of Forgiveness" conveys in contrast to the anemic "Assurance of Pardon." The second person "you" in the declarations is therefore preferred to the third person "we" in a declaration. The text "Know that you are forgiven and be at peace" (BCW 57), however, softens any authoritarian priestly note that some fear in the use of "you" in the declarations. It also makes clear that forgiveness is present and at work *before* we ask, and is not the result of our asking for it.

If not already standing at the font, the leader proclaiming the Declaration of Forgiveness could go to the font at this point, perhaps as the people are singing. While announcing the evangelical promise of forgiveness (BCW 56–57), the leader dips cupped hand(s) into the water of the font, lifts several handfuls high into the air, and lets the water cascade into the font. Another option is to pour water from a great height from a large pitcher into the font so that it can be seen and heard by the congregation. These dramatic actions link the promise of forgiveness to the promises made in the Sacrament of Baptism.

If the aim is to make the service of confession as simple as possible, then the simplest version is the sequence of Call to Confession, the Prayer of Confession, and the Declaration of Forgiveness. Even in this simple version, the enactment of the baptismal linkage at the font remains appropriate.

Note that at this point "The Service for the Lord's Day" offers an option of including an exhortation (BCW 57) or reading the summary of the law (BCW 29) or the Ten Commandments (BCW 28).

Although in the Reformed tradition, the service of confession normally follows directly after the hymn of praise, an option is to include it following the intercessions, before the Lord's Supper (BCW 35).

THE PEACE (BCW 57)

Following confession and pardon, this first part of the *ordo* ends with The Peace. (For alternative placements, see BCW 36, 84, and p. 24.)

The Peace is placed after the Confession and Pardon, because the focus has been on reconciliation with God. In the exchange of peace, there is a logical move toward reconciliation among the people of God. The intention is not to interrupt the service with an opportunity to engage in conversation as though it were fellowship hour, but to speak to one another, friends and strangers, with a reconciling and affirming word.

It is best for people to exchange symbolic words and gestures of peace with those near at hand rather than encouraging much movement around the room. Ministers and other leaders should also exchange the peace among their near neighbors, but do not need to move about the entire congregation. The exchange of peace is accompanied by handclasps, and saying something such as, "The peace of Christ be with you."

The *Book of Common Worship* offers the option of placing the exchange of peace *after* the prayers of the people (BCW 66). Following the exchange of The Peace, the congregation may sing a hymn, canticle, psalm, or brief acclamation of praise and thanksgiving, such as Gloria in Excelsis, "Glory to God in the Highest," or Gloria Patri (BCW 58, 59).

If the people have been standing for confession, they will have been standing since the Call to Worship. This is appropriate, and provides helpful encouragement to keep this section brief. It also serves to signal a shift of attitude as all then sit for the second movement of the *ordo*, the reading and preaching of the Word of God.

The Word (BCW 60)

Holy Spirit, Holy Scripture

The second movement of the *ordo* takes the congregation into the very heart of the service of Word and Sacrament. The person who has responsibility to read the first Scripture proceeds to the location where the reading occurs. If it is the preacher of the day, he or she may proceed to the pulpit. If it is another, that reader goes either to the pulpit or to a lectern. The physical location of the Bible and the demeanor of the reader's movement to that position need to reflect the importance of the reading and preaching of the Word. To accent the transition, it is appropriate to keep a brief silence.

The very Calvinistic act of a Prayer for Illumination precedes the first reading (BCW 60, 90–91). The reader/lector offering this prayer offers it on behalf of the congregation, inviting their participation with a simple "Let us pray." The prayer itself should be addressed to or offered in the name of Jesus Christ. At the conclusion of the prayer, the congregation adds their "**Amen**."

It is fitting that a large pulpit Bible be used for all of the readings. The very size of the book itself makes a statement. It is the community's book, and it is an important book. Reading from a small, hand-held book or from a piece of paper also makes a statement—that neither this book nor the required reading from it is very important. If there is a need to read from a translation of the Bible other than the one of the large pulpit Bible, one can insert a printed text within the pages of the large book in an unobtrusive way.

It is particularly incongruous to read from a smaller Bible while there is a large Bible displayed on the Communion table. While the table more appropriately displays a chalice and a paten (plate used for bread), the Bible should be placed where it actually can be used. The large Bible does make a symbolic statement, but the statement is related to and dependent on a function—to be read aloud in the assembly. Typically, a Bible on the Lord's table is never read. Thus, a Bible does not belong on the Communion table where it becomes an object of worship. If the Bible needs to be displayed, let the Bible from which the readings of the day are read, be displayed in some manner on the pulpit or lectern. For example, the Bible may rest on a slanted surface on the front of the pulpit. At the time of the readings, the Bible is removed, the Scriptures are read and, then, the Bible is returned to its place displayed on the front of the pulpit.

The reader may open the large Bible carefully and reverently, or if it is already opened, may turn to the place that has been marked beforehand. To leaf through the pages, first one way and then another, in search of the right chapter and verse is both distracting and unseemly. The reader, more fittingly, calls the people's attention to the service of reading, saying, for example, "Hear what the Spirit is saying to the church" (BCW 61). The reader may then introduce the reading briefly (for example, "A reading from the Book of Genesis about God's call to Abraham"). It is not necessary to state the chapter and verses, especially if there is a printed order of service.

The reading of Scripture was, from earliest times, an aural experience and not one of following along in a printed text. It is not necessary to have the readings printed in full in the bulletin or on an insert sheet, nor is it necessary to call attention to page numbers if there are pew Bibles. The aim is to prepare so carefully, and to read so well, that the reading of Scripture will be an event tuned to the ear rather than the eye.

Having worked with the text beforehand, and practiced reading it aloud, the reader will read with attentiveness to its meaning and the appropriate places to lay emphasis and to pause. A common error by otherwise good readers is inappropriate emphasis. For example, the sentence: "The dog ran down the street" can have four different meanings depending upon what is emphasized. The *dog* ran down the street (it was not the cat). The dog *ran* down the street (it did not walk). The dog ran *down* the street (it did not run up). The dog ran down the *street* (it did not run down the sidewalk). The meaning of Scripture can be distorted by poor emphasis.

If the reading is not the text for the sermon, and if it is a particularly difficult text or one that requires a context to make sense, the reader may make a brief statement to prepare the congregation to hear the Word of God. The reader can signal the end of the reading by saying, "The Word of the Lord," inviting the people's response, "**Thanks be to God**" (BCW 61).

The Psalm for the day is meant ordinarily to be sung, serving as a kind of reflection on the Old Testament reading (or the book of Acts from Easter Day through Pentecost), rather than to be read aloud. For Calvinists, psalm-singing has always been an essential element in public worship or daily prayer. Included in the *Book of Common Worship* are some various ways of "Singing the Psalms" (599) as well as "Instructions for Singing Psalm Tones" (600).

If circumstances require that the Psalm be read rather than sung, it requires a different conclusion than other readings. An ancient tradition is to conclude the Psalm with the Gloria Patri, sung or said. Still today, in many metrical settings in use by the Church of Scotland, the Gloria Patri in a metered version concludes the Psalm. If worship leaders wish to keep "Father, Son, and Holy Spirit" terminology to a minimum because they are concerned about the apparent masculine language, the one reading the Psalm could conclude with an ascription such as, "Glory be to the Triune God, three in One, One in three." Some believe that the use of the Gloria Patri inappropriately places the Psalm in a christological framework. It is perfectly fine to end the Psalm without any closing ascription. It is not appropriate to end the Psalm by saying, "The Word of the Lord."

"The Service for the Lord's Day" presumes three readings, ordinarily Old Testament (followed by Psalm), Epistle, and Gospel. Some churches read, on various Sundays, Old Testament and New Testament, or Epistle and Gospel.

The first reading is ordinarily from the Old Testament. (A regular exception is during the fifty-day Easter season of seven Sundays, from Easter Day to Pentecost, when the first reading is from the book of Acts.) The Psalm follows the Old Testament reading (or Acts) and has been chosen as a reflection upon it. Some believe that when the Old Testament reading is to serve as the text for the sermon, it is better to read it last rather than first (with the Psalm following it), in order that symbolically as well as homiletically text and sermon be clearly and unmistakably linked. Those who embrace the latter practice will likewise read the epistle last when it serves as the basis for the sermon. Most, however, prefer to maintain the value of the historic sequence of Old Testament, (Psalm), Epistle, Gospel consistently, no matter which reading will serve as the basis for the sermon.

In some churches, it is the custom to stand for the Gospel reading, as a sign of reverence in the presence of the Christ, as when people are addressed by a monarch or by one whom they deeply respect. Others believe it is the same voice that addresses the church in any or all of the readings, so that none calls for a gesture of respect to which all are not equally entitled. The ascription at the end of the Gospel reading may be, "The Gospel of the Lord," to which the people respond, "**Praise to you, O Christ**" (BCW 62).

Rather than reading two or three Scriptures consecutively, choral anthems, hymns, songs, or instrumental pieces of music may be offered between the readings, preferably related in some way to the theme of the Scripture on which the sermon is based. The Reformed understanding of the intimate relation between text and sermon suggests that the preacher of the day should read the text on which the sermon is based. If the architectural constraints of the worship space are such that the preacher feels the need to preach the sermon from some place other than the pulpit, the sermon text should be read from that place as well, and from the same large pulpit Bible as the other readings. Text and sermon need to be in close proximity both in space and in time.

Sermon (BCW 62)

The sermon is properly based on one of the texts read. There should be no attempt to relate to more than one text. While material from one of the other readings may be pulled in by way of illustration, allusion, connotation, amplification, or juxtaposition, it is a mistake to try to construct a sermon on more than one of the lectionary texts, even when they are clearly related "in season," and certainly not in Ordinary Time when they are definitely not related.

Biblical preaching is not just a matter of explaining the text. It is a mysterious process that begins with a serious study of and reflection on the text, accompanied by similar study of and reflection on the needs of the congregation and the times in which we live, all simmered together in the preacher's imagination, and appealing to the imagination of the congregation. Preaching is a task to be undertaken prayerfully and with the use of every scholarly and pastoral tool available. It is an awesome task to handle holy things. In the preaching of an ordinary, but committed human being, our hope and expectation is to hear and meet the risen Lord. This hearing and meeting is enabled by the Spirit, but the Spirit loves those who are prepared!

How does the preacher end a sermon? Not by saying "Amen"! If anybody is to say "Amen," it would be the congregation. A better way to end is with an Ascription of Praise from Holy Scripture (BCW 62–63, 91–92), to which the people can learn to say "**Amen**." In some churches, the preacher then sits, and all keep a moment of silence for reflection on the proclamation of the Word.

Invitation to Discipleship (BCW 63)

Some churches include at this point an Invitation to Discipleship (BCW 63, 92–93). The minister or other person offering the invitation should move to a position on the same level as the congregation, or stand at the baptismal font. It is the obligation of the minister to be clear about what sorts of responses to the invitation she or he expects. Is it for people to make a personal commitment or recommitment, remaining in their seats? Is it for persons to come forward? If so, will the minister offer a prayer for these persons, lay on hands, or enroll them in some course of preparation for making a profession of faith? The use of the invitation requires keen pastoral sensitivities and liturgical flexibility.

Affirmation of Faith (BCW 63)

With or without an Invitation, most congregations respond to the proclamation of the Word by singing a hymn, canticle, psalm, or spiritual song. An Affirmation of Faith, using a creed of the church, then follows. The Nicene Creed has been most often associated with occasions when the Eucharist is celebrated (BCW 64). The Apostles' Creed is well-known and often used by Presbyterians (BCW 65). Because of its association with the service of Baptism, the Apostles' Creed may be led from the font. There are also affirmations of faith in Scripture (BCW 94–98) as well as those of the Reformed heritage in the *Book of Confessions*. When baptism follows (BCW 403), or any Reaffirmation of the Baptismal Covenant (BCW 431), or new members are to be welcomed (BOS 229), the Apostles' Creed serves as a critical piece of those rites. Since a creed should not be used twice, it is omitted as a response to the Word on occasions when baptism or a baptism-related rite is celebrated, taking special care to use the Apostles' Creed in those cases (see

BCW 408, 409 regarding how the Apostles' Creed is used in baptism; and BCW 450, 451 regarding how it is used in a service of Reaffirmation of the Baptismal Covenant).

It is also possible to sing a creed, as was the custom in Calvin's Geneva. An example is "This Is the Good News" (PH 598), which is a setting of a scriptural affirmation of faith (1 Cor. 15). There are also creedal paraphrases such as "We All Believe in One True God" (PH 137), or "I Believe in God Almighty."[22]

While the *Book of Common Worship* also provides for using as an Affirmation of Faith "a portion of the *Book of Confessions*," this should be undertaken with caution. Most of the confessions were not written to be spoken aloud by a group of people, liturgically. Nor is the congregation likely to be familiar with them, particularly in any detail. It is hardly fair to expect the assembly to read dense prose aloud, especially when they have never seen the words before or pondered them.

The creed is not an occasion to reinforce the theme of the sermon or to catechize the congregation. For such purposes, it is entirely appropriate to print a portion of a confession in the bulletin for people's reflection before worship begins, or to take home. Neither should the Affirmation of Faith be something created for the occasion, or be one borrowed from a printed collection that has struck the imagination of those preparing the service. The Affirmation of Faith belongs to the whole church, and it should not come as a surprise to those who are expected to make it.

The faith being affirmed is the faith of the whole ecumenical church—a faith that is catholic and orthodox as well as Reformed. It is not a good occasion for novelty. The fact that the congregation knows it by heart is a plus, not a drawback. Creeds and prayers that are lodged in the memory, like the Lord's Prayer, work their way into our inner being over time. It is unnecessary to experience them every time as though it were the first time.

If announcements are to be made at this point, they can be made from the chancel steps, if there is a chancel, or from a position immediately in front of the congregation.

Prayers of the People (BCW 65)

The second part of the *ordo*, The Word, concludes with the Prayers of the People. These prayers should be offered from a position behind the Communion table, or adjacent to it, or from the midst of the congregation. In some congregations, it is customary to solicit from the congregation concerns or thanksgivings to be included in the prayers. In smaller assemblies, this might be done verbally. It is also possible to do it by including within the bulletin or in the pews a slip of paper on which concerns or thanksgivings can be written, to be collected before the prayers are offered.

Certain intercessions are appropriate to every congregation (BCW 66, expanded on 99), and the Directory for Worship also lists them, properly framing every occasion of prayers of the people so as to avoid merely local parochial concerns. They include prayers for:

> the church universal
> the world and the nation
> those in authority
> the community
> persons in distressing circumstances
> those with special needs

These prayers also often include a commemoration of those who have died (BCW 102, 106, 111, 116, and 121–122), and may close with a concluding collect (BCW 123, 124), or the Prayer of the Day if it has not already been used (BCW 50–52, 165–400). If altering or improvising these prayer models, it is important to take care to preserve the form or structure of the prayer chosen, in order that the prayer may flow naturally, give confidence to the people as to what is expected of them in responses, and to allow the style to communicate the contents of the prayer. If the Prayer of Confession has not been prayed earlier in the service, it may also be included at the conclusion of the Prayers of the People (BCW 53–54, 66, 87–89, 165–400).

A minister may lead the Prayers of the People, but it is also quite in order and a tradition of the ancient church for these prayers to be led by a deacon or deacons. Since the deacons have responsibility for caring for the congregation as well as providing various ministries of service beyond their boundaries, they can make a significant statement for someone ordained to this office to lead the people's prayers. In a congregation that chooses not to use the office of deacon, the prayers could be led by an elder.

Leading prayer is a skill to be learned. If a deacon or an elder is to lead the prayers, it is important that the pastor or someone delegated by the pastor spend time teaching this skill. If possible, the deacon will also serve as a member of a liturgical planning committee, or at least confer with the pastor(s) before planning the prayers.

If prayers are to be used directly from "The Service for the Lord's Day," or if they have been otherwise written out, a stand on the Communion table to hold the text will be useful, freeing the hands of the person offering them. In other instances, the one praying may have an outline firmly in mind and pray without any printed aids. The one offering the Prayers of the People may also lead them from the midst of the congregation, the person responsible stepping into the aisle from his or her seat, offering the prayers from a notebook pleasing to the eye, not just a piece of paper.

The one offering the prayers may call out to the congregation, "The Lord be with you," extending hands toward them,

while they respond, "**And also with you**," perhaps returning the gesture. While praying, it is fitting for the people to raise one or both hands,

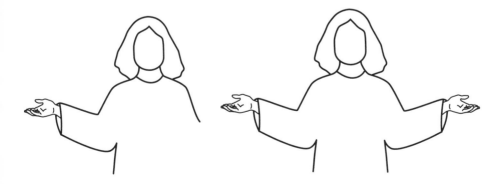

or to hold both hands together, palm to palm, in a gesture of prayer.

When praying for persons, we pray for them by name, using the first or given name only. This is not for reasons of privacy, but for reasons of intimacy. United with Christ and one another in Baptism, we are on first-name terms as sisters and brothers in Christ when we pray for one another. The practice is rooted in Baptism where only the given name is used. Through Baptism, one is united to the household of God, which transcends the family of one's birth. Do not use honorifics: no Mr., Mrs., Ms., Dr., Professor, or Senator, but simply, "for John, for your servant Mary, for Hans and other members of the family of your servant Greta, for your servant José . . ." The prayers are not occasions for making announcements. In other words, do not pray, "For little Maria, whose appendix was removed last night at County Hospital, but who is doing well and will be discharged to her home on Tuesday."

Rather than one, long, uninterrupted prayer, it is more effective to break the prayer into smaller units, ending each with a statement that cues a response from the congregation, such as "through Jesus Christ our Lord," to which they respond each time with "**Amen**," or "God of mercy," to which the response may be, "**Hear our prayer**." (Examples of other responses can be found in BCW 109, 115.)

A model for including spontaneous prayers, but following a traditional outline, is also included (BCW 118). These are very effective in incorporating spoken responsive lines, leader and people, fixed prayer and free prayer, and focusing on each subject of concern that should be included in all prayers of the people. It is also possible to sing responses after each intercession. Refrains of hymns or spiritual songs, the refrain of a psalm or canticle, or a chorus such as those used at Taizé or Iona will serve the purpose. Congregations appreciate adding their voices to the prayers, whether in speaking or singing, and follow the prayers more easily when the petitions are separated.

The Prayers of the People may also be omitted here and included in the Great (Prayer of) Thanksgiving (for example, BCW 72). In either case, if concerns and thanksgivings have not been solicited from the congregation, it is possible and appropriate to invite those present to call out the first names of persons for whom they desire prayer, all at once rather than in sequence, allowing however much time is necessary for them to do it.

The Eucharist (BCW 67)

Offering (BCW 67)

The service of the Word moves toward the Communion table at the Offering. While the most common practice is to circulate offering plates among the congregation, it is also possible for those bringing offerings to go forward and place their offerings in receptacles provided for them near, but not on, the Communion table, or on a table at the foot of the chancel steps. When ushers bring offering plates forward, they should place them on a side table or stand. The congregation could stand to sing a doxology, or some other sung praise, such as the refrain or verse of a hymn, psalm, or spiritual song. For suggestions of offertory sentences, see BCW 67; and for appropriate words to follow the presentation of the offering, see BCW 68.

In some churches, representatives of the congregation bring forward a flagon (pitcher) and a loaf of bread as the monetary offerings are presented. The presiding minister, standing behind the table, receives flagon and loaf, and places them on the Communion table. If the necessary table service and bread and cup are placed on the table prior to the start of worship, and if the table and/or the elements are covered, then the presiding minister prepares the table by uncovering them. Covering the elements simply serves to protect the bread and cup from flies; therefore, such a covering should not resemble a funeral pall.

Invitation to the Lord's Table (BCW 68)

Standing behind the table, the presiding minister offers an Invitation to the Lord's Table (BCW 68–69, 125). This is not a minisermon, nor an explanation of what the Sacrament means. The Invitation derives from Scripture. If the Words of Institution are not included in the Great Thanksgiving (the more typical ecumenical custom) (BCW 70–71), then they may be used here (BCW 68–69, B), but they should not be used more than once. While extending the invitation, the presiding minister may use arms and hands to indicate the breadth of Christ's hospitality, and to gesture toward the table, which represents the feast prepared for all the baptized.

Great Thanksgiving (BCW 69)

In some churches, the presiding minister is accompanied by elders gathered alongside or nearby. In others, children may be invited to stand with the presiding minister at the holy table, perhaps participating with a series of questions reminiscent of the children's role during the domestic liturgy of the Passover Seder: for example, "Why do we eat bread at this table?" After the opening dialogue, a Great Thanksgiving with a special role for children, perhaps during the Maundy Thursday service, might go like this:

> **Children :** Why do we give thanks and praise before this table?
> **All: We give thanks for God's work of creation, liberation, and salvation.**
>
> **Minister:** It is indeed right, our duty and delight, that we should at all times and in all places give thanks to you, O holy Lord, eternal God. You created the heavens and the earth and all that is in them; you made us in your own image; and in countless ways you show us

your mercy. Therefore, with choirs of angels, and the whole company of heaven, we worship and adore your glorious name, joining our voices in their unending praise:

All Sing: **Holy, holy, holy Lord, God of power and might,**
heaven and earth are full of your glory,
Hosanna in the highest.
Blessed is he who comes in the
name of the Lord.
Hosanna in the highest, hosanna in the highest.

Minister: All glory and blessing are yours, O holy God, for in your mercy you gave your only son Jesus Christ. He took our human nature, and suffered death on the cross for our redemption. There he made a perfect sacrifice for the sins of the whole world. We praise you that before he suffered and died, our Savior gave us this holy Sacrament and commanded us to continue it until he comes again.

Children: Why do we eat bread at this table?

Minister: On the night before he died, Jesus took bread. After giving thanks, he broke it, and gave it to his disciples, saying, "Take, eat. This is my body, given for you. Do this in remembrance of me."

Children: Why do we drink from the cup at this table?

Minister: The same night Jesus took the cup, saying, "This cup is the new covenant sealed in my blood, shed for you for the forgiveness of sins. Do this in remembrance of me."

Children: What do we remember at this table?

Minister: We remember God's gracious love for us, Christ's death and resurrection for us, and the Spirit's tender care for us. Let us proclaim the mystery of faith:

All sing: **Dying you destroyed our death;**
rising you restored our life.
Lord Jesus, come in glory.

Minister: Merciful God, pour out your Holy Spirit on these gifts of bread and wine, that in eating and drinking we may be made one with Christ and one another.

All: **Amen.**

Minister: Through Christ, with Christ, in Christ, . . . now and forever.

All: **Amen.**
Our Father, who art in heaven . . .

When the congregation is small and the space adequate, the whole congregation may be invited to stand in close proximity to the table.

From very ancient times, it was the practice of congregations to stand for the Great (Prayer of) Thanksgiving. It is best to stand at least for the first part of the prayer, which concludes with the sung "**Holy, holy, holy Lord. . . .**" This prayer, like the great creeds of the church, "is perhaps the primary liturgical repository of our collected theology."[23] One could say that this prayer is one that sings itself (HL 1–138). It is a prayer that is both prayed and proclaimed. It is a heads-up, eyes-open kind of prayer. The eyes of the congregation should be fixed on the action at the table. It is appropriate to invite those who are able to extend a hand toward the holy table as the presiding minister offers the Great (Prayer of) Thanksgiving.

From very ancient times, in both East and West, this prayer has begun with an opening dialogue between the presiding minister and the congregation. In order to keep hands free, the presiding minister may use a stand placed on the table to hold a copy of the prayer or notes for the prayer. The presiding minister calls out "The Lord be with you!" perhaps accompanied by a physical gesture, extending arms and hands in the direction of the people. They respond, "**And also with you!**" perhaps returning the gesture. Then the presiding minister cries, "Lift up your hearts!" while slowly raising hands on either side, palms up, in a lifting motion—the ancient *orans* ("praying") position.

They answer, "**We lift them to the Lord**." Then, the presiding minister says, "Let us give thanks to the Lord our God," perhaps bringing together both hands in a gesture of prayer.

The people answer, "**It is right to give our thanks and praise**." Then, with hands open and arms extended in such a way as to embrace both the congregation and the table, the presiding minister begins the Great Thanksgiving. If the minister chooses not to use the precise text of one of the eucharistic prayers in the *Book of Common Worship* or a similar service book (for example, *Lutheran Book of Worship*, United Methodist Church's *Book of Worship*, Church of England's *Book of Common Prayer*), it is possible to frame the Great Thanksgiving in his or her own words, being careful to follow the Trinitarian pattern that characterizes this prayer. (See Great Thanksgiving I or J, BCW 153; 156, or the Directory for Worship.) Note that Great Thanksgivings B, C, and D (BCW 126, 130, and 138) have been designed to be adapted to various liturgical seasons, festival days, or other occasions by the use of a Proper Preface (BCW 133–139).

The first part of the prayer reaches its climax in what has traditionally been known as the Sanctus ("Holy, Holy, Holy Lord . . ."), which should be sung, if at all possible, by everyone. The second part of the prayer recalls acts of

God in Christ accomplished for us, and reaches its climax in the Words of Institution (if following ecumenical usage) which segues into the Memorial Acclamation (BCW 71), which may easily be sung by the whole assembly. A lead-in line for each of the four models serves as the cue to the people for the appropriate text. The third part of the prayer prays for God to pour out the Holy Spirit both on the congregation and on the gifts of bread and wine. At this point, the presiding minister may hold hands over the loaf and the pitcher.

Then, resuming the earlier *orans* posture of prayer, the presiding minister may insert here the Prayers of the People—intercessions for the church and the world (bracketed example, BCW 72), if they have not been offered earlier. As described above, the people may also be invited to call out first names of people, or names of places or situations they would like to remember in prayer. The prayer concludes with an acclamation or ascription of praise to the Holy Trinity (BCW 73), to which from earliest times the people have given their vocal "**Amen**," either sung or said and, then, the minister leads the congregation in the Lord's Prayer, prayed aloud by all. Note that two translations of the Lord's Prayer are available, the first and preferred one listed being the one translated and approved by the International Consultation on English Texts (ICET) (BCW 73).

Breaking of the Bread

In what is called the "manual acts" (the use of hands), the presiding minister holds up the loaf of bread and breaks it in silence. Holding it high for all to see, the minister repeats words of Scripture such as those provided on BCW 74, or, if not used earlier, the Words of Institution. The words should be spoken slowly and in careful rhythm with the gestures. Gestures need to be expansive and smoothly paced. Nothing dare be rushed. Then the minister pours from the flagon into the cup (chalice), slowly and deliberately, for all to see. Lifting the cup as well as a part of the loaf, the minister invites the people to partake (BCW 75).

Communion of the People (BCW 75)

The people may come forward to commune at or near the Communion table, all participating in passing the bread and cup to one another; or they may go to persons who are prepared to serve them with the bread and cup; or, designated servers may take the elements to the people in the pews. Being called to the table rather than remaining fixed in place at a distance accents the fact that God's grace comes near to us and gathers us around. Moving to the table is reminiscent of our pilgrimage toward the heavenly city and the messianic banquet, where people "will come from east and west, from north and south, and will eat in the kingdom of God" (Luke 13:29). Approaching the table also requires an act of volition–choosing to receive the gift of God—that is important to many as a weekly renewal of commitment.

Whatever method is used, words of delivery should be spoken by those serving, or by the people to one another; for example, "The body of Christ, given for you" (BCW 75–76). The response to these words on the part of the receiver is "**Amen**." An increasing number of congregations have been restoring the long-standing custom of inviting the people to come to the Lord's table to receive the Sacrament. There are a variety of ways to serve the people when they come forward. In some churches, people come forward and form circles, the bread and cup circulating in both directions, with subsequent circles being formed until all have been served.

In other situations, servers receive the loaf and cup at the table, then station themselves to serve the people as they come forward, usually down the center aisle, then returning via a side aisle. More than one station for receiving the bread and cup is both acceptable and appropriate. In some churches, a server or servers go to the back of the sanctuary while others are serving in the front or the sides. It is far easier and more efficient to move large groups of people than to carry large, cumbersome vessels to persons seated in pews. One or two extra servers can be commissioned to keep an eye out for people who cannot easily leave their seats, and to make certain they are given the opportunity to receive the bread and cup in their seats.

It is possible to serve people with trays of small Communion glasses or with large chalices. One option is for the people to break off a piece of the loaf, then dip it into the cup, consuming the bread and wine together (this is called intinction). For two reasons, the better practice is for the server to break the bread and give it to the communicant. First, if the server's hands are properly washed, it has the argument for sanitation. Second, theologically, we are given and we receive—a fitting sign of being given and receiving the signs of God's grace. We are given, and in the giving we receive—we do not grasp and take. For the server to break and give is a more fitting sign. In gatherings of small numbers, some presiders break the bread into many smaller pieces to be served to the congregation.

It is also possible to buy "pouring chalices" (that is, a chalice with a pouring lip). A server can pour from this type of chalice into a smaller cup which has been given to the communicant before reaching the chalice-bearer. The older and ecumenical practice is for the people to drink from the common chalice, the server carefully wiping the rim after each communicant.

While people are communing, it is appropriate for the congregation or the choir to sing. Repetitive choruses, such as those in use at Taizé, or portions of a psalm, or a chorus, can be sung. Our long custom of funereal music at Communion runs the risk of canceling out the element of thanksgiving and disfiguring the service. Whether sung or played by organ or instruments, care should be taken that the music reflects the joy appropriate to eating and drinking with the risen Lord. It is not inappropriate to commune in silence, although this may convey an unduly somber mood.

If Communion is served in the pews, consider using bread in pieces large enough to be broken as it is passed. Some churches pass the bread in baskets lined with a napkin. The cup should immediately follow the bread, for bread and cup are not two separate courses. They are the meal. The custom of first serving the bread to everyone and then the cup needlessly prolongs the serving. Communicants should eat the bread and drink the cup as they receive them, not holding them to eat or drink in unison. Consumption of the elements in unison is an artificial practice, quite different from what people do at an ordinary meal.

The ancient custom was for the minister to receive Communion first, seemingly violating the rules of social etiquette when someone serves as the host at a meal. This practice made it clear that the minister was not the host, but a guest at Christ's table. However, in American culture, at least, the significance of communing first is likely to be lost on the congregation. It may be better, then, for the minister to commune last, as one of the servants of the servants of the Lord. However, in some cases, particularly when the congregation is communing in a new way, the minister and those charged with serving the elements might well receive first to model for the congregation how it will be done.

Prayer after Communion (BCW 76)

When serving is completed, the remaining bread and wine should be brought back to the table. The people may sing or say Psalm 103, or the presiding minister, standing behind the table, with arms extended, offers a Prayer after Communion (BCW 76, 77, or 157–158), which links God's nourishing us and God's sending us. The Directory for Worship requires that the remaining elements either be used or disposed of in a way approved by the session. In some churches, servers take the remaining bread to the door(s) of the church, or to the refreshment hour if one follows the service, to be consumed by the congregation. A member or members may take it home for use in their meal. In other cases, care is taken to distribute the remaining bread so that it may be consumed by the birds of the air.

When the Sacrament Is Omitted (BCW 79)

Clearly, "The Service for the Lord's Day" considers the norm of weekly practice to be Word and Sacrament—weekly Communion. If the congregation has not yet achieved this, however, there is a pattern for extending the second part of the *ordo*, in effect, eliminating the third part, Eucharist, of the *ordo*. This abbreviated Thanksgiving intends to be reminiscent of Eucharist even when there is no celebration of the Lord's Supper. On a noneucharistic occasion, the service moves from BCW 66 to 79.

As in the normative service, this part of the *ordo* also begins with the Offering. Then, moving to a position behind or alongside the holy table, the presiding minister offers a Prayer of Thanksgiving. Reminiscent of the Great Thanksgiving, the people may stand. The minister may introduce the prayer with part of the opening dialogue that ordinarily precedes the Great Thanksgiving. With arms extended in the same gesture used at celebrations of the Lord's Supper, the presiding minister offers the Prayer of Thanksgiving, climaxing with the people's "**Amen**," and leading into the Lord's Prayer. (For examples, see BCW 80–81, and 158–159, or seasonal prayers included in the liturgical materials for the Christian Year, BCW 165–400.)

Sending (BCW 77)

Charge (BCW 78)

The fourth and final movement of "The Service for the Lord's Day" is, like the Gathering, a threshold or transitional moment. In this instance, the threshold leads from the gathered assembly back into the world. Typically, this part of the service begins with singing: a hymn, spiritual song, canticle, or psalm. Then follows a Charge and a Blessing. Alternatively the Charge and Blessing may precede a final hymn. The congregation, in effect, goes out singing.

The Charge ordinarily precedes the blessing, although the *Book of Common Worship* suggests the possibility of reversing the order, with Blessing before the Charge (BCW 85). In such case, an alternative is: Blessing (minister), singing (procession out of worship space), Charge (deacon or elder). The Charge may be spoken (or sung) from the entrance to the worship space, from where people will depart. If there is no procession out of the worship space, then it could be hymn, blessing (minister), Charge (deacon or elder).

Drawn from Scripture, the Charge gives marching orders for the people of God. The Charge is hortatory. It exhorts us to do certain things, with the attendant promise of God's support as we undertake to do them. (See examples in BCW 82–83, 159–160.) However, it should not be a mini-sermon. The use of Scripture guards against the temptation to preach one more time. The Charge may be given by an elder or deacon, standing before the assembly.

If the Charge were not linked to the Blessing, the Charge might actually function as a counsel of despair. In the crosscurrents of daily life, it can be enormously difficult to "hold on to what is good," or "return no one evil for evil," or to "strengthen the fainthearted," "support the weak, and help the suffering." But a word of Blessing always accompanies the Charge.

Blessing (BCW 78)

The *Book of Common Worship* uses the word "Blessing" instead of the more familiar "Benediction" in order to make absolutely clear the nature of this last word. It is not a closing prayer. It is a "good word"—a blessing. Once again, in a service committed to and saturated in Holy Scripture, the forms of blessing are scriptural (BCW 83, 161). The Blessing should be given standing in front of the people, from near the Lord's table, or near the baptismal font. If the choir has recessed, the minister should remain behind in order to face the congregation while giving the Blessing. The minister also may give the Blessing before the processional hymn, then the charge from the door. Holding hands (or at least one hand) high, palm toward the congregation, the minister offers the Blessing, looking directly at the people, who need not close their eyes, but rather keep them open as they receive it.

The extended hands have the same function as the Laying On of Hands. In some churches, it is acceptable for the one offering the Blessing to trace the sign of the cross in the air with one hand, the other hand extended palm outward toward the people, particularly if using 2 Corinthians 13:13, or some other Trinitarian form. The sign of the cross reminds us, among other things, that God has claimed us in our baptism, and marked us as "Christ's own, forever."

After the Blessing, the congregation may sit in quiet reflection to listen to a postlude, or speak to one another as they leave the sanctuary, with particular care to greet those who may be visitors or infrequent worshipers.

In some congregations, it is the practice to be seated following the Blessing, during which time the pastor and/or others may make announcements related to congregational life, or offer invitations to participate in various forms of mission. In this case, either there may be no postlude, or the postlude will follow such announcements. A consideration regarding applause: Before applauding choirs or instrumentalists, remember that in worship both vocal and instrumental music are offered as forms of prayer. Music as prayer, therefore, is not for entertainment or artistic display. Music as prayer is a worthy offering to God on behalf of the people.

Preparing and Leading the Service for the Lord's Day

Worship as Symbolic Action

"The Service for the Lord's Day" is far more than written texts. The liturgy is not simply something we say, but something we *do*—an event with a shape. It is a series of actions, sometimes employing words or music, sometimes enacted in gesture or movement. The language of the liturgy is meant to *do* something rather than to communicate information. The fact that the liturgy is enacted week by week on schedule does not imply detachment. The liturgical action is entirely compatible with the heartfelt and the sincere, but it is more than merely the spontaneous outpouring of whatever may be in our hearts on any given Sunday morning. To enact the liturgy is to take our parts and do them as faithfully as we can, no matter what may be the status of our feelings at the moment, whether our faith is at full power or at low ebb. Faith may be given in and with the performance of the liturgy quite as easily as it may precede it.

The Directory for Worship rightly tells us that when the church responds to God and even when we try to speak of our experiences of God, we have no choice but to act and speak in symbolic ways. Symbolic words and actions must be rooted in the life, death, and resurrection of Jesus Christ.

Full Participation

"The Service for the Lord's Day" does not suggest that only one way of doing the liturgy is the "correct" way. Following the same *ordo* and using the same texts, the liturgy may be done quite differently. However enacted, it is important that the congregation learn to understand it as active rather than passive. The exercise of our "royal priesthood" (1 Pet. 2:9) takes place not only within the mind, but also requires engagement of the whole self, body as well as soul. Passivity weakens the ability to worship. Customs that require the congregation to sit for the greater part of the service contribute to passivity. The apostle Paul appealed to the Christians in the city of Rome to "present your bodies as a living sacrifice, holy and acceptable to God, which is your spiritual worship" (Rom. 12:1).

Whatever Paul may have had in mind, it is clear that from as early as the New Testament era itself, Christian worship involved more than simply listening and reflecting. It also involved washing, anointing, laying on of hands, eating and drinking, exchanging of the kiss of peace, singing, presentation of offerings, and quite probably the use of the Jewish posture for prayer, which involved standing with hands raised. More often than not—at least until the invention of pews in the thirteenth century—it involved physical movement by the congregation as well as by the leaders.

For various reasons, Presbyterians have become accustomed to a style of worship oriented almost entirely to the intellect. Many persons, but especially those born after World War II, do not find this style of worship attractive.[24] For many of those whose orientation is primarily to the sensibilities of the late twentieth and early twenty-first centuries, worship oriented primarily to the intellect represents a time past.

Too often our theology has tried to lead us in one direction while our worship practices have led us in exactly the opposite direction. One must never imagine that being authentically Reformed means that we must take a passive role in worship, smother authentic emotion for fear of emotionalism, remain glued to our seats, and disengage all the senses except the sense of hearing. Much Reformed worship has been like that, but those qualities do not make it Reformed. Such habits are rooted in historical circumstances rather than in Reformed principles. A recovery of a more biblical worship, engaging the body as well as the mind, not only brings us closer to the mainstream of Christian worship, but holds promise of more coherently integrating our practices of worship with our Reformed theology.

Contexts

For many Presbyterians, such a recovery will come hard. Certainly, it is wise to introduce unfamiliar practices tactfully and with discretion, expecting congregations to become at ease with them slowly, over a period of time. The aim is a renewal of the vitality of congregational worship in such a way as to win the hearts of the congregation as well as those of ministers and worship committees.

Nor is the aim uniformity. It is quite right that the way the congregation enacts the liturgy be appropriate to its context. "The Service for the Lord's

Day" will most likely look and sound and feel different in a primarily African American congregation than in a primarily European American congregation; in a small congregation than in a large one; a Korean American congregation than in one that is primarily Hispanic American. The rural congregation will enact the liturgy differently from an urban congregation, and both may celebrate it differently from one in a suburban setting. It will look and sound and feel different in one worship space than in another and, yet, the essential shape remains the same.

Worship Leadership

The following suggestions for leading the Lord's Day service are meant to stimulate the imagination of those responsible for introducing the service, or for leading congregations to grow into it more deeply. They are neither exhaustive nor limiting.

The chief responsibility for planning and leading the service generally falls to the pastor of the congregation, in close consultation with the person(s) responsible for music. Pastors and musicians can work together to teach each other and assist each other for the benefit of the whole congregation. Although some decisions regarding worship (such as the selection of Scripture to be read) have been reserved for the pastor, a session has overall responsibility for the worship of the congregation. In some cases, they may delegate this responsibility to pastor(s), musician(s), and worship committees. Liturgical planning always includes the key person(s) responsible for planning and organizing the music of the service.

Decisions about worship should be rooted in theological reflection informed by denominational guidelines rather than in personal tastes. Pastor, musician, and possibly others will consider the liturgical season, major festivals, and scriptural texts for each occasion far enough in advance to make it possible to coordinate the various personnel and resources necessary to realize the liturgy effectively.

The pastor commonly functions in the classical role of the presiding minister in "The Service for the Lord's Day." The presiding minister functions as host to the event and, as such, attends to its warmth and welcoming quality. It is not the presiding minister's responsibility to lead every part of the service, but to oversee the roles of others who share in leadership. This includes not only the presiding minister's attention to written texts, but also providing direction for others about the places from which they will exercise their leadership; their physical movement from one position to another; and planning the actions to accompany the spoken words of the service. Others who share in leadership are the musicians, readers/lectors, persons designated to lead in prayer, cantors, ushers, greeters, acolytes, persons receiving the offering, eucharistic ministers (those who serve Communion), elders representing the session on various occasions including the Sacrament of Baptism, persons who may be designated at particular times to join in laying on of hands or anointing, and so forth.

In concert with the Reformed tradition's distinctive accent on shared leadership between laity and clergy in governing congregations, ministers and members share leadership in worship. To lead corporate worship requires willingness and a particular gift to glorify God such as singing, speaking, playing a musical instrument, baking bread for the Lord's Supper, dancing, praying, lighting candles, serving the elements, or ushering. It is helpful for sessions (governing bodies) to establish some organized means by which many members may be invited to serve in leadership roles for corporate worship.

The role of a minister in a congregation is to preach and administer the sacraments, and to equip the saints. Lest that sound like a perfunctory commitment, consider that typically it takes far more energy, dedication, organization, and skill to empower and train people to do something than simply to do it oneself. Likewise, in the Revelation to John, images of no temples and no clergy in the new Jerusalem (for example, Rev. 21:22) speak clearly to us of the need in the present world for pastors to equip congregations to glorify and enjoy God. A challenge of one's pastoral call is to enact the various possibilities delineated above to make a congregation's worship experience truly *corporate*.

Why Preside from Table and Font?

Although it has been common in Presbyterian churches to lead worship from the pulpit, this practice is rooted not in principle but in practical circumstance. At the time of the Reformation, when reform of the liturgy required that worshipers understand and participate in worship in their native languages, and when preaching had been restored to its rightful place, actually *hearing* the spoken words of the liturgy became important for the first time in centuries.

Medieval churches had been designed to emphasize sight rather than hearing. Medieval church buildings had pulpits which were most often used for preaching on extraordinary occasions, outside the mass, and these pulpits were frequently placed at some distance from the chancel and altar, well into the nave, in order that preaching, when it occurred, be close enough to the people that they could hear it.

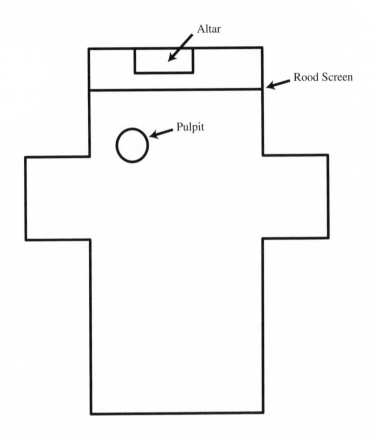

In the Protestant service, because hearing the whole service had become important, ministers serving in large church buildings led nearly the whole service from the pulpit. Leading from the pulpit serves as a practical solution to a practical problem, but it has the disadvantage of giving the appearance that all of worship is essentially a matter of listening to words spoken for our sake, as in preaching. Many modern churches are constructed with a lectern as well as a pulpit, and worship leaders are likely to lead from it as well as from the pulpit.

To lead worship from the table makes it clearer that the assembly has gathered to address itself to God as well as to listen for a Word from God. Where the space does not require sound amplification, or where electronic amplification is available, no practical reason requires leading worship entirely from pulpit or lectern. Leadership which moves among table, font, and pulpit offers the opportunity of clarifying and accenting the purpose and intention of each move of the service as well as providing visual focal points for worshipers.

"The liturgy requires focal points in space and time which are constant and stable."[25]

Printed Orders for Worship

Most churches provide worshipers with a printed order of service to aid their participation. Over time, congregations learn much of the service by heart. Most often, they will know at least a Gloria, doxology, the Apostles' Creed, and Lord's Prayer as they are sung and prayed in a particular church. Nevertheless, many church bulletins either print the texts or indicate where they may be found in the pew or chair rack resources, so that visitors and newcomers can find them and participate. In the same way, the printed bulletin can include unison or antiphonal prayers or readings, and other responses to be sung or said. It is unnecessary to print every word to be said by worship leaders; they can cue the congregation with gestures or words at appropriate points.

A printed order can aid visitors but it also can get in the way, communicating that a printed order is mandatory for worship and for those who are not new it may be an impediment. Visitors often will be more impressed by being present in a congregation participating in worship than being in the midst of worshipers whose faces are fixed on a piece of paper.

How Congregations Can Learn Acts of Participation

C. S. Lewis wrote in his *Letters to Malcolm: Chiefly on Prayer*[26] that we are not dancing until we no longer have to count the steps. The liturgy is a kind of dance. There are recurring pieces which, like the Doxology and the Lord's Prayer, congregations can easily learn. They also can be taught to the children, so that they can join in wholeheartedly and, in some cases, show the way to the larger congregation.

A good starting point is to recover the ancient traditional practice of the use of the little word "Amen," a Hebrew word meaning "So be it!" or "I agree!" "Amen" does not mean, "I'm finished now, so you can open your eyes." Rather, "Amen" means "I'm with you" or "I concur," and, therefore, belongs, by definition, to the assembled congregation. "Amen" is a word to be spoken or sung by the people, not the leader. For example, the great "Amen" at the conclusion of the Great (Prayer of) Thanksgiving (BCW 73, and elsewhere) is printed in **boldface** which indicates that the *congregation* may respond affirmatively to the prayer offered by the presiding minister. A leader in worship may voice a prayer, but the leader does so not by way of offering private devotions in public, but by articulating what is meant to be the prayer of the people. The people, then, embrace the prayer as their own with a sung or spoken "**Amen**." From ancient times, "Amen" has been used as the people's assent, especially to prayer (see biblical examples of 1 Chron. 16:36; Neh. 8:6; Ps. 106:48; 1 Cor. 14:16). When people fervently add "Amen" to prayers offered by a leader of worship, they actively participate in the prayers and embrace them as their own.

Assisting people to recover their "Amen" is an effective first step toward empowering their more active role in worship. Some worshipers may hesitate, at first, perhaps waiting for others so that they are not alone in their response. And, if leaders say "Amen" to their own prayer, then, typically, the congregation does not; thus, self-restraint is a watchword for leaders of prayer. In various ways, however, worship leaders (especially choirs), can support and encourage the development of congregational responses. For example, leaders can ensure their prayer text and voice inflection anticipate a response (even in the midst of a prayer) and, also, close a prayer with one of a familiar set of phrases, evidenced throughout the *Book of Common Worship*, such as:

> "in the name of our Lord Jesus Christ," *or*
> "through [Jesus] Christ our Lord [or Redeemer, or Savior]," *or*
> "for the sake of [Jesus] Christ our Lord [or Redeemer, or Savior]"

Thus, not only can prayer texts elicit natural responses as part of a congregation's engagement in prayer but also both vocal intonation and familiar expressions will invite the congregation, led by the choir, to affirm the prayer as their own. Some leaders also emulate the psalmist (Ps. 106:48) in saying at the end of a prayer or ascription of praise: "And let all the people say . . . ," pausing at that point to wait for the unison "Amen." The most effective keys, however, to enabling people to affirm a prayer as their own with a sung or spoken "Amen" are an evocative text and a familiar cadence and phrases.

Finding Our Voice

Congregations in many denominations already know portions of the liturgy by heart, and could profitably learn others. For example, when a worship leader offers the greeting, "The Lord be with you," the people can respond, "**And also with you**" (BCW 48). In one congregation, a minister used a time with the children to teach this response to them in the presence of all the other worshipers. The children's enthusiasm spread to their elders. In addition to the words, the minister also showed the children the gestures to accompany the greeting. When she said, "The Lord be with you," she stretched out her hands toward the children, palms open toward them.

When they answered, "**And also with you**," she taught them to return the gesture. It takes only a few repetitions before adults feel free to join the children in the response and the physical gesture that accompanies it.

If the congregation participates in an ecumenical service (for example, Ash Wednesday, Good Friday, Easter Vigil, Epiphany, Thanksgiving), members may already be familiar with a response after the reading of Scripture. The reader concludes with "The Word of the Lord," and it seems that almost everybody responds, "**Thanks be to God**" (BCW 61). When the leader says, "The peace of our Lord Jesus Christ be with you all," the congregation can readily learn to answer, "**And also with you**" (BCW 57, 66), and, then, to exchange similar greetings and responses with one another.

Many already sing the Kyrie ("Lord, have mercy") (BCW 55) after the Confession of Sin. Perhaps most important, the people of the congregation can learn the opening dialogue that introduces the Great (Prayer of) Thanksgiving at the Lord's Table (BCW 69). Once congregations learn to sing the "Holy, holy, holy Lord" (Sanctus) (BCW 70) or the Memorial Acclamation (for example, "Christ has died") (BCW 71) in the Great Thanksgiving, they sing it enthusiastically, and just as spontaneously as a familiar Gloria Patri or Doxology. Various language groups also sing or recite other confessional prayers and responses.

The "Amen" at the conclusion of the Great Thanksgiving, immediately prior to the Lord's Prayer (BCW 73), often has been called the "Great Amen." In its origin, it served as the people's ecstatic response, affirming what had been prayed. It particularly belongs to the people, and especially in a Reformed context, exhibits the conviction that it is the congregation who celebrates, while the presiding minister articulates the Great Thanksgiving on their behalf. Congregations can easily learn to sing or say the "Great Amen." Complete eucharistic musical settings for all the congregational responses during the Great Thanksgiving can be located in both *The Presbyterian Hymnal* (PH 568–570, 580–588) and *Holy Is the Lord: Music for Lord's Day Worship* (HL 1–138A).

It's Easier Than It Looks!

This can seem like a lot all at once. Such learning is, indeed, a major transition, because it requires congregations to shift from what often has been a passive to a more active mode of worship. Nevertheless, many Presbyterian congregations, small and large, have learned all the responses easily, sometimes a little at a time, and have begun to cherish them.

"The Service for the Lord's Day" offers other responses that congregations can learn over time and make their own. In fact, many commonly employ spoken or sung responses to the Declaration of Forgiveness, the Gospel reading, and the Charge and Benediction. During the Prayers of the People, the one praying could conclude each intercession with words such as, "Lord, in your mercy . . . ," to which the people sing or say in response, "**Hear our prayer**." Another pattern among many is "Let us pray to the Lord," to which the people respond, "**Lord, have mercy**." Frequently, a congregation will sing responses particularly appropriate to the culture of the people. Also, as a substitute for some of the customary responses, for example, a congregation can sing a stanza or refrain of a hymn, gospel song, or other spiritual song.

Worship planners and leaders will find other ways to encourage the active participation of the congregation. One effective teaching method to familiarize people with ways they can make their voices heard is to use worship occasions apart from the Lord's Day service. For example, the youth group, the church school, a Presbyterian Women's gathering or circle meeting, a men's breakfast, a weekend churchwide retreat, a brief service following a midweek program— all these offer opportunities to introduce people to ways of participating that can then increase clarity and confidence when employed on Sunday.

Training Liturgical Leaders and Worship Committees

Persons in the congregation who demonstrate the skill to work with readers/lectors may take responsibility to work one-on-one or with groups to prepare them to read Holy Scripture in the Lord's Day service. Such coaching could include discussing the Scripture passages, reading aloud the texts, working together on which words to accent and where and how long to pause, how to introduce the reading, and how to conclude it. Others in the congregation may be able to teach readers/lectors a certain demeanor: how to walk to the lectern or pulpit, how to open the pulpit Bible and handle it with reverence. The reader's body language will communicate to the congregation whether this book and this reading are important or not.

Some congregations may wish to organize liturgical planning committees to work with the pastor(s) and, possibly, a session committee to plan ahead, looking at particular Lord's Day services, keeping the *ordo* and the liturgical season in mind. Such a committee will benefit from study and discussion of the Scripture passages for the service, particularly given that preparing the worship of the people is an awesome responsibility requiring a careful preparation of mind and heart for the task. Members of the committee also could share or delegate leadership roles in the services they have helped plan. For wider participation, a weekly study group open to everyone could wrestle with the Scripture passage that will serve as the foundation of the sermon for the coming Sunday.

Resources for the Liturgical Year

(BCW 163)

Liturgical Time

It all began with the proclamation of the Word. The proclamation of the Word shaped the faith of the church concerning what God had done and was now doing in Christ.

The Inseparable Link between Story and Time

Throughout the church's history, hearing the stories of God's past freed people to have faith in God's future, and, therefore, to live in the present. "Faith comes from what is heard," writes Paul (Rom. 10:17). By continually hearing the stories of God's faithfulness in the past and God's promises for the future, people know to whom they belong and to what they are called in the present. God's unfinished story today inevitably moves toward God's promised future. From the very beginning, story and time have been inseparable.

That Jewish and Christian worship have instinctively linked story and time is no surprise. God's purpose directs the people of God toward an end. Jews annually retell, in the context of a communal meal, the exodus story about God redeeming them from bondage. The *Haggadah* (narrative story) for the *Seder* (order of service) at *Pesach* (Passover) is an all-encompassing, identity-shaping, direction-giving story of how God liberates from slavery. By telling their children year after year the story of the exodus—affliction, suffering, sorrow, and struggle—Jews lay claim to a promise in a living word that lies at the heart of their faith. The more they relive the story, the more it becomes a part of their present and future lives. Without the exodus story there is no people called Israel.

Likewise, the Easter Vigil shaped the people called Christians. The great saving acts of the Lord not only recorded in Scripture but read, contemplated, proclaimed, and lived over and over again provide a reality that lies at the heart of Christ's church.

Both Jewish and Christian worship include constantly retelling the memories from God's faithfulness in the past (story) and ritually enacting those memories (liturgical practice) in order to kindle hope in God's promised future and, thereby, be enabled to live freely in the present. Telling the story of God-with-us, and naming that presence in daily, weekly, monthly, seasonal, and annual cycles (ordered time) always have been and still are crucial to both Jewish and Christian worship.[1]

The Gospel story proclaimed over a period of time spawned the church's liturgical practices. That period of time, permeated by the proclamation of the Word and by the people's response to the Word, has come to be known as the liturgical calendar.

The major factor in shaping the liturgical year has been the inseparable link between story and time. Thomas Talley writes that the annual festivals and seasons grew out of the proclamation of the gospel in one locale after another over time. The drawing together of these "local customs" into one creates the complex calendar called the liturgical year. It all began with the proclamation of the Word.[2]

The Redeeming Work of Christ

What we hear in the Gospel stories of God-with-us is the redeeming work of Christ: incarnation-crucifixion-resurrection-outpouring of the Spirit:

> Christ was born.
> Christ taught.
> Christ was crucified.
> Christ was raised up.

And the Spirit was poured out on us. The saving work of Christ is the story behind the story of Jesus' life.

The liturgical calendar, therefore, commemorates not the historical life of Jesus but the redeeming work of Christ. Liturgy may be dramatic but it does not reproduce history. We are called not to reenact what Christ said and did, but to proclaim what Christ said and did.

Therefore, in our worship, extreme caution must be exercised with the fascination for reliving historical moments in the life of Christ.

Reenacting the life of Jesus historicizes a mystery that transcends time and place. Mimicking details of events in Jesus' life domesticates the holy awe of incarnation-crucifixion-resurrection-outpouring of the Spirit. We do not reproduce the Last Supper; rather, we celebrate the Lord's Supper. We do not perform Christmas liturgies that duplicate past events; rather, we rejoice in the present reality of Christmas. The festive liturgies throughout the liturgical calendar are not reenacted historical dramas of the past but contemporary encounters with Christ.

In the retelling and commemorating of the stories of God-with-us, the Spirit draws us into the mystery of the saving work of Christ. The liturgical calendar offers a series of celebrations that confront us with who we are in Christ and present us with a pattern for growth in Christ. The liturgical calendar permeates us with the mystery of Christ's redeeming work so we may conform our lives to Christ. It opens to us now the fulfillment of our lives for a future that is already with us in Christ and for which we were created.[3]

The Shape of the Liturgical Calendar

The nature and fullness of God's time is so radically different from our natural and arbitrary understanding of time that at best we can say: "Now we see in a mirror, dimly, but then we will see face to face. Now I know only in part; then I will know fully, even as I have been fully known" (1 Cor. 13:12). The liturgical calendar gives us a glimpse of the way God's time breaks into our time.

The Lord's Day

From earliest times, Christians have gathered on Sunday (the Lord's Day): "On the first day of the week, when we met to break bread, Paul was holding a discussion with them" (Acts 20:7). By the end of the first century, a church manual called the *Didache* instructed Christians to come together every Lord's Day for giving thanks and breaking of bread.[4] Justin Martyr, in the mid-second century, writes of worship on Sunday as the common time to celebrate the resurrection and the transformation of creation.[5] Sunday was and is the normative day for celebrating the fact that "everything has become new" (2 Cor. 5:17).

The reason the early Christians gathered for public worship on Sunday is found in the New Testament focus on the "first day of the week"—the day of Jesus' resurrection. All four Gospels affirm the first day of the week as the day of Christ's resurrection (Matt. 28:1ff.; Mark 16:2; Luke 24:1; John 20:1, 19). The risen and victorious Christ triumphed over the power of death. The Lord of life reigned. To honor God's work in raising Jesus from the dead, Christians gathered on the first day of the week to break bread and encounter the risen Lord. Sunday derives its meaning from Christ's resurrection, and it became a thankful celebration of being raised together with Christ.[6]

As the first Christians (primarily Jews) recalled the creation stories of Genesis, they remembered how God completed the work of creation in six days and rested on the seventh. On the eighth day of creation ("the first day of the week," according to all four Gospels), God continued the work of creation by raising Christ from the dead. This eighth day of creation/first day of the week is what became commonly known as the Lord's Day (Rev. 1:10), the day of resurrection.

The Lord's Day was characterized by recollecting Jesus' words and deeds, and celebrating the presence of the risen Christ among them in the bread and cup of the Lord's Supper. A story and a meal formed the heart of worship each Sunday. Sunday was and is a festival in its own right.

On Sunday, the church's worship focused on the presence of the risen Lord. And, since the church's definitive celebration and experience of the resurrection of the Lord is the Lord's Supper, the Lord's Day of resurrection, Sunday, is inseparably linked to the Lord's Supper.[7] The weekly cycle of Sundays also looks ahead to a final future fulfillment. The *Epistle of Barnabas*, written by a late-first-century Christian of Alexandria, urged rejoicing on the eighth day of creation/the first day of the week as "the beginning of a new world, because that was when Jesus rose from the dead."[8] Every Lord's Day (of resurrection) celebrates the unfolding presence of the new creation revealed in the risen Christ. In hearing the Scriptures and breaking bread each first day of the week, Christians celebrate the age to come.

Thus Sunday, the "original feast day," not only shaped the church's calendar but transforms all days. The standard or "ordinary" time for worship—the Lord's Day—reveals that which is becoming all creation's ordinary time. Sunday proclaims that all of time has been redeemed in Christ. The Lord's Day is the foundation of the way Christians keep time.

The Annual Calendar

While the whole gospel is celebrated on each Lord's Day, it is not surprising that early Christians found meaning in celebrating particular days that centered on a major event or aspect of the saving story. Gradually an annual calendar emerged. By the fourth century its major features were in place. That basic shape remains today. Whenever it has focused on the saving events of Christ it has played a major role in forming the faith of the people.

What we can faintly discern of God's time in our present calendar may be portrayed as two recurring cycles of extraordinary time undergirded by periods of ordinary time. Each cycle of extraordinary time commences with a period of preparation and anticipation, and culminates in a season of celebration. One cycle spirals around incarnation (Christmas), and the other around resurrection (Easter). Together they lead us through God's time.

An outline of the calendar that guides the "Resources for the Liturgical Year" (BCW 163–400) follows. Its major features reflect wide ecumenical concurrence.

THE CHRISTMAS (INCARNATION) CYCLE
Four weeks of Advent
Twelve days of Christmas
The Epiphany of the Lord

ORDINARY TIME
(January 7 through Tuesday before Ash Wednesday)

THE EASTER (RESURRECTION) CYCLE
"Forty days" of Lent
Fifty days of Easter
The Day of Pentecost

ORDINARY TIME
(Monday after the Day of Pentecost through Saturday before the First Sunday of Advent)

Particular days in and out of season offer a special focus or special occasions on which to begin or conclude a cycle:

The Baptism of the Lord (begins our marking of Ordinary Time)
The Transfiguration of the Lord (concludes our marking of Ordinary Time)
Ash Wednesday (begins Lent)
Passion/Palm Sunday
Maundy Thursday
Good Friday
Saturday of Holy Week (concludes Lent)
The Great Vigil of Easter
The Ascension of the Lord
Trinity Sunday (opens our marking of Ordinary Time)
All Saints' Day
Christ the King (or Reign of Christ) (ends our marking of Ordinary Time)

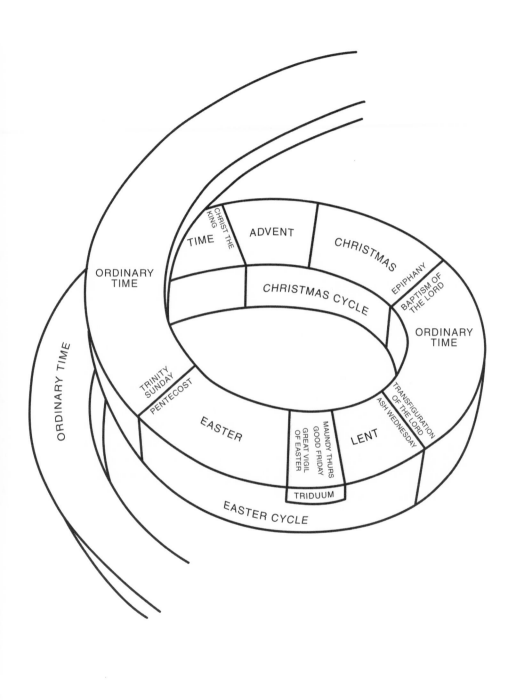

Texts Included in "Resources for the Liturgical Year"

The liturgical texts in "Resources for the Liturgical Year" (BCW 163–400) encompass the following elements:

Call to Worship: Sentences of Scripture
Prayer of the Day
Prayer of Confession
Great Thanksgiving
Prayer of Thanksgiving

The texts of these elements in the "Resources for the Liturgical Year" are intended for use *with* the *ordo* of "The Service for the Lord's Day" (BCW 31–161), namely, during the festivals and seasons in the liturgical calendar. "An Outline of [the Order of] the Service for the Lord's Day" (BCW 46) provides a practical worship planning tool for visual reference regarding the structure and sequence of each element in the order of service.

Call to Worship: Sentences of Scripture

Sentences of Scripture are provided for use as a call to worship. There is a text for each Sunday and festival. When a text relates to the lectionary readings for a particular day, it is identified in red print by Year A, Year B, or Year C, indicating the cycle for which its use is intended. A combination Year A, B, Year A, C, or Year B, C indicates that it is appropriate for use in either of the two cycles identified. If Year A, B, C, then the text is appropriate on that day in any of the three cycles.

Prayer of the Day

A prayer of the day is provided for each Sunday and festival. As with the Sentences of Scripture, many have a direct relationship with the lectionary readings for the particular day, and are also so indicated with Year A, Year B, Year C, Year A, B, C, and so forth.

The Prayer of the Day may be used in either of two ways. It may be used as an opening prayer, and would immediately follow the call to worship. This would enable a Prayer for Illumination to be used (BCW 60, 90–91). Or the Prayer of the Day may be used to conclude the opening rite, called "Gathering" (see p. 19).

Prayer of Confession

The prayers of confession supplement those in "The Service for the Lord's Day" (BCW 53–54, 87–89) and are provided for each season and festival. They may be used as alternatives to those in "The Service for the Lord's Day."

Great Thanksgiving

While recognizing that the norm of Christian worship is to celebrate the Lord's Supper as often as each Lord's Day, some Presbyterian churches have used the liturgical calendar as a means to recovery of the early church's pattern of Lord's Day Eucharist. Thus, on those days especially appropriate to celebrate the Sacrament, these congregations celebrate the Lord's Supper, namely:

First Sunday of Advent
Christmas Eve
Christmas Day
Epiphany
Baptism of the Lord
Transfiguration of the Lord
First Sunday in Lent
Passion/Palm Sunday
Maundy Thursday
The Great Vigil of Easter
Easter Sunday Through Seventh Sunday of Easter
Ascension of the Lord
Day of Pentecost
Trinity Sunday
All Saints' Day (or the Sunday after)
Christ the King (or Reign of Christ)

Churches following this pattern also ordinarily will celebrate the Sacrament at least monthly during Ordinary Time. This breaks the mode of mechanically scheduling an observance according to the secular calendar (for example, first Sunday of each quarter, or first Sunday of each month). By celebrating the Sacrament on the festivals that focus our attention on the saving acts of God in Jesus Christ, people may more readily associate the Sacrament with the Gospel story rather than the secular calendar. This especially will be true if the eucharistic prayer recounts the fullness of that story. The Eucharist will the more readily be received as a feast of celebrating the fullness of God's revelation, rather than simply as a memory aid to ponder the death of Jesus.

This increase in frequency of eucharistic celebration necessitates more eucharistic prayers to provide festival or seasonal images as well as variety. The "Resources for the Liturgical Year" addresses this need by supplementing the Great Thanksgivings for "The Service for the Lord's Day" (BCW 69, 126–156) with a eucharistic prayer for each festival and season (BCW 165–400). These prayers incorporate images and themes of the particular day or season. Also, among the Great Thanksgivings for "The Service for the Lord's Day" are three texts—B, C, D—that include proper prefaces (BCW 133, 138) for use on the various festivals of the liturgical calendar.

Prayer of Thanksgiving

At least one prayer of thanksgiving is provided for each season and festival. This prayer is for use when the Eucharist is not celebrated. It is used at the place in the order where the eucharistic prayer is normally offered (see outline of the service, BCW 46–47).

Other Texts

A Prayer of Adoration is provided for Christmas (BCW 178) and for Easter (BCW 315). This is for use immediately after the call to worship and may be used instead of the Prayer of the Day, when that prayer is used as an opening prayer.

A text for the lighting of the Advent candles (BCW 165) and a Litany for Advent (BCW 166) are provided. Also, three Litanies for Pentecost (BCW 340) are provided from which to choose. Each of the above is discussed in relation to Advent and Pentecost.

Music: Hymn Lines Can Be Used as Festival or Seasonal Refrains

Portions of hymns can be used as recurring refrains sung throughout the service in a variety of ways to emphasize the mood and import of a particular day or season in the liturgical calendar. A variety of suggested lines from hymns for seasons and festivals are offered throughout the commentary in this *Companion*.

A refrain may appropriately be interjected, sensitively and creatively, at several places in a service. Normally, only one refrain is used in a single service, although it may be repeated in several places, thereby contributing a sense of unity to the service. Examples include: following the Call to Worship, before and/or following the Confession of Sin, between the Second

Reading and the Gospel Reading, preceding the Prayers of the People (or between the petitions of the intercessions), after the Charge and Blessing.

Such hymn refrains can be printed in the bulletin or orally "lined out" by a cantor (soloist) or choir, making it unnecessary to print and also generating a greater sense of spontaneity. The refrain is always sung first by the cantor or choir; the congregation then repeats it. The "hymn refrains" are set to simple and often well-known hymn tunes or melodies that are easy for a congregation to sing.

The Christmas Cycle: From the Darkness of the World to the Light of Christ

The Christmas cycle evolved over several hundred years and, eventually, developed its shape in the latter half of the fourth century. Both Western and Eastern traditions helped to decide the central dates of this cycle: Christmas (December 25) and Epiphany (January 6). Both traditions also shaped how to celebrate these days that encompass the incarnation, the visit of the magi, the baptism of Jesus, and the marriage at Cana. As Easter is preceded by a time of preparation, Lent, so Christmas–Epiphany is preceded by a time of preparation, Advent. However, Advent is far more than preparing to celebrate the first coming of Christ, the incarnate Word. Advent is a season of hope, during which we anticipate the future coming of Christ to judge, and to establish his rule over all things. In the light of Christ's first coming, we have hope for fulfillment of the realm of God in the future. The Christmas cycle focuses on preparing for and celebrating the coming of the Word, Jesus Christ, in whom God's saving purposes are realized.

In the following description of the Christmas cycle, we begin with Christmas rather than Advent, because it is only when we understand what Christmas is all about that we can begin to consider appropriate ways to prepare for celebrating it.

Christmas: The Advent of the Messianic Savior (BCW 178)

There are currently two theories concerning the origin of Christmas.

The *first theory* proposes that Christmas is the result of the transformation, or Christianizing, of a pagan festival. The earliest empirical evidence of the celebration of Christmas has been found in fourth-century Roman documents. The civil calendar of A.D. 354 lists December 25 as the "Birthday of the Unconquered Sun." A list of martyrs' anniversaries compiled in A.D. 336

notes: "December 25: Christ, born in Bethlehem of Judea." The reason Christians identified December 25 as the day of Christ's birth, according to this theory, is that they took over the Roman "Birthday of the Unconquered Sun" that was celebrated on the winter solstice. On December 25 the sun completed its southward journey; when reborn, it began traveling northward with the promise of more light. Thus the pagan feast of the Unconquered Sun marked the winter solstice when days began to be longer. Christians in Rome appropriated this holiday for their purposes as the day when "the sun of righteousness" (Mal. 4:2) arose, when the "light of the world" entered (John 8:12).

The *second theory*, the "computation hypothesis," was proposed by Louis Duchesne in 1889, and revived a century later by Thomas Talley.[9] The theory notes the attention, as early as the third century, given to computing the date of Christ's birth. Calculation methods apparently followed the Jewish tradition of assigning the birth and death of significant people (for example, patriarchs) to the same date, thereby signifying a wholeness to their lives. For Jesus, conception and crucifixion were the events that offered such completeness. According to the computations of a mixture of calendars (Jewish, Julian, and Gregorian), Christ's death (and therefore conception) was either March 25 (in Western churches) or April 6 (in Eastern churches). By counting nine months forward, Christ's birth was further computed to have occurred on December 25 or on January 6. In Rome, the day became fixed on December 25, which coincided with the winter solstice and the celebration of the pagan feast of the Unconquered Sun. Thus, the computation hypothesis downplays, if not challenges, the common idea that December 25 was chosen simply as a Christian takeover of a secular holiday.

The Incarnation of God's Saving Purposes

On December 25, Christmas Day, more Christians pause in their frenzied lives to acknowledge Christ than on any other day of the year. Images of "the baby in the manger" and "peace among all on earth" (Luke 2:14) fill our minds. On Christmas Day, Christians unite in celebrating the birth of the Christ child.

What is "Christmas"? It is three words: God in flesh; or four syllables: in-car-na-tion. The Gospel According to John (1:14) tells us, "The Word became flesh and lived among us, . . . full of grace and truth." Christmas proclaims that God has come in flesh, has come "to save us all from Satan's power."[10] Christmas celebrates far more than a birthday; Christmas acclaims the advent of the messianic salvation. Christ was sent among us *in order to save us*. Note how the biblical "sending formula" ("God sent Christ in order to . . .") always reveals Christ's saving purpose:

I must proclaim the good news of the kingdom of God to the other cities also; for I was sent for this purpose. (Luke 4:43)

God did not send the Son into the world to condemn the world, but in order that the world might be saved through him. (John 3:17)

In this is love, not that we loved God but that he loved us and sent his Son to be the atoning sacrifice for our sins. (1 John 4:10)

And we have seen and do testify that the Father has sent his Son as the Savior of the world. (1 John 4:14)

Moreover, the "sending formula," with its purpose of human salvation, is combined with a reference to the birth of Christ:

But when the fullness of time had come, God sent his Son, born of a woman, born under the law, in order to redeem those who were under the law, so that we might receive adoption as children. (Gal. 4:4–5, read on the First Sunday after Christmas [Year B] as well as on The Name of Jesus [January 1, A, B, C])

What we pay homage to at Christmas, therefore, is that *the ultimate fulfillment of God's saving purpose begins with the birth of Jesus, the messianic Savior.* God's only Son is born among us in order to save the world. This is the message of Christmas.

From the beginning of time, God's saving purpose has been at work. God has raised up the seed of Abraham, including Moses and Gideon and Samson and John the Baptist. Through all these generations, God has been faithfully at work raising persons to bring us the Davidic Messiah, the messianic King, the Son of the Most High who will ascend the throne of David. Through all of human history, God has been bringing forth Jesus Christ. Now through the birth of the Savior, God's purpose will be fulfilled. God has acted to save God's people. The Christ child is born for the saving of the world.

The Day of Epiphany: Light to All People (BCW 191)

A part of the joy of Christmas lies in the utter improbability of the Nativity. Because of the new possibilities and hopes in Christ given to us by the sheer grace of God, we rejoice. Throughout the twelve days of Christmas we extol the advent of Jesus, the messianic Savior, for "the grace of God has appeared *(epephane)*, bringing salvation to all, . . . the manifestation *(epiphaneia)* of the glory of our great God and Savior, Jesus Christ" (Titus 2:11, 13).

On Epiphany, the incarnational "coming down" of the Savior is manifested to the whole world. At Christmas and Epiphany we rejoice in Jesus' "cross-shaped" advent, descending *and* spreading, among us. We celebrate during Christmas the entrance of the true Light into the world, and on Epiphany the showing forth of the true Light to the world.

Jesus is the light to all nations, races, classes, all peoples, the whole world. At Epiphany, Christ is revealed to the "Gentile world"; God's covenant with Israel is now open to people of every place and time. All are extended an invitation to the gathering of the New Israel in the New Jerusalem.

The Origins of the Feast of Epiphany

The word "epiphany" (from the Greek *epiphaneia* or *theophaneia*) means "appearance" or "manifestation" of God, and has roots in the word for sunrise or dawn. In ancient times, an epiphany meant either a visible manifestation of a god or the solemn visit of a ruler venerated as a god.

For Christians, Christmas marks the coming of God to us; Epiphany celebrates the appearance of the Lord in the midst of humanity. The Christmas stories of the birth of Immanuel declare the divine entry; Epiphany extols the revelation of God to the world in the person of Jesus of Nazareth. How did the church come to make this subtle distinction?

Epiphany probably evolved from a squabble over *the* christological moment when God revealed who Jesus was. According to Adolf Adam[11] the earliest traces of a feast of the Epiphany appear in the writings of Clement of Alexandria (Egypt), about A.D. 205. Clement reported that the followers of the Gnostic Basilides (ca. A.D. 150) celebrated a feast of the *baptism* of Jesus, which they regarded as being *the* real moment of the "birth" of the Son of God into the world.

Others, however, noted that for Luke and especially Matthew, the conception and birth of Jesus are the christological moment when God revealed who Jesus was. Christ's birth marks the entrance of "the Light of the world." Therefore, presumably in reaction to the Gnostic understanding, the following took place.

First, the feast of the Epiphany (that is, Christ's physical birth, considered the actual moment of the Son of God's entry into the world) was introduced into the church and became familiar to the churches of the East.

Shortly thereafter, the commemoration of Jesus' baptism in the Jordan was also linked with this feast of Jesus' birth. Thus, the day of the Epiphany became an important date for baptism in the East.

Also associated with this feast of the Epiphany was the commemoration of the first "sign" (or miracle) of Jesus, in which Jesus changed water into wine, once again revealing his glory (John 2:1–11).

Thus in its early stages, the feast of the Epiphany, as celebrated in the churches of the East, was a festival of the revelation of Christ's glory that united three elements: birth, baptism, and first "sign."

Churches of the West, however, accented the concept of the "sun of righteousness" (Mal. 4:2) as breaking into the world in the birth of Jesus as Savior. In the fourth century, therefore, the West began to celebrate Christ's birth on December 25 (probably because of its cultural context) with the East continuing its feast of the Epiphany on January 6.

About A.D. 375, Eastern and Western churches "appropriated" each other's "birthday feast" of Jesus, and adoration by the magi, the result being:

December 25

West celebrated	*East celebrated*
birth of Jesus	birth of Jesus and
	the coming of the magi

January 6

coming of the magi	baptism of Jesus
baptism of Jesus	Jesus' miracle at Cana and
wedding feast at Cana	reserved the day for the
	conferral of baptism

What East and West share in common, however, is Epiphany's celebration of Jesus' manifestation to the whole world. In our celebrations of Christmas and Epiphany we rejoice in the dawning and the arising of Light in darkness, stability amid chaos, assurance and anxiety for the whole creation. Epiphany not only discloses the Savior to the world but also calls the world to show forth Christ, to be witnesses to God's true Light. The timeless mystery of the incarnation, God in flesh, leads us forth to show and tell of Christ as God's gift of grace and salvation for all persons. Some call this ongoing epiphany the work of Christmas.

Advent: Come, Lord Jesus! Our Lord Has Come! (BCW 165)

Since the first century, as Christians await the advent of the true Light in prayer and liturgy they have uttered the word *Maranatha,* often translated "Our Lord, come!" Maranatha is a Greek transliteration from the Aramaic in 1 Corinthians 16:22, and often printed in Greek New Testaments as one word—maranatha.

In Aramaic, as in Syriac, maranatha may be two words, with differing translations:

> *marana tha* = an imperative form oriented toward the *future,* translated as: "Come, our Lord!"
> *maran atha* = the perfect form expressing a completed event in the *past,* translated as: "Our Lord has come."[12]

The two directions in these translations are crucial for our Advent liturgies. The cry of maranatha and the season of Advent emphasize both our remembrance of the past and our hope for the future. In Advent, the beginning and end times meet. In fact, in mid-sixth-century Rome, Advent was considered as the end of the liturgical year, while today we regard Advent as the beginning.[13] We live between *marana tha,* our prayer for the future coming of the Lord, and *maran atha,* our belief that the Lord has come as God's ultimate acting history.

In Advent we expectantly wait for the One who has already come. We anticipate the promised justice of God's new world, yet we praise God who raised the "righteous branch" to rule with justice and righteousness. We hope for the restoration of the afflicted, the tormented, and the grieving, yet we delight that healing has come in Christ. We long for the beating of swords into plowshares, yet we rejoice that the Prince of Peace has appeared. We yearn for the barren deserts of our inner cities to flourish, yet we laud the desert Rose that has bloomed. We dream of the land where lions and lambs live in harmony, yet we acclaim the child born to lead us into the promised land.

Christ has come! Christ is risen! Christ will come again! In Advent, we are living between the first and the second coming of the Lord.

The dialectical tension of maranatha—placing us between memory and hope, past and future—may strengthen our Advent liturgies. Perhaps we need to cling to the ancient cry of *Maranatha!* and its paradoxical meanings so we may freely embrace "the new thing" prophesied by Isaiah (Isa. 43:19) that God is doing among us right now. The tension and the paradox we find in Advent shapes our celebrations during the season.

Waiting for the One Who Has Already Come

Though at Christmas we rightly retell the story of the babe in the manger nearly two thousand years ago, Christmas ultimately focuses on the mystery of Immanuel (God is with us) breaking into our world. Though we paint pictures of the sweet baby in a manger "asleep on the hay," Christmas centers on the Christ who inaugurates God's realm of justice and peace. Though we sing of the baby with "no crib for His bed" and "no crying He makes,"[14]

Christmas holds before us Jesus of Nazareth whose human life fulfills God's saving purpose by preaching, teaching, liberating, healing, and living according to the rule of God. On Christmas Day, we celebrate the mystery of the incarnation.

How? We can retell the birth narratives of Matthew and Luke, display the wide-ranging artistic interpretations of the Christ child's birth, and sing the powerfully evocative hymn texts. These stories, images, and songs are all vehicles for telling the astounding story of incarnation, of a Savior breaking into our world.

Advent, however, is the time to prepare for the One who is coming to us as our judge and redeemer. During these weeks, we anticipate the second coming of Christ, the coming peace and justice of the Lord. Our Advent call is, therefore, to prepare the world for Christ's coming now and in the end time.

Since we believe that the Lord is coming to judge the world, then we must prepare the world for judgment. Since we believe that the Christ is coming, Advent becomes a time for words and deeds that witness to Christ's new age. Our Advent witness to the coming of Christ requires caring about our world, our neighbors, our enemies—everyone. Advent is the time to care about peace and justice in the world, since we believe Christ has come and, therefore, everything that has come in Christ will be fulfilled in the world. Maranatha! Come, Lord Jesus! Maranatha! Our Lord has come!

Christmas is the time for celebration. "Joy to the world!" God has inaugurated a new realm in Jesus Christ. God has established the new age. The time of justice and peace has arrived. Clap your hands! Dance for joy! Sing a new song to the Lord, for the Lord has done marvelous things! Each year we have twelve days in which to celebrate these incredible acts of God. Twelve days in which to taste and experience Christmas.

When the church embraces an Advent season of waiting, preparing, and serving in both its worship and mission, twelve days of Christmas joy will naturally follow. By beginning and maintaining a tone of suspense, anticipation, and expectation regarding the coming Savior, the opportunity is present to sustain it through the four weeks and then build on it at Christmas.

For example, on the first Sunday of Advent, we begin our watch and preparation for the coming of the Lord. In the midst of human disorder, anguish, desolation, and uncertainty we hear the promises of Jeremiah (Year C of the Revised Common Lectionary) that the days are coming when God will raise up "a righteous Branch" from David's line who will rule with "justice and righteousness" (Jer. 33:14–16). We believe that God has raised up the "righteous Branch" from David's line in Jesus Christ, who rules with justice and righteousness.

We also hear Luke's (21:25–36) apocalyptic vision of the end of the world: signs in the sun and moon and stars, distress of nations, people fainting with fear, and the "Son of Man" coming. As we listen for the Word of God in these signs, we raise our heads, look up, and see that Christ's redemption is near. We do not know when, but we watch, pray, prepare, and gladly expect the coming of the Lord. Christ has come! Christ is risen! Christ will come again!

During Advent, therefore, our eyes are focused on God's future promised in Jesus Christ. At Christmas, we rejoice that it has arrived.

Commentary on the Christmas Cycle
(Advent—Christmas—Epiphany, January 6) Services

Advent (BCW 165–177)

Advent originated as a three-week fast in preparation for baptism at Epiphany, and it evolved into a period of preparation for the coming of Christ as judge, and so assumed a penitential mood, a shorter Lent. In contrast, Advent today is seen as a season of hope and joy, anticipating the fulfillment of the rule of God in Christ's coming in the future. The Scripture that is read, the liturgical texts used, the music, the environment, and the ceremonial actions should all convey this sense of expectant, joyful longing for the fulfillment of God's promised reign.

Lighting of the Advent Candles (BCW 165–166)

The lighting of a wreath during the season is a common feature of Advent. The Advent wreath is a large wreath with four candles in the wreath itself, and often with another candle in the center. A candle is lighted the first week and an additional one each week thereafter, culminating in the lighting of the center one on Christmas. Ordinarily, the wreath candles are blue or purple, the color traditional to the season, and the center candle white. In some traditions the candle that is lighted on the Third Sunday of Advent is rose-colored. Some congregations replace the candles with white candles for Christmas Eve.

The origin of the Advent wreath is obscure. It apparently emanated from the Lutheran tradition, but it has been appropriated by almost all other traditions. A review of the origin of the wreath makes it clear that the candles do *not* represent any single event, person, or doctrine. What the candles do signify and communicate is the increasing crescendo of light throughout the season. The dominant natural symbol is *increasing* light during Advent. As Advent draws nearer to Christmas, the congregation experiences the increasing brightness radiated by the wreath. This is the significance of the wreath, and should not be lost by trying to give each candle some special meaning such as hope, joy, shepherds, angels. Let the focus be not on the proper meaning of the candles, but on the light generated by the candles. The tradition of lighting candles on the Advent wreath is simply a symbol, powerful though it may be, that intensifies the anticipation of our waiting for the One who has already come.

People remember the action of lighting an increasing number of candles throughout the weeks of Advent. Conversely, the lighting of the Advent wreath often triggers memories and hopes of the season. Music, mood, colors, signs, biblical texts are recalled, and, above all, the symbol of lighting candles on a wreath.

A model for lighting the Advent wreath, based on the Revised Common Lectionary's Old Testament readings for the weeks of Advent (Cycle A), is provided for congregational use (BCW 165–166). No attempt is made to identify each candle with any person, event, or doctrine. Rather, the natural symbol of light is accompanied by biblical word pictures of the coming Savior. The act of reading or reciting our biblically based Advent hopes and of lighting a greater number of candles on the wreath reinforce an understanding that the increasingly bright light both flows from and reflects on the Word.

Instructions for Lighting the Advent Wreath. Invite different persons for each of the four Sundays of Advent, as well as for Christmas Eve, to *light* a candle on the Advent wreath, and/or *read* an appropriate text.

In selecting people, try to include a broad range of persons—a cross section of the entire congregation (for example, young child, older adult, college student, teenager, middle-aged parent or single person). "Twosomes" or even "threesomes" are encouraged, particularly during the second half of Advent when the reading portion becomes longer and, therefore, can be shared. (NOTE: Since, this is *not* a nuclear family event, but a *church family* ritual, nuclear family teams are ordinarily discouraged, and combinations of random members of the congregation are encouraged.)

Distribute to each person, well in advance, appropriate instructions for lighting the wreath. To be sure everyone understands what is expected, rehearse the lighting of the candle(s).

Third Sunday of Advent (BCW 174–176)

A frequently asked question is, Why do some churches light a pink or rose-colored candle on the Third Sunday of Advent?

During the fourth century in Gaul, Advent evolved as a period of preparation for the coming of Christ as judge and, therefore, its mood was penitential.

In the Middle Ages, the appointed epistle for the Third Sunday of Advent was Philippians 4:4–6, which begins with the Latin word *Gaudete,* meaning "rejoice": "Rejoice in the Lord always; again I will say, Rejoice. Let your gentleness be known to everyone. The Lord is near." Philippians 4:4–6 also served as the introit for the day (entrance song), which was interspersed with the antiphon of Psalm 84:2: "My soul longs, indeed it faints for the courts of the LORD; my heart and my flesh sing for joy to the living God."

Thus, the penitential mood of Advent was momentarily suspended by the joyous character of the Philippians text. Since this anticipated joy of the end time was an exception during a penitential Advent, Paul's injunction to the Philippians, *Gaudete in Domino semper* ("Rejoice in the Lord always") had the effect of interrupting the period of fasting. Therefore, the opening word of the text gave its name to this Third Sunday of Advent, Gaudete Sunday, by which it is still known in some traditions. And, a candle on the Advent wreath was changed to pink or rose as a sign of a brief delight in the midst of fasting in preparation for the Christmas feast. In traditions where the Third Sunday of Advent is observed as Gaudete Sunday, the paraments are also often rose-colored.

In the Revised Common Lectionary, this Philippians text is the appointed epistle for the Third Sunday of Advent in Year C. On that same day and cycle, we also hear Zephaniah's psalm of celebration (Zeph. 3:14–20): "Rejoice and exult with all your heart."

In Year B, the Revised Common Lectionary's appointed epistle for the Third Sunday of Advent is 1 Thessalonians 5:16–24, in which, at the close of one of his earliest letters, Paul offers some final admonitions, beginning with the words, "Rejoice always."

In Year A, the Revised Common Lectionary's appointed Old Testament text for the Third Sunday of Advent is Isaiah 35:1–10, in which the opening metaphor concerns the transformation of the land: "The desert will rejoice, and the rose will bloom in the wastelands. The desert will sing and shout for joy." Do you believe the messianic rose can bloom in the wilderness?

The decision to use or not to use a pink or rose-colored candle on the Third Sunday of Advent is at the discretion of particular churches. With or without the pink candle, the biblical note of joy on this Third Sunday of Advent does intensify the anticipation, for truly, "The Lord is near" (Phil. 4:5b).

Litany For Advent—O Antiphons (BCW 166–167)

The Litany for Advent incorporates a series of texts called the O Antiphons, so-called because all seven of them begin with the interjection "O."

The O Antiphons, with their recurring "Come, Lord Jesus," poignantly capture the hope of Advent. During the season, the biblical readings selected from Isaiah and other prophets announce the coming of the Messiah. The closer Christmas comes to us, the more the liturgy accentuates its call to the Savior with the cry, *Veni!* ("Come!"). Ultimately, "Come" is humanity's only valid prayer: it sums up all of our needs of God. Ever since the expulsion from paradise, "Come" has been the ceaseless cry of humanity.[15]

Although we do not know for sure when or by whom the O Antiphons were conceived, they probably originated in Rome about the ninth century. They enjoyed great popularity during the Middle Ages.

For centuries, each O Antiphon has been sung on one of the seven days (December 17–23) preceding the Vigil of Christmas (December 24). Traditionally, they are sung in full both before and after the Canticle of Mary (the Magnificat [Luke 1:46–55]) during Vespers (evening prayer) on the following days:

Dec. 17 – "O Wisdom . . ."	Proverbs 8:22
Dec. 18 – "O Adonai . . ."	Exodus 20:2
Dec. 19 – "O Root of Jesse . . ."	Isaiah 11:1, 10
Dec. 20 – "O Key of David . . ."	Isaiah 22:22
Dec. 21 – "O Radiant Dawn . . ."	Zechariah 6:12
Dec. 22 – "O Ruler of the nations . . ."	Haggai 2:8
Dec. 23 – "O Immanuel . . ."	Isaiah 7:14

Each antiphon is addressed to the Son, and begins with an exclamation which is a scriptural title: "O Wisdom!" "O Adonai!" The title is then amplified with other biblical images.[16] The antiphon concludes with a petition to the coming Savior. Each is structured in this way:

> *Address*—invocation to the Messiah with a title inspired by the Old Testament (for example, "O Wisdom")
>
> *Amplification*—stating an attribute of the Messiah, and foreshadowing the petition (for example, "coming forth from the mouth of the Most High, pervading and permeating all creation, you order all things with strength and gentleness")
>
> *Appeal/Petition*—commencing always with "Come" and referring to the initial invocation (for example, "come now and teach us the way to salvation")

The litany incorporating the O Antiphons is provided for use on the Sunday that falls on or between December 17 and 23. It may be used at the beginning of the service instead of the Prayer of the Day, and is especially effective when sung.

In using the litany in the liturgy, a cantor (soloist) sings the O Antiphons, either improvising or using a chant tone (PS 341–346), and the congregation sings the refrain "Come, Lord Jesus." In the service, the cantor first sings the refrain. The congregation then repeats it. This familiarizes the congregation with the refrain. The cantor then sings each of the O Antiphons. At the conclusion of each O Antiphon, the cantor with a simple motion of the hand invites the congregation to sing the refrain. Silence follows the singing of the refrain after the last O Antiphon. The concluding petition is then spoken by a worship leader. The litany is most effective when sung without organ accompaniment, with a handbell striking the note at the beginning of each O Antiphon.

Congregations may find use of the O Antiphons enriching in other ways as well. Most congregations do not currently conduct evening prayer on the seven days (December 17–23) preceding Christmas Eve, when the O Antiphons traditionally are sung. An alternative to daily use might be to sing all seven of the O Antiphons throughout the service on the Fourth Sunday of Advent. A fine series of settings of the O Antiphons by John Weaver may be found in *The Psalter: Psalms and Canticles for Singing* (1621–1620). Or, stanzas of the familiar hymn "O Come, O Come, Emmanuel" (tune: VENI EMMANUEL) also may be used in the same way.

The text for the hymn "O Come, O Come, Emmanuel" derives from the Latin O Antiphons and originally was sung responsively by two choirs seated opposite each other in the chancel. In the twelfth century, the antiphons were reduced from seven to five, and made into the hymn "O Come, O Come, Emmanuel," with a refrain added. It is this hymn with which we are now familiar.[17]

Since the O Antiphons allow worshipers to express their "ceaseless cry," the O Antiphons should be played and sung boldly. O Antiphons are neither mournful nor plaintive in mood, but insistent, outspoken, almost a demanding cry for the Lord to come. Because they are very poetic and symbolic, the O Antiphons increase the feeling of expectancy and longing for the coming of Christ.

Customarily, the largest bell was rung throughout the singing of the O Antiphon and the Canticle of Mary, or the Magnificat (Luke 1:46–55), which it accompanied. Thus, it is desirable to ring the largest bell available during the singing of the antiphons during Advent but, particularly, on the Fourth Sunday of Advent if all the O Antiphons are sung.

Music and Environment for Advent

Music. Given our cultural contexts, the selection of music for Advent, understandably, can be difficult for many congregations. The Scriptures invite us to wait, watch, and prepare. Musical responses reflect these messages and bid Christ come: "Maranatha," "O Come, O Come, Emmanuel." The music of the season should move *from* reflection on Christ's coming at the end of time *to* preparing for celebrating Christ's first coming. Careful consideration of instrumentation can enhance the mood of Advent. Consider, on occasion, use of a cappella singing to create a sense of longing (for example, PH 2, 4). Consider also instrumentation of hymns intended to convey expectancy. The Advent section in *The Presbyterian Hymnal* (1–20), and some responses from *Music from Taizé*, will assist a congregation in understanding the dual nature of the season.

Neither the Revised Common Lectionary scriptural texts for Advent nor the historic understanding of the nature of the season of Advent lend themselves to the use of Christmas carols during Advent. These should be saved for the celebration of the incarnation at Christmas. Concerts of Christmas music are best scheduled during the twelve days of Christmas and not during Advent.

A Suggested Hymn Line That Can Be Used as a Refrain during Advent (see "Music: Hymn Lines Can Be Used as Festival or Seasonal Refrains," p. 90):

> "O come, O come, Emmanuel, And ransom captive Israel."
> From hymn text: "O Come, O Come, Emmanuel" (PH 9)
> hymn tune: VENI EMMANUEL

Setting. The counsel regarding music pertains also to decorating the place of worship. Let Advent speak its own message by delaying any Christmas decorations in the space for worship until Christmas Eve. Allow the symbol of light in the Advent wreath to speak without ambiguity. In addition, the Advent message could be accented in designing banners using the signs of the season (for example, messianic rose, the peaceable kingdom, root or tree of Jesse), or the principal figures in focus during Advent (Isaiah, John the Baptist, and Mary), or the symbolic, eschatological words: *Maranatha,* or *Come, Lord Jesus.*

Liturgical Color. The traditional color for Advent is purple, although use of blue is increasingly used. Blue is expressive of the hope that is at the heart of Advent, and is less penitential than purple.

Christmas and Epiphany (BCW 178–190, 191–197)

Christmas–Epiphany engages us in joyful praise of the incarnation, God's coming to us in Jesus Christ. When Advent is observed as a time of preparation and anticipation and is characterized by the plaintive sounds of the Advent hymns, Christmas comes to us as a time for jubilant praise of Christ's coming to dwell with us.

Let the Christmas Eve service be the first occasion for the church to be dressed in the manner that is the local custom for Christmas. Let the decorations communicate the Advent to Christmas shift in mood and tone. Upon entering the transformed worship space, people will readily sense their joy in the coming of the feast of the incarnation of the Lord. Decorations should be simple, well-planned, and artistically done. In decorating, care should be taken to ensure the integrity of the pulpit, font, and table. Nothing should impede any of the liturgical actions or obstruct any exit.

The meaning of the season is conveyed in a variety of ways. Christmas Eve, Christmas Day, and Epiphany are all occasions for celebrating the Eucharist. A candlelight Communion on Christmas Eve is a common practice. Epiphany and the Sunday following (The Baptism of the Lord) are appropriate times to celebrate baptism. Many congregations set up a Christmas crèche on Christmas Eve, maintain it for the twelve days of the season, and then remove it after the Epiphany service. Banners and bulletins can portray the many symbols of the season.

Gold and white are the traditional colors of the season. Congregations are encouraged to use the finest and most elegant fabrics available for vestments and paraments, to express the joy of the incarnation.

In contrast to the sometimes difficult task of selecting service music and hymns for Advent, the task of planning for Christmas music is easy. We find ourselves dealing, for the most part, with the favorite and familiar carols that have been sung and played in our secular environs since before Thanksgiving. A challenge could be having sufficient opportunities to sing enough carols in the services on Christmas Eve, Christmas Day, the First and Second Sundays after Christmas, and Epiphany, to satisfy congregations that have not sung Christmas carols during Advent. A Festival of Lessons and Carols and caroling activities during the twelve days of Christmas will help meet this need. In addition to the two or three hymns ordinarily sung on Sunday, selected carol fragments or stanzas of carols can be incorporated as responses to the Call to Worship (for example, refrain, "Angels, from the Realms of Glory," PH 22; refrain, "O Come, All Ye Faithful," PH 41), Declaration of Forgiveness (for example, stanza 3, "Joy to the World!," PH 40), Offering (for example, stanza 3, "Of the Father's Love Begotten," PH 309), during Communion, after the Blessing (refrain, "Angels We Have Heard on High," PH 23; refrain, "Hark! The Herald Angels Sing," PH 31), and so forth. This is both effective and pastoral. Various instruments may be used to complement the organ (for example, trumpets, handbells, tympani, cymbals, recorders, French horn, harp, glockenspiel). On Christmas Eve and Christmas Day, carolers on the front walk or in the narthex could welcome worshipers with carols.

A Suggested Hymn Line That Can Be Used as a Refrain during Christmas (see "Music: Hymn Lines Can Be Used as Festival or Seasonal Refrains," p. 90):

> "Joy to the world! the Lord is come."
> From hymn text: "Joy to the World!" (PH 40)
> hymn tune: ANTIOCH

Epiphany music needs to be selected with theological breadth. The congregation is cheated if Epiphany represents only the visit of the three magi. The baptism of Jesus is well reflected in *The Presbyterian Hymnal* (for example, PH 70–72). There are also appropriate hymns that focus on light and the Light of the Word (for example, PH 63, 67–69, 340, 411, 425, 462/463). Hymns that center on the miracle at Cana, another traditional focus of Epiphany (now Third Sunday after Epiphany in Cycle C), are not generally available in most hymnals. "Songs of Thankfulness and Praise" (tune: SALZBURG), in *Rejoice in the Lord,* is one of the only hymns from the classical hymn tradition that reflects the miracle at Cana. There are, however, instrumental selections and anthems that can balance this lack of hymns.

A Suggested Hymn Line That Can Be Used as a Refrain on Epiphany (see "Music: Hymn Lines Can Be Used as Festival or Seasonal Refrains," p. 90):

> "Go, tell it on the mountain Over the hills and everywhere;
> Go, tell it on the mountain That Jesus Christ is born!"
> From hymn text: "Go, Tell It on the Mountain" (PH 29)
> hymn tune: GO TELL IT

The Easter Cycle: From the Ashes of Death to the Fire of the Spirit

Easter is the oldest of the annual festivals, and it celebrates the central event of the story of our salvation. The Easter cycle consists of six Sundays in Lent, seven Sundays of Easter, and one Sunday of Pentecost ("the fiftieth day"). Throughout these fourteen Sundays, the emphasis on cross *and* resurrection expresses the unity of the cycle. Cross and resurrection are inseparable, both in the Christian faith and in our liturgical celebration. We observe Lent in anticipation of the resurrection, and we celebrate Easter remembering the cost of the cross's life-giving victory.

We shall examine first the nature of the resurrection joy of Easter and then turn to the Lenten preparation for such joy. Finally, we shall focus on the gift of the Spirit to the church at Pentecost, setting it on fire to witness to the crucified and risen Christ. We begin with Easter rather than Lent because it is only when we understand what Easter is all about that we can begin to consider appropriate ways to prepare for celebrating it.

Easter (Pascha): Celebrating the New Order (BCW 294)

The early church's annual paschal festival functioned as both culmination and initiation of the church year—in that way it is a "big Sunday." Pascha is the English transliteration of both the Greek and Hebrew words for "Passover," the central festival for Jews. The early Christians appropriated this term for the annual celebration of the death and resurrection of Christ. Pascha signified the great deliverance accomplished in the Lord's new Passover.

For Christians, Pascha was initially a feast that included everything from the incarnation, through the death and resurrection of Christ, to the gift of the Spirit. The Lord's life-giving victories were proclaimed and celebrated each year in a fast and vigil near the time of Passover. Throughout the Roman Empire, Gentile Christians gathered for this yearly celebration on a Sunday—the day of the Lord's resurrection. In Asia Minor, where Jews constituted the bulk of the church, Jewish Christians observed this annual festival of Pascha on the actual date of Passover (14 Nisan), which had now been transformed by Christ's resurrection. The annual Paschal Vigil was celebrated on these two different dates until the Council of Nicaea (A.D. 325) declared the Sunday Pascha as the official day.[18]

As the principal service of the year, since at least the second century, the Paschal Vigil celebrated the promise of new life, of forgiveness of sins, and of victory over death. Lighting of the fire and the paschal candle symbolized Christ passing through darkness into light. This was followed by singing the Exsultet, the great hymn in praise of the redemption. On this night of nights, stories of creation, of Israel passing through the waters from oppression to liberation, of God preparing the world for the coming of Christ, and of Christ's bursting the bonds of death and rising victorious from the grave were recalled.

It was furthermore the occasion for baptism. "What time is more appropriate for baptism," wrote St. Basil of Caesarea, "than this day of the Pasch. It is the memorial day of the resurrection. Baptism implants in us the seed of resurrection. Let us then receive the grace of resurrection on the day of the resurrection."[19] On this night of nights, new converts to the faith were baptized into Christ Jesus, and so into his death and resurrection: "We have been buried with him by baptism into death, so that, just as Christ was raised from the dead by the glory of the Father, so we too might walk in newness of life" (Rom. 6:4).

The Paschal Vigil concluded in the early hours of Sunday morning, the great resurrection day, as the community of faith gathered at the table of the Lord to celebrate the Lord's Supper.

Pascha *is* the central event, the time of transformation, of becoming a resurrected people, God's new people. On this Sunday of all Sundays, Pascha, we celebrate our transformation as a new people.

When Christ rose from the grave, death and all other "principalities and powers" that seek to entomb God's will were forever defeated.

Easter is not simply the miracle of a dead person raised from a grave, but a celebration of power that can shatter death in order that people can freely serve the God of life. In the resurrection of Christ, God's awesome purposes were on display, revealing a radically new world of peace and harmony and equality and mutuality, about which we can only dream. The Lord of the future has been disclosed to us. Both the incarnation at Christmas and the resurrection at Easter testify to the lordship of Christ.

Resurrection Faith

Resurrection shouts "no" to everything in our world that works against God's will, and "yes" to God's victory. At the same time, Easter draws us toward a future salvation for which we wait with patience. History is marching to a final end. What Christ accomplished on Easter is a glorious revelation of the future, for resurrection implies a totally new order. "We will be changed," writes Paul (1 Cor. 15:52). The new age will transform the old age. "So if anyone is in Christ, there is a new creation: everything old has passed away; see, everything has become new!" (2 Cor. 5:17). The Scriptures offer confidence in the power of God who raised up Jesus, and an invitation to trust God's grace for life and for death.

God reversed the judgment on us by raising Christ from the dead. The great hymn in Ephesians (2:14–16) tells of Christ breaking down the walls that separate us from each other and from God, to make us one people. Out of a divided humanity, Christ formed a new humanity that transcends differences in race, religion, nationality, politics, and economic class. Christ's resurrection not only absolved humanity from sin; it established a new reality. Post-Easter history is history in a new dimension. Post-Easter Christians are new people, citizens of the city without walls.

Behold the New Order

On Easter we glimpse a new landscape—the age to come—and experience a sense of holy awe at the significance of the resurrection for human life. The shape of the age to come reveals a new people of God, a new humanity.

When Christ was crucified, humanity died with him on Calvary. But on Easter morning, a new world was born—raised up with the crucified and risen Christ. Bursting the bonds of death, the first human being of a new human race, Jesus Christ, appeared among those who crucified him. In the midst of the old sin-struck world, God gave the world a new beginning, a new humanity. By faith the old guilt-ridden humanity was born again into the new forgiven humanity of Jesus Christ. Ever since, here and there, clusters of the new people of God live according to the new social order of the new age.

Therefore, Easter faith recalls the past, especially the awesome act of God in raising the crucified Christ from the grave. Easter hope looks to the promised future, to that which awaits us. Easter love celebrates the presence of the crucified and risen Christ who is now among us, reconciling us as one people. Resurrection faith asserts that by grace we are born again into the new humanity of Jesus Christ. We are called to new life for God and for neighbors. As representatives of the new humanity we walk in newness of life.

Ascension Day (BCW 332)

The seven weeks of the Easter season include the festival of the ascension of our Lord—Ascension Day.

Throughout the earliest centuries of the church, every Sunday celebrated the unitive festival of the paschal mystery: the passion-death-resurrection-ascension of Christ, the giving of the Spirit, and Christ's coming in glory at the end of time. Over the years, however, Christ's redeeming work was gradually separated into individual feasts on specific days. For instance, by the late fourth century, the Lord's ascension and the outpouring of the Holy Spirit were commemorated as two distinct aspects of Christ's redeeming work. Ascension Day's exaltation of Christ, however, still looks both back to Transfiguration and Easter and forward to Christ the King (or Reign of Christ).

Adhering to the Lukan sequence of events in Acts 1:1–11, Christ's ascension was celebrated on "the fortieth day" after resurrection. This custom probably originated in the Constantinople-Antioch area of Asia Minor and then spread westward to northern Italy and eastward to Jerusalem. Obviously, Ascension Day was and is observed always on the fortieth day after the resurrection (the Thursday after the sixth Sunday of Easter), or on the Sunday following.

In that John Calvin's theology placed great importance on the ascended and regnant Christ, Ascension Day is in some ways *the* Presbyterian feast day. Christ is Lord of the world and head of the church, we proclaim. Christ's ascension, therefore, concerns us not only with ecclesiastical matters but also with social and political ones. If Christ has ascended, then Christ's word rules the world as well as the church. If Christ has ascended, then there are no other rulers—all others are merely pretenders. Christ reigns supreme.

With the raising of Christ to a position above all worldly powers, the earthly ministry of Christ begun at Christmas's incarnation now concludes. The path of faithfulness obediently followed by Christ traveled through the suffering of the cross to the exaltation of the glory. From glory to suffering to glory again is the shape of Jesus' ministry as well as ours. We, too, are destined for the glory we share now in Christ only by faith. "It does not yet appear what we shall be, but we know that when Christ appears we shall be like him" (1 John 3:2).

Lent: The Way of the Cross to Easter (Pascha) (BCW 235)

Pascha (Easter) quickly evolved into a cycle that we now celebrate as a day and a season of the Great Fifty Days ending with Pentecost and preceded by a period of preparation. Though the earliest traditions are unclear, Lent apparently evolved as a time for training, particularly as a time of final preparation of candidates for baptism at Easter. Lent also became a time for the renewal of the faithful, as well as a time for the excommunicated to prepare to return to the community of faith.

By the fourth century, Lent had developed from a two-day fast, through a weeklong fast, to a biblical "forty days." Originally, though Lent contained elements of penitence, it was primarily a time devoted to preparing those who were to be baptized. The Lenten season seems to have developed as a period of learning with a focus on what it means to be a follower of Christ. Those preparing for baptism learned the creed, the teachings of Jesus (perhaps the Sermon on the Mount), and the disciplines of the Christian faith.

The period of Lent had and still has an emphasis on reaffirming baptismal identity, of knowing and living the faith. During Lent, we have the opportunity to reaffirm who we are and always will be, in anticipation of Easter.

Commencing the Journey of the Cross to Easter (Pascha)

The Lenten journey from the ashes of death to resurrected life begins on the first day of Lent, Ash Wednesday, which signifies a time to turn around, to change directions, to repent. This first day of Lent reminds us that unless we are willing to die to our old selves, we cannot be raised to new life with Christ. The first step of this journey calls us to acknowledge and confront our mortality, individually and corporately. In many traditions, this is symbolized through the imposition of ashes—placing a cross of ashes on one's forehead. During the imposition of ashes the words: "You are dust, and to dust you shall return" (Gen. 3:19) are repeated again and again. We are to remember that we are but temporary creatures, always on the edge of death. On Ash Wednesday, we begin our Lenten trek through the desert toward Easter.

Ashes on the forehead is a sign of our humanity and a reminder of our mortality. Lent is not a matter of being good, and wearing ashes is not to show off one's faith. The ashes are a reminder to us and our communities of our finite creatureliness. The ashes we wear on our Lenten journey symbolize the dust and broken debris of our lives as well as the reality that eventually each of us will die.

Trusting in the "accomplished fact" of Christ's resurrection, however, we listen for the word of God in the time-honored stories of the church's Lenten journey. We follow Jesus into the wilderness, resist temptation, fast, and proceed "on the way" to Jerusalem, and the cross. Our Lenten journey is one of *metanoia* ("turning around"), of changing directions from self-serving toward the self-giving way of the cross.

What we hear during Lent is the power and possibility of the paschal mystery, and that the way of the cross, the way to Easter, is through death. To appropriate the new life that is beyond the power of death means we must die with Christ who was raised for us. To live for Christ, we must die with him. New life requires a daily surrendering of the old life, letting go of the present order, so that we may embrace the new humanity. "I die every day!" asserts Paul (1 Cor. 15:31). Resurrection necessitates death as a preceding act. The church's peculiar Lenten claim is that in dying we live, that all who are baptized into Christ are baptized into his death. To be raised with Christ means one must also die with Christ. In order to embrace the resurrection, we must experience the passion of Jesus. The way of the cross, the way to Easter, is through death of the "old self." In dying, we live.

Therefore, at the beginning of Lent, we are reminded that our possessions, our rulers, our empires, our projects, our families, and even our lives do not last forever. "You are dust, and to dust you shall return" (Gen. 3:19). The liturgies throughout Lent try to pry loose our fingers, one by one, from presumed securities and plunge us into unknown baptismal waters, waters that turn out to be not only our death tomb, but surprisingly our womb of life. Rather than falling back into nothingness, we fall back on everlasting arms. Death? How can we fear what we have already undergone in baptism?[20]

It is the power of the resurrection on the horizon ahead that draws us in repentance toward the cross and tomb. Through the intervention of God's gracious resurrection, lifelong changes in our values and behavior become possible. By turning from the end of the "old self" in us, Lenten repentance makes it possible for us to affirm joyfully, "Death is no more!" and to aim toward the landscape of the new age. Faithfully adhering to the Lenten journey of "prayer, fasting, and almsgiving" leads to the destination of Easter.

Completing the Journey of the Cross to Easter (Pascha)

During the final week, Holy Week, we hear the fullness of Christ's passion, his death, and resurrection. From Jesus' triumphal entry into Jerusalem and on to the Triduum (Maundy Thursday, Good Friday, and Holy Saturday), all of Holy Week focuses on the passion. As his followers, we travel Christ's path of servanthood through the Lord's Supper and the suffering of the cross toward the glory of Easter, all of which underscores the inseparable link between the death and resurrection of Jesus.

Passion/Palm Sunday (BCW 251)

The service for Passion/Palm Sunday maintains the inherent tension that exists between the joyful entry of the palm processional and the somberness of the passion, the focus of Holy Week. The triumphal entry as a gateway to the week can be celebrated by a congregational procession into the sanctuary. Christ's suffering and death for all is then proclaimed through the passion narratives in Matthew, Mark, or Luke.

The question is frequently asked, Why combine the passion and the palms?

First, it is in accord with historical tradition. Since at least the fourth century, the focus of the first day of Holy Week, or Great Week, has been the passion of Christ. After a palm processional, a Gospel passion narrative has been read. Western churches have kept the first day of Holy Week by concentrating on both the glory and the passion of Christ, recalling both the passion and the palms. Presbyterians, Methodists, and Roman Catholics call this day Passion/Palm Sunday; the United Church of Christ calls it Palm/Passion Sunday; Lutherans and Episcopalians call it The Sunday of the Passion: Palm Sunday. Though the name may differ, what all the churches share is the Western tradition of linking the joy of Christ's triumphal entry into Jerusalem with sober meditation on the suffering and death of Christ.

Pastoral values result from combining the passion and the palms. Many people simply do not attend worship on Good Friday. The result is that, for them, there is a distortion in the story. A story that skips from Jesus' triumphal entry into Jerusalem to Jesus' resurrection from the dead evades the question,

What happened in between? If we leap from Palm Sunday's "Hosannas" to Easter Day's "Hallelujahs" we overlook the pivotal event of Christ's suffering and death on the cross. The journey to Jerusalem has the cross as its goal, and the cross needs to be kept in sight even during the triumphal entry into Jerusalem. Where the long tradition of reading the whole passion narrative on Passion/Palm Sunday is appropriated, congregations have found the value of hearing the entire passion story. Also, those who do not attend the Good Friday service hear the fullness of Christ's passion.

Combining the passion and the palms furthermore provides for a critical understanding of entire passion narratives. Instead of hearing only bits and pieces of the various Gospel accounts of the passion of Christ, congregations may hear an entire passion narrative, including differences and similarities with other accounts. The unique character of each Gospel account of the passion helps parishioners understand the theological and apologetic viewpoint present in each Gospel account, especially since the writers of each Gospel saw and understood Jesus Christ differently.

Though the passion narratives have been misused as a foundation for anti-Judaic sentiments in Christian theology and in the life of Christian churches, caution is urged in combining biblical texts into one harmonious story. Such efforts typically smooth over the different christological emphases of each Gospel, and consequently each evangelist's version loses its distinctive theological and apologetic contribution. If we allow the differences and similarities of the Gospels to stand, we allow the Word, through the work of the Spirit, to open to us a fresh critical understanding of each passion narrative.

The most important reason for combining the passion and the palms is the relationship between the death and the resurrection of Jesus. To understand the resurrection, we must contemplate the passion of Jesus. Long, careful meditation upon the mystery of the cross must precede the glorious message of Easter.

On the one hand, an *oversimplified theology of glory* can *under*value death by implying that it is merely a stepping-stone on the path to resurrection. Therefore, in order to experience resurrection, one simply dies, and on dying will automatically ascend from the grave to glory. On the other hand, an *oversimplified theology of the cross* can *over*value death as a "work," by implying that resurrection is merely a consequence of the passion; therefore, if one suffers and dies for the faith, one will have earned resurrection. Instead, the cross *and* resurrection must be held together theologically. The extent to which we understand the resurrection of Jesus will be determined by our understanding of his passion.

Thus, the palm procession with ringing Hosannas symbolically foreshadows the Hallelujahs of God's promised future when the risen Jesus will lead his people into a new Jerusalem. Interwoven with such liturgical experiences are the stories of the passion of Christ. Thus, the eight-day week from Passion/Palm Sunday to Easter Day is framed by resurrection and death on one side, and death and resurrection on the other.

The need to affirm, as Holy Week begins, the inseparable relationship between the death and the resurrection of Jesus is precisely the reason the passion of Christ and the palms are linked together as Passion/Palm Sunday.

The Triduum ("The Three Days") (BCW 268–314)

All of Holy Week points toward the passion—the death and resurrection of Christ. The week's three final days (from sunset Thursday through sunset on Easter) complete the commemoration of Christ's passion. These three days are called the Triduum.

The Triduum engages us from Thursday until Sunday in a unified act. What happens on Maundy Thursday, Good Friday, and the Easter Vigil forms a continuous dramatic story. These days are to be seen together rather than separately. The services of the three final days of Holy Week connect with one another and, together, comprise the oneness of the Triduum.

Because of this interrelationship of the three days, each service of the Triduum needs the others to tell the whole story. For example, resurrection is incomprehensible without Christ's self-giving in crucifixion and at the Lord's Supper. Therefore, Easter needs Good Friday and Maundy Thursday to be fully understood. The way to the triumph of Easter is through the Triduum.

All of Holy Week, and particularly its three concluding days (the Triduum), provides an opportunity to undertake a pilgrimage of renewed commitment and joy; to travel Christ's path of servanthood, through the Lord's Supper and the suffering of the cross, as we move toward Easter.

Our joy during the great festival of resurrection will be enhanced by faithful participation in worship during the preceding week, especially during the whole of the Triduum.

Maundy Thursday (BCW 268–279)

Maundy Thursday (or *le mandé*; Thursday of the *Mandatum,* Latin, commandment). The name is taken from the first words sung at the ceremony of the washing of the feet, "I give you a new commandment" (John 13:34); also from the commandment of Christ that we should imitate his loving humility in the washing of the feet (John 13:14–17). The term *mandatum* (maundy), therefore, was applied to the rite of the foot-washing on this day. So, sometimes, understanding what we do in worship is as simple as remembering the name of the day. Ash Wednesday is linked with ashes, dust, and mortality. Palm Sunday displays palms and Hosannas. Maundy (or Commandment) Thursday presents the model of the footwashing commandment.

The opening service of the Triduum is not inherently mournful. The penitential acts of Maundy Thursday have celebratory aspects as well: restoration through the bold declaration of pardon; the act of footwashing connoting humility and intimacy; the celebration of the Lord's Supper embodying the mystery of Christ's enduring redemptive presence. Maundy Thursday's acts provide the paradox of a celebratively somber and solemnly celebrative service.

Footwashing. A powerful symbolic response to the Word, representing the way of humility and servanthood to which we are called by Christ, is the act of footwashing, practiced within the church since at least the fifth century.

The practice of footwashing in first-century Palestine may have been as common as when today a host helps guests take off their coats, a waiter seats diners, or a driver holds the taxi door for passengers. Hospitality underlies all such welcoming gestures.

However, if the focus of footwashing today is primarily on the act itself and not its meaning, then footwashing often is perceived as a quaint rite that can become a fad to enliven worship. Churches should be cautioned to resist including footwashing for its quaintness, and rather to consider its dramatic, potent message.

The difference between yesterday's footwashing and today's common courtesy is that the person expected to wash guests' feet was at the bottom of the household pecking order. In the prevailing practice, according to the way of the world, therefore, footwashing was a lowly task performed by menials, with or without pay. What is startling if not jolting about the footwashing story in John is not the act of footwashing, but the identity of the servant who washed others' feet—Jesus, God-with-us, the least likely person. The focus is on the *person* washing feet, not on the *act*. Following the footwashing, Jesus took on himself the humiliation of the cross, the ultimate symbol of his selfless love for others.

The life of servanthood is affirmed again and again by Jesus as the life to which he calls people. Recall such poignant sayings of Jesus as "The Son of Man came not to be served but to serve, and to give his life a ransom for many" (Matt. 20:28; Mark 10:45); "The greatest among you must become like the youngest, and the leader like one who serves. . . . I am among you as one who serves" (Luke 22:26, 27b). In response to the command of the gospel, footwashing is an example of the servanthood that Jesus urges on all who follow him. In essence, Jesus' act of footwashing says to us, "I have descended; you, too, descend."

In the priesthood of all believers (not hierarchies of power), *all* members of the body of Christ can "kneel" before each other and wash one another's feet as did our Lord and Savior himself—neighbor to neighbor, perhaps even stranger to stranger. More important, as the priesthood of all believers, our corporate kneeling before others for the earthy task of footwashing symbolizes our servanthood within and beyond the body of Christ.

Churches whose members dare to wash one another's feet may find themselves transformed so that they also turn toward other neighbors in service—the family next door, the single parent, the retired, the unemployed, the unwanted child, refugees, prisoners—and begin to see the image of God in the face of the world. Washing another's feet may help us minister in the church by joining other Christians in caring, not only for one another, but for the world God loves.

Therefore ask *who* is washing feet. Not a hired butler or maid, not a person paid to perform what the world views as menial tasks, but someone called to Christ's ministry of serving others. Focus on the person washing feet, for he or she symbolizes the radical nature of servanthood.

The Lord's Supper. Though on this night we remember and celebrate the final supper Jesus shared with his disciples in the context of Passover, we are neither celebrating a Seder ("order of service"), nor reenacting the Last Supper, but sharing with our risen Lord a foretaste of the heavenly banquet.

In recent years, some congregations have begun to celebrate a Maundy Thursday Eucharist in the context of a Christianized Seder (Passover meal). Before deciding to celebrate a Christian Passover, remember that seeking to experience the historical origins of the Last Supper presents an almost impenetrable path through which to walk.

1. Since no Jewish Seder texts earlier than the ninth century exist, any attempt at historical reconstruction of an authentic first-century Seder is suspect because it cannot possibly represent what Jesus did. The Gospels themselves present conflicting data regarding the day of the meal. The Eucharist was instituted either *during* the Passover meal (Matthew, Mark, and Luke) or *before* the feast of the Passover (John 13:1).

2. At a contemporary "Christian Passover Seder," the attempt is sometimes made to "Christianize" the rite by adding the words of institution of the Lord's Supper, or by appending "through Jesus Christ our Lord" to the prayers. Both practices may offend Jews.

3. The focus of the Lord's Supper is not the annual reactualization of the exodus, but the celebration of salvation in Christ. The annual liturgy of liberation for Christians is the Easter (Paschal) Vigil (BCW 294–314).

4. The term "last supper" suggests that it was only one of many meals

shared by Jesus and his disciples, and not *the* meal. The Eucharist is rooted not only in the Last Supper but also in Jesus' eating with sinners, and in his feeding the crowd with the loaves and fishes, and it foreshadows the meals after his resurrection. All together they connote the multiple meanings of the Lord's Supper. To reduce the Lord's Supper to the Last Supper is to cut off the Sacrament from its eschatological significance (that is, as it relates to the unfolding of God's purpose and in the ultimate destiny of humankind and the world).

5. What constitutes the Eucharist is a ritual meal that combines the sharing of bread and cup with the offering of a great prayer of thanksgiving. Therefore, the Eucharist as a ritual meal eliminates the need for an actual meal of multiple courses.

6. The quest to imitate Jesus' Last Supper with his disciples in the upper room is a historicism that inevitably undermines the symbols of offering of a great prayer of thanksgiving and sharing of bread and cup as effective means of conversion or nurture.

It may be far better, therefore, for Christians to participate in Jewish Seders as guests, rather than entangling themselves in the hazards of celebrating "Christian Passover" meals.

Good Friday (BCW 280–293)

The Good Friday service is a penitential service, yet it is also a celebration of the good news of the cross. So, retain the paradox of the day in the form, mood, and texts of the service. Good Friday is a day in which to allow for numerous contemplative moments, and to permit the power of silence to speak for itself.

No colors, flowers, candles, or decorative materials are appropriate on Good Friday, except, perhaps, "representations of the way of the cross."

The passion narrative according to John is read on Good Friday, because at the heart of John's passion narrative is the good news of the cross—the victory of the cross. Thus, John's emphasis on crucifixion and glory corresponds to the tension and ambiguity of the day.

Easter Vigil (BCW 294–314)

On the final night of this Easter journey we pause in vigil, at which time we remember stories about who we have been and are now becoming. As the community of faith we recount our centuries-long pilgrimage culminating in the renewal of baptismal promises. The Easter Vigil is akin to sitting around a campfire while listening to the stories of generations past and future. During the Easter Vigil, we tell our name to ourselves and to those not of the household of faith. Our name is a very long story of how we were made, of how God chose us from among all peoples, of how God liberated us from bondage, of how God planted us in the promised land, of how, in these last times, God has given the story a new twist in the life, death, and resurrection of Jesus. Because we have been here for so long, it takes a long time to tell who we are. We will not be hasty folk on that night.[21]

To hear Christ's teaching is one of the traditional disciplines of the season of Lent. Hear what the Spirit is saying to the church throughout all of Lent and, perhaps, this season will become a *turning from* the mind of this age *to* that of Christ, and a renewing of baptismal identity (who we are and always will be), all in anticipation of Easter.

Pentecost: Set on Fire as Witnesses to the Crucified and Risen Christ (BCW 338–347)

For seven weeks, a week of Sundays, we acclaim the resurrection of Christ by the power of God. The period of seven weeks of jubilation can be traced back to its Jewish roots of the fifty days celebrated from the day after Passover to Shavuot (Feast of Weeks, Exod. 23:16). For Jews, the Feast of Weeks closed the season of harvest, which had been initiated by the Feast of Unleavened Bread. In a similar manner, early Christians observed a fifty-day period of celebration from Easter to the Day of Pentecost. To underscore the uninterrupted rejoicing of these fifty days, fasting and kneeling in prayer were forbidden at least as early as the end of the second century. On the *pentecoste* ("fiftieth") day, not only was the fifty-day period concluded, but a festival with its own proper content was celebrated. The Jews observed a feast of covenant renewal and eventually commemorated the giving of the Law. Christians celebrated the gift of the Spirit as preparing the way for the day of the Lord. What Moses and the Law did for the Jewish community, the Holy Spirit now does for the community of Christ.[22]

The Gift of the Spirit

According to the Day of Pentecost story in Acts 2:1–13, God gave the gift of the Holy Spirit to empower witnesses to the resurrection. Sounds from heaven, cosmic language, the rush of a mighty *ruach* (wind, spirit, breath) invaded the house in which the apostles gathered, and appeared to them as a burning fire. Tongues of fire touched their nerve centers. A power—the unseen power of God—moved among them and gripped them. The Holy Spirit is unseen, like the wind, which is why the Old Testament calls it *ruach*

YHWH, "the wind, or breath, of God" (cf. John 3:8). The Spirit is the "unseen-ness of God" working among us.

According to Joel (2:28–29), the *ruach* is to open everybody to God's future. People young and old will dream and will have visions of hope; they will be able to loose themselves from the way things are now, because God is establishing a whole new economy of creation. The Holy Spirit breaks us out of our preoccupation with ourselves and frees us to serve neighbors, loosens our grasp on possessions, and sets us to loving people. New creation is what Joel is talking about. Pentecost is new creation.

The book of Acts tells the story of the outcome of Pentecost's new creation: people witness in word and in deed to the risen Christ. At the outset, the new-born church immediately tumbled out into the streets to witness to God's mighty works in the languages of people all over the world. By the end of the story, a tiny, Spirit-filled community of faith that broke from its present order has spread across the continents with incredible power to bring new things into being. With the gift of the Spirit, all things are possible.

The Spirit-filled experience ignited the faithful and sent them outward, giving utterance in word and deed to the good news. "The cause of good works, we confess," states the Scots Confession (chapter 13) "is not our free will, but the Spirit of the Lord Jesus."[23] Our call as disciples of Christ is not only to celebrate but also to show and tell neighbors about God's new world coming in the name of the crucified and risen Christ.

The same Spirit that empowered Jesus to love enemies was the Spirit that enabled the Corinthian church to love their antagonists. A living fellowship means living as the body of Christ by preaching the Word with freedom, breaking bread together, reconciling with adversaries, and serving neighbors, near and far. What makes possible the church's witness to the resurrection of Christ is the Spirit of God.

Life Together in Christ, Filled with the Holy Spirit

Note that the Spirit is conceived, first of all, as God's presence within the whole community of faith, rather than the private possession of solitary individuals. The essential mark of the Spirit's presence is obedience to the will of God within the context of the community of faith. Both Old and New Testament witnesses to Spirit-filled life portray an experience of new community.

Therefore, on the Day of Pentecost, we celebrate God's gift of Holy Spirit which draws us together as one people, helps us comprehend what God is doing in the world, and empowers us to proclaim, in word and in deed, God's plan of reconciling all people in the name of Christ (Eph. 1:10).

Without the gift of the Spirit, Christ's church dries up and withers away, and we are left with only our broken selves. With the gift of the Spirit, all things are possible. A spirit-filled community of faith opens eyes to needs in the world and sees its mission as God's new people. The Day of Pentecost is the climax of the Great Fifty Days of Easter, celebrating as it does the gift of the Spirit to the body of Christ—the church.

Commentary on the Easter Cycle
(Lent–Easter–Day of Pentecost) Services

Ash Wednesday (BCW 220–234)

Ash Wednesday centers on both human mortality and the confession of sin before God. The service provided in the *Book of Common Worship* maintains this dual focus in the light of God's redeeming love in Jesus Christ.

Entrance

When a procession begins the service, it is to take place in silence in keeping with the austere character of the Ash Wednesday service, thus encouraging thoughtful meditation on the meaning of the day.

Confession of Sin

Psalm 51 is *always* used as a Confession of Sin in this service. Since the time between Ash Wednesday and Maundy Thursday is traditionally a time of penitence, some churches embrace the tradition of *not* including a declaration of pardon on Ash Wednesday and throughout Lent, until Maundy Thursday.

Ashes

Traditionally, the ashes for this service are prepared by burning the palm branches from the previous year's Palm Sunday. Ordinarily, the palms from the service are returned on the Sunday before Ash Wednesday (The Transfiguration of the Lord). No empirical historical reason seems to exist for the burning of the previous year's palms for Ash Wednesday. But, it is often suggested that the returned palms signify the enthusiasm from the last year's palm procession that has now wilted to brittle, dry, dead fronds. Burned to ash, they remind us of our dashed dreams of faithful discipleship and, ultimately, our mortality: "You are dust, and to dust you shall return" (Gen. 3:19). In this sense, the burning of the previous year's palms can imply a relationship between one year's Passion/Palm Sunday and the following year's Ash Wednesday. The natural symbols of palms that are part of the conclusion of Lent become part of the subsequent year's introduction to Lent.

Ignite the dried palms in a container (A large coffee can will do). Then put the ashes into a bowl and crush them into a fine powder. A mortar and pestle are not required. Use a small bowl and the back of a spoon. Working them through a screen will make them even finer. Shortly before the service, mix the ashes with water to form a paste. Small wooden salad bowls can be used as simple vessels for the ashes. Be sure to have a moist towel (or large paper tissues) available for the hands of those who have imposed ashes.

The issue of imposition has clear educational implications, and it could take time to prepare a congregation for participation in a service that includes imposition. In an initial year, for example, ashes simply could be present in the service. A second step could be for the congregation to see the ashes poured from one container into another. Another step could be for worshipers to pass before the ashes, or for a worship leader holding a container of ashes to pass before the people. Whatever the progression of specific steps, each can be seen as an opportunity to grow toward the actual imposition of ashes. Still, for pastoral reasons, some congregations may choose not to impose ashes.

Before the thanksgiving over the ashes, the worship leader should observe a brief period of silence. The silence should be more than a pause.

People proceed to the front of the church to receive the imposition of ashes. The minister imposes ashes on the forehead of those who come forward to receive. The person imposing the ashes dips his or her thumb in the ashes, and marks the forehead in the form of a cross, while saying the words, "Remember that you are dust, and to dust you shall return" (Gen. 3:19).

Music

Music for Ash Wednesday will probably be the most somber of the year, except for Good Friday. A musical setting of the biblical text of Psalm 51 may be found in PH 196. Some appropriate choices of hymns for the service include:

> Forty Days and Forty Nights (PH 77)
> God of Compassion, in Mercy Befriend Us (PH 261)
> Have Mercy on Us, Living Lord (Psalm 51, paraphrase) (PH 195)
> Just as I Am, Without One Plea (PH 370)
> Lord Jesus, Think on Me (PH 301)
> Lord, Who Throughout These Forty Days (PH 81)

A Suggested Hymn Line That Can Be Used as a Refrain during Ash Wednesday (see "Music: Hymn Lines Can Be Used as Festival or Seasonal Refrains," p. 90):

"Teach us with Thee to mourn our sins, and close by Thee to stay."
From hymn text: "Lord, Who Throughout These Forty Days" (PH 81)
hymn tune: ST. FLAVIAN

A Suggested Hymn Line That Can Be Used as a Refrain during Lent (see
"Music: Hymn Lines Can Be Used as Festival or Seasonal Refrains," p. 90):

"There is a balm in Gilead to heal the sin-sick soul."
From hymn text: "There Is a Balm in Gilead" (PH 394)
hymn tune: BALM IN GILEAD

Liturgical Color

The liturgical color for the day is purple, the color traditional to Lent, although
some prefer the use of gray. Consider rough textured fabrics, such as monk's
cloth or burlap, perhaps using earth tones for Ash Wednesday and the weeks
that follow during Lent.

Passion/Palm Sunday (BCW 251–267)

The Service for Passion/Palm Sunday maintains an inherent tension between
the joyful entry of the palm procession and the somberness of the passion (the
focus of Holy Week). The triumphal entry is celebrated as a gateway to the
week by a congregational procession into the sanctuary. Christ's suffering and
death for all is then proclaimed through the passion narrative according to
Matthew, Mark, or Luke.

The Setting

Liturgical Color. Red is often used for part of the service on Passion/Palm
Sunday. Some traditions begin the service (the entrance rite of prayer, proclamation, and palm processional) with red vestments in celebration of Christ's
impending sacrificial death. The color red also manifests the triumphant
singing and joyful excitement of this opening part of the service. At the conclusion of the hymn of praise, or immediately prior to the liturgy of the Word,
vestments are changed to the traditional purple which continues the penitential color of Lent. Some traditions reverse this color sequence, understanding
the purple to represent the majesty of the entering king, and red the blood of
Christ shed for our salvation. Other congregations dress the church and vest
solely in purple.

Congregations using somber earthen tones of gray or brown throughout
Lent may wish to continue such colors on this day, but still might use red during the entrance rite.

Other Visual Signs. As with liturgical colors, each congregation will decide for itself what visual signs are consistent with the day as well as in the particular setting of the liturgy. Remember, it is the first day of Holy Week with shifts in music, mood, texture, and tone from joyfulness to solemnity. The shadow of the cross in the passion narrative falls on the exuberance of the triumphal entry.

Therefore, visual signs of the triumphal entry—crown, palms, and donkey—as well as signs of the passion—whip, flogging post, crown of thorns, seamless robe, dice, nails, ladder—are appropriate.

Music. Since Passion/Palm Sunday moves us from the procession into Jerusalem through the crucifixion, the selection of hymns for this service will need to be conducted carefully. Suggestions are offered at appropriate places below.

Gathering of People

If possible, the congregation gathers at a designated place outside the usual worship space. A brief introduction to the service may be given, noting any unfamiliar elements, musical responses, and so forth. Perhaps special instruction or practice may be required to ensure not only awareness but also smoothness in the conduct of the day's service.

Palm branches, or flowering branches indigenous to the area, may be distributed to all the people so they may carry or wave them as they sing the hymn(s) of praise during the palm processional.

Call to Worship and Proclamation of the Entrance into Jerusalem. Consider enhancing the entrance rite and/or the reading of the Gospel account of Jesus' entrance into Jerusalem by encouraging the people to sing the *Benedictus qui venit* ("Blessed is the one who comes . . . ," [Psalm 118:26]) as it appears in: (a) the entrance rite; (b) each Gospel reading of the Entrance into Jerusalem (Matt. 21:9; Mark 11:9; Luke 19:38); (c) concluding the entrance rite, *or* as introductory words to the Prayer for Illumination. Sources of musical settings are noted below under "Response" (p. 123).

Procession into the Church. A palm procession (used since at least the fourth century) involving sight, hearing, and touch heightens a congregation's appreciation of the story of Jesus' triumphal entry into Jerusalem. Therefore, the possibilities of a palm procession should be considered. Distance and degree of incline (including steps) must be considered in order sensitively to incorporate people who may have difficulty walking with ease.

If an outdoor procession is not possible, a congregation can gather in the worship space and conduct a palm procession within that space by inviting the people to proceed around the outside aisles to the rear and then down the center aisle(s) to their seats. The action of the procession is a symbolic move-ment by the congregation from outside to the inside of the worship space.

Since the ninth century, "All Glory, Laud, and Honor" (HB 187, WB 284, PH 88) has been sung on this day. This hymn relates to the Scripture just read as the Call to Worship and expresses a festive spirit. Consider varying the voices singing the stanzas and refrain of the hymn among combinations of alto and soprano voices, and tenor and bass voices. Enhancing the accompa-niment with varied instrumentations adds to the festive nature of this proces-sional hymn. An alternative to this hymn is the singing of Psalm 118:19–29. A setting of this psalm is found in *The Presbyterian Hymnal* (232).

During the processional hymn or psalm, choirs, liturgical leaders, dancers, musicians (brass and percussion instrumentalists are particularly suitable), with the whole congregation proceed into the place of worship bearing their palms. Since it may prove cumbersome for some people to hold a hymnbook in one hand and a palm branch in the other, consider printing the text of the hymn in the order for worship or on a separate sheet. It will be necessary to secure per-mission to reprint the hymn if a hymn is chosen that is under copyright.

Response. Echoing the opening of the service, the responsive words "Blessed is the one who comes . . ." from Psalm 118:26 frame the entrance rite, as well as assist transition to the Liturgy of the Word with its distinctly different mood. A response can be formed from the "Blessed is the one who comes . . ." portion of the "Holy, holy, holy Lord," used in celebrations of the Eucharist such as in *The Presbyterian Hymnal* (568, 581) or *Holy Is the Lord* (Lord's Supper: Complete Settings 1–22).

A prayer of confession is usually omitted from the service, particularly if a palm procession is incorporated in the entrance rite. In keeping with the pen-itential discipline of the entire season of Lent, as well as the ensuing reading of a passion narrative, a prayer of confession is redundant on this day.

A Suggested Hymn Line That Can Be Used as a Refrain during Pas-sion/Palm Sunday (see Music: Hymn Lines Can Be Used as Festival or Sea-sonal Refrains, p. 90):

> "All glory, laud, and honor to Thee, Redeemer, King!"
> From hymn text: "All Glory, Laud, and Honor" (PH 88)
> hymn tune: VALET WILL ICH DIR GEBEN

The Word (BCW 254)

Gospel Reading. Various modes of proclaiming the passion narrative could include any one or combination of the following. All require advance plan-ning and careful practice:

Choral Reading. At the reading of Matthew 27:31; Mark 15:20; or Luke 23:26, it is customary for the congregation to stand and remain standing through the remainder of the reading. An extended period of silence follows the reading of Matthew 27:50; Mark 15:37; and Luke 23:46. A most usable resource providing the texts for the passion narratives from Matthew, Mark, and Luke (as well as the narrative in the Gospel of John) arranged for choral reading is The National Liturgical Office's *Passion Narratives for Holy Week* (Ottawa, Canada: Canadian Conference of Catholic Bishops, 1985). This resource provides suggestions for acclamations (p. 77) to be sung throughout the reading of the narrative. It may be ordered from the Canadian Conference of Catholic Bishops, Publications Service, 90 Parent Avenue, Ottawa, Ontario, K1N 7B1, Canada. The text arranged for choral reading may also be found in Hoyt L. Hickman, Don E. Saliers, Laurence Hull Stookey, and James F. White, *Handbook of the Christian Year* (Nashville: Abingdon Press, 1986), pp. 135–52, 181–86. The text is also available in an eight-page folder (5" x 8") suitable for including in a church bulletin: "The Passion of Our Lord According to Matthew [or Mark or Luke] for Congregational Reading" (Philadelphia: Fortress Press, 1975).

Dramatization. This could include art forms such as mime, readers' theater, dance, music, or visual arts.

A *Vocal setting* may be sung by the choir or an individual, perhaps including congregational responses.

A *Lessons and Hymns format* may be used, such as the following:

	HB	WB	PH
Cycle A			
Matthew 26:14–35			
An Upper Room Did Our Lord Prepare (st. 1, 2)	—	—	94
Matthew 26:36–75			
Go to Dark Gethsemane (st. 1, 2)	193	—	97
When We Are Tempted to Deny Your Son (st. 1, 2)	—	640	86

Matthew 27:1–32

At the words: "Then they led him away to crucify him" (Matt. 27:31), it is customary for the congregation to stand and remain standing through the remainder of the reading.

	HB	WB	PH
Ah, Holy Jesus	191	280	93
O Sacred Head, Now Wounded	194	524	98

Matthew 27:33–50
An extended period of silence follows the reading of Matthew 27:50, after
which one of the following may be sung:

Alas! And Did My Savior Bleed	199	—	78
Throned Upon the Awful Tree	197	605	99
Why Has God Forsaken Me?	—	—	406

Matthew 27:51–66

Deep Were His Wounds, and Red	—	—	103
O Love, How Deep, How Broad, How High!	—	518	83
Were You There?	201	—	102
What Wondrous Love Is This	—	—	85
When I Survey the Wondrous Cross	198	635	100/101

Cycle B
Mark 14:1–31

An Upper Room Did Our Lord Prepare (st. 1, 2)	—	—	94

Mark 14:32–72

Go to Dark Gethsemane (st. 1, 2)	193	—	97
When We Are Tempted to Deny Your Son (st. 1, 2)	—	640	86

Mark 15:1–37
At the words: "Then they led him out to crucify him" (Mark 15:20), it is
customary for the congregation to stand and remain standing through the
remainder of the reading.

An extended period of silence follows the reading of Mark 15:37, after
which one of the following may be sung:

O Sacred Head, Now Wounded	194	524	98
Throned Upon the Awful Tree	197	605	99
Why Has God Forsaken Me?	—	—	406

Mark 15:38–47

Deep Were His Wounds, and Red	—	—	103
Were You There?	201	—	102
When I Survey the Wondrous Cross	198	635	100/101

Cycle C
Luke 22:14–38

An Upper Room Did Our Lord Prepare (st. 1, 2)	—	—	94

	HB	WB	PH
Luke 22:39–71			
Go to Dark Gethsemane (st. 1, 2)	193	—	97

Luke 23:1–31
At the words: " . . . they laid the cross on him, and made him carry it behind Jesus" (Luke 23:26), it is customary for the congregation to stand and remain standing through the remainder of the reading.

	HB	WB	PH
Ah, Holy Jesus	191	280	93

Luke 23:32–46
An extended period of silence follows the reading of Luke 23:46, after which one of the following may be sung:

	HB	WB	PH
Alas! And Did My Savior Bleed	199	—	78
He Never Said a Mumbalin' Word	—	—	95
Jesus, Remember Me	—	—	599

Luke 23:47–56

	HB	WB	PH
Deep Were His Wounds, and Red	—	—	103
Were You There?	201	—	102
When I Survey the Wondrous Cross	198	635	100/101

Sermon. The proclamation of the readings for the day may replace the sermon, or a brief sermon may precede, interweave, or follow the readings for the day.

Prayers of Intercession. Consider using a seasonal sung or spoken response following each intercession, such as one of the above *Responses* (123).

The Solemn Reproaches of the Cross (see Service for Good Friday, BCW 288–291). The Reproaches are probably more effective on Good Friday, but some congregations may wish to use them on Passion/Palm Sunday, especially if the congregation will not gather again for corporate worship until Easter Day. If a prayer of confession has been included earlier in the service, do not use the Reproaches.

The Eucharist (BCW 256)

Music that attends the Sacrament needs to be carefully selected to be in keeping with the reading of the passion narrative. A hymn such as "Bread of Heaven, on Thee We Feed" (PH 501), which reflects on Christ's death and is set in a minor key, is especially appropriate for use during the serving of the people.

Sending (BCW 262)

The Service for Passion/Palm Sunday draws people into contrasts of mood: the exuberant entry of the palm procession, the solemn reading of the passion of Christ, and a celebration of the Lord's Supper—"the joyful feast of the people of God." The conclusion of this service, therefore, needs to be carefully planned.

The people depart in silence. Or, a hymn anticipating the import of the week may be sung immediately prior to departing, for example, "Ah, Holy Jesus, How Have You Offended" (PH 93), perhaps accompanied by the playing of the melody only. An appropriate hymn refrain also could provide a dramatic close to the service, for example:

> "Your will, O God, be done."
> From hymn text: "When We Are Tempted to Deny Your Son" (PH 86)
> hymn tune: PSALM 22

Maundy Thursday (BCW 268–279)

How can we respect the paradoxical nature of the Maundy Thursday service—somber and celebrative?

Since most services will occur in the evening, perhaps lighting the worship space by many candles, or by illuminating the worship space in subdued fashion, can effectively assist. Periods of silent meditation juxtaposed with joyful expression may also help. We need not fret about trying to create a proper mood, because the acts of confession, the declaration of pardon, the reading and preaching of the Word, the footwashing, the Lord's Supper, and the stripping of the church will draw us all into the paradoxical mood of this first service of the Triduum.

Arrangement of the Worship Space. Services on Maundy Thursday demonstrate a wider variety of celebration than perhaps any other day of the year. Modest to fancy fellowship meals, unadorned church meeting halls to elegantly decorated sanctuaries, reserved to convivial moods, simple to elaborate services are all common to Maundy Thursday. At root, all communities of faith gather on the first night of the Triduum to hear the Word and to break bread together.

Pastoral sensitivity to adapt to local circumstances is a necessity in order to conduct the service for Maundy Thursday "decently and in order" and with dignity, while avoiding a contented mood or uncomfortable setting. Decide how to arrange the worship space in order to establish an environment suitable to the solemn celebration of this day.

Depending on the flexibility of the worship space and the intended mood and movement of the service, some congregations arrange the space so that the bread and the cup are served to the people seated at tables.

For example, small groups of people may be seated at individual tables located throughout the room, with the Lord's table serving as a "head table" from which the liturgical leaders preside. Congregations are discouraged, however, from setting up only tables of twelve as a means of reliving a historical moment in the life of Christ. Liturgy may be dramatic and historic but it is not a reenacted historical drama.

Another example consists of one, room-sized Lord's table around which all the people gather. This may be achieved by arranging a series of tables, all connected in some fashion, the length of a hall or around the room.

A third example, among a limitless number, consists of a semicircular or half-wheel arrangement with the Lord's table as the hub and the tables, at which the people sit, as the spokes.

Congregations desiring to serve the bread and the cup to people who come forward to the Lord's table or to stations where the bread and the cup are served, may also arrange their worship space in varying ways to accommodate easy movement of the congregation.

Liturgical Color. Continue the same colors and worship environment employed throughout the season of Lent. Though the traditional color is purple, some churches use somber earth tones of brown or gray. Whichever color is used, consider rough textured fabrics as a suitable means of conveying the mood of the season. Special visual art or use of shades of colors appropriate to the day can be added to enhance the stories and the shifting moods of this service. Keep in mind that the concluding act is the stripping of the church (worship space) when the stark, bare environment reflects the tone of the concluding days and services of the Triduum in preparation for Easter.

Gathering: The Entrance Rite (BCW 269)

Gathering of the People. Music played or sung as the people gather for worship will set the mood of the service. Therefore, first decide the tone to be established, then carefully choose instrumental or choral music to match.

Call to Worship. The sentences of Scripture proclaim who God is and what God has done in Christ, mindful of the overarching themes of the day.

Confession and Pardon. Either a prayer or penitential psalm, spoken or sung, is appropriate. Use of a sung Kyrie ("Lord, have mercy") will reinforce the penitential note. Choices include *The Presbyterian Hymnal* (565, 572–574); *Holy Is the Lord* (157–169); *Music from Taizé* (vol. 1, pp. 12–14); *Lutheran Book of Worship* (pp. 57, 78, 99); and *The Hymnal 1982* (pp. S85–S98).

For many Christians, the "penitential season" commences on Ash Wednesday and culminates finally in a great absolution on Maundy Thursday (the custom of reconciling penitents on this day is an ancient practice). Thus, Ash Wednesday to Maundy Thursday is kept as a time of penitence, with the long-awaited absolution on Maundy Thursday concluding the Lenten discipline.

In response to the pardon, a hymn of praise, such as the first stanza of "There's a Wideness in God's Mercy" (PH 298), or Hal Hopson's "We Are Forgiven" (HL 178) represent but two appropriate responses to the joy of forgiveness.

The Peace. The momentous words of forgiveness call for action. We have been forgiven, and we have sung praise. Now we extend forgiveness to neighbors and embody a reconciled community. Therefore, the first act of the community following the climax of the penitential season is the exchange of the peace. The community, thus, symbolizes its reconciliation with God and with neighbors by exchanging signs of peace following the announcement of our forgiveness in Jesus Christ.

Since the peace is exchanged at this point in the service, it should not be repeated later. If the peace is not exchanged at this point in the service, another possible location would be immediately preceding the celebration of the Lord's Supper, again as a sign of a community reconciled to God and with neighbors.

The Word (BCW 272)

Scripture Readings. Following the completion of the season of penitence with the declaration of pardon, the last three days of Lent truly begin, with an intense meditation on the mystery of redemption through the cross and resurrection of Christ. Thus, Scripture readings according to the Revised Common Lectionary focus on a range of texts over its three-year cycle, including:

> preparation and celebration of the Passover (Exod. 12:1–14)
> sealing of the Mosaic covenant (Exod. 24:3–8)
> promise of a new covenant and the fulfillment of this promise through
>   Christ's sacrifice (Jer. 31:31–34; Heb. 10:16–25)
> understanding our sharing in the body and blood of Christ (1 Cor.
>   10:16–17)
> footwashing by Jesus (John 13:1–17)
> Pauline and Gospel accounts of the institution of the Lord's Supper
>   (1 Cor. 11:23–26; Mark 14:12–26; Luke 22:7–20)

Creed or Affirmation of Faith. In keeping with the solemnity of the service, most Christian traditions omit a creed on Maundy Thursday. The act of footwashing is itself an act of professing faith, and the eucharistic prayer also is an act of confessing the faith. We are doing what Jesus did for the reason he did it—in love and service of our brothers and sisters. However, since the Reformed tradition is a confessional tradition, particular churches may wish to use suitable segments of historic confessions (see current edition of *The Book of Confessions* of the Presbyterian Church (U.S.A.)).

Footwashing. If a footwashing is included in the service, it should be conducted in an open area of the worship space, preferably in view of the whole congregation.

Depending on the size of the congregation and the amount of space available, either all who wish to may participate, or representative members of the congregation may be selected. The simple yet powerful act of washing the feet of another person best represents the intention of the "new commandment." Therefore, try to avoid having minigroups of two people wash only each other's feet as mutual footwashing may connote "mutual back-scratching" and, therefore, diminish the radical nature of the unilateral action of footwashing. Some of the possibilities that symbolize servanthood, include the following: (a) a person washes the feet of another person, whereupon both return to their seats; (b) on completion of having one's feet washed, that person then turns to a neighbor and washes his or her feet.

It is usually prudent to prepare the persons whose feet will be washed so they may wear easily removable footwear and socks. The specific people to engage in the footwashing could be arranged beforehand, or an opportunity could be offered to those so moved by the Spirit to step forward at the time of footwashing.

A sufficient number of pitchers of warm water, basins, and towels must be provided for the people washing the feet of another person. Fill the pitchers with hot water before the service so the water may cool to a tepid temperature for the actual washing.

The procedure for the footwashing is as follows:

1. People go to the location of a pitcher (ewer), basin, and towels.
2. A pitcher, basin, and towels are passed from one person to another.
3. People whose feet will be washed remove their footwear, while those who will wash the feet of others kneel before them, place the basin under the feet, pour the water over the feet, letting it cascade into the basin, "wash" the feet with the hands, dry the feet with the towel, and assist with replacing the footwear.

An especially appropriate hymn for the congregation to sing during the footwashing is "Where Charity and Love Prevail." This hymn is a paraphrase of the ancient Latin hymn *Ubi Caritas* and appears in *The Worshipbook* (641). Particularly effective is an ostinato (repetitive singing) version included in Jacques Berthier, *Music from Taizé.*[24] This particular hymn has long been associated with Maundy Thursday footwashing. The choir may also provide an anthem or responsorial music during the footwashing. Perhaps a combination of hymns, anthems, and silence may enhance the footwashing ritual.

Plan for everyone to participate through acts of washing, being washed, singing, or observing. Also, recognize that footwashing will require movement by at least some people. Plan accordingly for graceful and natural movement.

The Eucharist (BCW 273)

Words of Institution. If the Words of Institution were not spoken before the Great Prayer of Thanksgiving, or included in it, then the minister, standing before the people, speaks them in relationship to the breaking of the bread.

Serving. Possible room arrangements for churches with flexible seating are suggested in "Arrangement of the Worship Space" (p. 127). Whatever the room arrangement, plan a mode of distributing the elements so that the bread and the cup, as always, are *served* (that is, given) to the people rather than *taken* by the people.

For example, people can be served at the Lord's table or at one of several stations within the worship space. Or, if people are seated at various tables, the bread and the cup can be passed around or across each table, with each person serving the elements to others at the table. Careful planning is necessary to ensure that people understand what is expected of them so that the method of distribution facilitates rather than frustrates the Communion of the people.

Stripping of the Church (Worship Space) (BCW 279)

The final act of this service is the evocative stripping of the worship space. This is most effectively done in absolute silence, and in an unhurried, orderly fashion. Designate several people to extinguish the candles, strip the Lord's table of all cloths and vessels, and remove all textile hangings, candles and candelabra, flowers, and so forth, carrying all the items out of the room. The stark, bare, unadorned church now reflects Jesus' abandonment during the night in Gethsemane.

The visual aspect of the transformed worship space gives people a dramatic depiction of Christ's desolation. The church remains bare until the Easter Vigil when the process is reversed and the worship space is "dressed" again.

Ordinarily, neither a blessing is given nor a postlude played on this night, as the services for Maundy Thursday, Good Friday, and Holy Saturday (The Great Vigil of Easter) are actually one unified ritual. The opening service of the Triduum continues on Good Friday and concludes with the Easter Vigil at which time a blessing is pronounced.

Some congregations may desire to conclude the service with a psalm, hymn, or spiritual. A setting of Psalm 22 would be appropriate, or a hymn, such as, "I Greet Thee, Who My Sure Redeemer Art" (PH 457), which focuses on our redemption in Jesus Christ.

The church remains in semidarkness, and all depart in silence, thus making the transition from the eucharistic celebration to Jesus' crucifixion and death. Symbolically, Christ, stripped of his power and glory, is now in the hands of his captors.

Good Friday (BCW 280–293)

The Good Friday service is intentionally in concert with the broad ecumenical tradition, and representative of many ecumenical aspects. It, therefore, reflects a commonality with many strands of Christian tradition.

It is important to retain the paradoxical nature of the day in form, mood, and texts. Good Friday is a day for many contemplative moments, so let the power of silence speak for itself.

No paraments on the table or pulpit, no flowers, candles, or decorative materials are appropriate on Good Friday, except, perhaps, representations of the way of the cross. On Good Friday, some traditions drape the cross with red (or black) where it remains until the paschal vigil.

While the nature of music on Good Friday is somber, hymns that include reflections on resurrection need not be avoided, such as:

	HB	WB	PH
In the Cross of Christ I Glory	195	437	84
O Love, How Deep, How Broad, How High!	–	518	83

A Suggested Hymn Line That Can Be Used as a Refrain during Good Friday and Passion/Palm Sunday (see "Music: Hymn Lines Can Be Used as Festival or Seasonal Refrains," p. 90):

> "Were you there when they crucified my Lord?"
> From hymn text: "Were You There?" (PH 102)
> hymn tune: WERE YOU THERE

The Word (BCW 282)

Gospel Reading. We read the passion narrative according to John on Good Friday, because at the heart of John's passion narrative is the good news of the cross—the victory of the cross. Thus, John's emphasis on crucifixion and glory corresponds to the tension and ambiguity of the day.

Various modes of proclaiming the passion narrative could include any one or combination of the following, all of which necessitate not only advance planning but careful practice:

Choral Reading. At the words: "So they took Jesus; and carrying the cross by himself, he went out to what is called The Place of the Skull, which in Hebrew is called Golgotha" (John 19:16b, 17), it is customary for the congregation to stand and remain standing through the remainder of the reading. An extended period of silence follows the reading of John 19:30 ". . . and gave up his spirit."[25]

Dramatization. This could include art forms such as mime, readers' theater, dance, music, or visual arts.

A *Vocal setting* may be sung by the choir or an individual, perhaps including congregational responses.

A *Lessons and Hymns format* may be used, such as the following:

	HB	WB	PH
John 18:1–27			
When We Are Tempted to Deny Your Son			
(st. 1, 2)	–	640	86
John 18:28–19:16a			
Ah, Holy Jesus	191	280	93
An extended period of silence follows the reading of John 19:30 ". . . and gave up his spirit," after which one of the following may be sung:			
Deep Were His Wounds, and Red	–	–	103
He Never Said a Mumbalin' Word	–	–	95
Were You There? (st. 1, 2 in HB, st. 1, 2, 3 in PH)	201	–	102
Throned Upon the Awful Tree	197	605	99
John 19:31–42			
Were You There? (st. 3 in HB, st. 4 in PH)	201	–	102
When I Survey the Wondrous Cross	198	635	100/101

Sermon (BCW 283)

The proclamation of the readings for the day may replace the sermon, or a brief sermon may precede, interweave, or succeed the readings for the day. Those who plan the liturgy may consider letting the gospel speak through the power of silence, or through an appropriate liturgical dance or offering of music, which may help deepen reflection on the cross for all worshipers.

The Solemn Intercession (BCW 283)

A fitting response to the hearing of the passion of Christ is intercession in the form of bidding prayers for the whole family of God and the afflictions of the world. This is an important element of the Good Friday tradition. Such bidding prayers are signs of our joining in Christ's priestly ministry of fully extending his arms in order to embrace all God's people (that is, his posture on the cross).

Solemn Reproaches of the Cross (BCW 288)

The Solemn Reproaches are an ancient text of Western Christendom associated with Good Friday. They need to be read slowly and clearly.[26]

The Solemn Reproaches take the place of confession in this service, so no Confession of Sin and Declaration of Forgiveness are included in the service. If, however, a Prayer of Confession with a Declaration of Forgiveness are included earlier in the service, or if the Reproaches were used on Passion/Palm Sunday, then the Solemn Reproaches are not used.

Consider enhancing the people's response to the Solemn Reproaches by inviting the people to sing the Kyrie ("Lord, have mercy") (for example, PH 565, 572–574; HL 157–169).

In some traditions, the people's response during the Reproaches is the "Holy God" (*Trisagion*, Greek, literally "the thrice holy"), the name of a hymn in the ancient rite of the Eastern church:

Holy God,
Holy and mighty,
Holy immortal One,
have mercy upon us.

The Trisagion may be spoken or sung by the congregation adapted from musical settings (for example, HL 170, 171; *The Hymnal 1982*, nos. S99–S102).

Instead of printing the entire text of the Solemn Reproaches in the order for worship, simple rubrics will suffice. Here is an example:

Each reproach ends with the leader saying:

. . . you have prepared a cross for your Savior.

and all the people respond by singing:

Lord, have mercy.

Dismissal (BCW 291)

The Service for Good Friday draws people into the story of the passion of Christ. It is composed of contrasting actions and moods of the solemn reading of the passion of Christ and, yet, a hopeful look toward the resurrection. What is an appropriate way in which to be dismissed to continue serving?

Following the Solemn Reproaches (BCW 288), some congregations find it meaningful to depart in silence, while others find it useful to sing a hymn of the good news of the cross, extolling the victory of the cross of Christ. For example, a hymn appropriate to the day and the week, such as "Ah, Holy Jesus, How Have You Offended" (PH 93), could be sung either a cappella, or softly accompanied by only a simple melody. An effective alternative is to sing a response such as "Jesus, Remember Me" (PH 599), sung repetitiously (that is, ostinato) with a flute accompaniment.

Following the singing, it is most dramatic and meaningful when all depart in silence. The service continues with The Great Vigil of Easter on Saturday, or an Easter Day service.

The Great Vigil of Easter: First Service of Easter (BCW 294–314)

The Great Vigil of Easter is the brightest jewel of Christian liturgy traced to early Christian times. It proclaims the universal significance of God's saving acts in history through four related services held on the same occasion.

1. *Service of Light.* The service begins in the darkness of night. In kindling new fire and lighting the paschal candle, we are reminded that Christ came as a light shining in darkness (John 1:5). Through the use of fire, candles, words, movement, and music, the worshiping community becomes the pilgrim people of God following the "pillar of fire" given to us in Jesus Christ, the Light of the World. The paschal candle is used throughout the service as a symbol for Jesus Christ. This candle is carried, leading every procession during the vigil. Christ, the Light of the World, thus provides the unifying thread to the service.

2. *Service of Readings.* The second part of the vigil consists of a series of readings from the Old and New Testaments. These readings provide a panoramic view of what God has done for humanity. Beginning with creation, we are reminded of our delivery from bondage in the exodus, of God's calling us to faithfulness through the cry of the prophets, of God dwelling among us in Jesus Christ, and of Christ's rising in victory from the tomb. The

readings thus retell our "holy history" as God's children, summarizing the faith into which we are baptized.

3. *Service of Baptism.* In the earliest years of the Christian church, baptisms commonly took place at the vigil. So this vigil includes baptism and/or the reaffirmation of baptismal vows. As with the natural symbol of light, water plays a critical role in the vigil. The image of water giving life—nurturing crops, sustaining life, and cleansing our bodies—cannot be missed in this part of the vigil. Nor is the ability of water to inflict death in drowning overlooked. Water brings both life and death. So also there is death and life in baptism, for in baptism we die to sin and are raised to life. Baptism unites believers to Christ's death and resurrection.

4. *Service of the Eucharist.* The vigil climaxes in a joyous celebration of the feast of the people of God. The risen Lord invites all to participate in the new life he brings by sharing the feast that he has prepared. We thus look forward to the great messianic feast of the kingdom of God when the redeemed from every time and place "will come from east and west, from north and south, and will eat in the kingdom of God" (Luke 13:29). The vigil thus celebrates what God has done, is doing, and will do.

Background of the Great Vigil

The Great Vigil of Easter is an exciting liturgical recovery. Churches of many traditions have rediscovered the vigil and experienced its potential for renewal of the faith. It is an occasion for worship and fellowship; an annual remembering of all that is fundamental in the history of the faith; an event rich with the mystery and power of the gospel.

The Tradition of the Great Vigil

In the early centuries of the church, Holy Week was observed by a rigorous fast followed by a celebration of the mystery of Easter Eve and Easter Day in one unified liturgy. The Great Vigil contained everything: lighting the new fire and the paschal candle; reading and telling of the mighty acts of God; baptizing persons into the body of Christ; renewing baptismal vows for the entire community of faith; retelling the story of our Lord's dying and rising; and celebrating the Eucharist as a foretaste of the messianic banquet in the kingdom of God.

Originally, the Great Vigil continued through the night climaxing with the celebration of the resurrection as dawn approached. Like the dawning sun ending night, so Christ arose in the splendor of his glory, conquering forever the night of sin.

Clearly, the Great Vigil was the high point of the church's annual liturgical calendar. It was the greatest moment during the year in the life of the church. It was a great occasion when the church baptized the converts to the faith. The vast majority of baptisms were at this service.

The Great Vigil has both historic and symbolic roots in the Jewish Passover. So, many of the images in the vigil are drawn from the Old Testament. In the four liturgies of the vigil, we experience our passage from slavery to freedom, from sin to salvation, from death to life.

In medieval times, the proclamation of the gospel was virtually lost from the vigil, smothered by practices which distorted its original purpose. Consequently, the sixteenth-century Reformers saw little worthwhile retaining in the vigil. For this reason, the vigil has not generally been observed in the Protestant tradition—until recently, in the light of reforms of the vigil.

The liturgy in the *Book of Common Worship* is based on ancient texts and contemporary editions of the vigil used in many churches, including Roman Catholic, Episcopal, Lutheran, Orthodox, and Methodist. Many Presbyterian congregations throughout the United States, as well as other Reformed churches throughout the world, have begun to observe paschal vigils. Often they are creative and innovative celebrations based on the tradition of the ancient texts.

Introducing and Planning the Great Vigil

Since the vigil is the most glorious liturgical celebration of the entire year, it requires careful preparation. It takes many weeks or months of planning and education to prepare a congregation for such an occasion.

Congregations planning their first vigil should strongly consider establishing an educational program to introduce the concept to the church several months before Easter. Possibilities include Sunday morning classes, a program centered around a church supper, or whatever day and time seems suitable in the life of the congregation. Materials in both the *Book of Common Worship* and this *Companion to the* Book of Common Worship should be used.

It is also wise to form a group or committee responsible for planning the vigil. For example, special attention needs to be given to the details involved in all of the settings for the various components of the vigil. Lighting, processions, the details surrounding the baptisms, the serving of Communion, the lighting of the new fire, and the readings, all need to be carefully planned and rehearsed.

Music should be selected with great care, with particular attention given to the musical settings, hymns, and instrumental music used. Brass fanfares and accompaniment to the hymns in the last portion of the vigil add greatly to the service. The choir's main role will be to assist the congregation in its singing, and during Communion it may sing appropriate music.

A paschal candle needs to be purchased or made. This candle is of central importance in the vigil. The paschal candle is a large candle at least two inches in diameter, and at least two feet tall. It is placed in a stand at least three feet high. Traditionally, the paschal candle has a cross inscribed on it with the numerals of the current year and the Greek letters *alpha* and *omega*. A new candle is used each year. Paschal candles may be purchased from church supply houses, or may be made by someone in the congregation.

Movement adds a great deal to the vigil, particularly if the church facilities enable the congregation to move to different places during the vigil. As the community moves from place to place around the church property and buildings, there is a symbolic sense of identification with God's pilgrim people. The community also experiences a sense of physical participation in the vigil.

Since each vigil takes on its own life, those who plan the vigil will need to make some localized decisions about movement, readings, music, timing, and placement that may not be addressed in this book or any liturgical resource. The Easter Vigil is an ancient part of Christian liturgical tradition, but one should not be overly concerned about the *right* way to celebrate it. The Easter Vigil should reflect the spirit and essence of the particular community of faith.

It is appropriate for the Great Vigil to commence about 10:30 P.M., and end after midnight. The most dramatic time, of course, would be for the vigil to begin in the middle of the night so that the vigil would end at dawn. However, the vigil can be observed anytime after dark on Holy Saturday and before sunrise on Easter Sunday.

Service of Light (BCW 297)

The community gathers in silence at an appointed place for the new fire. As worshipers gather, each person is given a candle, which may be purchased at religious supply stores.

Lighting of the Paschal Candle (BCW 298). The new fire should be a simple open fire that can be set up somewhere on the church property. A large metal container on legs about three feet high also may be used to contain the fire. The paschal candle is lighted from the flames of the fire. It is best to light the paschal candle with a taper or stick from the new fire since it is difficult to light the paschal candle from a blazing, open fire without risking meltdown of the candle.

If an outside fire is not possible for practical considerations, such as inclement weather, a simple fire in a brazier inside the church building, at the main entrance, can be most effective. It is important that the fire be lighted in as dark a setting as possible. The symbols of light and darkness are far more powerful when the contrast is greatest.

After the lighting of the fire and the paschal candle, the procession into the church begins. The fire is carefully extinguished after the paschal candle and the candles of the people are lighted. A cover may be placed over the fire container to smother the flames.

The lighting of worshipers' candles can be accomplished by having the people come to the paschal candle and light their candles from the paschal candle. If the congregation is large, those nearest the paschal candle may light their candles and then pass the light to those nearby until all of the candles are lighted. Or, the candles of the worshipers may be lighted after the congregation has been seated in the church.

If the lighting of the paschal candle takes place inside the church building, a procession is still included, although it may consist only of the worship leaders and choir. The paschal candle is carried at the head of the procession, as with all processions throughout the vigil.

Customarily, the procession moves in silence, with the silence punctuated at three places when the worship leader sings: "The light of Christ." The congregation responds, singing: "**Thanks be to God**" (BCW 299).

Worship leaders are encouraged to memorize the texts in the Service of Light, since much of the service is conducted in darkness or limited light.

Easter Proclamation (BCW 300). The Exsultet is the ancient Easter proclamation sung in conjunction with thanksgiving for the paschal candle. It is sometimes known as *Laus Cerei* ("praise of the candle"). It takes its more familiar Latin name, *Exsultet jam Angelica turba*, from its opening words: "Rejoice, heavenly powers! Sing, choirs of angels! Exult, all creation around God's throne! Jesus Christ our King is risen!" The text comes from the third or fourth century and is intended to imitate the style of the psalms. It is often attributed to St. Ambrose, bishop of Milan (340–397).

The traditional setting of the Exsultet (Setting I, BCW 300, PS 196) is sung without accompaniment, by a choir (or cantor) with the congregation singing the recurring refrain as indicated in the text. Organ accompaniment is provided for Setting II (BCW 300; PS 197). In using either setting, the congregation needs to be provided the text of the Exsultet with the melody line of the appropriate refrain, and responses as displayed on BCW 300–302. If it is not possible for the full text of the Exsultet to be sung, it may be read with the congregation singing the refrain at the appointed places. If it is read it should be carefully rehearsed to ensure that its message is effectively conveyed.

A hymn inspired by the Exsultet may be found in the *Lutheran Book of*

Worship, no. 146. An alternative to the tune in the *Lutheran Book of Worship* is the familiar tune MIT FREUDEN ZART.

The worshipers hold their lighted candles throughout the singing of the Exsultet. After the Exsultet the worshipers' candles are extinguished.

Service of Readings (BCW 304)

Traditionally, this part of the service includes the reading of as many as twelve readings from the Old Testament.[27] Some Eastern liturgies have included as many as seventeen lessons. Nine readings are here provided from the Old Testament, together with an epistle lesson and a reading from one of the Synoptic Gospels. If the situation does not permit all nine Old Testament lessons to be read, a sufficient number should be read to convey a sense of the broad sweep of salvation history. There should always be at least three readings from the Old Testament, one of which always is Exodus 14:10–31; 15:20–21. The reading of each lesson is followed by a brief silence. The appointed psalm or canticle (or a suitable hymn) may then be sung. A brief prayer follows.

The lessons should be read with care and sensitivity. The planners of the Easter Vigil should be as creative as possible in considering a variety of methods to present the reading. Drama, choral readings, slide, film, and video presentations, liturgical dance, and choral music are some of the possibilities one can consider.

Following each reading are some suggested settings for singing the appointed psalms and canticles (for example, Psalm 136, BCW 304).

Following are some suggestions for congregations that choose to substitute hymns for some of the psalms:

	HB	WB	PH
Following Genesis 1:1–2:2			
Father Eternal, Ruler of Creation	486	362	—
God of the Sparrow	—	—	272
God, You Spin the Whirling Planets	—	—	285
Many and Great, O God, Are Thy Things	—	—	271
Creating God, Your Fingers Trace	—	—	134
Following Genesis 7:1–5, 11–18; 8:6–18; 9:8–13			
Our God, Our Help in Ages Past	111	549	210
A Mighty Fortress Is Our God	91	274	260
Following Genesis 22:1–18			
God of Our Life	108	395	275
O God of Bethel, by Whose Hand	342	496	269

	HB	WB	PH
Following Exodus 14:10–31;15:20–21			
Call Jehovah Your Salvation	123	322	—
Come, Ye Faithful, Raise the Strain (esp. v. 1)	205	344	114/115
Following Isaiah 55:1–11			
God Is My Strong Salvation	347	388	179
Following Proverbs 8:1–8, 19–21; 9:4b–6			
Immortal, Invisible, God Only Wise	85	433	263
Be Thou My Vision	303	304	339
Following Ezekiel 36:24–28			
Breathe on Me, Breath of God	235	—	316
O Spirit of the Living God	—	528	—
Spirit of God, Descend Upon My Heart	236	575	326
Following Ezekiel 37:1–14			
Breathe on Me, Breath of God	235	—	316
Come, Holy Ghost, Our Souls Inspire	237	335	125
Come, Holy Spirit, God and Lord!	—	336	—
Following Zephaniah 3:14–20			
Father, We Thank You that You Planted	—	366	—
Joy to the World!	161	444	40
The Church's One Foundation	437	582	442
Following Romans 6:3–11			
The Church of Christ in Every Age	—	—	421

The "Glory to God in the highest . . ." (Gloria in Excelsis) is commonly sung after the last Old Testament reading (BCW 308, 578; PH 566, 575, 576; PS 173; HL 173–176). Some traditions accompany the singing with the ringing of the church bells. In some traditions, the "Glory to God in the highest . . ." is not sung until *after* the singing of Psalm 114 following the reading of Romans 6:3–11, where it occurs immediately before the reading of the resurrection narrative from the Gospel.

A brief sermon may follow the Gospel reading. Instead of a sermon, in some congregations a portion of the paschal homily of St. John Chrysostom is read.[28]

Service of Baptism (BCW 309)

At this place in the liturgy, baptisms take place (BCW 403–415). An alternative service of baptism is also provided: one ecumenically prepared by the

Consultation on Common Texts[29] in which Reformed, Anglican, Catholic, Lutheran, and other traditions participated (BCW 418–429).

When there are no candidates for baptism, the Service of Baptism essentially becomes the reaffirmation of baptismal vows (BCW 464–471). Worship leaders may move among the people liberally sprinkling the worshipers with water while repeating "Remember your baptism and be thankful . . ." (BCW 470) as a symbol of forgiveness and reconciliation we have in Christ. An evergreen bough may be used in sprinkling the people. The bough is dipped into a large basin of water that is carried by the person doing the sprinkling. If an evergreen bough is not available, the water can be lifted out of the font with cupped hands and either returned to the font or splashed over the worshipers. The sprinkling of the people as a reaffirmation of baptismal vows is most dramatic when it immediately follows a baptism.

Appropriate hymns for use in procession to the font include:

	HB	WB	PH
Glorious Things of Thee Are Spoken	434	379	446
The Church's One Foundation	437	582	442

Appropriate hymns for use during baptism or the reaffirmation of baptismal vows include:

	HB	WB	PH
Baptized in Water	—	—	492
Dearest Jesus, We Are Here	—	310	493
Come Down, O Love Divine	—	334	313
Lord Jesus Christ, Our Lord Most Dear	452	461	496
O God, This Child from You Did Come	—	501	—
Out of Deep, Unordered Water	—	—	494
We Know That Christ Is Raised	—	—	495
With Grateful Hearts Our Faith Professing	—	—	497
Wonder of Wonders, Here Revealed (after baptism)	—	—	499

Service of the Eucharist (BCW 310)

The passing from darkness to light, from death to resurrection, is now fully consummated. Congregations who have not yet removed the red (or black) drape of Good Friday do so at this time as well as display the Easter flowers. The sanctuary is decorated with white and gold, the traditional colors of Easter.

If the baptism or renewal of baptismal vows took place in a space other than the sanctuary, then this part of the vigil lends itself to a grand procession into the sanctuary. Colorful banners, preferably without words, can add to the beauty of the procession. The entire worshiping community follows the paschal candle and banners.

Hymn suggestions for use during the celebration of the Eucharist include:

	HB	WB	PH
Come, Risen Lord	—	340	503
Deck Yourself, My Soul, with Gladness	—	351	506
I Sing As I Arise Today	—	428	—
O Sons and Daughters, Let Us Sing!	206	527	116

Hymn suggestions for use before the charge and blessing or during a recessional include:

	HB	WB	PH
Alleluia, Alleluia! Give Thanks	—	—	106
The Day of Resurrection	208	584	118

In traditions where fasts have been maintained during Lent, the fast is broken after the vigil with a breakfast of bread, cheese, milk, honey, and fruit. Such a meal could take place in a fellowship hall or other rooms of the church or, weather permitting, outside on the church grounds.

Easter Sunday through Seventh Sunday of Easter (BCW 315)

Congregations are encouraged to celebrate the resurrection throughout the Great Fifty Days of Easter. During these days we remember Christ's rising from the tomb, his postresurrection appearances, his ascension, and the outpouring of the Holy Spirit at Pentecost. This is the most festive period of the year.

Some congregations, moving toward weekly Communion, celebrate the Eucharist on each Sunday throughout the Easter season, even when they celebrate it less frequently during the rest of the year. Congregations are thus introduced to weekly Communion, making for an easier step toward the ultimate commitment of celebrating the Eucharist each Lord's Day. Weekly Communion during the Easter season further helps congregations to understand that this Sacrament is a resurrection feast. The Lord's Supper derives as much from the postresurrection meals as it does from the Last Supper. Music that attends the Sacrament should, therefore, not be funereal but joyful in tone. Adequate preparation and instruction of the congregation should precede weekly Communion during Easter, even if only for the season.

The environment for worship should sharply contrast with the austerity of the preceding season of Lent. The traditional Easter colors of white and gold, in the finest and most elegant fabrics, can express the joy of the season. Other festive colors, of course, may also be used. Since in the early church the Great Fifty Days was as much the Season of Pentecost as it is the Season of Easter, red possibly could be added (beginning on the Second Sunday of Easter) to the white and gold used at the Great Vigil and Easter Sunday. This would remain until red becomes dominant on Pentecost Sunday. Symbols common to the Easter season may be incorporated on banners, church bulletins, and so forth.

The paschal candle is particularly important throughout the season. First lighted at the Easter Vigil, it is lighted for each Sunday of the Easter season through the Day of Pentecost. During the Great Fifty Days it will remain in its stand beside the Communion table. After Pentecost, it is placed beside the baptismal font for the rest of the year.

The paschal candle is lighted for every baptism throughout the year, signifying the relationship of our baptism with the death and resurrection of Jesus Christ (BCW 403, rubric). It is also lighted at each funeral (where it is placed in its stand at the head of the coffin) and memorial service (BCW 911).

Music that proclaims Christ's victory over death and our joyful response befits the season. It is a wonderfully appropriate time to sing lots of hymns with Alleluias as well as a variety of Alleluias (HL 180–187). Use of trumpets to punctuate portions of the liturgy, especially the call to worship, will remind us of the significance of the season. A seasonal refrain can add further focus.

A Suggested Hymn Line That Can Be Used as a Refrain during the Easter Season (see "Music: Hymn Lines Can Be Used as Festival or Seasonal Refrains," p. 90):

> "Come, Christians, join to sing Alleluia! Amen!"
> From hymn text: "Come, Christians, Join to Sing" (PH 150)
> hymn tune: MADRID

> "Alleluia! Alleluia! Alleluia! Alleluia! Alleluia!"
> From hymn text: "From All That Dwell Below the Skies" (PH 229)
> hymn tune: LASST UNS ERFREUEN

Ascension of the Lord (BCW 332–335).

Ascension Day was a festival retained by the sixteenth century Reformers. As noted previously (p. 108), the doctrine of the ascension of Christ has had an important place in Reformed theology. Congregations are encouraged to restore a service on Ascension Day. To introduce it, a congregation could precede it with a congregational meal. A celebration of the Eucharist is most fitting. The environment should help convey a sense of the transcendent, of Christ enthroned in glory as ruler of all. The Pantocrator iconography of Eastern Orthodoxy could be used in a creative way, such as in visual projections. What is done on Ascension Day needs to carry through the following Sunday, lest the Ascension be seen as an isolated event and not integral to the season that leads to the celebration of Pentecost.

Day of Pentecost (BCW 338–347)

The Day of Pentecost draws the Great Fifty Days of Easter to a glorious climax.

The Litany for Pentecost, options A, B, and C (BCW 340–343), may be used as an alternative to the Prayer of the Day as well as an alternative to a Prayer of Confession. As with the Litany for Advent, the Pentecost litany is particularly effective when sung (see pp. 101–102 for instructions on singing a litany). In fact, the Litany for Pentecost may be sung in a manner similar to that suggested for the Litany for Advent (BCW 166–167) in which a cantor (soloist) sings the opening lines, either improvising or using a chant tone (PS 341–346), and the congregation sings the **boldface** refrain. Unlike the Advent litany, however, it is preferable for a choir to sing the text of this litany, and the singing should be accompanied with the organ.

A Litany of Intercession for Pentecost is also provided (BCW 341–342).

Red is the traditional color for the day, symbolizing the fire of the Spirit that rested on the disciples of Christ, and gives life to the church in every age. The use of gold (as throughout the rest of the Great Fifty Days), is common, along with the red on Pentecost Sunday. The colors may be used in a variety of ways, including vestments, paraments, and banners. Congregations have been very creative in the use of textiles on Pentecost. For example, some congregations have employed red, orange, and gold streamers of "fire" throughout the worship space. To symbolize the "wind of the Spirit," some congregations have placed a collection of wind chimes in the worship space where they would be in the path of the currents of air which would produce a gentle, joyful sound throughout the service. The use of a readers' theater presentation of Acts 2:1–21 or Ezekiel 37:1–14 (Cycle B) is another possibility. Many congregations read the Acts lesson in a variety of languages known to members in the congregation. In planning this service, let it be evident that Pentecost is a major festival. A sense of triumphant joy should characterize the liturgy.

The powerful images of rushing wind and tongues of flame lend themselves to use of a variety of instrumentation which might otherwise be resisted in a worship setting. Percussion effects, especially using cymbals, both rolled and crashed, tympani, and synchronic or diachronic music in almost any instrumentation will convey some sense of this extraordinary event and perhaps even the powerful symbolism of being commissioned for ministry through the gift of the Holy Spirit.

Ordinary Time (BCW 205–219; 354–384)

In calendar reforms following Vatican II, the periods between Epiphany and Lent, and between Pentecost and Advent, are called Ordinary Time. This term now enjoys wider acceptance across the church.

In the past, the common practice was to identify time *after* Epiphany (January 6) and the Day of Pentecost as, for example, the "Fifth Sunday after Epiphany," or the "Twelfth Sunday after Pentecost." Unfortunately, these expressions were often misunderstood to be part of an "Epiphany Season" or a "Pentecost Season." Neither Epiphany nor Pentecost is a season. Each is a single day. This misunderstanding tended to distort the nature of these two periods in the liturgical calendar. Since the span of time following Epiphany and Pentecost does not center on a dominant event or theme, the practice of keeping time in reference to the immediate past festival (Epiphany or Pentecost) was merely a way to keep track of time. Continued use of the terminology "Sundays after Pentecost" also engendered much confusion regarding the use of the Revised Common Lectionary and resources based on it.

More important, the term "Ordinary Time" can make its own unique and valuable contribution to the way we understand liturgical time. Since Ordinary Time is not a season, this period allows Sunday to be preeminent. This is in accord with the insights of the Reformed tradition, for which the Lord's Day has always had a dominant role, whether or not annual festivals were maintained.

In Ordinary Time, the focus is on the Lord's Day. In lectionary understanding, Ordinary Time is a sequence of Lord's Days to reflect on the ministry of the Lord, Pauline and Johannine materials, and appropriate Old Testament texts.

Time between Epiphany and Lent, and
Time between Pentecost and Advent

Ordinary Time is the norm of time kept by the church. The Sundays of Ordinary Time celebrate the good news of Christ's death and resurrection, and the unfolding presence of the new creation. Ordinary Time presents us with an ongoing opportunity to witness to the living Lord who makes all things new. The standard time of the church is Ordinary Time.

The (liturgical) term "ordinary" means that which is standard, normative, usual, or typical. For example, ordinary or invariable elements of worship (for example, the Lord's Prayer, Doxology, Creed, Kyrie ["Lord, Have Mercy"], Gloria, Alleluia, Sursum Corda ["Lift up your hearts"], and so forth) are said or sung week after week. As the standard elements of worship, they are called "ordinaries." They are the elements common to worship every Sunday.

In like manner, week after week, Sunday "ordinarily" celebrates the resurrection and the unfolding of the new creation. The standard for worship is, therefore, the ordinary time of Sunday in the week-to-week progression of time.

Twice each year, however, Ordinary Time is heightened by the extraordinary time of the Christmas and Easter cycles. They are extra-ordinary in that they intensify the foundational doctrines of incarnation and resurrection. The liturgical contribution of these cycles is to supplement the "ordinaries" of worship with additional or seasonally reflective elements, the "propers," those elements which change from Sunday to Sunday (prayers, hymns, carols, rituals, and so forth). Thus, the ordinary time of the church is made extraordinary during the Christmas and Easter cycles.[30]

This interruption of Ordinary Time by the Christmas and Easter cycles results in two segments of Ordinary Time: a period of four to nine weeks following Epiphany, and a period of about one half of the year (from 23 to 28 weeks) following Pentecost.

At the beginning and end of each of these periods are transitional Sundays that move the church from what has preceded to what follows. The first two Sundays that follow Epiphany develop some of the emphases of Epiphany, namely, Jesus' baptism on the Sunday immediately following Epiphany, and the wedding in Cana on the Second Sunday in Ordinary Time (Year C). The Sunday that concludes this part of Ordinary Time, the Transfiguration of the Lord, serves as a transition to focusing on what is to happen in Jerusalem, Christ's dying and rising. The Sunday that follows Pentecost, Trinity Sunday, underscores the Trinitarian nature of the Easter cycle that preceded it. The Sundays that conclude this part of Ordinary Time, and especially the final Sunday before Advent, are eschatological in character. These Sundays move the church toward Advent with its focus on the new age that is to come.

A Suggested Hymn Line That Can Be Used as a Refrain during Ordinary Time (see "Music: Hymn Lines Can Be Used as Festival or Seasonal Refrains," p. 90):

"Rejoice! rejoice! Rejoice, give thanks and sing!"
From hymn text: "Rejoice, Ye Pure in Heart!" (PH 145)
hymn tune: MARION

"Lord of all, to Thee we raise This our hymn of grateful praise."
From hymn text: "For the Beauty of the Earth" (PH 473)
hymn tune: DIX

"Sing praise to God, who reigns above, The God of all creation."
From hymn text: "Sing Praise to God, Who Reigns Above" (PH 483)
hymn tune: MIT FREUDEN ZART

Festivals in Ordinary Time

We turn now to a closer look at each of the festivals that begin and end the two segments of Ordinary Time, and at All Saints' Day, a major festival in November.

The Baptism of the Lord (BCW 198–204)

The Baptism of the Lord is closely related to Epiphany and should be considered in relation to that feast. Jesus' ministry to bring in God's rule was inaugurated in his baptism. As he came out of the water, the Spirit rested on Jesus, and a sign of God's approval was heard. On this day, we celebrate not only Jesus' baptism but our own as well, for our baptism is rooted in Christ. Baptism joins us to Christ and his church, and with all of the baptized we are called to share in Jesus' ministry. In the waters of baptism we are buried with Christ, cleansed of our sins, and raised to share in his resurrection. The Spirit is given to us and we are declared the children of God.

The Transfiguration of the Lord (BCW 214–219)

From ancient times, the Feast of the Transfiguration has been important in Eastern Orthodox traditions. In 1457, it was adopted in the Western church with its date of August 6. In recent lectionary alterations, the Transfiguration of the Lord has gained greater prominence because it is given focus on a Sunday before or just after the beginning of Lent. The Sunday immediately prior to Ash Wednesday is an appropriate time to celebrate the Transfiguration of the Lord, because this event marked a transition in Jesus' ministry in which he "set his face to go to Jerusalem" (Luke 9:51), where he would die.

In Jesus' transfiguration, we are assured that Jesus is the hope of the ages. Jesus is the One who fulfilled the Law given through Moses, the One dreamed of by the prophets, of whom Elijah is the greatest.

In celebrating this event, we rejoice in the divine majesty of Christ, whose glory shone even when confronted with the cross. It is given us for our journey through Lent toward the agony of the cross and the victory of the empty tomb. We celebrate this mystery in order that our faith may be renewed. We are transformed into the new being in Christ as we join Christ in his death and resurrection in Lent and Easter.

"Locking Up Our Alleluias" Prior to Ash Wednesday. The Hebrew word *hallel* means "a song of praise." Combine the Hebrew words *hallel* and *YHWH*, and you get *Hallelyhwh*, commonly pronounced "Hallelujah" or "Alleluia," which is usually translated into English as "Praise the Lord." In the fourth century, the blending of the Lenten emphasis of prebaptismal training with a penitential mood led the Western church to suppress the joyful Alleluias during the Lenten season. By forgoing the Alleluias for the "forty days and forty nights" of Lent, they then could return to it with renewed vision and spiritual perception when Easter, the "Feast of Feasts" broke forth.

Some churches, near the end of this service, "put away" or "lock up" the Alleluias in a chest for the entire "forty days and forty nights" of the Lenten season. For example, children in church school could make some decorative "Alleluia" banners. During the Easter Vigil, the chest is opened, and the Alleluia banners displayed as part of the Easter decorations, and once again the assembly boldly sings "Alleluia" as a glorious proclamation of Easter joy.

A Suggested Hymn Line That Can Be Used as a Refrain during Transfiguration of the Lord (see "Music: Hymn Lines Can Be Used as Festival or Seasonal Refrains," p. 90):

> "Still be my vision, O Ruler of all."
> From hymn text: "Be Thou My Vision" (PH 339)
> hymn tune: SLANE

Trinity Sunday (BCW 348–353)

Unlike other festivals in the church's liturgical calendar, Trinity Sunday centers on a *doctrine* of the church, rather than an *event*. It celebrates the unfathomable mystery of God's being as Holy Trinity. It is a day of adoration and praise of the one, eternal, incomprehensible God.

Trinity Sunday, in a sense, synthesizes all we have celebrated over the past months which have centered on God's mighty acts: Christmas–Epiphany celebrating God's taking flesh and dwelling among us in Jesus Christ; Easter celebrating Christ's death and resurrection for us; Pentecost, celebrating God the Holy Spirit becoming our Sanctifier, Guide, and Teacher. It is, therefore, a fitting transition to that part of the year when Sunday by Sunday the work of God among us is unfolded in a more general way.

The triune God is the basis of all we are and do as Christians. In the name of this triune God we were baptized. As the baptized ones we bear the name of the triune God in our being. We are of the family of the triune God. We affirm this parentage when, in reciting the creeds, we say what we believe. Our discipleship is rooted in the mighty acts of this triune God who is active in redeeming the world. The triune God is the basis of all our prayers—we pray *to* God the Father, *through* Jesus Christ, *by* the Holy Spirit. The Trinity holds central place in our faith.

Earliest evidence of celebration of a Trinity feast dates from early in the eleventh century. It gained official standing in 1334.

In celebrating Trinity Sunday, remember that every Lord's Day is consecrated to the triune God. On the first day of the week, God began creation. On the first day of the week, God raised Jesus from the grave. On the first day of the week, the Holy Spirit descended on the newly born church. Every Sunday is special. Every Sunday is the day of the Holy Trinity.

A Suggested Hymn Line That Can Be Used as a Refrain during Trinity Sunday (see "Music: Hymn Lines Can Be Used as Festival or Seasonal Refrains," p. 90):

"God in three Persons, blessed Trinity."
From hymn text: "Holy, Holy, Holy! Lord God Almighty!" (PH 138)
hymn tune: NICAEA

All Saints' Day (November 1) (BCW 385–391)

All Saints' Day is a time to rejoice in all who through the ages have faithfully served the Lord. The day reminds us that we are part of one continuing, living communion of saints. It is a time to claim our kinship with the "glorious company of apostles . . . the noble fellowship of prophets . . . the white-robed army of martyrs" (Te Deum). It is a time to express our gratitude for all who in ages of darkness kept the faith, for those who have taken the gospel to the ends of the earth, for prophetic voices who have called the church to be faithful in life and service, for all who have witnessed to God's justice and peace in every nation.

To rejoice with all the faithful of every generation expands our awareness of a great company of witnesses above and around us like a cloud

(Heb. 12:1). It lifts us out of a preoccupation with our own immediate situation and the discouragements of the present. In the knowledge that others have persevered, we are encouraged to endure against all odds (Heb. 12:1–2). Reminded that God was with the faithful of the past, we are reassured that God is with us today, moving us and all creation toward God's end in time. In this context, it is appropriate for a congregation on All Saints' Day to commemorate the lives of those who died during the previous year.

Christ the King (or Reign of Christ) (BCW 394–400)

The festival of Christ the King (or Reign of Christ) ends our marking of Ordinary Time after the Day of Pentecost, and moves us to the threshold of Advent, the season of hope for Christ's coming again at the end of time.

The day centers us on the crucified and risen Christ, whom God exalted to rule over the whole universe. The celebration of the lordship of Christ thus looks back to Ascension, Easter, and Transfiguration, and points ahead to the appearing in glory of the King of kings and Lord of lords. Christ reigns supreme. Christ rules in peace. Christ's truth judges falsehood. As the Alpha and Omega, the beginning and the end, Christ is the center of the universe, the ruler of all history, the judge of all people. In Christ all things began, and in Christ all things will be fulfilled. In the end, Christ will triumph over all the forces of evil.

Such concepts as these cluster around the affirmation that Christ is King or Christ reigns! As sovereign ruler, Christ calls us to a loyalty that transcends every earthly claim on the human heart. To Christ alone belongs the supreme allegiance of our lives. Christ calls us to stand with those who in every age confessed, "Jesus Christ is Lord!" In every generation, demagogues emerge to claim an allegiance that belongs only to God. But Christ alone has the right to claim our highest loyalty. The blood of martyrs, past and present, witnesses to this truth.

Behold the glory of the eternal Christ! From the beginning of time to its ending, Christ rules above all earthly powers!

Suggested Hymn Lines That Can Be Used as a Refrain During Christ the King (or Reign of Christ) (see "Music: Hymn Lines Can Be Used as Festival or Seasonal Refrains," p. 90):

> "Alleluia! Sing to Jesus! His the scepter, His the throne."
> From hymn text: "Alleluia! Sing to Jesus!" (PH 144)
> hymn tune: HYFRYDOL

"Crown Him, crown Him, crown Him, And crown him Lord of all!"
From hymn text: "All Hail the Power of Jesus' Name!" (PH 143)
hymn tune: DIADEM

Liturgical Color

In recent decades, it has been customary for Presbyterian congregations to vest their clergy with stoles and other vestments, and to adorn their worship spaces with paraments, banners, and other textiles in colors that are traditional to the days and seasons of the liturgical calendar. Congregations often ask, What are the *correct* colors? To help congregations, the *Presbyterian Planning Calendar* of the Presbyterian Church (U.S.A.) has for many years displayed the colors most commonly used.[31]

A brief examination of the use of liturgical colors throughout church history quickly leads to the conclusion that no pattern of liturgical color is "correct" in and of itself. For over a thousand years the church gave little attention to the use of color. White vestments predominated. It was not until the twelfth century that schemes assigning colors to seasons and festivals began to appear in wealthier cathedrals, abbeys, and churches. Local custom predominated, practice varying from place to place with great freedom in the use of color. It was common, for example, to reserve the newest and most beautiful vestments, regardless of their color, for the great festivals, and to use the older ones for the rest of the year.

In 1570, the Roman Catholic Church for the first time defined a sequence of color usage. Local differences still continued until the nineteenth century, when attempts were made to standardize practice. Since Vatican II (1962–65), the Catholic Church has been less prescriptive in the use of liturgical color, resulting in a new sense of freedom and spontaneity.

Calvinists in the sixteenth century saw no value in the use of mass vestments of varying colors, so they abolished them. Black vestments predominated. Their origin, though, seems a bit obscure—probably a teaching robe, perhaps a gentleman's gown? In the nineteenth and twentieth centuries, however, Protestants began to recognize the value of involving people's eyes as well as their ears in worship. The result is that liturgical colors are now widely used. It ought to be stated, however, that their use is attributed more to the influence of church supply houses promoting matching sets of vestments and paraments in the "correct" colors, than it is from ecclesiastical pressures. Furthermore, their use often reflects little more than an aesthetic concern or desire for variety.

The traditional liturgical color schema is fairly simple. *White* and *gold* are for festivals of great joy that focus on the work of our Lord. *Red* is the color for the festival of the Holy Spirit and the commemoration of the lives of the martyrs.

Purple marks seasons of penitence or preparation. *Green* is used at all other times. Recently, *blue* has often been used instead of purple during the season of Advent. Blue is expressive of hope (expectation, anticipation), which is the dominant mood of Advent. Light shades of blue should be used rather than dark blue.

The use of the seasonal color is ordinarily not affected by baptisms, Holy Communion, or marriage services. For funerals, however, white is the standard color. Red is sometimes used for ordinations and installations (since ordained ministry enriches the life of the whole church), and for church dedications and anniversaries.

While the use of liturgical colors does not have the antiquity of the liturgical calendar itself, there is value in displaying the colors presently associated with festivals and seasons. The colors are helpful in teaching, prompt within us responses appropriate to the season, unite us ecumenically with the whole church past and present, and add beauty to our worship. These values, inherent in the traditional liturgical colors, ought to be kept clearly in mind. We should use them, however, with an informed and creative freedom, rather than simply adhering to what is considered correct.

We are also free to use other colors in ways that enhance the celebration of the saving work of our Lord. Sensitivity to the psychology of color, and the emotions each color prompts, can help us to use effectively more of the full range of color in worship. It is also important to understand the different moods that hues can evoke. Before choosing the color(s), ask: What mood, tone, effect is intended? What color(s) will fulfill that intention? For example, the color associations of the warm and sometimes hot colors of red, orange, and yellow are suitable for fast-paced, upbeat, active, exciting experiences. On the other hand, the cool colors of blue and violet are more appropriate for passive, calming, subdued, meditative, pensive times. While a light or medium blue may speak of hope, a dark blue may speak of despair. It is also helpful to be aware of what is communicated by the texture of a fabric. A rich piece of silk says something far different from a piece of monk's cloth or burlap, even though they are dyed the same color. Colors and textures do prompt various moods and, therefore, consistency with such moods is important.

Also, consider the many ways in which color(s) may be displayed throughout worship: vestments, paraments, choir robes, banners, bulletin covers, vessels (of metal, wood, stone, and so forth). When based on an adequate understanding of the nature and meaning of the season and festivals, fabric and color and texture can be used in fresh ways to enhance the meanings and mood of the time being celebrated. The depth of our involvement in the mighty acts of God, which we celebrate in the liturgical calendar, will thus be enriched.

Following is the predominant practice concerning use of liturgical color:

Christmas Cycle

Advent	blue or purple
Christmas (12 days)	white and gold
The Epiphany of the Lord (January 6)	white and gold

Ordinary Time

January 7 through the Tuesday before Ash Wednesday	green

except for:

Baptism of the Lord	white
Transfiguration of the Lord	white

Lent

Ash Wednesday through first five weeks	purple
Passion/Palm Sunday	red and/or purple
Monday, Tuesday, and Wednesday of Holy Week	purple
Maundy Thursday	purple (until church is stripped bare)
Good Friday and Saturday in Holy Week	No color since the church remains stripped bare

Easter Cycle

Easter Season (including Ascension of the Lord)	white and gold
Day of Pentecost	red

Ordinary Time

Monday after Day of Pentecost through Saturday before the First Sunday of Advent	green

except for:

Trinity Sunday	white
All Saints' Day (or First Sunday in November)	white
Christ the King (or Reign of Christ)	white

Baptism and the Reaffirmation of the Baptismal Covenant

(BCW 401)

Recovering the Meaning of Baptism

The baptismal rites in the *Book of Common Worship* reflect an effort to recover the full meaning of baptism from perspectives both ecumenical and Reformed. Baptism is a rite of profound significance. It is the symbol of initiation into the household of faith, a sign of cleansing from sin, and a dramatic proclamation of dying and rising with Christ. Baptism is a Christian's "ordination" to the "royal priesthood" and the mark of belonging to a community of saints that extends beyond time and space. Baptism signifies the presence of the Holy Spirit working among us to comfort, strengthen, and empower us in God's service.

A radical act of commitment in response to the pure grace of the triune God, baptism is at the center of the Christian life. When the church baptizes persons in ways that evidence the centrality and importance of baptism, baptism will more effectively point us to God, who is the source of strength and comfort of life until our baptism is made complete in death.

Many modern American Presbyterians do not appreciate these multiple facets of baptism. The fact that so many church members have witnessed baptisms all their lives and still regard the sacrament as a "lovely ceremony" meant for babies testifies to the challenge faced by ministers and sessions. The *Book of Common Worship* rites, used with appreciation for their language and actions, and linked to sound preaching, can help the church claim and celebrate its baptismal vocation.

Obstacles to Recovery

Recovering the full meaning of baptism, however, will require changes in many congregations. Many congregations regard baptism as an "add-on" to the "regular" service. The rite itself, then, takes place before the reading of

Scripture and the sermon, and is rapidly concluded. In many congregations, children are excluded from witnessing the Sacrament and, thus, are deprived of the opportunity to remember their own baptisms with gratitude and to join the congregation in welcoming the newly baptized.

Some sessions also experience pressure to approve baptisms that are little more than exercises in liturgical theater. For instance, parents indifferent to baptism's radical commitments are sometimes allowed to "go through the motions," standing before a congregation they do not know and making promises they have no intention of keeping.

If the church is to recover the fullness of baptism, sessions and ministers must correct practices in the congregation's worship and life that obscure or distort baptism's meaning.

Reformed Emphasis

Emphasizing the sovereignty of the triune God, Reformed theology tends to see baptism less as something *we do* and more as something *God does*. "In baptism God claims us, and seals us to show that we belong to God" (BCW 404). The water of baptism is God's sign that "You did not choose me but I chose you" (John 15:16). The rite of baptism is both God's gift and our response to the gift of God's saving grace, not a means of securing salvation for ourselves and our children. "Obeying the word of our Lord Jesus, and confident of his promises, we baptize those whom God has called" (BCW 404). We baptize in response to the God who first loved us (1 John 4:19). Our faithful response does not end at baptism, but continues our whole life.

Since the days of John Calvin, this tradition has also viewed infants and children of believers as heirs to the covenant of grace. An infant or adult is baptized not only into the fellowship of a local congregation but also into the church universal.

Preparation for Baptism

The minister and session shall prepare those presenting children for baptism and those being baptized to participate in the rite with understanding. The children of believers are to be baptized without undue haste, but without undue delay. It is advisable for the pastor and session representatives to make a home visit, if possible, where, in a familiar setting, the members of the family can review the actions and meaning of the Sacrament. Baptismal education can also take place in classes provided by the session. A visit to the church for a rehearsal is also strongly advised. Reviewing the words and actions not only prepares parents, candidates, and children, it also provides an opportunity for those who have already been baptized to remember their baptism and be thankful. Some congregations also are developing more extended processes of baptismal preparation rooted in the ancient catechumenate.

Commentary on the Baptism Rites (BCW 401–488)

Baptism is the same Sacrament whether the person being baptized is an infant, child, youth, or adult. The BCW does not have different rites for children and adults. Three very similar rites are presented, however: The Sacrament of Baptism (BCW 403–417), An Alternative Service for the Sacrament of Baptism (BCW 419–430), and Baptism and Reaffirmation of the Baptismal Covenant: A Combined Order (BCW 431–446). The structure for all the baptismal rites is the same.

In addition, five orders for Reaffirmation of the Baptismal Covenant are provided (BCW 447–488), each for use in particular circumstances.

The Place and Time for Baptism

Baptism ordinarily takes place as part of the worship of the congregation. The congregation should have an opportunity to be part of the celebration and welcome the new members of the body of Christ. Moreover, except for extraordinary circumstances, baptism takes place in the congregation where it is expected the person being baptized will be nurtured. Children, who can be especially attentive to the actions in baptism, should be present.

Ordinarily baptism is celebrated as part of the congregation's worship on the Lord's Day. Early in the church's history, baptism usually occurred in the annual Easter Vigil on the Saturday night before Easter Day, the culmination of a long period of preparation and teaching. As part of the Easter celebration, baptism was clearly related to Christ's death and resurrection. The Easter Vigil, therefore, provides an especially appropriate setting for baptism. Other times in the liturgical year also are significant times for baptism. They include Baptism of the Lord (the first Sunday after Epiphany), the Sundays of the Easter season, Day of Pentecost, and All Saints' Day. Celebrating baptism on these occasions proclaims that our life as Christians is rooted in the mighty acts of God in Jesus Christ.

Because of Lent's character as a penitential season and a period for baptismal preparation, and in accord with the long tradition of the church universal, sessions (governing boards) usually choose to refrain from celebrating baptisms during Lent. Some are known to extend this prohibition to Advent as well, although Advent is not a penitential season. Some sessions reserve certain Sundays in the church year for baptisms while others try to accommodate candidates and parents who request baptism on a Sunday when extended family and friends can be present. Factors such as the size of the congregation and the number of baptisms celebrated in a typical year may also affect the session's determination of appropriate Sundays for baptisms.

The Setting of Baptism in the Lord's Day Service. Baptism follows the reading and preaching of the Word. This placement emphasizes that baptism is the sign and seal of God's promises proclaimed in the Word. Baptism enacts the very grace the Word proclaims.

The Sacrament of Baptism: The Elements of the Rite
(BCW 401–417)

1. Presentation (BCW 403)

An elder presents the person to be baptized. Regardless of the candidate's age or situation, each is presented. This act of presentation makes it clear that no one presumes to *come* to baptism but is brought through the prevenient work of the Holy Spirit.

The presentation begins with a gathering at the font. This may include a procession to the font during the singing of a hymn, spiritual, or psalm (Psalms 8, 23, 29, 32, 42:1–3 with 43:3–4, 51:1–17, 63:2–8, 103, and 116 are particularly appropriate when baptism is celebrated). If space permits, the entire congregation may assemble about the font. It is especially appropriate to invite children to gather near the font so they may hear and see the action of the Sacrament.

The minister presides at the baptism, acting on behalf of the universal church as the servant of Christ. After the baptismal group has assembled, the minister reads verses from Scripture that express the meaning of baptism and gives a brief explanation.

Sponsors. Some sessions appoint baptismal sponsors. Sponsors are members of the congregation who accept a particular responsibility for the spiritual nurture of those to be baptized. Their presence emphasizes that baptism is integral to the life of the Christian community and that the congregation has a serious obligation to nurture those it baptizes. Sponsors may be appointed for adults as well as for children. The Reformed tradition has always emphasized that the entire congregation shares responsibility for the baptized. The appointment of sponsors does not diminish the role of the session and congregation in nurturing the baptized, but rather seeks to give it functional and personal expression.

The use of sponsors is optional. If sponsors are used, they are appointed by the session, which needs to exercise care in their appointment and instruction. Sponsors are to help nurture the new Christians as they are incorporated into the church. This responsibility continues throughout life.

Announcing the Name. The elder announces the name of the candidate as part of the presentation. The use of a person's name in baptism is its most important use in all of the Christian liturgy, for it marks adoption into the family of God. One's name is an extension of one's identity, a sign of one's uniqueness as a human being. Both the given name(s) and the surname may be used in the presentation, but the rest of the rite uses *only* the given name(s).

Accepting Responsibility for Baptism. The minister asks two questions of the parent(s) presenting children for baptism (BCW 405, 406). In these questions, the church seeks to be assured that those presenting infants and children for baptism will nurture them in the faith.

The minister asks adults and older children to affirm their desire for baptism. The question, "N., do you desire to be baptized?" (BCW 405) may be addressed to children who express a desire for baptism, but who are not old enough to assume adult responsibilities of church membership.

The minister asks sponsors to commit themselves to the support of the newly baptized.

The minister asks the congregation to share in the nurture of the baptized (BCW 406).

2. Profession of Faith: Renunciations and Affirmations (BCW 406)

The Christian life involves both a *turning from* sin and bondage to evil and a *turning to* Christ and the way of righteousness. It is to turn our backs on the kind of life that is destructive and to embrace the new life that is promised in the Gospel. Both renunciation and affirmation are aspects of the Christian life and, therefore, they are important aspects of the baptismal liturgy. Both are equally dependent on God's grace active in our lives and in the community of faith.

In apostolic times, as evidenced in the Acts of the Apostles, candidates for baptism expressed their faith in Christ before the washing with water. From as early as the third century, the baptismal rite included a twofold profession of faith, in which the candidates, on entering the water, were asked to "renounce Satan, and all his works" and to confess Christ.

In the ancient church, this was expressed in a dramatic way. Immediately before baptism, candidates were asked to face west and renounce evil. The west, as the place of the setting sun and gathering darkness, symbolized the abode of evil. The candidates then *turned from* the west and *turned to* the east and professed the Christian faith. The east, the place of the rising sun, symbolized Christ, the Light of the World. At that time, church buildings were laid out so that the altar was in the east end of the worship space. Therefore, those early Christians literally turned their backs on the ways of Satan and his darkness as they faced the altar and affirmed the ways of Christ.

Renunciation. Renunciation marks the ethical change implicit in the Christian life (for example, Col. 3:8–10; 1 Pet. 3:18–22). Turning from evil is part of one's faith commitment, because Christian discipleship is a way of life that contrasts with the ways of death, which prevail in the world.

The age in which we live is no exception to the need to renounce evil. Both in personal life and in the life of society, destructive forces are at work, forces such as greed, lust, selfishness, pride, materialism, militarism, racism, sexism, and economic exploitation. The renunciation of evil in the baptismal liturgy reminds us that turning from sin is a critical aspect of discipleship and continues throughout the Christian's life. Since the baptismal liturgy marks the beginning of the Christian life and focuses on the life Christians are to live, the renunciation is appropriate even in the baptism of infants. In any case, parents (and sponsors) are affirming their own faith, not professing faith on behalf of the child. Note that the renunciations in the Alternative Service (BCW 425) may be sung (HL 143).

Affirmation. In turning *from* evil, Christians turn *to* the way of the gospel. To profess faith is to affirm that as Christians we live out of a particular stance of faith. Personal faith is rooted in the faith of the church and is, therefore, expressed in baptism within the context of the faith of the church.

The oldest surviving baptismal liturgy, dating from about the year A.D. 200 (Hippolytus), describes the candidate standing in the water and affirming the faith by responding to three questions, each centering on a person of the Trinity. To each question, the candidate responds, "I believe," and after each response is immersed in the water or water is poured (affused) over the candidate. The candidate's profession of faith was made in the context of articulation of the faith into which the new Christian was entering, and by which he or she would be refashioned.

This ancient pattern of baptismal vows is the basis for the Apostles' Creed. For many centuries, the Apostles' Creed has been the dominant one in the baptismal rites of the West. As an ecumenical creed, it summarizes the faith of the church, acknowledging that we are baptized into the one holy catholic church.

The church's ancient baptismal creed, the Apostles' Creed, shall be used in baptism. As an ecumenical creed it summarizes the faith of the whole church, linking the particular baptism with the believing community throughout history. Baptism is not an occasion for using a statement of faith that is sectarian or local in nature, for we are baptized into the universal faith. To show that personal faith is not separate from the church's faith, the entire congregation professes its faith in the words of the Apostles' Creed in the baptismal rite.

The interrogative form of the creed (BCW 408–409) is in keeping with the most ancient form of the Apostles' Creed noted above. Using it expresses the historic and universal faith of the church. The interrogative form is now the form that is used in baptism in many branches of the church. Singing the creed is both in harmony with the early churches of the Reformed tradition, and an enlivening mode of affirmation in a congregation (HL 139, 151).

3. Thanksgiving over the Water (BCW 410)

Water is the primary and essential symbol in baptism. In early civilizations, water was regarded as one of the four basic elements in the universe. Still, today, water is a powerful symbol for us. Water is basic to life. Before each of us was born, water protected us in our mother's womb. We cleanse our bodies with it. It brings cooling refreshment. It sustains life on our planet. Without water we will die. But by it we may die, for water also has power to kill. We can drown in it. Floods destroy life and property. This is why water speaks so forcefully in baptism when used in abundance.

The power of the symbolism of water is particularly dramatic where a baptismal pool or font is kept full of flowing water. Throughout history, the place of baptism has been regarded as a *bath* by which we are cleansed of sin, a *womb* from which we are reborn, a *tomb* in which we are buried with Christ and from which we are raised with him. This is more readily apparent when the baptismal space is ample and the baptismal font or pool is prominently located.

In the early history of the church, when baptisms were by immersion or affusion, no particular care was needed to emphasize the power and centrality of water in baptism. But in our day, fonts have become so small that they no longer are able to hold enough water to symbolize its meaning and power.

In cases where the font must be filled before the baptism, the centrality of the water is heightened if the font is filled as a part of the baptismal service. The minister pours water into the font from a ewer, or large pitcher, held high enough above the font so that the falling water is visible and audible to all. An appropriate time for this action to take place is immediately before the Thanksgiving over the Water.

Prayer over the Water. This historic prayer recalls God's saving acts with thanksgiving and invokes the Holy Spirit so that those who are baptized may have their sins washed away, be reborn to new life, be buried and resurrected with Christ, and be incorporated into the body of Christ.

This prayer parallels the Great (Prayer of) Thanksgiving of the Lord's Supper. The people stand for this act of praise and proclamation just as they do for the eucharistic thanksgiving. The prayer recalls biblical images of water: the waters of creation, the flood, the exodus, and the baptism of Jesus. When both sacraments are celebrated in the same service, it may be prudent for the minister to condense this prayer, although not when it is sung (HL 141, 142, 152, 154).

When invoking the Spirit, it is natural for the minister to touch the water. This action emphasizes the physical element of the Sacrament and adds drama. The minister may even scoop water up in both hands, allowing it to cascade into the font.

As an alternative to the prayers in the BCW, the minister may offer free prayer. Suggestions are offered as a guide (BCW 412).

4. The Baptism: The Act of Baptizing (BCW 413)

Addressing the Candidate by Name. In the act of baptism, the minister addresses the candidate, using only the candidate's Christian (given) name(s). Thus "Alexandra Jean, I baptize you . . ." and not "Alexandra Jean Walker, I baptize you . . ." The reasons for this lie in both ancient tradition and baptismal theology.

In the West, it was long regarded that a person's name was officially bestowed at baptism, hence the common reference to one's "baptismal name" or "Christian name." Certainly, baptism is more than bestowing a name, but there is a good reason for using only the given name in baptism. In baptism, we are reborn into a new family, the family of the triune God. Baptized, we are made sisters and brothers together in a family that transcends the family of our physical birth. In a sense, we are given a new surname: the name Christian. Thus the minister uses only the candidate's Christian (given) name.

Because this is the most important use of the individual name in the entire liturgy of the church, it is crucial that the minister speak or sing the name(s) clearly and accurately (BCW 427; HL 144). If the minister is in doubt, he or she may ask of parents, "What is this child's name?" or of older candidates, "What is your name?"

Washing with Water. The washing with water in the name of the triune

God is at the heart of the Sacrament, both theologically and dramatically. In the early centuries, baptism was usually by immersion. However, this need not have meant full submersion in the water. Early Christian mosaics portray persons kneeling or standing in the baptismal pool as water is poured over them (that is, affusion). Whatever the practice, baptism connoted *going down* into the water (dying) and *coming up* out of the water (rising). In later centuries, when the baptism of adults was rare, fonts were still large enough to immerse infants. Eastern Orthodox churches continue to immerse infants to the present day.

While the quantity of water applied in baptism does not affect the validity of the Sacrament, lavish actions are best for enacting this Sacrament of lavish grace. As the rubric indicates, water should be used "visibly and generously."

The *Book of Common Worship* provides three modes of baptism: pouring, sprinkling, and immersion (BCW 413). Each mode has roots in Scripture and has found a place in baptismal tradition. It is important that the action convey washing. When immersion is not used, the preferable mode is to pour water over the head of the person being baptized (affusion). Following ancient practice, the minister may use a cup or baptismal shell to pour water over the person's head, or the minister may use a cupped hand as a way of making direct contact with the water.

The minister may pour the water only once, but it is better to pour the water three times—once for each person of the Trinity. Thus, while pouring water the first time the minister says, "in the name of the Father," while pouring water the second time, "and of the Son," and while pouring water the third time, "and of the Holy Spirit." The people respond, "**Amen**."

While it is not necessary for the minister to hold infants while baptizing them, some ministers prefer to receive the child into their hands for baptism. The elder, parent, or sponsor also may hold the child. The child should be held with the child's head over the font so the water can wash over the child's head and into the font. Experience teaches that warm, but not hot, water is best used in the Sacrament.

Older persons being baptized should place their heads over the font, facing the water. The minister pours generous amounts of water so that it runs over the person's head and, perhaps, even onto clothing. A towel should be provided for each person baptized. A puddle on the floor by the font is an appropriate result of baptismal washing.

In the Name of the Triune God. Christian baptism is "in the name of the Father and of the Son and of the Holy Spirit," in fulfillment of the command of the risen Christ (Matt. 28:19). Grounded in Scripture, this formula has been used throughout Christian history in the initiation of Christians into the community of faith. All branches of the church regard this formula and the use of water as the essentials of a valid baptism. These words thereby mark "the one baptism" that unites all Christians in the one holy catholic and apostolic church. No other words can link us with this heritage or maintain our unity with the rest of the church.

Today, many in the church have raised serious questions about the Trinitarian formula with respect to its gender-specific language and its roots in ancient theological controversies. Some have proposed substituting "Creator, Redeemer, Sustainer," for "Father, Son, and Holy Spirit." Substituting functional titles to correspond to the persons of the Godhead distorts the doctrine of the Trinity. All three persons of the Godhead take part in the creation, redemption, and sustenance of the world.

Although the church continues to struggle with this issue, the Trinitarian formula remains essential to Christian baptism. This is one of the very few instances in which a Presbyterian minister is not free to alter a liturgical action. The Trinitarian formula is essential to celebrating the Sacrament of Baptism.

5. The Laying On of Hands (and Anointing) (BCW 413)

The laying on of hands appears many times in the Bible as a solemn act of blessing. In the Acts of the Apostles, it is associated with baptism. As the baptismal liturgy developed in Christian history, the laying on of hands came to be related to the gifts of the Holy Spirit.

By at least the third century, anointing with chrism accompanied the laying on of hands in the baptismal liturgy. In the West, the laying on of hands and anointing with chrism were separated from baptism and became the rite of confirmation. In the East, this division never occurred.

While baptism with water needs nothing to complete it, the laying on of hands and anointing help to convey the richness and abundance of the Holy Spirit and to demonstrate that Christian baptism is a baptism with water *and* the Holy Spirit. The early church developed this ritual based on the baptism of Jesus, on whom the Holy Spirit descended as he emerged from the waters of the Jordan.

Anointing with chrism has a very ancient origin and was assimilated by the early Christians from Old Testament times. In ancient Israel, it was associated with the anointing of kings and priests. So also, as God's baptized and Spirit-filled people, we share in the priesthood and rule of Christ, the Anointed One (Rev. 1:6; 5:10; 1 Pet. 2:5, 9).

The anointing with chrism is a literalizing of New Testament imagery (1 John 2:20; 2 Cor. 1:21, 22; Eph. 1:13, 14; see also 1 Pet. 2:9 and John 3:3–6) and is a sign of the meaning of the name "Christian" (both *Christian* and *chrism,* as their similarity in sound implies, derive from the same Greek root, translated Christ, meaning "the anointed one"). The anointing of new Christians emphasizes their union with Jesus the Christ and their claim to the name "Christian." . . . The act of anointing is therefore particularly illustrative of one's "taking the name of Christ" in baptism.[1]

If candidates are anointed with oil, the procedure is for the minister to trace, with the oil, the sign of the cross on the forehead of the newly baptized. The minister's thumb traces the sign, with the hand resting on the candidate's forehead. As the sign is made, the minister declares: "N., child of the covenant, you have been sealed by the Holy Spirit in baptism, and marked as Christ's own forever" (BCW 414). An alternate form is also provided. The minister addresses the person being signed as a "child of God" regardless of the person's age.

Specially prepared oil can be purchased from Christian bookstores or liturgical supply houses. Chrism can be kept in a small vial or in a small metal container, called a stock, also available from liturgical supply houses. It is useful to place a cotton wad in the stock to absorb the chrism and to prevent it from leaking. Be sure to remove the cap from the vial or stock before the anointing rite begins. Unscrewing the cap immediately prior to the act of anointing is an unnecessary distraction.

The prayer for the gift of the Holy Spirit (BCW 413) and the declaration ". . . you have been sealed by the Holy Spirit in baptism and marked . . ."(BCW 414) are used whether or not there is laying on of hands or anointing with oil, because the meaning applies whether or not the actions accompany the words.

It should be understood that the laying on of hands and anointing with oil are part of a single action and, with the prayer and the washing, express the fullness of the biblical teaching about baptism.

6. Welcome (BCW 414)

As those baptized are welcomed, the elder declares that the new Christians are "members of the household of God." They are not alone, left to their own resources to live as Christians. In baptism, the congregation therefore assumes a responsibility to nurture the new Christians. The congregation, in accepting responsibility, welcomes the newly baptized "with joy and thanksgiving." Congregations that sing their Welcome can add a memorable dimension of richness to their joy and thanksgiving in celebrating the Sacrament of Baptism (HL 140, 153).

7. The Peace (BCW 415)

Since baptism is not a private affair but is the entrance into the family of God, the church of Jesus Christ, it is fitting to express our kinship by sharing signs of peace as the concluding act of baptism. If the peace is shared at this point in the service, it is not shared following the Declaration of Forgiveness or immediately preceding the Lord's Supper (BCW 36).

Baptism within the Whole Liturgy

Prayers of Intercession and Supplication for Inclusion in the Prayers of the People (BCW 416–417). Intercessions for those baptized, parents, and sponsors should be included in the prayers of the people. Forms for these prayers are provided.

Baptism and the Lord's Supper. It is highly appropriate to follow baptism with a celebration of the Lord's Supper. When the two sacraments are celebrated in the same service, their intimate relationship is emphasized. God creates the church through baptism and sustains the church with the Supper. From ancient times, Christian initiation culminated with the new Christians joining the congregation at the Holy Table. Thus Christian initiation has traditionally included three actions: washing with water, anointing with oil, and celebration of the Eucharist.

Other Actions and the Reformed Tradition. The Reformed tradition long resisted what it considered extraneous actions, lest the centrality of water in baptism be weakened and the people confused as to what baptism is. It was frequently insisted that baptism was to be with water alone, with no other ceremony added.

Baptism with water in the name of the triune God is all that is required of a valid Sacrament, but adding other signs from the church's baptismal tradition can enrich and give deep meaning to the baptismal event. We need to keep in mind the sixteenth-century ecclesiastical situation that caused the Reformers' strong reactions. We live in times that are very different. Unlike the Reformers, we are called to witness in the context of secularism, where sterile rituals leave us spiritually malnourished. Recovering from our broader Christian heritage those signs which are rich with theological significance can mark the presence of God in our day and link us with the faith tradition of the centuries. Such worship will once again unite our bodies with our minds.

In addition to water, the major traditional ritual acts that have been a part of baptism are the laying on of hands and the anointing with oil, marking with the sign of the cross. If water is used generously and dramatically, these other acts will not obscure its centrality, but rather add to the meaning of the Sacrament.

Giving of a Candle to the Newly Baptized. Other signs have also been and continue to be a meaningful part of the celebration of baptism. Of these other signs, perhaps the most useful is *the giving of a candle to the newly baptized* (BCW 428). Since ancient times, the candle given to the candidate has been lighted from the paschal candle of the Easter Vigil. It is given as a sign of the light that comes from the risen Christ, and it expresses the link between every baptism and Christ's death and resurrection. It further signifies the life the baptized are to live.

In order that the significance of the action not be distorted, it is important that candles be given to the baptized *only* if the paschal candle is a part of the Easter tradition of the congregation. We are the light of the world only as we are in relation to Christ who is the Light of the World (John 8:12; Matt. 5:14–16).

The meaning of the action is obscured if candles are given to the newly baptized where there is no symbolic representation of the risen Christ who is the Light of the World. In congregations where a paschal candle is used, however, the action can emphasize an important aspect of the meaning of baptism and direct the new Christian toward the life the baptized are to live.

The paschal candle signifies the death and resurrection of Jesus Christ and is central to the Easter Vigil. It then remains near the Communion table through the Easter season. It is lighted each Sunday from Easter through the Day of Pentecost. After Pentecost, it is placed beside the baptismal font and lighted only on occasions of a baptism or funeral. When candles are given to the newly baptized at their baptism, they are lighted from the paschal candle and then given to the newly baptized or parent(s). If a sponsor is a part of the baptismal celebration, the sponsor may be invited to receive the unlighted candle from the hands of the minister. The sponsor then lights the candle from the paschal candle and gives it to the newly baptized or parent(s). As the candle is given, the minister, sponsor, or representative of the session may say "Receive the light of Christ," and the people may speak or sing in response, **"You have been enlightened by Christ . . . "** (BCW 428; HL 146). The candle is extinguished when those gathered at the font return to their seats.

A candle given in baptism can be particularly useful in helping persons "remember" their baptism. The candle may be lighted on the anniversary of baptism, as part of a family's worship. The story of Jesus' baptism (Matt. 3:13–17; Mark 1:4–11; or Luke 3:15–17, 21–22) may be read, prayers may be said, and gifts having spiritual significance may be given. Parents can describe the occasion of the child's baptism. It is a growing practice for church school teachers to send greetings to their pupils on anniversaries of baptism as well as sessions who oversee the nurture and care of those on the baptized members roll. In ways such as these, children can "remember" their baptism as an important event in their life, just as they "remember" their physical birth on each birthday. Even for adults, such a marking of the anniversary of baptism can reinforce the importance of the event and remind us that as Christians we live out of our baptism. Sessions could consider celebrating "baptismal anniversaries" for the whole congregation.

Some sessions and congregations employ other means to help people remember their baptism. Some write letters to or visit people on their baptismal anniversary. Some present banners or small quilts bearing the baptized person's name and the date of baptism. Others display session records and encourage people to look up their names on the baptismal roll. Sessions are free to create their own customs and traditions.

Processions. In addition to the procession to the font, in some churches it is the custom for the minister or elder to lead or carry the newly baptized into the congregation while singing a baptismal hymn (for example, PH 492–499). This can be an effective way of linking the congregation to the newest members of the household of faith and dramatizing the inclusion of the baptized into the covenant community.

An Alternative Service for the Sacrament of Baptism (BCW 419)

This service is an ecumenical form prepared by the Consultation on Common Texts. It closely resembles the preceding service, and provides for dressing the newly baptized in a white garment (BCW 428) and for the presentation of a lighted candle (BCW 428), as discussed above.

Baptismal Space

The place of assembly has three focal points: font, pulpit, and table. These three foci accommodate the actions of Christian baptism, reading and interpretation of the Scripture, and the Lord's Supper. The pulpit has long dominated Protestant worship space, but during the latter part of the twentieth century, the Lord's table has increasingly returned to prominence along with the pulpit. The space for baptism is only now beginning to be taken seriously.

Minimal baptismal space reflects the lack of attention the church has given to baptism. Too often, no recognized space is provided; instead, a small bowl is brought out and used when a baptism occurs. Even when a font is provided, it often has no place of prominence. The result is that many church buildings provide little or no evidence that Christians baptize. If baptism is to have the centrality in Christian worship that belongs to it, along with Word and Holy Communion, careful attention needs to be given to the space for this Sacrament.

The location of the space for baptism is important and can convey significant sacramental meaning. There are four possibilities for locating the baptismal pool or font:

1. Locating the water at the entrance to the worship space calls attention to baptism as initiation into the community of faith and reminds those who pass it of their own baptism.
2. Placed at the center of the worship space, the pool or font emphasizes the centrality of baptism to our common life in Christ.
3. Placing the water near the pulpit emphasizes the link between baptism and the Word.
4. When situated near the Communion table, the baptismal water points to the link between both sacraments.

The space surrounding the font or pool should be uncrowded so the importance of baptism may be symbolized without distraction or competition from either the pulpit or the Communion table. Ample space about the font or pool also provides room for at least a portion of the congregation to gather together at the water when a baptism is celebrated.

In some recently built churches, a baptismal pool with recirculating water is located in the back of the sanctuary, between the major entrance and the pews. The continually flowing water evidences life. It can be seen and heard by the worshipers. Such a provision for baptism gives strong focus to the importance and centrality of baptism in Christian worship.

The advantage of a pool is that it is of sufficient size to signify the importance of the sacrament and stands prominently as a reminder of the living water of baptism. Some of the pools are large enough for immersion or affusion, although all enable water to be used in abundance in baptism. Whether a church has a pool or a font, it should be designed to accommodate the use of a generous amount of water in baptism. Water should dominate both in the space for baptism and in the baptismal action itself.

Occasions for the Reaffirmation of the Baptismal Covenant

It is appropriate, at various times and on various occasions, to acknowledge and to celebrate the grace of God bestowed on us in baptism and to lay claim to that grace. This was Luther's point in his oft-repeated phrase, especially upon waking, "I am baptized." Whenever Luther's faith was weakening, he would remember his baptism and find new strength and courage. It is not too much to say that by remembering his baptism, Luther experienced again its power and meaning.

Baptism is the primary referent point for our daily lives. Its meaning is revealed and reinforced through daily acts of repentance and discipleship. In the words of the Westminster Larger Catechism, "The needful but much neglected duty of improving our Baptism, is to be performed by us all our life long . . ." (7.277).

For centuries, certain communions have encouraged individuals who have been baptized to reaffirm their own baptism when others are baptized. Moreover, reaffirmation of one's baptism is bound up in each celebration of the Eucharist. It is also appropriate, from time to time, to celebrate the power and grace of our baptism with a special service for reaffirmation.

Therefore, in addition to the liturgy for baptism, the *Book of Common Worship* provides several orders for the reaffirmation of baptism. These services point to the meaning of baptism as well as to occasions for recommitment and reaffirmation. To make clear the many and varied occasions when reaffirmation of baptism is appropriate, each service is adapted to particular situations in the lives of Christians.

Baptism and Reaffirmation of the Baptismal Covenant: A Combined Order (BCW 431)

This rite can be used for a confirmation class composed of both baptized and unbaptized catechumens, and for other occasions calling both for the Sacrament of Baptism and for reaffirmation of the baptismal covenant.

When it occurs, baptism must stand on its own as the central act of this service. Therefore the act of baptism, that is, washing (and, if desired the laying on of hands and anointing), should be completed for each baptismal candidate.

Following the baptism of each candidate, those who have been previously baptized and are making a profession of faith (for instance, young people) make their vow to fulfill their Christian calling (BCW 442–443), and receive the laying on of hands (and anointing) (BCW 444).

If space allows, each group should stand together, slightly apart from the other groups:

1. candidates for baptism
2. those presenting children for baptism

3. those previously baptized who are reaffirming their baptismal covenant
4. those previously baptized who are making their public profession.

This will help the minister and congregation distinguish one group from the other. The minister should plan this combined order carefully. A rehearsal is prudent.

Reaffirmation of the Baptismal Covenant for Those Making a Public Profession of Faith (BCW 447)

This service may be used for a confirmation class or for others who were baptized as children and are now making a public profession of faith.

Reaffirmation of the Baptismal Covenant for Those Uniting with a Congregation (BCW 455)

This rite is for those uniting with a congregation by transfer of letter or reaffirmation of faith, and for those who are coming from active membership in a church that does not issue certificates of transfer. It is also appropriate for those who wish to renew their participation in the life of a church following a period of inactivity.

Reaffirmation of the Baptismal Covenant for a Congregation (BCW 464)

This order may be used in a Lord's Day service, and is especially appropriate for Baptism of the Lord, during Lent, on any Sunday in Easter, on the Day of Pentecost, and/or on All Saints' Day. This order may also be used in the Easter Vigil when there is no baptism.

Reaffirmation of the Baptismal Covenant Marking Occasions of Growth in Faith (BCW 478)

This service provides for an individual to reaffirm baptism in recognition of a sense of renewed commitment, a new growth in faith, or a new sense of calling. It can be a public or a private ceremony. When used in "The Service for the Lord's Day," it follows the sermon.

Reaffirmation of the Baptismal Covenant in Pastoral Counseling (BCW 485)

This is a private ceremony for use within a counseling relationship. It includes the reaffirmation of vows and may include the laying on of hands.

Daily Prayer

(BCW 489–595; BCW-DP 26–163)

The Nature of Daily Prayer

In his First Letter to the Thessalonians (5:17), Paul admonishes his Christian friends to "pray without ceasing": to live all of life in the presence of God. This is the calling of every Christian.

In practical terms, however, regular daily prayer seems difficult to many and nearly impossible to most. So it is tempting for many Christians today to consider any full schedule of daily prayer more a luxury than a necessity. Those who desire to pray throughout the day are frustrated by an inability to "find the time" and may envy those whose life is ordered in such a way as to have prayer time "built in," such as those in religious communities. Additionally, some Christians are confronted by the great paradox of prayer. Prayer, which is a gift given to us by God, is perceived as work, a religious chore, even a burdensome duty. So they postpone it or try to avoid it and, then, wonder why they have so much trouble praying.

"Daily Prayer" offers a response to this double frustration, for it is possible to experience a profound prayer life even in the busiest of schedules. It is, perhaps, the busyness of schedules that makes us see more clearly our need for prayer in our lives. When we experience prayer as a joyous gift from God, we can begin to grasp for ourselves the life-giving power of daily communion with God. Only by venturing forth in prayer can we discover new vistas of life lived in the presence of God.

Within each one of us, a human impulse to pray seems to reside. As Calvin said, "Genuine and earnest prayer proceeds first from a sense of our need and, next, from faith in the promises of God."[1] For the Christian, then, prayer is a means of grace as well as a result of it. Prayer is not merely an expression of established faith; it is also the food that nourishes faith, giving it strength and energy. By the moving of the Holy Spirit, prayer brings us to new life in the

173

fullness of Jesus Christ. Praying, then, is not a burden under which we labor, but the release of energy for joyful living.

"Daily Prayer," therefore, offers a pattern of prayer designed for us by Christians in the latter part of the twentieth century. Yet, it is a pattern that draws on the experience and traditions of the Christian church in all centuries.

Discipline and Commonality

Two aspects of daily prayer need our attention because they are so easily neglected.

The first is *discipline*. Daily prayer deserves a discipline. Sometimes we associate "discipline" with rigidity, and consider it to be opposed to "freedom" that allows the Spirit to work. To some, discipline in prayer may seem to be an obstacle to relevant prayer, preventing prayer from being timely and responsive to the Spirit of God, but this need not be so. The Holy Spirit is the Spirit of order present at the creation. By the Spirit prompting our prayers, we are delivered from aimlessness and emptiness in our praying. A discipline of prayer, therefore, can work with the Spirit as we relate our prayers to the circumstances of our daily life.

The need for a discipline in prayer is apparent. Without some discipline, human frailty prevails. Being a disciple of Jesus Christ does not occur without our commitment and effort, and that part of our discipleship called prayer deserves no less. The common root of the two words "disciple" and "discipline" indicates that they are related in meaning. To pray without discipline means too often to pray randomly, superficially, and infrequently, thus falling into the trap of irrelevance. A discipline of prayer can open us to the presence of God in everyday situations and keep us alert to the moving of God's Spirit within, among, and around us.

Furthermore, to be a disciple is to be one who learns. With the first disciples, we are constantly asking the Lord to teach us to pray. The model prayer (Matt. 6:9–13; Luke 11:2–4) Jesus gave in answer to this request is a guide to us in our praying, a reminder that we are always to be learning as disciples of Jesus Christ. A discipline of prayer, then, tutors us in prayer so that we continually grow in faith.

The discipline of prayer modeled in the *Book of Common Worship* is a modification of the most common of all disciplines of daily prayer used by Christians for centuries, harking back to the early church and even to the ancient Jews. It is a durable discipline, having lasted for ages, adapted repeatedly in different times and situations.

The second aspect of daily prayer easily neglected is that of *commonality*.

Too often, individual selves are emphasized regarding prayer, suggesting that all that really matters is our one-to-one relationship to God. On the contrary, individual prayer grows out of communal experiences of prayer, rather than daily prayer being a personal discipline for individuals out of which communal prayer grows. Inherent in Christian prayer is a corporateness that draws us to others in the experience of prayer. Even when we pray separately, we have a sense in which we pray together, because we come before God as a people, not as a collection of individuals. The opening words of the prayer Jesus taught his disciples instructs us as well about our commonality before God in prayer. And the promise of Jesus is for us also: "Where two or three are gathered in my name, I am there among them" (Matt. 18:20). This is the "Christian quorum" and requires us to be aware of the commonality of our prayer.

We do not live our lives in isolation from those around us, our families, our friends in faith, even strangers. Praying together, we discover that Christ is present, binding us in a community of faith. Common prayer is itself an act of faith in the promised presence of Jesus Christ with his people.

When we pray for others, we discover a new dimension of the discipline of prayer. In order to pray together, we have to make practical commitments to one another, and we find ourselves encouraged and even challenged to greater constancy in prayer. Mutual discipline is expressed in mutual support.

Beyond the immediate circle of family and friends with whom we pray daily, we become conscious of the wholeness of Christ's church, the people of God in prayer everywhere. When we adopt a *discipline* of prayer having much in *common* with how other Christians pray, we are conscious of being at prayer "with" them as well. Now our prayers are not just our own, nor are they reserved for our immediate community. They are joined to prayers of the whole people of God around the world. We are not preoccupied with personal or local concerns; rather, we are inspired to a broader perspective of prayer. As we pray for others, we are confident that we are lifted up in their prayers as well, and we glimpse something of the fullness of Christ's church at prayer. An objective, therefore, is to introduce daily prayer into the life of the church in a variety of ways, and out of that to encourage individual prayer to reinforce the communal experience.

Many of the prayers offered in the *Book of Common Worship* derive from a variety of traditions, and from times other than our own. This reminds us of the resource of the whole Christian church, as the Spirit working in the prayers of others enables us to pray. The prayers suggested here may be used as they are, or may be accepted as the promptings of the Spirit to help us articulate our own prayers. In any case, they remind us of our oneness in Christ with men and women and children around the world.

Hours of Prayer and the Meaning of Time

Praying at designated hours of the day is one way of acknowledging the rhythm of time. As the sun rises and sets, so we are summoned by time itself to pray to God who rules over time. Naturally, therefore, morning and evening have become the primary times for prayer. They seem particularly appropriate times to praise the God of creation who gives us the years of our lives. As finite creatures, we humans are subject to the limits of time, and our lives find their rhythms in the cycles of nature, the seasons of the year, even in the daily round of light and darkness. Daily prayer, morning and evening, puts us in touch with the Ruler of creation and all time.

The rhythm of daily prayer is rooted in the experience of ancient Judaism. The day begins with sundown, evening before morning, just as it is recorded in the biblical account of creation (Gen. 1:1–2:4). The onset of night reminds us that the God of creation begins with nothingness and shapes it into new life, just as our day begins with the "nothingness" of sleep anticipating the "new life" that comes with the dawn. The church has often continued this perspective by seeing every morning as a celebration of the resurrection that can follow only the "death" of sleep, thus beginning daily prayer with evening. Whether daily prayer is understood as beginning with morning or evening, there is an overlapping effect so that at the end of one day we already anticipate the beginning of the next, looking forward to God's future.

God's redemption in Jesus Christ involves the redemption of time. Jesus Christ, who took on human nature, accepted and entered into the limitations of human time, thereby transforming the meaning of time itself. "Eternal life" offered in Christ is not simply eternal in the sense of duration or a quantity of time; it has more to do with the *quality* of time. Life that has this eternal quality is life lived before God. Daily prayer, morning and evening, structures our day in such a manner as to remind us that all our times are lived in God's presence. Time is transformed from a measuring device that marks off our chronology into a kind of time that is filled with the presence of God and divine promises for the future.

Daily prayer, therefore, challenges us to think differently about time. Ordinarily, we think of the times of our day being blocked out in terms of various activities: meals, work, relaxation, sleep. A certain amount of time is allotted for each, and specific times noted, so that those activities provide a structure for the rest of the day. In this framework, we may want to find a time for prayer, but we tend to see it as one of a number of activities to be inserted in the daily schedule.

If time is transformed, however, so that we are conscious of being in God's presence all the time, then daily prayer becomes itself the framework for our common activities. Time for meals, work, play, and sleep is set in the context of prayer and praise to God. Those activities are thus filled with new meaning, the new quality of life called eternal. All we do, the business and busyness of living, is done before God, and our daily prayer makes us conscious of that fact. At meals we will recognize Christ as our host in the breaking of bread and the sharing of food. Our work will be offered as a part of our Christian discipleship and service. Our play and relaxation is also transformed into an experience of God's renewal of our whole lives in Christ. Sleep becomes an act of trust and surrendering ourselves to the eternal care of God. Daily prayer, morning and evening, enables time to be transformed from a round of activities into events of worship because of the presence of God in Jesus Christ.

History of Daily Prayer

Our daily prayer has a long tradition. The history of daily prayer is a complex one and is the subject of scholarly study. A brief sketch of that history, however, reveals something of the rich heritage that is our legacy.[2] It is clear that early in Judaism, a pattern of prayer evolved including morning and evening sacrifices in the Jerusalem Temple, along with psalms and prayers at midmorning and midafternoon. Devout Jews also engaged in private prayers in the evening and morning and at noon, possibly in preparation for the times of common prayer. Daily prayer was *not* casually observed by a few, but was highly important in the worship of the synagogue.

The early Christian church continued this pattern built on morning and evening prayer. The book of Acts tells us that the first converts to the Christian faith "devoted themselves to the apostles' teaching and fellowship, to the breaking of bread and the prayers" (Acts 2:42). The prayers referred to are services of morning and evening prayer, probably held in homes.[3] An example of such a prayer service is mentioned later in Acts as Peter and John and their friends praise God in the words of the Second Psalm (Acts 4:25–26). As it did with much of its Jewish inheritance, the early church adapted the daily prayer experience to its uniquely Christian understanding. They saw in the Psalms a prophetic witness to Jesus Christ, and even the hours of the day set for prayer reminded them of the story of Christ's suffering and death.

Evening and morning, the reckoning of the day at this time, continued to be the normative times for daily prayer. While the goal was constant prayer, assigned times were recognized as a helpful means toward its accomplishment.

The fact that Christians gathered for prayer is also important to note; common prayer was also normative, encouraging constancy in prayer.

In the fourth century, following the establishment of Christianity under Constantine, the structure of daily prayer became more formalized. Actually, it developed in two separate strands. The *congregational* style of daily prayer included selected psalms as well as participation by parish people in responses and hymns, and centered on morning and evening as the principal times. *Monastic* prayer developed simultaneously in religious communities and among the clergy, and concentrated on praying the *entire* Psalter on a regular basis. Additional times were set for prayer appropriate for the concentrated prayer life of the monastic community. Throughout the Middle Ages, the congregational and the monastic styles of daily prayer were woven together in a variety of configurations. Eventually, however, the discipline of daily prayer was carried by the clergy and those in the religious orders, and no longer followed by the common people. It became highly complicated and cumbersome, totally impractical for all but the most diligent of religious orders.

In the sixteenth century, the Reformers, especially in Germany, attempted to revive a congregational use of morning and evening prayer. They were firmly committed to daily prayer as essential in the life of the church. And, they understood it to be corporate worship.[4] Among the reforms instituted were the concentration on morning and evening prayer and the use of the common language rather than Latin. The Reformers were also anxious to continue the use of the psalms in daily prayer, as well as other biblical songs. These, then, would have to be translated and arranged for the singing of the common people. Scripture was read in continuous fashion (*lectio continua*), straight through the Bible, often accompanied by instruction.

In Protestantism, daily prayer found *a focus in the family*. By the end of the sixteenth century, it was common for families to gather each morning to begin the day with prayer. At the evening dinner table, following the meal, the family would sing a psalm, listen to Scripture, and join in prayer, the essential ingredients in any service of daily prayer.

Another Protestant focus of daily prayer was as *a discipline for pastors*. The pastor was to be a student of Scripture, but was also to be diligent in prayer and devotion. The pastor's study was also a chapel; the place of learning was a place of piety as well.

The Free Churches, those who have their origin in the radical wing of the Protestant Reformation, have been intentionally free of prescribed forms or liturgies so as to allow the worshiper to be freely guided by the Holy Spirit. Still, this tradition has given emphasis to daily prayer, including the reading of Scripture and its exposition, and extemporaneous prayer. Some of this "free church" tradition is expressed within our Presbyterian experience. The affirmation of community before God in praise, and holding up the needs of the existential situation in prayer, are characteristic of this discipline. Singing is extremely important in involving people fully in praising God. While this approach to prayer is "free" in the sense of being free of prescribed forms, it is nevertheless disciplined. It brings prayer to focus on immediate struggles of living, and is thus intensely practical. It also recognizes the need for a strong sense of community in coming before God in prayer.

Presbyterians have incorporated much of this "free" tradition and, at the same time, have persisted in providing prayer books with resources for family worship in the home on a daily basis. In recent decades, worship books in Presbyterian and Reformed lineage have explicitly encouraged the practice of daily prayer by providing prayers and liturgies.

The rise of ecumenism in the past century has witnessed cooperation by Reformed Christians in developing daily worship liturgies, as in the Taizé Community in France, the Iona Community on the Scottish island of Iona, and in the Church of South India. And, Presbyterians in Scotland and in the United States have given renewed attention to daily prayer in recent publications. Common study and worship have taken place among Protestants, Roman Catholics, and Eastern Orthodox Christians, and virtually all major faith communities have taken a fresh look at daily prayer.

Components of Daily Prayer

1. Psalms and Canticles

Psalms

The book of Psalms is a collection of songs of prayer and praise. These songs were used by the ancient Jews for both corporate and individual worship. Evidently, they were sung rather than spoken, and they find their fullest expression of praise of God in musical settings.

Christians quickly adopted the Psalms for their worship. One reason was that Jesus himself used and quoted the Psalms (for example, Mark 15:34). Another was that the early Christians were Jews and brought with them the heritage of the Hebrew psalms. Still another reason was that Christians had interpreted the psalms christologically (or, in terms of their faith in Jesus Christ). Not only were the Psalms used by Jesus, they seemed in the eyes of Christians to articulate his voice and prayer. So the Psalms were adopted and adapted by the followers of Christ for their prayers.

The Reformers easily adopted the Psalms as Christian prayer, recognizing the continuity between the Old Testament and the New.[5] Bucer, Calvin, and others interpreted the Psalms from a Christian perspective. The Psalms have always been central in Reformed piety and worship, and prayer books in the Reformed tradition are often referred to simply as psalters. As early as 1523, Luther called on German poets to translate the Psalms so they could be sung by the people "in meter." In 1539, assisted by the poetic talents of Clément Marot and Theodore Beza, Calvin introduced nineteen metrical psalms, inspired no doubt by the singing of psalms in German in Strasbourg.[6] The entire Psalter was completed in 1562. It was a significant achievement in its literary and musical qualities. The tunes were to accentuate and carry the words, for it was the lyrics that spoke of Christ.[7] Yet, singable tunes were chosen as a way of restoring the Psalms to the people.

The Psalms provide for us today a basis for our prayers as they have for Christians through the centuries. By singing them we lift our praises to Almighty God. By offering them as our own prayers we are guided in candid prayer. Some of the psalms seem very unchristian in their attitude, yet even these are directives for us as we intercede for those who feel pain and injustice as the psalmist did. Above all, they are realistic prayers, and they call us to realism in our daily prayer.

The Psalms are an essential part of daily prayer. The persistent praying of psalms over a period of time gives one a repertoire of prayers learned by heart. The prayer language of the Psalms finds a natural use in our own prayers, enabling us to articulate the deepest prayers of our souls.

The Psalms also may be sung in a variety of settings, with refrains or responses, chanted, or in metrical versions. They may be shared in improvised ways, as when a single verse is selected as a refrain to be sung by all to a simple tune.

Psalm Prayers

Psalm prayers follow each psalm (BCW 611–783; BCW-DP 181–390), and are suggested for use with all psalms except the opening psalms in Morning Prayer. At the conclusion of a psalm, a psalm prayer restates the essence of the psalm and may include Christian implications recognized in the psalm. Psalm prayers appeared in the French Psalter in 1561, and were translated into English for inclusion in the Scottish Metrical Psalter of 1595.[8] Psalm prayers, thus, reclaim part of our Reformed heritage.

Typically, each psalm prayer captures some theme or image from the psalm and often adds Christian implications drawn from the psalm. The prayer helps us to reflect on the psalm as well as to pray the psalm ourselves. Psalm prayers may be composed in this way to focus on emphases of immediate need to the worshipers. *After* the psalm is sung or read, follows a period of silent reflection, whereupon the psalm prayer is spoken by the leader. The psalm prayers in the *Book of Common Worship* are from various traditions; many are based on psalm prayers from the Scottish Psalter (1595).[9]

Canticles (Biblical Songs) and Ancient Hymns

In addition to psalms, daily prayer incorporates the singing of other biblical texts. Biblical songs other than the Psalms are called "canticles." Three canticles (songs) from the Gospel of Luke are traditionally used in Daily Prayer in Western Christianity: the Canticle of Zechariah, or the Benedictus (Luke 1:68–79), the Canticle of Mary, or the Magnificat (Luke 1:46–55), and the Canticle of Simeon, or Nunc Dimittis (Luke 2:29–32). They are called Gospel Canticles, not only because they come from a Gospel, but because they witness to the message of the gospel. Since these are used most often, several musical settings are provided in *The Presbyterian Hymnal* (600–605) and *The Psalter* (158–166).

A variety of other biblical songs are suggested in the orders of the services, appropriate for the changing liturgical seasons. When the traditional song is not used, it is suggested that a biblical song from the Old Testament be used in the morning and one from the New Testament be used in the evening. Texts of canticles (biblical songs) and ancient hymns are provided (BCW 573–591; BCW-DP 137–158). They may be sung or said in the same manner as suggested for the psalms.

Many other biblical texts also lend themselves to song. Ancient hymns such as the Te Deum Laudamus ("We Praise You, O God") (BCW 577; BCW-DP 141; PH 460, PS 170, 171) are also called canticles. Any of the canticles for which texts are provided (BCW 573–591; BCW-DP 137–158), or which are listed below, may be used at any time, as provided in the daily services.

As noted above, worshipers traditionally sing the Canticle of Zechariah in the morning, the Canticle of Mary in the evening, and the Canticle of Simeon in Prayer at the Close of Day, as suggested in the services. Other texts are provided as alternatives for seasons and festivals to the traditional canticles (BCW 524–543; BCW-DP 65–104). A Canticle of Creation, the Canticle of Judith, and the Te Deum ("We Praise You, O God") are especially appropriate for use on Sundays and festivals.

Other texts to those listed in the rubrics of the *Book of Common Worship*, provide additional choices that may be sung as canticles during particular seasons and festivals. These include:

For General Use

Deut. 12:1–12
1 Sam. 2:1b–10
Isa. 26:1b–4, 7–8, 12
Isa. 40:10–17
Isa. 40:28–31
Isa. 41:17–20
Isa. 45:5–8, 18, 21–25

Isa. 61:10–62:5
Isa. 66:10–14a
Jer. 14:17–21
Jonah 2:2–9
Rom. 8:28, 31–35, 37–39
1 Tim. 3:16; 4:10; 1:17
Wisdom (Apocrypha) 9:1–6, 9–11

Advent

Deut. 32:1–12
Isa. 2:2–5
Isa. 11:1–9
Isa. 25:6–9
Isa. 40:3–11
Isa. 42:10–16
Isa. 55:1–5

Isa. 55:12–13
Jer. 31:10–14
Mic. 5:2–5a
Zeph. 3:14–18
Eph. 3:1–10
Rev. 19:1b–2a, 5b, 6b–8
Rev. 22:12–13, 16–17, 20

Christmas

John 1:1–5, 10–12, 14

Eph. 1:3–10

Epiphany

Isa. 40:9–11

Isa. 60:4–9

Baptism of the Lord

Isa. 11:1–5
Isa. 42:1–8

Rom. 6:3–5

Lent

Isa. 38:10–20
Isa. 53:1–6
Isa. 53:6–12

Isa. 55:1–5
Jer. 31:31–34
Ezek. 36:24–28

Maundy Thursday

John 15:4–5, 9–10, 12–14

Good Friday

Hab. 3:2–4, 13a, 15–19

Phil. 2:5c–11 (*Jesus Christ Is Lord*) (BCW 589, #25; BCW-DP 156, #25)

Holy Saturday

Isa. 38:10–14, 17–20

Phil. 2:5c–11 (*Jesus Christ Is Lord*) (BCW 589, #25; BCW-DP 156, #25)

Easter

1 Sam. 2:1–10

Isa. 12:2–6 (*Canticle of Thanksgiving*) (BCW 580, #10; BCW-DP 145, #10)

Isa. 38:10–14, 17–20

Isa. 42:10–16

Isa. 66:10–14a

Jer. 31:10–14

Hos. 6:1–3

2 Cor. 4:6–11, 14

Eph. 1:3–10

1 Pet. 1:3–4, 18–21

1 Pet. 2:4–10

Rev. 5:9–10, 12, 13b (*Worthy Is the Lamb*)

Rev. 11:17–18; 12:10b–12a

Rev. 19:1b–2a, 5b, 6b–8

Ascension (those for Easter, and the following)

Isa. 42:10–13

1 Tim. 3:16

Rev. 11:17–18; 12:10b–12a

Pentecost

Ezek. 36:24–28

Trinity Sunday

Eph. 1:3–10

Rev. 4:8, 11

Rev. 15:3–4 (*Canticle of the Redeemed*) (BCW 587; #21; BCW-DP 152, #21)

All Saints' Day (November 1)

Rev. 1:8, 17c–18, with 2 Tim. 2:11–13 and Rom. 8:17

Rev. 2:8b, 7b, 10c, 17bc, 26; 3:5, 7b, 12, 21, 14b

Christ the King (Reign of Christ)

Rev. 4:11; 5:9–10, 13 (*A Canticle to the Lamb*) (BCW 586, #20; BCW-DP 152, #20)

Hymns

Hymns may be sung as noted, some familiar hymns being particularly suited for Morning Prayer (for example, BCW 492; BCW-DP 28) and others for Evening Prayer (for example, BCW 507; BCW-DP 45).

2. Scripture Readings

Lectionary

Daily Prayer engages us in prayerful reading of the Scriptures, providing us with a systematic discipline of Bible reading. The Daily Lectionary (BCW 1050–1095; BCW-DP 459–506; see also BCW 1096–1097; BCW-DP 508–509 for a table indicating the assignment of years 1 and 2 to particular calendar years) guides us through the Scriptures that we may hear God speak to us not only through the familiar portions of the Bible but also through parts unfamiliar to us. A description of this lectionary and suggestions for its use are included (BCW 1049; BCW-DP 459). Many of the readings in this lectionary are a series of consecutive readings (*lectio continua*) from a book of the Bible. This lectionary, therefore, has its greatest value when used daily, since the reading for a particular day is read in relation to the readings that have immediately preceded.

When Morning and Evening Prayer are not held daily (as may be the case in a congregation, meetings of committees or governing bodies, or retreats), it may be preferable to select readings according to the Revised Common Lectionary (RCL). One possibility is to choose readings appointed for the nearest Sunday in the table of readings for the years not in current use. For example, on a day following the Fourth Sunday of Easter during a year when Cycle B is being used, readings may be chosen from Cycles A and C for the Fourth Sunday of Easter. Other possibilities for text selection could evolve from noting that during Ordinary Time, many of the readings in the RCL are a series of consecutive readings (that is, *lectio continua*) from a book of the Bible. These readings offer great value when used daily or at sequential meetings of a particular group, since the reading for a service is read in relation to the readings that have immediately preceded.

The daily lectionary is on a two-year cycle that does not necessarily relate to RCL. Currently, the Consultation on Common Texts (CCT) is preparing a three-year daily cycle which will relate to RCL, loosely patterned in the following manner: Monday, Tuesday, and Wednesday are devoted to texts reflective of the preceding Sunday, and Thursday, Friday, and Saturday are devoted to texts anticipating the coming Sunday. (For a similar pattern, see Gail Ramshaw, *Between Sundays: Daily Bible Readings Based on the Revised Common Lectionary;* Minneapolis: Augsburg/Fortress, 1997.)

The Scripture reading may be briefly interpreted or discussed. While a sermon is not ordinarily a part of daily prayer (that is, it is not a "preaching service"), occasions do occur when the proclamation of the Word may be desirable, or other devotional readings from Christian literature may be shared.[10] In any event, the reading of Scripture should be followed by a period of silence, time for personal reflection and meditation on the Word, and listening for that Word spoken personally.

Other Uses of Scripture in Daily Prayer

It is fitting that a resource for daily prayer in the Reformed tradition be firmly rooted in Scripture. Not only do the services include psalms, biblical songs, and Scripture readings, but much of the liturgical text is also in words of Scripture. The versicles, the verses that begin the service and introduce the prayers, are taken from Scripture. Morning Prayer begins with words from Psalm 51:15, "O Lord, open my lips . . . ." (BCW 491; BCW-DP 27). Evening Prayer begins with Psalm 124:8, "Our help is in the name of the Lord . . .", or Psalm 70:1: "O God, come to our assistance . . ." (BCW 513; BCW-DP 53). Midday Prayer also begins with Psalm 124:8 (BCW 545; BCW-DP 106). And, Prayer at the Close of Day begins with Psalm 70:1 (BCW 551; BCW-DP 113). The opening sentences that follow are ordinarily verses from Scripture. The references are displayed in the text.

Biblical verses also introduce the prayers of thanksgiving and intercession. The verse used in Morning Prayer, "Satisfy us with your love in the morning . . . ," is based on Psalm 90:14. The verse used in Evening Prayer on Sundays and Saturdays, "Receive my prayer as incense . . . ," is Psalm 141:2. The verse used in Evening Prayer on Mondays through Fridays, "Let us walk in love . . . ," is Ephesians 5:2. Psalm 31:5 and Psalm 17:8 comprise the major part of the versicles introducing the prayers in Prayer at the Close of Day. The dismissals are also in words of Scripture. The references for these are included in the text of the services.

3. Prayers (Thanksgiving and Intercession)

Prayers of Thanksgiving and Intercession

The *Book of Common Worship* includes two series of thanksgiving and intercessions for use in daily prayer: Morning Prayer (BCW 496–499; BCW-DP 33–37) and Evening Prayer (BCW 517–520; BCW-DP 56–60). These prayers can prompt us in thanksgiving and intercession over a broader range of concern than we might otherwise pray. They are structured to include free prayer by providing an opportunity for the leader or worshipers to offer those concerns which are currently paramount. The ellipses (". . .") at the end of lines (for example, BCW 496; BCW-DP 34) denote places where the leader provides an unhurried pause for silent prayer or verbal offering of prayer. In using these prayers each day, in the course of a week, prayer will be offered for churches throughout the world in the morning, and for Christians in the various traditions of the church ecumenical in the evening.

Other prayers throughout the *Book of Common Worship* are appropriate for use in Daily Prayer. Throughout the week, prayers are provided for use both for "ordinary days" (BCW 496–501, 517–522; BCW-DP 33–39) and for the seasons and festivals (BCW 524–543; BCW-DP 65–104). Also included are selected prayers for use during seasons and festivals:

> Advent [131] (BCW 166–167, 525, 527; BCW-DP 67–68, 70)
>
> Christmas [148], [149], [150], [151] (BCW 178–180, 529, 530; BCW-DP 72–73, 75–76)
>
> Epiphany [170], [171], [177], [178] (BCW 192–193, 199–200, 532, 533; BCW-DP 77–78, 80–81)
>
> Lent [213], [214], [216], [217] (BCW 235–237, 535, 536; BCW-DP 84–86, 90)
>
> Passion/Palm Sunday [243], [244/486] (BCW 266–267, 537; BCW-DP 86–87, 90)
>
> Good Friday [251], [253] (BCW 282, 292–293; BCW-DP 87–88, 90)
>
> Easter [267], [268], [269], [270] (BCW 315–317, 538, 540; BCW-DP 93, 94, 97–98)
>
> Ascension of the Lord [300] (BCW 333, 538, 540; BCW-DP 94, 97)
>
> Pentecost [310], [313], [314], [315], [316], [317], [318] (BCW 339, 340–343, 542, 543; BCW-DP 100–101, 103–104)

Since the section "Prayers for Various Occasions" (BCW 785–837; BCW-DP 391–455) is a rich treasury of prayer embracing a broad spectrum of concern, it is included in the daily prayer, as well as Prayers of the People: E [95], [96] (BCW 112–114; BCW-DP 399–402), a favorite sung prayer for use in Evening Prayer (BCW 516; BCW-DP 56). This Litany is an ancient prayer and comes from the Eastern Orthodox tradition. It is most effective when sung.

The Great Litany (BCW 787–791; BCW-DP 393–398) is very old, having roots in a variety of sources in Western Christianity. In the sixteenth century, it was revised and incorporated in both Lutheran and Anglican service books. A version of it appeared in *The Book of Common Worship* (1946). The rubrics (BCW 533, 787; BCW-DP 81, 393) describe the Great Litany's traditional uses in Daily Prayer, particularly during Advent and Lent. At penitential times, "when used alone or as the entrance hymn, the Great Litany may be sung in procession as a dramatization of our passage through this world toward that which is to come."[11] Both the *Lutheran Book of Worship*[12] and the *Lutheran Book of Worship: Ministers Desk Edition*[13] include a musical setting for the Great Litany.

The prayers of thanksgiving and intercession may be used as they are, or may serve as models for free prayer. In any event, the prayers of thanksgiving and intercession should be offered in a manner appropriate for the particular group. (See also BCW 99–122, 792–837; BCW-DP 399–455.)

Biblical and Written Prayers

The prayer Jesus taught his disciples, which we call the Lord's Prayer, serves as a model for our prayers. The biblical texts (Matt. 6:9–13; Luke 11:2–4) serve as the basis for versions of the prayer used repeatedly in Christian worship. Our "personal prayers" as well are shaped by this model, for it is the standard by which all prayers are measured.

In addition, many other prayers in Scripture serve as a great resource for Christian prayer. The Bible provides for us the content, context, and norm for our praying. Not only do we adopt and adapt scriptural prayers for our use, but the whole of Scripture provides us with the language and imagery of prayer. Narratives and histories give us images of the Lord whom we worship, and pictures of the faithful life we seek to follow. Prophetic voices instruct and challenge us to see a hurting world and people in need. Doctrinal passages teach us "orthodoxy," which literally means not only "right opinion" but also "right worship," to guard our prayers from eccentricity and narrowness. The reading of Scripture is integral to daily prayer, therefore, so that our prayers may be rooted in biblical soil.

Similarly, prayers from all generations of God's people (that is, tradition) are passed down to us in written form. Although they do not have the same authority as Scripture, they nevertheless aid and encourage our practice of prayer. In our own generation we find resources in the prayers of others.

A prayer book, therefore, offers continuity with our heritage and community with our contemporaries. Those who write prayers risk sharing what is most personal and intimate. In reading the prayers of others, we are encouraged to give voice to our own personal prayers. We may even be moved to risk sharing aloud in prayer, and by the grace of God our words may articulate another person's prayer. A prayer book is supposed to be *suggestive* to us, the first words we pray, perhaps, but by no means the last.

4. Silence

Silence is particularly important in these services, for they are services of prayer. Silence helps us to be more deliberate than rushed in our worship, and encourages a contemplative attitude.

The services could begin with silence as a way of "centering" and beginning to focus one's whole person on God in prayer. This is particularly desirable in Morning Prayer, when silence is broken with the first words of the service, "O Lord, open my lips." (BCW 491; BCW-DP 27; Ps. 51:15). For Evening Prayer, the church should be very dimly lighted *before* the service, the people waiting in silence.

In addition to a period of meditation and reflection following the hearing of Scripture, silence is incorporated in other places in the service.

A time of silence should follow the singing or speaking of each psalm. This is not only for reflecting on the meaning of the psalm but more especially for absorbing the psalm as a personal prayer. In this way, the words of the psalmist give guidance to the words of our own prayers, and we learn to listen to the promptings of the Spirit within us.

Similarly, silence is incorporated into the prayers of thanksgiving and intercession (indicated by the ellipses ". . ."). Again, this allows the prayers of the people to be personalized.

During these periods of silence, a comfortable posture of prayer should be adopted as one's breathing is allowed to deepen and one fulfills the command, "Be still, and know that I am God!" (Ps. 46:10).

The Services of Daily Prayer

The *Book of Common Worship* offers a resource for daily prayer in a variety of circumstances, and it will need to be adapted by those who use it to fulfill the requirements of the occasion.

The services are ordered along traditional lines. This pattern of daily prayer has developed over many centuries and has been useful to people of faith. Nevertheless there is considerable flexibility in these services, and they may be shaped according to particular needs.[14]

It is important to remember that the *Book of Common Worship* is not intended to be a substitute for our most personal prayer, but to prompt and encourage us in our daily worship of Almighty God. The prayers offered here can help us pray our own prayers, serve as models for our prayers, or even suggest language to give voice to our deepest prayers.

Music is important in daily prayer. Song can transform what otherwise might be a rather pedestrian service into a liturgy that effectively leads worship into prayer. At least the psalms and biblical songs, as well as the hymns, should be sung.[15]

Morning Prayer (BCW 490–503, 524–543; BCW-DP 27–41, 65–104)

The gift of *creation* is one theme celebrated in Morning Prayer. Each day is a gift fresh from God, unspoiled and pure, filled with possibilities. It is as though we are given a new creation every morning, and in our prayer together we praise God for the gift of this day and this world, the time and space in which we live.

Morning Prayer is also a time to praise God for the *re-creation* that we see in the *resurrection* of Jesus Christ. In a sense, each morning is a reflection of Easter, and we all receive new life daily because Christ is raised from the dead. Our waking from sleep is a daily "resurrection" as we are offered the gift of new life.

Commitment is another aspect of Morning Prayer. As we begin a new day, we seek God's power in living more faithfully throughout the day before us. We anticipate our day's work and recreation, consciously giving ourselves in it to the service of God. Praising God for all Christ has done for humankind, we pledge ourselves to seek to reflect the compassion of Christ in all our relationships. Our prayers focus on those around us, our families and friends, and strangers too. We intercede for them in prayer as we commit ourselves to serve them in the name of Christ.

Certain psalms have long been associated with Morning Prayer. Those included in the *Book of Common Worship* are Psalms 95, 100, 63, and 51 (BCW 492–494; BCW-DP 28–31). One of these is suggested for use each morning. Psalms 67 and 24 have also been long used in Morning Prayer. They provide further alternatives.

The "Canticle/Song of Zechariah" or Benedictus (BCW 573; BCW-DP 137; PH 601, 602) is traditionally sung in Morning Prayer. It is particularly appropriate for use in the morning because of the words, "The dawn from on high will break upon us" (Luke 1:78). In this song, Zechariah, the father of John the Baptist, sings, assured of the fulfillment of God's ancient promise. He addresses his son, "You, child, will be called the prophet of the Most High" (Luke 1:76). This song looks toward the future, to the dawn of the day when God's purpose for humanity will be fulfilled, when we shall dwell in the full light of the kingdom of God.

Evening Prayer (and Service of Light) (504–543)

Evening Prayer comes at the end of the workday. So *commitment* is also an evening theme, but now it is the offering of the day past to God. We reflect on what has happened, offering to God our praise for the gifts of opportunity and love and power we received, and confessing our failures as well. So we commit it all, good and bad, to God, recommitting ourselves at the same time.

The theme of *resurrection* is also celebrated in Evening Prayer, but with a different emphasis. As the daylight fades and darkness enshrouds, we celebrate the light of Jesus Christ that will not be extinguished, even by darkness of death. Evening Prayer is a time of preparation for sleep, and the theme of death and resurrection is even more clearly accented in Prayer at the Close of Day. Here there is a consciousness that we are surrendering our lives into God's keeping in anticipation of our own death, confident that God will "raise us to new life" in the morning as we look toward our resurrection in Jesus Christ.

Evening Prayer also celebrates the theme of *creation*, yet from a different perspective from that of Morning Prayer. To the ancient Hebrews, the day began with sundown, evening and night being times of preparation and rest for the next morning's work. Christians too have recognized that the end of one day is the beginning of the next, and the sleep of night is in preparation for the morning's work.

The Service of Light (BCW 505–513; BCW-DP 43–52)

Since the beginning of civilization, people have lighted lamps as darkness approached. It has always been more than a utilitarian act, for associated with it have been the ancient symbols of darkness—light and fire. In Jewish worship the Sabbath begins with the blessing of the evening light. In Christian worship the lighting of lights as worship begins has continued.

The service of light is a dramatic portrayal of creation and resurrection. The candle symbolizes Christ the Light of the World, who shines in the midst of this world's night. The God who in the darkness of the first creation said, "Let there be light" (Gen. 1:3), in the new creation called forth Christ from the darkness of death. We are reminded that the darkness of chaos, fear, and defeat, though always threatening, is driven back by the coming of the light of Christ.

In early centuries, Christians marked the eve of Sundays and major festivals in cathedrals and parish churches in a special way in the service of light *(lucernarium)*. This ancient service of light is incorporated into the services of the *Book of Common Worship* on all Saturday and Sunday evenings and on the eve of major festivals. The services include the lighting of a candle and carrying it in procession into the midst of the assembly.

The traditional hymn sung at the lighting of the candles at Evening Prayer is the ancient Greek hymn Phos Hilaron, referred to in this resource as the Hymn of Light. Its use dates from very early in Christian history. Basil the Great in the fourth century spoke of the singing of this ancient hymn as a cherished tradition. Three metrical settings (PH 549; PS 165, 167) and one responsorial version (PS 166) are readily available.

The Thanksgiving for Light concludes the portion of Evening Prayer called the Service of Light. The service continues with Psalm 141 and the remainder of the order for Evening Prayer.

The "Canticle/Song of Mary," or the Magnificat (BCW 575; BCW-DP 139; PH 600), is traditionally sung in Evening Prayer. As the darkness deepens and the lamps are lighted, Mary's song (Luke 1:46–55) becomes the church's song. Like Mary bearing the fulfillment of the promise of the ages in her womb, so we wait for the fulfillment of God's promises in the kingdom of God.

The Canticle of Simeon (without refrain) (Luke 2:29–32) is an appropriate alternative to the optional hymn or spiritual at the end of Evening Prayer when there is to be no Prayer at the Close of Day.

Prayer at the Close of Day (BCW 551–561; BCW-DP 113–124)

The "Canticle/Song of Simeon," or the Nunc Dimittis (BCW 576; BCW-DP 140; PH 603–605), is traditionally sung in Prayer at the Close of Day. The aged Simeon had long awaited and watched for the coming of Christ. At last, he held the Savior in his arms. Knowing that the ancient promises were now fulfilled, he was content to die.

Other Services: Midday Prayer (BCW 544–549; BCW-DP 106–111); Vigil of the Resurrection (BCW 562–572; BCW-DP 125–136); Prayers at Mealtime (BCW 592–595; BCW-DP 159–163)

Morning and evening are the principal times for prayer, but certainly not the only ones. Calvin mandated prayer on arising in the morning, before starting work, at meals, and at retiring for the night.[16] In fact, the times of morning and evening prayer will tutor us in praying at other times. To this end, we may also want to have prayer in the middle of the day and at night before going to sleep. Midday Prayer and Prayer at the Close of the Day are sometimes observed along with Morning Prayer and Evening Prayer. However, Midday Prayer is simply an extension of Morning Prayer, and Prayer at the Close of Day is an auxiliary of Evening Prayer.

Midday Prayer picks up themes similar to Morning Prayer. We are conscious of being in God's world and give continual praise for the creation around us, filled with wonders and opportunities. We rejoice throughout the day, celebrating the new life in Christ that enables us to live life fully in his service. And we draw on the power of God's Spirit to fulfill the moral and ethical responsibilities of Christian discipleship.

Preparing and Leading Daily Prayer

There are certain things that should be completed in advance of a service of daily prayer.

1. The leader should be selected or determined. Usually it is helpful for one person to be in charge of a particular service, although many may have different leadership roles.

2. The structure of the service should be determined. The leader will want to decide the specific order, and which optional parts to include. For instance, if it is Evening Prayer, the leader will have to decide whether to include the Service of Light. If so, a suitable candle will need to be secured. If not, will a candle be lighted anyway, and will a hymn be sung? Other choices will be made similarly. Which opening psalm or hymn, which psalms selected from those listed, and which biblical song will be used, are also among other choices to be made.

3. Responsibilities should be assigned to other leaders. For example, who will lead the opening sentences and the psalter; who will read the Scripture, lead the prayer?

4. Those with assigned leadership roles should prepare their individual parts. For instance, the person leading a psalm should decide (in consultation with the leader in charge) how it will be shared—responsorially, antiphonally, sung in a metrical version, or in some other way. The person reading Scripture should, in consultation with the leader in charge, determine which passages in the daily lectionary are to be read, or decide on other appropriate texts. The person leading the prayer may want to solicit concerns (such as, joys and sorrows) to include in prayer, or needs to decide how to invite the voicing of concerns during the service.

5. The room or place should be prepared so that the setting is conducive for worship. Where seating is movable, a decision needs to be made relative to the arrangement of the seats, the location of a reading desk, and the placement of candles if it is Evening Prayer. In the home, the family dinner table may be arranged with an open Bible and candles. Or another place in the home may

be similarly set aside for such prayer services. Other arrangements may be made according to the liturgical season and time of day. Bibles and songbooks or hymnals or other worship resources should be made available.

6. A time should be set. For individuals, this may be a regular time each day; for families it may be at meals or other times in the day; for church groups the times of prayer may be determined in relation to meeting times. In all cases, a regular time clearly set aside for daily prayer works most effectively. The time should be announced to all concerned in advance.

7. Elders, deacons, or other visitors on behalf of the church as well as families or individuals who engage in daily prayer will find most helpful the user-friendly, pocket-sized edition of *Book of Common Worship: Daily Prayer* (Louisville, Ky.: Westminster/John Knox Press, 1993), which contains the "Daily Prayer" section of BCW 112–114, 489–837, 1049–1097.

The Environment for Daily Prayer

Effective services of prayer require a sensitivity to environmental aspects of the actions. The space and all of the visual aspects should contribute to the spirit of prayer.

Worship leaders ought not to dominate in services of prayer. Since the services center on praise and prayer, and unordained as well as ordained persons may lead them, a simple alb (Latin, *alba,* "white") without stole is a fitting vestment for leaders.

Since services of daily prayer are not centered on the Eucharist, and normally do not include preaching, a different kind of worship space is desirable. *Neither* the Lord's table *nor* the pulpit is the focus. A different seating configuration is preferable to one designed to gather the people around the Lord's table or to hear a sermon. Furthermore, a configuration in which everyone faces forward militates against this form of prayer.

If the seating is movable, an effective configuration consists of arranging the seats in rows facing each other across a broad center aisle, with a "reading desk" closing one end of the aisle. For Evening Prayer, candles may be placed beside the reading desk. If the Service of Light is used, the large candle is placed in front of the reading desk between the rows. In this configuration, leaders of worship do not dominate, since they are in the midst of the worshipers (see Diagram A).

Diagram A. Arrangements for Daily Prayer

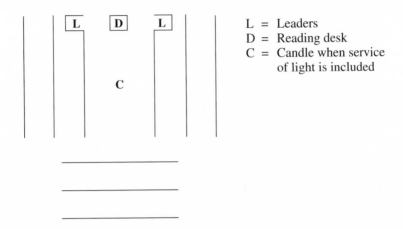

In buildings having a divided chancel in which the choir is divided into two sections facing each other, small groups could gather in the choir stalls for daily prayer. The reading desk is placed at the open end opposite the Lord's table (see Diagram B).

Diagram B. Daily Prayer in Chancel

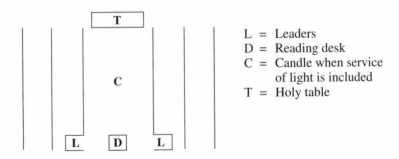

Sight and Sounds in Daily Prayer

For Presbyterians, with a long history of minimizing the sensory, these aspects can be approached both positively and negatively—that which enhances the experience and that which distracts from the experience. Those preparing for worship need to identify, as much as possible, everything that distracts in sight and sound, and develop the most obvious in enhancing the sensory aspects. In worshiping in the same space all of the time, for instance, we become blind to visual things that are distracting to one entering the space for the first time (for example, books piled on top of a piano). Other distractions are extraneous sounds: people gathered in a far corner of the room talking and laughing, oblivious to those gathered across the room engaged in prayer; musicians practicing their parts (failing to recognize that liturgy starts on entering the space set apart for worship); noises in a nearby kitchen by those preparing a simple refreshment after the service, and so forth.

So also sights, sounds, and smell on entering a space set apart for worship need to be prepared to the end that people are drawn quickly into prayer. One's time is too precious to waste it in waiting "for something to happen." A service of daily prayer is to engage people in prayer and contemplation, and this should begin on entry into the space. It is amazing how even Presbyterians, at evening prayer, become hushed when they enter a space "filled" with silence and illumined only by candlelight. It is accentuated when there is the subtle smell of incense, and a focal point that draws one beyond oneself. Then in such a setting, the simple music of Taizé begins to flood the room, in a crescendo as people feel comfortable in joining in song. Music—song—as prayer. Very powerful. In such a setting, casual prayer seems inappropriate: only one filled with metaphoric images, and capturing the rhythm of fine prose, seems fitting. Furthermore, how can anyone simply "read" the text? And, of course, evening prayer is most effective if it occurs as the sun is setting. The setting is of great importance in making the services of daily prayer effective. The remark one hears sometimes, "Oh, I can worship in a barn" simply does not work.

Evening prayer may be the easiest, but there are abundant opportunities for morning prayer as well. Perhaps a very plain room with the morning light streaming through a window, freshly cut flowers beside an icon (no candles, please), probably no incense, leaving that for evening prayer. The gathering music will be somewhat different, but still not so different that it fails to draw people into prayer (remembering that prayer includes praise as well as supplication—no sleepy time music. We are not resting from the labor of the day, but preparing to go out into a day filled with activity).

Sights and sounds call for careful preparation and use. The use of a piano, for example, is often not conducive to services of daily prayer. Taizé music, however, is often effective in daily prayer, probably because it arises principally out of the experience of a community—daily prayer in the Taizé Community. For example, evening prayer and prayer at the close of day could include Taizé music as gathering music, people joining in the singing as they enter the worship space, perhaps flooded with candlelight. Moving into the liturgy is thus gracefully facilitated by singing the Taizé chants.

Even the placement of leadership and the manner in which leaders assume their roles, the manner in which they move about, enhances or distracts from the visual dimensions of prayer. The "babble" of a leader offering comments on what worshipers are doing, or ad-libbing the "script" becomes a distraction. Adding such to our liturgical "vocabulary" would enhance our liturgies.

Service of Light (BCW 505–513; BCW-DP 43–52)

The inclusion of the ancient *Lucernarium,* here titled Service of Light, is appropriate on any day, and is particularly appropriate on Saturday and Sunday evenings, and other occasions when a special service of evening prayer is called for.

The worship space should be very dimly lighted *before* the service begins, the people waiting in silence. The service begins with a large lighted candle being carried in procession into the midst of the assembly gathered in semidarkness. A large unadorned candle is used. Although the candle should be the size of the paschal candle, the paschal candle should not be used, to avoid confusing the symbolism. The person carrying the candle leads the procession, since the candle, as the representation of Christ, is the principal focus of attention. The one carrying the candle sings the verses responsorially with the congregation, during the procession, or after the candle is placed in its stand. The stand for the candle should be placed in the center of the assembly. Alternatively, if a procession is not included, a candle already in place is lighted as the opening sentences are sung. Other candles, artfully arranged, may then be lighted. Musical settings for the Opening Sentences are included in *Daily Prayer: Supplemental Liturgical Resource 5* (Philadelphia: Westminster Press, 1987) in a section between pp. 324 and 375 (nos. 102–109). The Opening Sentences may also be sung to a tone provided in the *Lutheran Book of Worship,* p. 142.

On Epiphany (January 6), the people may be given candles as they enter. These may be lighted from the large candle during the singing of the Hymn to Christ the Light, thereby filling the space with light.

Other lights may be turned up after the candle(s) is lighted. Nevertheless, the light should not be bright, in order to ensure an environment conducive to a meditative spirit.

The Hymn of Light (Phos Hilaron) follows (musical settings in *The Presbyterian Hymnal* and *The Psalter: Psalms and Canticles for Singing* are noted in the heading of the hymn) (BCW 507; BCW-DP 45). The William G. Storey translation set to music (PH 548 and PS 169) is particularly effective in evening prayer, especially when sung without accompaniment (as with all of the music in the service), the tone struck by a handbell.

The Thanksgiving for Light is then sung or spoken (BCW 507–511; BCW-DP 46–51). Some of these prayers derive from ancient sources. Prayer [448] is from the *Apostolic Constitutions* (ca. 380) based on even earlier sources. Prayer [449] is a Jewish berakah of the evening, based on Jewish texts. Prayer [451] is from the Apostolic Tradition of Hippolytus (ca. 215). Musical settings for the thanksgivings for liturgical seasons [452–455] (BCW 510–511; BCW-DP 48–51) may be found in *Praise God in Song*, ed. John Allyn Melloh, S.M., and William G. Storey (Chicago, Ill.: G.I.A. Publications, 1979). When a musical setting for the Thanksgiving for Light is sung, the versicle introducing the prayer is also sung (BCW 507; BCW-DP 46). Musical settings for the thanksgivings also include music for the versicle.

Evening Prayer then continues with the psalmody (BCW 515; BCW-DP 55), as noted in the rubrics (BCW 513; BCW-DP 53). The use of Psalm 141 in Evening Prayer (BCW 512; BCW-DP 51) is rooted in a long tradition. This psalm leads us to reflection and repentance. It is suggested for use on each Saturday and Sunday evening.

Effective musical settings for Psalm 141 abound, including a metrical version (PH 249) and two responsorial settings (PS 144, 145). Employing incense with these settings increases their effectiveness. In fact, since Psalm 141 speaks of our prayers rising like incense before God, it is appropriate that incense be used as the psalm is sung. The Christian use of incense is rooted in Jewish Temple worship. In the Bible, as is clear in Psalm 141, incense symbolizes our prayer ascending before God. Heaven and earth are thus joined in a visible and sensuous way.

An unthreatening way to introduce the use of incense is to place one or two pieces of self-starting charcoal in a metal bowl filled with sand. The bowl is placed on a small stand. The charcoal is lighted in advance of the service so that it is red hot by the time the service begins. As the words from Revelation 8:3–4 and Psalm 141 are sung or said, grains of incense resin are sprinkled on the charcoal. Such use of incense is unobtrusive, yet the fragrance of the incense fills the space. Epiphany is a particularly fitting occasion to use incense, since on that day we recall the visit of the magi, who brought frankincense as a gift for the infant Jesus.[17]

Singing Other Texts

There may be occasions when it is desirable to sing more of the liturgy than only the psalms, hymns, and biblical songs. Certain litanies are effective when sung. The opening sentences and the dismissal could be sung. Such occasions for singing the full service could include vespers on an occasional Sunday evening, or on the eve or evening of major festivals. The singing of Prayer at the Close of Day is an effective way to end the day and is usable after an evening committee meeting, or by a group in a retreat setting. A musical setting is provided in PS 165.

In building a service, careful attention should be given to each detail. Care should also be taken to select musical settings that are in keeping with the mood of the liturgical season, for example, musical settings during Lent will be more restrained than those used during the season of Easter.

Daily Prayer and the Church Year

The services of daily prayer in the *Book of Common Worship* reflect the seasons of the church year while keeping the focus on the morning and evening. Alternative responses and prayers appropriate to the seasons of Advent (BCW 524–528; BCW-DP 65–71), Christmas (BCW 528–530; BCW-DP 71–76), Epiphany (BCW 531–533; BCW-DP 76–81), Lent (BCW 533–537; BCW-DP 81–91), Easter (BCW 538–541; BCW-DP 91–98), and Pentecost (BCW 541–543; BCW-DP 98–104) are provided. The psalms as incorporated into the services are also coordinated to the seasons of the church year and help us see daily prayer in that broader context.

Flexibility of Daily Prayer

In the use of the Psalms and in arranging daily prayer for particular situations, considerable flexibility is needed. Above all, however, it is important to remember the essential elements of daily prayer—psalms, Scripture, prayer, silence. There may be flexibility in their use, but these four elements are the foundational elements on which to build. Obviously, no one resource could be prepared that would be equally useful in every situation without some adaptation. The resources in the *Book of Common Worship* are intended to be adapted from place to place according to the particular need and circumstance. This flexibility is inherent in the history of daily prayer and should still guide us today, with one caveat: remember the essential elements of daily prayer—psalms, Scripture, prayer, and silence. They may be flexible in their use, but they are the critical elements.

Daily prayer does not require leadership by clergy. It is truly the worship of the people, and anyone can lead any prayer service. The sharing of leadership of daily prayer, in fact, gives opportunity for broad participation in planning each prayer service, making it as meaningful as possible for the worshipers. In a family, for instance, the children may assume the leader's role from time to time and have ownership of the worship experience in a fuller way.

Place, time, and size of group also are adaptable. Daily prayer is not confined to any physical setting. It may be scheduled for mealtimes at home around the table, or at the beginning or end of various church meetings in a particular congregation. It can be shared by a few people in any number of locations from schools to offices. Daily prayer may offer the basis for worship in governing bodies or church conferences, delivering them from attempting to provide miniature Sunday worship services each day. The flexibility of daily prayer regarding setting, time, and number witnesses to the fact that Christian prayer is not escapism, but is born in the circumstances of everyday living.

While daily prayer is intended to be a shared experience for two or three or more gathered in the name of Christ, there are times when an individual cannot be present with others. That individual may pray privately using these same resources, with the assurance that his or her prayers are joined with those of others.

Adapting the Prayer Services

When worshiping *alone* one may wish to abbreviate the services as suggested on the outline pages facing the opening of the services for morning, evening, and midday prayer (BCW 490, 504, 544; BCW-DP 26, 42, 105). The basic elements of psalm, Scripture, prayer, and silence may be sufficient. Individuals, however, may sometimes choose to include the opening sentences and dismissal, speaking them aloud, and singing the hymns. While the prayers may be altered from plural to singular, retention of the plural can remind one that though we may be alone when worshiping, we are still part of the fellowship of Christ's church.

In a *family*, the services may be used at meals or other convenient times of the day. Children should be encouraged to take part in the leadership of the services. Younger children may help with lighting the candle, and older children may read Scripture. Leadership of the services may be rotated among family members. Special decorations may be made by family members for particular days or seasons of the year. Familiar hymns or songs may be sung from memory, or from songbooks or hymnals kept handy. The service may be streamlined as desired.

In a *small church group*, the services may also be useful. Morning Prayer may be adapted for the beginning of church staff meetings or other group meetings at church. Evening Prayer may begin the meetings of boards or committees. Or a time may be set aside in advance of regular church group meetings for daily prayer. Meetings may incorporate Midday Prayer or end with Prayer at the Close of Day as appropriate.

Large church groups may also find use for daily prayer services in this format. Annual church meetings or dinner meetings may incorporate Evening Prayer. Longer meetings, such as those of presbyteries or retreats, may make use of several times of worship according to the outline of daily prayer. Particular Scripture readings appropriate to the theme or emphasis of such meetings, or related to the Sunday Lectionary, may be used. Sermons may be preached as the "interpretation" of Scripture.

A welcoming sign of Daily Prayer's possibilities in congregations is the increasing number of churches introducing Taizé prayer into their life together in Christ. The characteristics of Taizé evening prayer, for example, are easily incorporated into Daily Prayer. For instance, (a) conducting evening prayer in candlelight, thus muting the plainness of the environment. (b) Forgoing use of a piano or organ, and using instruments such as flute, guitar, cello, or oboe. (c) Singing the Taizé music as it is intended to be sung, repeatedly to allow it to permeate the minds and spirits of the participants. Too often, after singing something a few times, there is a temptation to think it is time to quit, that all is completed, yet worshipers have not allowed it to imbue their spirit. (d) Allowing the environment to be conducive to prayer: people gather in silence, the music is prayer, the prayers are effectively led, not simply something the leader has been assigned to read. Leaders often wear an alb, symbolic of the egalitarian baptismal garment of all Christians. The current popularity of the Taizé experience can help introduce and even implant Daily Prayer in the life of the church. Out of this kind of communal experience it can be much easier to extend Daily Prayer to personal experience when a communal experience is unavailable.

It is difficult to suggest all of the possibilities because of their limitless number as well as the various circumstances that call for different and creative adaptations. Worshipers are encouraged to develop their own style and particular expressions. It is important to remember that a prayer book is a resource to encourage our prayer life rather than to be used slavishly.

Finally, while these services may be adapted to very brief time constraints, it is helpful if they are not rushed. The Orthodox tradition explicitly states in its Guidance for Morning Prayer: "If the time at disposal is short, and the need to begin work is pressing, it is preferable to say only a few of the suggested prayers, with attention and zeal, rather than to recite them all in haste and without due concentration."[18] Daily prayer should not be driven, but should be relaxed so that the Spirit of God can be given opportunity to prompt our prayers and surprise us.

The Psalms

(BCW 597–783; BCW-DP 165–390)

Singing the Psalms

The core of daily prayer is the Psalter. We follow an ancient tradition of God's people when we pray the Psalms.[1] The Psalms are sung prayer, and across the centuries a rich variety of ways to sing the Psalms has developed. All of these are readily available for use today. A congregation will be richly rewarded if it cultivates the use of each form, incorporating those settings which are in keeping with the spirit of prayer.

Gregorian Chant

Fidelity to the prose text of the psalms, such as those in the *Book of Common Worship* and the Bible, requires a melodic system that accommodates lines and stanzas of varying lengths. In both Christian and Jewish traditions, the prose text of the psalms has been chanted throughout the centuries. Historically, the most widely used system in Western Christianity for singing the psalms has been the Gregorian psalm tones. These melodies have long been associated with the psalms and give them a musical expression that is conducive to sung prayer. They are essentially "sung recitation" (that is, not solo or group *singing* but "musical speaking"), since they are expressive of the inflections of speech. Modern psalm tones share the same principle.

Psalm Tones and Refrains

The eight psalm tones and refrains in the BCW (599–610) are an example. The tones and refrains enable the singing of all of the psalms in the BCW (611–783). A tone and refrain are provided for each type of psalm. Each tone has its own refrain. They range from Tone 1, with its refrain "Alleluia,"

202

through Tone 8, with its refrain "Lord, You Are My Strength, Hasten to Help Me," each tone becoming progressively more somber in nature. The particular refrain assigned to a tone is appropriate to any psalm of the type for which the tone is provided. In order to ensure that the appropriate tone and refrain are used for a particular psalm, the tone to be used is designated in the heading for each psalm. By learning the eight refrains, a congregation will be enabled to sing a familiar refrain to any psalm that may be used. Alternatively, a refrain may be created for a psalm or a canticle by simply intoning the text of the refrain to the first reciting note of the psalm tone being used. See the notes (BCW 599, 600) for an overview of the use of these tones and refrains.

Throughout the *Book of Common Worship*, the psalms and canticles are pointed, enabling them to be sung to psalm tones. A comment, however, needs to be made concerning the shortcomings of the pointing in the *Book of Common Worship* that became evident after the book was published, the result of inadequate testing prior to publication. The *Book of Common Worship* introduced a tie (for example, *labor*) (for example, BCW 616; Ps. 7:9, 12–14) indicating that the syllables above the tie were to be sung to a single note. The objective was to improve the rendition of the text. Whatever the merits might be in the use of a tie, it introduces a complication into an otherwise simple system. Furthermore, in singing, there is a tendency to emphasize the tied syllables, which is invariably inappropriate. Some musicians have corrected this by using white-out to blot out the tie, and have placed a dot over the last syllable above the tie, thereby giving consistency to the rest of the text. This correction removes any confusion that may result when using tones that are commonly available.[2]

Use of the tones in the *Book of Common Worship*, along with those in other readily available resources for psalmody, provide a rich variety for singing the psalms and canticles. Two resources provide instructions for pointing any psalm or biblical text to be used as a canticle: *The Psalter: Psalms and Canticles for Singing* (Louisville, Ky.: Westminster/John Knox Press, 1993), and Hal H. Hopson, *Psalm Refrains and Tones for the Common Lectionary* (Carol Stream, Ill.: Hope Publishing Co., 1988; revised in 1992 to be in harmony with the RCL). These resources are perhaps the best available for introducing a congregation to the use of tones in singing the psalms.

Responsorial Singing

Tones and refrains, such as those in the *Book of Common Worship*, may be used in singing the psalms *responsorially*. That is, a person (called a cantor) or a choir, sings the stanzas of the psalm, and the congregation sings a refrain after each verse or group of verses. Singing the psalms responsorially is the earliest form of singing the psalms in Christian worship, taken into the church from Jewish usage.

To enable singing of them responsorially, the psalms in the *Book of Common Worship* are divided into sections, each followed by a boldface "**R**" (for refrain) printed in red. The "**R**" denotes appropriate places for the congregation to sing a refrain—at the beginning, following particular blocks of verses, and finally to conclude the psalm. Psalm 1 (BCW 611), for example, displays an "**R**" prior to verse 1 (the refrain sung first by the cantor to line it out, with the people repeating it). All then sing the refrain following the cantor's singing of verses 1 and 2; again, after the singing of verses 3 and 4, and finally after verses 5 and 6 are sung to conclude the psalm.

Responsorial psalmody is sprinkled throughout the section of psalms in *The Presbyterian Hymnal* (158–258). In addition, some excellent responsorial psalmody (over 150 settings) drawing from a variety of sources is provided in *The Psalter: Psalms and Canticles for Singing*. Its "Introduction" (pp. 9–22) includes brief substantive essays on "Singing Psalms in Christian Worship," "Responsorial Psalm Singing," and "Resources for Singing the Psalms." When a psalm in the *Book of Common Worship* has a corresponding setting in either PH or PS it is so noted in the heading of the psalm.

Gelineau Psalmody

Another system for singing the psalms responsorially is Gelineau psalmody. Joseph Gelineau, b. 1920, a French Jesuit, based psalm tunes on ancient psalm tones from Gregorian, Ambrosian, and other sources. Since their introduction in 1953 (in French; 1963 in English), Gelineau psalms have found an established place in psalmody. This method depends on a particular text of the psalms, the Grail translation and corresponding melodies. Unlike psalm tones, Gelineau psalmody is organized on an accentual basis, called sprung rhythm. Each line has a prescribed number of accented syllables, even though the total number of syllables in a line will vary. An example of this rhythmic principle is "Three Blind Mice," in which the rhythmic structure of each line is the same (three beats), although the number of syllables in each line varies between three and eleven. The text in Gelineau psalmody follows this accentual structure. In the United States, G.I.A. Publications is the best source for both the Grail translation of the psalms and the Gelineau tones. A valuable booklet explaining the Gelineau system of singing the psalms is J. Robert Carroll, *Guide to Gelineau Psalmody,* (Chicago: G.I.A. Publications, 1979).

Antiphonal Singing

Psalms can also be sung *antiphonally*, in which two segments of the gathered community alternate in singing lines of the psalm. For example, the choir could sing antiphonally with the congregation, or treble clef voices could sing antiphonally with bass clef voices, or one "side" or "portion" of the congregation with the other side or portion, according to the same divisions as in responsorial singing, or simply alternating lines. In singing antiphonally, no refrains are included.

Singing the psalms antiphonally makes possible the use of Hebrew parallelism. For example, Psalm 23 (BCW 634; BCW-DP 209) could begin as follows:

Cantor, choir or group 1: The LORD is my shepherd;
Congregation or group 2: **I shall not be in want.**
Cantor, choir or group 1: You make me lie down in green pastures;
Congregation or group 2: **and lead me beside the still waters.**

Psalms sung to psalm tones are most effective when sung without accompaniment. There is great power and beauty in unison unaccompanied singing. Handbells may be used to establish pitch at the beginning and at appropriate places during the singing.[3]

Accompaniment is provided in most available resources for circumstances where it is felt that organ accompaniment is needed. Use of the organ, however, needs to be restrained. The accompaniment provided with most sets of psalm tones illustrates the restrained style of accompaniment that is required.

Metrical Psalms

For many, the most familiar way to sing the psalms is metrical psalmody. A metrical psalm is a psalm in which the psalm text is paraphrased into poetic meter (usually rhyming) and sung to a hymn tune. Familiar metrical psalms include: Psalm 23, "The Lord's My Shepherd, I'll Not Want" (PH 170); Psalm 95, "O Come and Sing Unto the Lord" (PH 214); Psalm 100, "All People That on Earth Do Dwell" (PH 220); and Psalm 121, "I to the Hills Will Lift My Eyes" (PH 234).

Introduced in the sixteenth-century Reformation, metrical psalms returned the Psalms to the lips of the people. The result was that metrical psalms implanted the spirit of the Psalms deep within Reformed piety. In this period, a metrical doxology also had to be "added," just as with a chanted prose psalm, in earlier centuries, a metrical Gloria Patri was added to give Trinitarian completion. The best-known example of a metrical doxology is LONG METER 8.8.8.8 (LM), in "Praise God, from Whom All Blessings Flow" (PH 591, 592, 593).

Metrical psalms have played an important role; however, they can lose something of their lyrical quality when forced into the restrictions of meter and rhyme.[4] Since by their very nature, metrical psalms are paraphrases of psalm texts, they reflect a manipulation of the text not required in prose translations. The result is that they do not fully convey the original poetic text of the psalms. They often suffer from contorted syntax that obscures a sense of the poetry. Often the tune overpowers the words of the psalm. Furthermore, most congregations are unaware that a metrical psalm is anything other than a hymn. Nevertheless, metrical psalms have a continuing place of importance in psalmody, and should be embraced alongside other ways of singing the psalms.

Metrical psalms are readily available in many hymnals, particularly in *The Presbyterian Hymnal* (158–258), *El Himnario Presbiteriano* (405–441), and *Come, Let Us Worship: The Korean-English Presbyterian Hymnal and Service Book* (394–535). Another source is the Reformed Church in America's *Rejoice in the Lord* (Wm. B. Eerdmans Publishing Co., 1985). An excellent collection of metrical psalms is *The Psalter Hymnal* of the Christian Reformed Church, 1987, most of its texts new versifications in contemporary English, with tunes ranging from Genevan to contemporary.

In examining offerings of metrical psalms, one should analyze the text, comparing it with a prose translation of the psalm, to determine whether it is really a translation of the psalm in meter, or simply a hymn inspired by a psalm. It is not uncommon to find hymns identified as a metrical psalm, though they may be loosely based on a psalm, or simply inspired by a psalm. These merit no claim to being a metered translation of the psalm. In such instances the music may be used as a hymn, but ought not to be graced with an identity as a psalm.

Reading the Psalms

Though, ideally, psalms are sung, in circumstances where that is not possible, they may be read. An overview on ways to read the psalms may be found in the BCW (600).

Numbering of the Psalms

In many psalters prepared for liturgical use, the numbering of the psalms is taken from the Greek Septuagint. This numbering differs from that in the

Hebrew text and the Bibles we use. The result is that in these psalters, many of the psalms have a different number from that to which we are accustomed. For example, Psalm 23 in our Bibles is Psalm 22 in the Greek Septuagint. The following comparative numbering of the two systems will be helpful when different numbering is encountered:

Greek Septuagint	Hebrew
1–8	1–8
9	9–10
10–112	11–113
113	114–115
114–115	116
116–145	117–146
146–147	147
148–150	148–150

Prayers for Various Occasions

(BCW 785; BCW-DP 391–455)

The Great Litany (BCW 787–791; BCW-DP 393–398)

The *Book of Common Worship* has gathered a variety of prayers from diverse sources. The first is The Great Litany, which probably originated in the churches of the East. Originally, the assembly either recited it or sang it following the sermon, in the place reserved for the prayers of the people. In about the ninth century, it became detached from its traditional place and drifted to a position after the entrance, near the beginning of the Orthodox service.

In the Western churches, there developed traditions to guide its use. The rubrics (BCW 787; BCW-DP 393) list the occasions on which it has been considered most appropriate to use The Great Litany: as a separate service on Wednesdays and Fridays of Lent (after Ash Wednesday); on Sundays of Advent and Lent, and at penitential times. Martin Luther used it to conclude the service after the sermon on Sundays when there were no communicants present, thus restoring it to its original position. He published both a corrected Latin version and a German translation of The Great Litany in 1529.[1]

The Great Litany may be used as the chief prayer on other occasions than those prescribed by tradition. It can be used in an abbreviated form, as the rubrics indicate, using only the Prayer of Approach to God (BCW 787; BCW-DP 393) and the Concluding Prayers (BCW 791; BCW-DP 398), with other portions of the Litany in between as may be appropriate to the occasion. The main headings of the Litany are For Deliverance, Recalling Christ's Saving Work, and Intercession (for the Church, Our Country, and for All People). The Lord's Prayer follows the Concluding Prayers, then a final Collect after the Lord's Prayer. There are a variety of Collects to be found in the several services of Daily Prayer in the *Book of Common Wor-*

ship. The one provided (BCW 791; BCW-DP 398) is an altered version of a familiar and beautiful Collect from *The Book of Common Prayer*.

Other Litanies (BCW 792–795; BCW-DP 399–455)

Two other litanies follow, both of more recent origin. Both A Litany of Thanksgiving (BCW 792; BCW-DP 402) and A Litany of Confession (BCW 794; BCW-DP 404) appeared originally in *The Worshipbook*. Either can be used in services of Daily Prayer or at appropriate points in "The Service for the Lord's Day," or as devotional pieces for a small group, session meeting, or other church gathering.

Prayers for Various Occasions (BCW 795–837; BCW-DP 391–455)

The prayers in this section are in traditional prayer form rather than the litany form. There are 122 of them, each numbered by a red numeral, and divided into seven general categories:

Prayers for the World (13)
Prayers for the Natural Order (9)
Prayers for the Church and Other People of Faith (36)
Prayers for the National Life (8)
Prayers for the Social Order (12)
Prayers for the Family and Personal Life (29)
Prayers for the Human Condition (15)

The source of each prayer can be located in Harold M. Daniels, *To God Alone Be Glory: The Story and Sources of the Book of Common Worship* (Louisville, Ky.: Geneva Press, 2003), pp. 240–246.

Prayers for the World (BCW 795–799; BCW-DP 406–411)

Among these prayers are ones for peace, racial diversity, world religions, and times of international crisis.

Prayers for the Natural Order (BCW 799–803; BCW-DP 411–415)

This section includes St. Francis of Assisi's "Canticle of the Sun" (BCW 800, #15; BCW-DP 412, #15).

Prayers for the Church and Other People of Faith
(BCW 803–815; BCW-DP 416–430)

This largest single category includes: prayers for a new church building, meetings of governing bodies, new members, courage in Christ's mission, moderators, church musicians and artists, deacons, elders, ministers, church secretaries and teachers. There is also a prayer in Remembrance of Those Who Have Died. This section concludes with a prayer for Jews and one for Muslims, both prayers of generous and loving spirit.

Prayers for the National Life (BCW 816–818; BCW-DP 430–433)

Prayers for the National Life include prayers for the nation, government leaders, the courts, state and local governments, and the military.

Prayers for the Social Order (BCW 818–822; BCW-DP 434–438)

In Prayers for the Social Order, there is a prayer for those suffering from addictions, and prayers for people in business and industry. There are prayers for cities, students, graduates, and those who suffer for the sake of conscience.

Prayers for the Family and Personal Life
(BCW 822–832; BCW-DP 438–450)

Prayers for the Family and Personal Life include petitions for the newly married, families, single people, parents, children, and people of various ages and stages. There are prayers for a birthday, for the divorced or separated, and for those having difficulty in their marriage. There are prayers for an illness, for healing, and for those who are absent.

Prayers for the Human Condition (BCW 832–837; BCW-DP 450–455)

Prayers for the Human Condition are equally diverse, including persons who are lonely or outcast, poor, bereaved, sexually confused, or—somehow not quite the same—retired! There is a prayer for travelers and one for the unemployed.

A Variety of Uses

These prayers can be used, as appropriate, in personal or household devotions. They can be used in services of Daily Prayer. Some can be used in the

Prayers of the People in "The Service for the Lord's Day." They can be used in pastoral visitation, or visitation by deacons, elders, or parish nurses. Those who pray at circle meetings or youth gatherings or committee meetings or other semipublic occasions will find in this collection helpful materials.

Some will wish to use the prayers exactly as they are. Others will find them useful models as they learn to frame prayers in their own words. There is great value in listening to the concerns, the cadences, the biblical images and allusions that others have used in prayer. Acquaintance with prayers first made by others can help us to get out of the ruts that we so easily fall into, and learn, when we pray in public, to pray more profoundly. When we pray in private, they can lead us to places we have never been before, but need to be.

Christian Marriage

(BCW 839)

Pastoral Challenge and Evangelical Opportunity

Christian marriage presents both challenges and opportunities for ministers and sessions. Some couples, seeing their wedding as a matter of personal expression and the church as a provider of consumer services, approach marriage as customers who expect to be satisfied. Such couples are surprised to discover that the church and its minister are not for hire. Other couples express a sincere desire to have their marriage "blessed by God," but have little concept of marriage as an act of Christian discipleship. They may be perfectly willing to "go through the motions" in order to have a church wedding.

Those who attend the marriage rite are also likely to have mixed expectations. While many may be Christians accustomed to taking an active role in worship, others may find hymns and other elements of Christian liturgy unfamiliar and disconcerting. Some see themselves as "spectators" or "guests," not as members of a worshiping assembly. They are surprised to be invited to take part.

Despite these challenges, the marriage rite also provides opportunities. Sessions can claim their responsibility for overseeing worship and managing church property. Ministers can guide couples toward a deeper Christian understanding of marriage. The rite itself can proclaim the steadfast love of God which makes human faithfulness possible. Guests can become *participants* in a service of worship that affirms marriage as God's gift to humanity and invites those present to "rejoice that marriage is given by God, blessed by our Lord Jesus Christ, and sustained by the Holy Spirit."

In short, the marriage rite, though a challenge, can also become an evangelical opportunity through which the Spirit testifies to God's love in Jesus Christ, opens hearts, and quickens faith.

212

Theological Convictions

Christian theologians have tended to view marriage from two important perspectives. First, marriage is grounded in the doctrine of creation, and thus, the gift of God to all humanity. From this perspective, marriage is not the exclusive possession of the Christian faith; it belongs to the whole of human society. Just as Christians rejoice when the civil government justly rules, they also rejoice when marriage is honored and wisely administered in the public realm. Christians therefore marry by "the authority of the state," participating in the same social reality as all others who marry.

Second, Christians view marriage as a dimension of discipleship. They seek to bring their marriages into accord with the will of God and to allow their relationship with Christ to form the pattern for the covenant of marriage (Eph. 5:21ff.). In baptism, Christians are called to a life of service in the name of Christ, and marriage is one of the settings for such service. The promises of marriage are connected to the promises of baptism, and it is therefore fitting that these promises take place in worship, witnessed by the community of faith.

The rites in the *Book of Common Worship* are services of Christian worship. They express praise and thanksgiving to God for the gift of marriage, and they embody the Trinitarian faith of the Christian community. They assume that at least one of the marriage partners is a Christian. Moreover, they assume that the promises of marriage are to be made in response to the Word of God, in the context of prayer, and in the presence of the community of faith.

Freedom and Form

The marriage rites in the *Book of Common Worship* attempt to preserve a healthy balance between liturgical form on the one hand, and liturgical freedom on the other. Because weddings are particularly subject to being misunderstood as private and family events rather than as services of corporate worship, it is especially important that the marriage rite proclaim the faith of the church, and not merely express the feelings of the couple.

Ministers may invite the couple to participate in the planning of the service, but the popular misconception that the couple can "write their own wedding" assumes that the service belongs only to the bride and groom. As public worship, the marriage rite includes affirmations about the nature of worship and marriage that transcend the concerns of any one couple. The wedding comprises claims and promises, prayers and blessings, which together depict a vision of marriage broader, deeper, and more helpful than any of us can see apart from the witness of the larger church.

The *Book of Common Worship* rites contain, therefore, much that is traditional in language, theological claim, and order, but there is also room for flexibility and adaptation. Authentic worship is "in the Spirit," and the Spirit's action cannot be expressed by any single liturgical pattern. Free prayer, a different sequence of elements, or careful changes in the language of the service are options open to the minister who leads the service.

Flexibility is also built into the rites themselves. Options are given for alternative orders of worship, declarations of intent, vows, and prayers. The choices regarding music and Scripture provide other opportunities for adapting the service to particular needs and settings. Although weddings do not "belong" solely to the bride and groom, it is appropriate for the marriage rite to reflect the couple's ethnic, cultural, and personal situation.

Scripture

Because the marriage rites are services of worship, Scripture has a prominent place in each of them. Christian marriage is a response to the Word of God and is governed by that Word. This is expressed in the rites not only by the fact that Scripture lessons are read in the service but also by the many biblical phrases and allusions found throughout the services.

Several passages in the Bible speak directly about marriage, and others employ marriage as a metaphor for the nature of the kingdom of God (for example, the "wedding" parables, Revelation 19). The biblical witness regarding marriage is not confined, however, to these texts. Any passage containing one of the prominent theological themes of marriage (for example, creation, covenant, blessing, discipleship) illumines the nature of Christian marriage. A selection of Scripture readings traditionally read at weddings appears on BCW 893–902, but many other passages are also suitable. It is strongly recommended that every service of marriage include a brief sermon.

Marriage and the Sacraments

Although marriage is not itself viewed as a sacrament in the Reformed theological tradition, it is firmly connected to both of the sacraments, baptism and the Lord's Supper.

In baptism, Christians are given a new identity and called to a special way of life. Christians who marry reaffirm their baptismal calling as disciples. The oneness of husband and wife and the steadfast promises they make to each other reflect the unity and love between Christ and the church (Eph. 5:32).

The Lord's Supper is the Sacrament of Christ's continual presence, feeding, and sustaining the people of God. At the Lord's Table, Christians are called to serve Christ by serving each other and the world, a call that encompasses every relationship, including marriage. Christ is present in the Lord's Supper, and the promises of marriage cannot be kept nor the responsibilities of marriage fulfilled without Christ's continual and strengthening presence.

Including the Lord's Supper

It is sometimes quite fitting for the marriage service to include a celebration of the Lord's Supper. When deciding whether to include the Supper in a marriage service, the session should consider these factors:

1. There should be no hint of a "private ceremony."
2. The Lord's Supper should be observed only in the context of a full service of worship, including the reading and preaching of the Word.
3. Because the congregation at a wedding may include both non-Christians and Christians who are not comfortable receiving Communion in traditions other than their own, the presider should take special care to be hospitable without compromising the Supper as the feast of the baptized.
4. A statement such as the following may appear in a printed order of service and/or spoken by the minister: *The Sacrament of the Lord's Supper is open to all baptized Christians. All present are invited to take part in this service as fully as your conscience allows.*
5. The service may include oral or printed instructions to worshipers on how to take part in the Sacrament (see pp. 33–40, 61–69).

Participation in Worship

The *Book of Common Worship* rites are built on the conviction that witnesses to a marriage are part of a worshiping community. Therefore the rites begin with a call to worship and provide several opportunities for congregational participation. The congregation sings the hymns of faith and assumes a commitment to support the couple in their covenant vows. The congregation may also join the minister in saying, "Those whom God has joined together, let no one separate."

Printed orders of service that provide an outline of the rite and the text of congregational responses are especially helpful at weddings. Printed orders may include the Lord's Prayer, the words of hymns or their number in the hymnal, the chapter and verse of Scripture readings, and instructions for receiving Communion.

The Roles of the Minister and Other Leaders

The primary function of the minister at a wedding is to lead the people in worship. The minister does not "perform the marriage," but rather leads the service of worship during which the couple, through their vows, bind themselves to each other as husband and wife. Ministers do not function in weddings on their own authority, or merely as agents of the state, but as ministers of the Word and Sacrament in the church, subject to the vows of ordination.

Other leaders may also take part in weddings, including ushers, musicians, and readers of Scripture. Their role is to assist the congregation in corporate worship, not to perform for the congregation's entertainment.

The Role of the Congregation

The congregation assembles in worship for the reasons given in the Statement on the Gift of Marriage: to give thanks for the gift of marriage, to witness the couple's covenant promises, to surround them with prayer, and to ask God's blessing upon them.

Selecting the Appropriate Rite

The *Book of Common Worship* offers three marriage rites from which to choose:

Rite I: A Service for General Use (BCW 840–851) is a brief service that is suitable in almost every setting. This service can, if necessary, proceed without hymnbooks or printed orders of service. It can be used in the regular worship space, in a home, out-of-doors, or in other locations.

Rite II: A Service Based on the Service for the Lord's Day (BCW 852–881) contains an ordering of the elements that is very much like that found in the classical pattern of Sunday worship. It can be used when the wedding is to be incorporated into Lord's Day worship or on any day when the full order of Christian worship is desired. The service includes the option of celebrating the Lord's Supper.

Rite III: A Service Recognizing a Civil Marriage (BCW 882–892) is to be used when a couple, having been previously married in a civil ceremony, wish to have their marriage promises witnessed by the community of faith. Except for a few changes in language, made to conform to the fact that the couple are already legally married, this service is the same as Rite I.

The decision of which rite to use is the responsibility of the minister, but in most cases this choice can best be made in consultation with the couple.

The Wedding Rites and Pastoral Care

People shape liturgies. Liturgies, in turn, shape people. The liturgy is not only the instrument for worship, it also teaches. Ministers should include, as a part of their program of premarital counseling, a review of the marriage rite itself. This can provide the opportunity both for the couple to help shape the marriage service and for the minister to teach the church's convictions concerning marriage. Because the marriage rite expresses, in liturgical language, the basic theological affirmation of the church in regard to marriage, it is an effective instrument for teaching.

For example, having been formed by a culture of self-expression, couples may ask for works of poetry or literature, both religious and secular, to be read at their wedding. Premarital counseling can provide an occasion for the minister to explain that a wedding is not a platform for self-expression, but is, as worship, an offering to God.

A copy of the marriage rite and the text of the sermon preached at the wedding may be given to the couple after the service. Reading and remembering the service can be for the couple an act of reaffirmation.

Some couples seeking marriage will have been previously married, and then divorced. The high view of marriage and the permanence of the vows expressed in the marriage rite provide the minister an opportunity to discuss the love and forgiveness of God. No one is fully able to keep the marriage vows, and every married person depends on the grace of the triune God, who is faithful even when we are not, to sustain the covenant of marriage.

The pastoral relationship developed with the couple need not end with the wedding. The minister may find it helpful to talk with the couple during the first few weeks of their marriage, to make a pastoral visit on the occasion of the first anniversary of their wedding, and to provide special programs of education, counseling, and support for the newly married.

Preparation for the Marriage Rite

Preparation for the marriage rite should be made in at least the following four areas:

1. *Session Approval.* The marriage service is under the supervision of the session and the direction of the minister. While it is usually desirable to delegate to the minister most of the responsibility for the specific planning of each wedding, sessions should develop general guidelines for weddings, including policies on such matters as music, flowers and other decorations,

photography during the service, fees, and other matters. (See suggested list, pp. 230–31.) In most cases, the minister will be responsible for seeing that the session's policies are followed.

2. *Legal Requirements*. The laws regarding marriage vary from state to state. Ministers need to become familiar with the legal requirements for clergy in their localities and take care to fulfill them.

3. *Preparing the Couple*. The minister shall meet with the couple to provide pastoral care and to assist them to prepare for their marriage. Marriage preparation may take the form of meetings with the minister, referral to pastoral counselors, or participation in classes led by ministers, counselors, or married couples who have been trained to provide this ministry. Part of this preparation should include reviewing the marriage liturgy itself.

4. *Rehearsal*. In most cases, the couple and other members of the wedding party should have an opportunity to rehearse their responsibilities for the service. Not only does this prepare and reassure the participants, it also gives the minister an occasion to interpret, for the full wedding party, the character of the marriage service as worship. Even in those cases when a wedding "director," or "consultant," is involved, the minister is in charge of the rehearsal. (See "Suggestions for Conducting a Wedding Rehearsal," p. 231.)

Ordering the Service

Wedding customs vary, and notions of "the proper way" for a wedding to proceed may have more to do with etiquette and fashion than with theologically informed worship. The minister is in the best position to distinguish between what is essential, what is distracting, and what is of little importance to the wedding as a service of worship, and is responsible for shaping the liturgy accordingly.

Children in the Service

As full members of the household of God, children are welcome in Christian worship. Children participate, however, at the level of their own development. If children are in the wedding party, they should not be assigned roles that exceed their maturity. If they serve as flower girls, ring bearers, and so forth, they should be old enough to carry out their roles without suffering exploitation or causing distraction.

In cases where the couple wish to involve children from a previous marriage, the service should not contain symbolic actions which imply that the children are "marrying" their stepparent. For example, the groom should not present gifts to the bride's children after giving a ring to the bride. It is appropriate, however, for the minister to offer prayer for the new household created by the marriage, asking God's blessing on the children by name.

Authenticity in Worship

Insincere actions and empty symbols are inappropriate for worship. Two examples:

1. A couple wishes to have a child serve as a ring bearer during an entrance procession. The "rings" to be carried in the procession, however, are ceremonial substitutes, not the rings the couple will give and receive as a sign of the marriage covenant. Sham rings are not appropriate.

2. A couple who has been married in a civil ceremony asks the minister to use Rite I in order to give the impression that they are not already married. Rite III remains the appropriate service for this couple.

Photography and Video Recording

Worshipers should not take photographs or operate video equipment during the service. This expectation can be conveyed by a brief announcement, by a notice near the entrance of the sanctuary, or by a note in the printed order for worship (for example, *Worshipers are kindly requested to refrain from using photographic equipment during the marriage service. Thank You!*).

If the session allows designated photographers or videographers, they should be given explicit guidelines. For instance, many sessions forbid flash photography and restrict the movement of video camera operators during the service. If the service is being disrupted by photography or videography, it is the minister's prerogative to suspend the liturgy until it can proceed without disruption.

Time and Setting for Marriage

Although true worship can take place anywhere, the site where the Christian community is accustomed to gather for worship should be the setting for Christian marriage. "The Service for the Lord's Day," which takes place in most congregations on Sunday morning, is a particularly appropriate context for Christian marriage (as in sixteenth-century Reformed churches).

Sessions should reserve Holy Week as a period for the church to give its full attention to the mystery of the redemption and Easter Sunday as a day for exclusive celebration of the resurrection. Moreover, because of Lent's character as a penitential season and a period for baptismal preparation, and in accord with the long tradition of the church universal, sessions should seriously consider choosing to refrain from celebrating marriage rites during Lent. Sessions may also choose not to schedule marriages during other days or seasons in the life of the church.

Before agreeing to lead a wedding, the minister should determine whether its setting is suited for Christian worship. The minister who leads a wedding out-of-doors, in a home, in a commercial establishment, or in some other setting should adapt the service to its setting. For instance, congregational singing can be omitted because of poor acoustics or the lack of suitable musical accompaniment, and the shorter form of the prayer following the vows can be used.

Music and the Wedding

The music selected for the wedding should embody the same high standards applied to the music chosen for worship generally. Wedding music should focus on God and emphasize the faith of the Christian community rather than romantic love or sentimentality.

The minister has the final authority for the ordering of worship and the selection of music. The minister should consult with the church musicians and others with musical expertise regarding the best available music for use in the marriage rite. Musical standards and aesthetic judgment are subjective, but the trained musician can be helpful regarding standards of musical excellence and theological integrity. Ordinarily, musicians on the church staff should play for the marriage service, but they may defer to a guest musician if they choose.

Suggestions of musical selections suitable at various places in the marriage rite are available in the current edition of "Weddings and Funeral Music" prepared by the Presbyterian Association of Musicians (Presbyterian Church (U.S.A.), 100 Witherspoon Street, Louisville, KY 40202–1396), with an emphasis on music that is within the scope of small- and medium-sized congregations. This list is not exhaustive; many other compositions are also appropriate for marriage services.

Commentary on the Marriage Rites

Rite I: A Service for General Use (BCW 841–851)

Entrance (BCW 843). The purpose of the entrance rite is simply to bring the bride, groom, and other members of the wedding party to a position in front of the minister and in view of the congregation, who will witness the marriage promises. This may be accomplished in *many* ways, for instance:

1. The bride and the groom enter together.
2. The entire wedding party gathers in view of the congregation, without ceremony.
3. The parents of the bride accompany the bride and the parents of the groom accompany the groom in procession.
4. In those churches where it is the custom for worship to begin with the bearing of a cross in procession, the minister and wedding party enter in this order: cross, minister, attendants, parents, bride, and groom.
5. The minister leads the groom and his attendants to the front of the church, then, leaving them in place, the minister goes to the back of the church and leads the bride and her attendants to the front in this order: minister, bride (and her father), maid of honor, other bridal attendants.
6. The minister, groom, and the groom's attendants enter from a side door and stand in the front of the church, facing the congregation. The bride's attendants enter in procession from the back of the church, the maid of honor entering last. The bride enters. The bride may or may not be accompanied by her father or other escort.
7. Another practice suitable to the particular circumstances may be used.

If the father of the bride accompanies her during the entrance, he may take leave of her when the two of them arrive at a position near the minister. Alternatively, he may stand with her until the affirmation of the families is completed.

The bride and groom may face the minister with their backs to the congregation, or they may face the congregation, with the minister standing nearby.

If music is used during the entrance, it should be suitable for worship, directing attention to God and expressing the faith of the church. As an alternative to "processional music," the congregation may sing a hymn. It is appropriate for the congregation to stand for the whole of the entrance rite, but the custom of standing only for the bride's entrance has no theological warrant.

A suggestion for placement of the wedding party:

(M)

Attendants (B) (G) Attendants

Bride's Parents   Groom's Parents

_____ _____
_____ _____
_____ _____

(M)

Attendants (B) (G) Attendants

| Parents and | Parents and |
| other family | other family |

(M) = Minister

(B) = Bride

(G) = Groom

Sentences of Scripture (BCW 841). Three selections from Scripture are available to serve as a call to worship, each alluding to an important theological theme related to marriage. The minister may use one of these or some other passage from Scripture to call the people to worship.

Statement on the Gift of Marriage (BCW 842). These words, spoken by the presiding minister, serve three purposes: (1) They remind the congregation of why they have gathered. (2) They provide a summary of what the church understands about marriage biblically and theologically by announcing the promises and actions of God in regard to marriage. (3) They provide ethical instruction regarding the responsibilities of marriage, not only for the bride and groom but also for the whole congregation.

"We gather . . ." The opening paragraph reminds the congregation that they are not passive spectators at the wedding. Theirs is to be an active role. They are to worship God, giving thanks for the gift of marriage. They are to pray for the couple and to express the support of the community of faith by witnessing the couple's vows.

"God created us male and female . . ." Biblically, marriage has its origins in God's creation of human beings as male and female, to provide for them steadfast companionship and mutual support (Gen. 2:18–25; Mark 10:7–8).

"God gave us marriage for the full expression of the love between a man and a woman." This is the first of three statements that begin with the refrain, "God gave us . . ." Marriage, which from a sociological perspective is a product of human society, is also understood theologically to be a good and gracious gift of God. A wedding is the only service of worship in the life of the church where sexuality and sexual union are major themes, and the phrase "the full expression of the love between a man and a woman" acknowledges

this fact. In the lifelong covenant of marriage, the sexual relationship between a man and a woman finds its richest physical, emotional, and spiritual expression. "They are no longer two, but one flesh" (Mark 10:8). The statement "In marriage a woman and a man belong to each other" further points to the depth of the marriage covenant and echoes the word of Paul (1 Cor. 7:3–7) regarding the sexual mutuality of marriage.

"God gave us marriage . . . for the birth and nurture of children." This statement affirms the role of marriage in sustaining humankind and the place of marriage as a basic unit of ordered human society. The birth and nurture of children are essential for the continuation of the human race and are an expression of hope and confidence in God's providential care. Since this statement is part of a general declaration about the church's understanding of marriage, it is appropriate to say these words even if the particular couple being married, for reasons of health, age, or personal choice, are unlikely to have children themselves. At this point in the service, the theological affirmations are about marriage in general. Later in the rite the language will become more focused on the specific marriage being celebrated this day.

"God gave us marriage as a holy mystery . . ." This statement is based on Ephesians 5:31–33, in which the relationship between a husband and a wife is presented as a profound mystery, analogous to the relationship between Christ and the church. This does not imply that the husband is superior to the wife but their relationship is one of mutual love and self-giving. Marriage points beyond itself to the redemptive activity of God in Christ.

"In marriage, husband and wife are called to a new way of life . . ." Here the church affirms that marriage is a form of vocation. In baptism, all Christians are called to a new way of life, and Christians who are married are to express that baptismal call in and through their marriages.

"We rejoice . . ." The closing statement is a Trinitarian affirmation of the presence and blessing of God in marriage and a call to the community to respond by upholding the honor of marriage (Heb. 13:4).

Prayer (BCW 843). This brief prayer rejoices that God is faithful in keeping promises, and seeks the presence of the Holy Spirit for the couple as they make their promises. Marriage vows are radical promises, promises that cannot be kept relying on human resources alone. This prayer invokes the sustaining and strengthening power of God's Spirit.

Declarations of Intent (BCW 843). This element replaces the betrothal vows found in many older services of marriage. The church has declared, in the Statement on the Gift of Marriage, its convictions about marriage, and now, in the light of this understanding, the man and the woman are asked if they wish to be married. By responding, "I do," the bride and groom indicate that they come as free, discerning, and willing partners to the covenant of marriage.

Two choices for the Declaration of Intent are given. One specifically connects marriage to baptism and thus assumes that both bride and groom are baptized. The other does not make the baptismal connection explicit and, while it is suitable for any wedding, it should always be used when one of the marriage partners is not baptized. The same declaration should be used for both the man and the woman.

The rite calls for the minister, both here and at the point of the marriage vows, to address the man first and then the woman. This order is no doubt shaped by custom and cultural considerations, and there is no theological basis for it. The minister may use one ordering for the declaration of intent and then reverse the sequence for the marriage vows.

Affirmations of the Families (BCW 844). This element provides opportunity for the families of the bride and groom to express their love for the couple, to offer their blessing to them, and to pledge their support for the marriage. The Affirmations of the Families emphasize not only the willingness of the families to bless the couple but also their readiness to release them into this new relationship.

People are not property. There are therefore no provisions in this service for "giving away the bride." This custom had its roots in the understanding that every woman must belong to some man. At marriage a woman was delivered by her father (or some other male guardian) to the hand of the (male) minister, who placed her hand in the hand of the groom. The *Book of Common Worship* rite affirms that the man and woman "freely give themselves to each other."

The minister addresses the families of the bride and groom in a way deemed appropriate. Depending on the circumstances, the question may be addressed only to the parents of the bride and groom or to other members of the family. For instance:

1. "John and Mary, do you give . . . ?"
2. "Do you, the parents of Mary, give . . . ?"
3. "Do you, the members of the Smith family, give . . .?"

Two responses are provided as alternatives. The minister may prompt the families by saying, "You may say, 'We do.'" It is preferable that both families, if present, give affirmations. If the parents are standing with the bride and groom, they may be seated among the congregation after the affirmations. If the parents are sitting when the minister addresses them, it is appropriate for them to stand to make their affirmations.

The Affirmations of the Families may not be appropriate for some weddings, for instance, in the case of a couple marrying after divorce or a couple marrying in middle age. The minister may decide, for pastoral reasons, to omit this portion of the service, and to invite the families of the bride and groom to join in the Affirmation of the Congregation.

Affirmation of the Congregation (BCW 844). Marriage is the concern of the whole community, and depends on the community's support. In this element, the congregation is given the opportunity to voice its support and to pledge continuing responsibility toward the marriage. The congregation may remain seated or may stand. The minister may prompt the congregation by saying, "You may say, 'We will.'"

Scripture and Sermon (BCW 844–845). Christians seek in their marriages, as in the rest of life, to be obedient to the Word of God. Now God's Word is proclaimed in Scripture and sermon. Scripture lessons particularly suitable for weddings are included (BCW 893–902), but many other scriptural texts, especially those that refer to the praise of God, the love of Christ, the calling of Christians, and the disciplines of the Christian life, are fitting.

The reading from Scripture may be preceded by the singing of a psalm, hymn, spiritual, or anthem, and a prayer for illumination. Members of the family, the wedding party, or other members of the congregation may serve as readers.

In most cases the Scripture readings should be followed by a brief sermon. The sermon should be based on one or more of the readings, and, while acknowledging the special circumstances of the occasion and the needs of the bride, the groom, and their families, it should be addressed to the whole congregation.

In most settings it is appropriate for the wedding party to sit for the reading of Scripture and sermon. This action reiterates that they are members of the worshiping congregation and helps to focus attention on the Word read and preached. Following the sermon, the wedding party stands to resume the positions they had after the entrance.

Vows (BCW 845). The essence of the marriage rite is the making of promises. The man and the woman make public promises to each other in the context of promises made by their families, promises made by the congregation, and, most important, promises made by God. The promises contained in the marriage vows are phrased in the present tense, but they are oriented toward the future. They are therefore expressions of hope as well as of faith and love.

Because the marriage of a man and a woman is a sign of the covenant relationship between Christ and the church, the promises made in marriage are

expressed in unequivocal language. The man and the woman pledge themselves to each other "as long as we both shall live." This lifelong commitment
is a sign both of God's steadfast covenant and of the high responsibilities of
marriage.

This act of covenant-making must be both visible and audible. The minister and the couple may move to another location (for example, up into the
chancel area) in order to give visual emphasis to this portion of the service.

The bride and the groom face each other, joining their right hands as they
speak their vows. Either of two customs may be followed here.

1. The couple joins their right hands, keeping them joined through both
   vows.
2. The one saying the vow takes the right hand of the other, releasing the
   hand after the vow is spoken.

During the rehearsal, the couple should be encouraged to speak their vows
clearly and loudly enough to be heard by the congregation. It is the custom in
some places for the congregation to stand during the speaking of the vows. In
some settings, however, standing prevents many members of the congregation from seeing and hearing the couple. If this is the case, the congregation
should remain seated.

Though the text of the rite preserves the traditional custom of presenting
the man's vow first, the minister may, as noted on page 224, employ one order
for the declarations of intent and reverse the order for the vows.

The common practice is for the minister to speak small sections of the vows
and for the couple, in turn, to repeat the words spoken by the minister. This
practice is better than the couple memorizing and reciting the vows, not only
because lines are easily forgotten under stress, but also because the vows
themselves do not belong to the bride and groom. The vows of Christian marriage express the church's long liturgical tradition and centuries of careful
reflection.

Two forms are given for the vows. The same form of the vow is used for
both the bride and the groom, thus affirming the mutuality and equality of
both in the marriage covenant.

Exchange of Rings (or Other Symbols) (BCW 846). The exchanging of
rings, or other symbols, serves as a visible and tangible confirmation of the marriage promises. Since the exchanging of gifts simply underscores the promise-
making that has already taken place, it is an optional element in the service.

Most Americans are familiar with rings as the symbols that are exchanged.
In some geographical locations and in some ethnic traditions, other symbols,

such as coins or food, are exchanged. With minor changes in language, this element can be adapted to embrace these other symbols.

Customs vary as to who presents the rings at this point in the service. The most straightforward action is for the bride to carry the groom's ring and the groom the bride's. When this is the case, the minister addresses the couple, saying, "What do you bring as the sign of your promise?" Then the couple either gives the rings to the minister for the blessing of the rings, or holds them while the minister says the blessing. If others carry the rings, they may give them to the minister or the couple for the blessing, and the question "What do you bring . . . ?" may be omitted. In any case, the focus of the ring blessing is not on the rings themselves but on the relationship between the man and the woman signified by the rings.

Two texts are presented in the rite. The first involves a statement by the one giving the ring, followed by a response from the one receiving the ring. The second text does not call for a verbal response.

Both texts end with the traditional Trinitarian formula, "in the name of the Father, and of the Son, and of the Holy Spirit." This reaffirms that Trinitarian grounding of marriage which has already been expressed in the Statement on the Gift of Marriage. The Trinitarian formula can be omitted, however, and should be omitted for *both* bride and groom when one of the marriage partners is not a Christian.

Prayer (BCW 847). After the marriage promises have been made (and, if desired, confirmed by the exchange of rings or other gifts), the minister prays, seeking God's grace for the couple, for all marriages, for the community, and for the church's mission. Unless the congregation kneels for this prayer, it is not appropriate for the couple to do so.

The rite provides two prayers as models. Each can be modified to fit the circumstances. The first prayer includes a section, enclosed in brackets, regarding the gift of children. In some situations, because of the age or health of the couple, or because of other pastoral considerations, this section of the prayer should be omitted. If the couple brings children to their marriage, it is appropriate to include petitions for them. Extemporaneous prayer is also appropriate.

Lord's Prayer (BCW 850). It is better for the whole congregation to pray aloud or sing the Lord's Prayer than for it to be sung by a soloist or a choir. Prayers sung by soloists or choirs can, of course, be understood as prayers offered on behalf of all the worshipers. The Lord's Prayer, however, is widely known, and provides a good opportunity for active congregational participation. Because English versions of the Lord's Prayer vary, it is helpful to provide the congregation the text of the version being used.

Announcement of Marriage (BCW 850). The minister announces to the congregation that the man and the woman are married by virtue of the vows they have made to each other. The words, "Those whom God has joined together let no one separate," based on Mark 10:9, are said either by the minister or by the minister and the congregation together. An appropriate gesture to accompany these words is for the couple to join both hands and for the minister to place his or her hands around the couple's. Another gesture is for the minister to remove the stole he or she is wearing and use it to wrap the couple's joined hands, symbolizing that they have been "joined together." Neither gesture is required.

Charge to the Couple (BCW 851). Here the minister charges the couple, using words of Scripture to remind them of the ethical responsibilities of marriage. Two texts, both based on the language of Colossians 3, are given as alternatives. The reference to crowning in the first option has a rich symbolic association with marriage.

Blessing (BCW 851). The blessing is intended both for the couple and for the congregation. Two textual options are given. The first is an adaptation of the traditional Aaronic blessing from Numbers 6:24–26. The second is built on a Trinitarian structure. The congregation stands for the blessing.

The blessing marks the conclusion of the service. As a concession to tradition, the couple may share a kiss after the benediction, but this action has no theological warrant. The wedding party may leave along with the other members of the congregation, or they may leave in procession as music is played or sung. If the mothers and grandmothers of the bride and groom or others are escorted out of the church, care should be taken not to prolong this action.

Incorporating Other Customs. In many cultures other customs are included in weddings. In such places as Hawaii, Mexico, and India, garlands of flowers are hung around the necks of the bride and groom or a large circle of flowers is placed on their shoulders. In other cultures, crowns of flowers (chaplets) are placed on the heads of the bride and groom. In Eastern churches, the bride and groom are crowned as the king and queen of the family—a symbolic reference to the presence of the kingdom of God in the world.

The service may incorporate these or other symbols, providing they do not distract from the central actions of the rite: the exchange of promises and the holding of hands (and, if desired, the exchange of rings). If other ceremonies symbolic of the marriage bond are used, they should follow the announcement of marriage.

Not all customs, however, enhance the marriage rite. For instance:

1. The bride and groom each bears a lighted candle with which they light a single candle. Whatever meaning this action is intended to convey, it adds little to the symbolic actions that have already taken place.
2. The minister introduces the couple to the congregation as "Mr. and Mrs. John Smith." This announcement abrogates the equality of the marriage covenant so carefully conveyed in the rest of the rite and is redundant. The minister has already pronounced the couple "husband and wife."

Contrived or misleading actions, such as these, should be avoided.

Rite II: A Service Based on the Service for the Lord's Day (BCW 852–881)

This rite is based on the *ordo* of "The Service for the Lord's Day" (p. 14). It may serve as a wedding service, per se. It may also serve as the Sunday service at the place and time that is customary for the congregation. As a Service for the Lord's Day, it includes all the elements for a liturgy of Word and Sacrament, placing emphasis on theological themes integral to marriage. For example:

1. The alternative texts for the call to worship emphasize the themes of joy and love.
2. The call to confession, from Jeremiah 31, and the prayer for illumination present the covenant image.
3. One of the alternative texts for the prayer of confession acknowledges that "we have broken the promises we have made to you and to one another."
4. The Great (Prayer of) Thanksgiving (to be used when the Lord's Supper is included) and the Prayer of Thanksgiving (to be used when the Lord's Supper is omitted) praise God for the gift of marriage.
5. The prayer after the Lord's Supper employs the biblical imagery of the marriage feast.

Following the sermon (and, if desired, a creed and a congregational song), the bride, groom, and other members of the wedding party present themselves in front of the congregation. This does not require an elaborate procession, and may be accomplished while the congregation sings.

The service proceeds in the same manner as Rite I through the charge to the couple. At this point there are several options for completing the service:

1. The service may continue following the Lord's Day pattern including the Lord's Supper. The Blessing for the Couple is followed by Prayers of the

People, the Offering, Preparation of the Table, the Invitation to the Lord's Table, the Great Thanksgiving, the Breaking of the Bread, the Communion of the People, the Prayer after Communion, Congregational Singing, a Charge, and a General Blessing.

If the Great Thanksgiving provided (BCW 869–872) is not used, other eucharistic prayers from the BCW, especially Prayers B and C (BCW 126–132) with the Preface for Christian Marriage (BCW 137), may be used.

2. The service may follow the pattern of a Lord's Day service that does not include the Lord's Supper. The Blessing of the Couple (BCW 886–887) is followed by Prayers of the People (BCW 99–120), the Offering, a Prayer of Thanksgiving, the Lord's Prayer (BCW 877–879), Congregational Singing, a Charge, and a General Blessing.

3. The service may conclude following the Blessing of the Couple (BCW 866) with the Charge and Blessing of the People (BCW 880–881).

Rite III: A Service Recognizing a Civil Marriage (BCW 882–892)

This rite, designed for use when the couple have been married in a civil ceremony, is almost identical to Rite I, and it can be conducted following the suggestions given for that rite. The following changes in the language of Rite I reflect the fact that the couple are already married:

1. The statement of marriage indicates that the couple "have been married according to the law of the state."
2. The couple are called "in faith" to make their promises to each other "as husband and wife."
3. The vows state, "You are my wife (husband)."

Some Questions to Address in a Session Marriage Policy

1. Who may apply for marriage? Must both bride and groom be church members? Must both be Christians?

2. When and how should the request for marriage be made?

3. When may weddings take place? Are weddings allowed during certain liturgical seasons, such as Advent, Lent, and Holy Week?

4. Must the wedding take place in the sanctuary? If not, what other settings are approved?

5. May other Christian congregations use the sanctuary for weddings in their own traditions? May congregations of other faiths use the sanctuary?

6. Is the couple required to undergo marriage preparation?

7. Who is authorized to conduct marriage preparation? The pastor? Other counselors?

8. Who may conduct marriages on church property? Only the pastor? Other clergy? Civil authorities, such as justices of the peace and notaries?

9. What music is allowed? Who approves musical selections? May guest organists or instrumentalists be involved? May prerecorded music be used?

10. May the sanctuary be decorated? Where may flowers and candle stands be placed?

11. What precautions must be observed to avoid damage from dripping candles, tacks driven into pews, and tape attached to painted surfaces? When must decorations be removed following the wedding?

12. May symbols of the faith, such as the Communion table, font, and pulpit, be moved from their customary places or obscured by candles and decorations?

13. In addition to the holding of hands, and the giving and receiving of rings, may other symbolic actions take place, such as lighting a Unity Candle?

14. May photographers and/or videographers operate during the service? What guidelines apply to prevent interruptions of, or distraction from, the service of worship?

15. May children be members of the wedding party? Is there a minimum age?

16. May rice, confetti, birdseed, or other matter be thrown on church property?

17. May alcoholic beverages be served on church property?

18. What fees or honoraria are expected? When and to whom shall they be paid?

19. Has the session designated a person or a group to serve as agents of hospitality for weddings? Some churches have wedding committees who help couples with planning, and assure that the sessions' guidelines are followed.

Suggestions for Conducting a Wedding Rehearsal

These suggestions are for a rehearsal in a church sanctuary with a musician present, but in many cases it is not necessary for the musician to attend the rehearsal. Other adjustments should be made to these suggestions, depending on the circumstances.

1. All members of the wedding party assemble in the front pews. The families of the bride and groom sit in their designated places during the wedding.

2. The minister opens with prayer, introduces himself or herself, and welcomes everyone on behalf of the session.

3. The bride and groom introduce their family, their attendants, and the other friends who are present.

4. The minister reviews any session policies that apply to the wedding party, for instance, the use of alcohol, decorating the sanctuary, and so forth.

5. The wedding party arrange themselves in the places they will take following the entrance rite and just before the call to worship.

6. The wedding party practice the mode of entering (or leaving) the sanctuary. This often involves a procession. The musician plays the music appointed for the entrance rite.

7. After the entrance (leaving) has been mastered, the wedding party practice the exit (entrance) rite with the appropriate music.

8. After the entrance and the exit have been mastered, the wedding party resume the positions they had following the entrance rite.

9. If hymns are to be sung, the wedding party practice them. The minister provides hymn sheets for this purpose, which are carried by the wedding party at the wedding. If there is no other music to be rehearsed, the musician may leave. (*This is a gesture of courtesy to busy church musicians.*)

10. The minister explains what happens in the call to worship, the statement on the gift of marriage, the prayer, the declarations of intent, the affirmations of the families, and the affirmation of the congregation. The family and wedding party practice their responses.

11. If the wedding party are to sit during the reading and preaching of the Word, they practice moving to their seats for this portion of the service.

12. The readers practice reading the lessons from the pulpit Bible. If a public-address system is used, it is adjusted so that the readings can be heard clearly at the wedding.

13. If they have been seated for the readings, the wedding party resume the positions they had following the entrance rite.

14. The minister explains what happens during the vows, and reads the words of the vows so that the couple can become familiar with them.

15. The minister practices receiving the ring(s) from the person(s) who will carry them in the service. As a precaution, it is helpful to designate a member of the wedding party as the person to pick up a ring if it is dropped. (This is usually the best man.)

16. The bride and groom practice giving and receiving the rings while the minister reviews the words that accompany this action. (It is customary for the bride to hand her flower bouquet to the maid of honor when the minister says, "Join your right hands.")

17. The minister reviews with the wedding party the appropriate posture during the prayer and the Lord's Prayer. (The text of the Lord's Prayer may be printed on the hymn sheets.)

18. The minister reviews the actions that accompany the announcement of marriage. If the congregation is to join the minister in saying, "Those whom God has joined together let no one separate," the wedding party practices saying the words.

19. The minister reviews the actions following the charge to the couple and the benediction. These usually are: (1) The bride and groom kiss. (2) The bride receives her bouquet from the maid of honor. (3) The couple turn toward each other and face the congregation. (4) The couple leads the wedding party out of the sanctuary.

20. The minister reviews the procedure, if any, for escorting the mothers and grandmothers of the bride and groom out of the sanctuary. (This ritual is easily forgotten on the wedding day, leaving the mothers and grandmothers anxiously awaiting their escort!)

21. The minister asks for questions and then announces the times for arriving at the church for the wedding.

22. The minister closes the rehearsal with prayer.

The Funeral: A Service of Witness to the Resurrection

(BCW 903)

Bearing Witness to the Resurrection

The central doctrine of the Christian faith is the resurrection. Christians confront the reality of death, with its attendant sorrow and feelings of loss, as "Easter people." They grieve, but not as those who have no hope (1 Thess. 4:13). Their hope is in Christ, who died and now lives, and whose death and resurrection have robbed death of victory (1 Cor. 15:55). Christians affirm that they belong, in life and in death, to their faithful Savior, Jesus Christ (Heidelberg Catechism, Question 1). Ministry to the grieving is shaped by this affirmation, and the funeral rites of the church bear witness to it.

Funerals pose a special challenge to pastors and sessions. The funeral of a loved one may be the first occasion in years for those on the periphery of church life to acknowledge their need of the church's ministry. In such circumstances, the funeral provides the church with an opportunity to express the love and compassion of a gracious God. For those active in the church, the funeral can be an occasion to express grief, to give thanks for the life of the deceased, to receive the consolation of brothers and sisters in Christ, and to celebrate the hope of the life to come. Funerals can be an occasion for the church's most effective witness to the gospel.

American culture is diverse, however, and not everyone who approaches the church for a funeral sees the service as "A Witness to the Resurrection." Many will come with vague notions about the immortality of the soul, and will speak of the deceased as having "passed on" to a better life. Others expect a celebration of the deceased's personality, complete with videos of special moments and tape recordings of the deceased's favorite show tunes.

While the church cannot accommodate every expectation (or indeed, every heresy), pastoral sensitivity is especially important in ministry to those who want to do what is best for the sake of the deceased, but do not know how best to proceed. What the church believes must take precedence over what some families desire, but ministers and sessions are free to exercise both pastoral discretion and common sense.

The funeral rites in the *Book of Common Worship* express the highest standard for the church's ministry at the time of death. Sessions and pastors who use them as their model will find that they offer wisdom, beauty, and theological depth, and comprise a treasury far richer than that which much of modern culture offers.

Ministry at the Time of Death

Although they appear separately in the *Book of Common Worship*, A Service for Wholeness for Use with an Individual (BCW 1018–1022), Prayer at the Time of Death (BCW 1025–1030), and the service for Comforting the Bereaved (BCW 905–909) are closely related. Portions of all three services could be used in ministry to the dying and to the grieving.

Notifying the Pastor. It is most important to encourage church members to notify the pastor or church when death is imminent or has occurred. Pastoral care at this time can help the bereaved to receive the consolation of the gospel and, if funeral arrangements have not been made, to make sound decisions regarding them. If the person has died at home, in a hospital, or in a nursing home or other institution, it is usually helpful for the pastor to meet with the family *before* the body has been removed, in order to offer prayers of consolation and commendation.

Comforting the Bereaved (BCW 905–909)

In some communities it is customary to gather on the evening before a funeral at the home or the funeral establishment, to pray for those who mourn and to offer assistance to the bereaved. The pastor or member of the congregation leads a brief service of prayer. The order Comforting the Bereaved is provided for this purpose. As indicated, prayers, psalms, and readings from Scripture contained in the funeral rite are appropriate for this service and may be substituted for the resources in this order. This service also resembles what is referred to, in the Roman Catholic tradition, as the wake which is conducted either at a funeral home or at the deceased's home. During this wake, eulogies are offered. This makes eulogies unnecessary during the funeral or memorial service because they were already offered during the wake.

Arrangements

Pastoral care surrounding the funeral rites includes helping people prepare for their own death. Ministers and sessions should encourage members to prepare a written statement of their preferences regarding their own funerals. A way to accomplish this is to provide a form that can be filled out and kept in the church office or in some secure place readily available at the time of death. The form can provide preferences about:

1. viewing the body
2. burial, cremation, or donation for medical purposes
3. music and selections from Scripture
4. leaders in the service, such as musicians, readers, and pallbearers
5. flowers
6. memorial gifts
7. place of burial or committal
8. whether to hold the committal before or after the funeral or memorial service
9. the location of a will or other papers
10. names of the person's lawyer and funeral director
11. other important information.

The session can provide settings for education, at which members can discuss the funeral rites, sing some hymns appropriate for funerals, and explore the theological affirmations contained in the rites. Such educational programs should be offered *regularly*. Making known one's wishes for one's own funeral can be a much-appreciated form of ministry to the living. Sessions should encourage members to share their wishes with those who will carry out their funerals, and to make advance financial arrangements.

As important as it is to know the deceased's desires, funerals are services of worship that bear witness to the faith of the church. They are not merely occasions to fulfill the wishes of the deceased or platforms for self-expression by family and friends. As with all worship in the Reformed tradition, the rites should glorify God, the author of life and salvation, rather than the deceased.

In most cases, the family should discuss arrangements for the funeral with the pastor before meeting with a representative from a funeral home. For instance, the pastor can visit with the family at home or meet the family at the funeral home before the family meets with the funeral home representative. The pastor can explain the nature of the funeral service, the options open to the family, and the importance of exercising sound stewardship by avoiding overspending. The pastor's counsel in these matters can prepare the family to make informed decisions when meeting with the funeral home representative. This is especially important when the wishes of the deceased are not known.

The Funeral: A Service of Witness to the Resurrection
(BCW 910–938)

The Christian funeral service is a service of worship and should be approached as such. The singing of hymns, reading of Scripture, preaching of the gospel, confession of sin, affirmation of faith, and the celebration of the Lord's Supper are all appropriate to the Christian funeral service.

Ministers are occasionally asked to lead funeral rites for a person who did not embrace the Christian faith. In these circumstances, the service, nevertheless, can bear witness to the hope of the gospel and the love of God for the world. The minister may adapt the rite to the circumstances, but should not compromise the gospel of grace it proclaims.

Funeral or Memorial Service

If the deceased's body or ashes (cremains) are present, the service is called a funeral. If neither the body nor the ashes are present, then the service is called a memorial. Either way, the service will be substantially the same.

Location of the Service

The Service of Witness to the Resurrection ordinarily should be held in the building set apart for the corporate worship of God. In ambiance, architecture, and association, the church building interweaves the major events of the life of faith: baptism, public profession of faith, Communion, marriage, and hope in the resurrection.

Some circumstances, however, could preclude the use of the church building. These could include the need to accommodate a large number of people or concerns about accessibility of the building to those whose mobility is limited. If the funeral takes place at a funeral home, crematorium, or columbarium, it is still a rite of the church and a service of worship. Weather permitting, the service can be held at the graveside.

Dressing the Place of Assembly

Elaborate and numerous flower arrangements are not in keeping with the Reformed tradition's emphasis on sound stewardship and lack of ostentation. Banks of cut flowers can also be troublesome to those who suffer from allergies. One or two arrangements are adequate for the place of assembly. Additional arrangements can be placed outside near the entrance to the sanctuary.

If the church uses pulpit hangings (paraments) and stoles, they typically are white, the color for resurrection, but could be the color of the current season of the liturgical year. If the paschal candle is part of the church's tradition and is not carried in procession, it is lighted and placed near the head of the coffin.

Viewing the Body of the Deceased

If the service takes place at the church and the family desires that a viewing of the deceased be made possible, it should be arranged so that those who attend the service have the option not to view the body. For instance, the coffin may be placed in the church lounge or hall before the service. The coffin is closed before it is taken inside the sanctuary. If the service takes place in a funeral home or at the graveside, the coffin is closed before the service begins.

The Pall

A pall is a cloth used to cover the coffin. It corresponds to the alb (Latin, *alba,* "white"), the garment of baptism. The white pall reminds us of our faith in resurrection, and symbolizes our having put on the robe of Christ's righteousness in baptism (Gal. 3:27). The use of a pall avoids calling attention to the relative costliness of the coffin and any invidious comparisons with other funerals. A well-designed pall can employ the symbolism of color, fabric, and design that are clearly Christian and the same for all persons, no matter what their status in life (Jas. 2:1–9). When the coffin is brought to the sanctuary, the pall is placed over it. When the coffin is taken out of the sanctuary, the pall is removed.

A flag is sometimes used to cover the coffin. When the pall is used for the service, the flag is removed.

Two alternative liturgical texts are provided for use in placing the pall on the coffin (BCW 911–912). Each text recalls the centrality of baptism in the life of a Christian. Galatians 3:27 reminds us that in baptism we put on the robe of Christ's righteousness. Romans 6:3–5 reminds us that in baptism we are buried with Christ in his death and raised with him in his resurrection. In the funeral of a Christian, it is particularly appropriate to recall one's baptism. For Christians, death marks the completion of their baptism.

The words from Galatians or from Romans (BCW 912) may be said or sung as the pall is placed over the coffin at the time the body is received at the entrance of the church. These words recall the beginning of the Christian life in baptism as the body enters the church for the last time. If the pall is placed over the coffin immediately before the procession, the words are sung or said in the hearing of the congregation. The words are not then used in the procession.

Because of the importance of the baptismal focus, Romans 6:3–5 is highly appropriate for the funeral of every baptized person. Therefore, if the Romans 6 passage is said before the people assemble, or otherwise not heard by the congregation, it should be included in the sentences of Scripture at the beginning of the service.

Procession

By long tradition the most liturgically effective way of bringing the body of the deceased into the place of worship is in procession, *after* the congregation has assembled and been seated. The usual order: minister(s), lay leaders, pallbearers with the coffin (feet first), and the family (if not previously seated). Where the customary liturgical practice of a particular church includes the use of a processional cross and paschal candle, their use in the funeral service would be natural and appropriate. In this case, the processional cross leads the procession, followed by the paschal candle, the minister(s), lay leaders, pallbearers with the coffin (feet first), and the family (if not previously seated). As the procession moves forward, a psalm (for example, 23, 90, 118, 130) or hymn may be sung by the congregation. Alternatively, the minister may say the scriptural verses, or sing them using a simple tone.

Placement of the Coffin or Urn

The closed coffin should be placed (if architecturally possible) in a position perpendicular to the Communion table, rather than crosswise (as if on view).

If a processional cross and paschal candle are part of the procession, the paschal candle is placed in its stand at the head of the coffin, and the cross in its usual place.

If the body has been cremated and the urn is present, it may be carried by a pallbearer in procession and placed on an appropriate stand in full view of the congregation as the people assemble. Alternatively, the urn may be placed on its stand before the people assemble.

Scripture Sentences

Sentences of Scripture (BCW 912– 915) proclaim the comfort and hope of the gospel as the service begins. Printed orders of service containing the people's portion of the liturgy help the congregation participate as fully as possible. Nonscriptural texts that compromise or contradict the affirmations in the rest of the rite are not appropriate.

Music of the Funeral

It is especially important that all music be as carefully chosen as are the Scripture selections, so that everything may be done with dignity, simplicity, and consistency.

Trust and hope in the resurrection, which is proclaimed in the spoken parts of the liturgy, is also proclaimed in the church's music. By singing psalms and hymns, Christians express the victory of Christ that is central to the faith, and are renewed and rooted more firmly in the faith. Music for the funeral needs to express the resurrection faith.

If a hymn begins the service, either in procession (BCW 912) or following the Scripture sentences (BCW 915), it should be one of adoration and praise of God and may reflect the liturgical season. A hymn suited to the liturgical season can assist the congregation to see this service in relation to other services of worship of God.

Most of the singing in the service should be done by those gathered. There is no better way to express the unity of the family of God, and to express the joy and comfort that is integral to the gospel, than for a congregation to sing psalms, hymns, spirituals, and responses together.

In churches where choirs regularly sing in worship on Sunday, it is especially appropriate for the choir to sing for this service as well.

All the music of the service should serve the liturgy and have an integral relationship to it. It should never dominate, but always contribute to the spirit and flow of the liturgical action.

Suggestions of musical selections suitable at various places in the funeral service are available in the current edition of "Weddings and Funeral Music" prepared by the Presbyterian Association of Musicians (Presbyterian Church (U.S.A.), 100 Witherspoon Street, Louisville, KY 40202–1396), with an emphasis on music that is within the scope of small- and medium-sized congregations. This list is not exhaustive; many other compositions are also appropriate for funeral services.

Prayers

The Prayers (BCW 915–917) may be offered verbatim, or used as guides for the preparation of prayers suited to the particular circumstances. Those who lead the service may augment the selection with prayers of their own choosing or composition. Prayers should be simple and direct, giving voice to enduring faith rather than wordy sentimentality.

A prayer of confession may be said by the people followed by a declaration of pardon given by the minister. The prayer of confession provided (BCW 917–918) is intentionally simple and universal, avoiding subjectivity.

Scripture Readings and Sermon

A number of suggested Scripture readings are offered (BCW 947–963). Selections of Scripture may be read by the minister or by others, especially those who sustained a close relationship to the deceased.

The sermon ought always to be a clear proclamation of the gospel, but may quite appropriately include grateful reference to the life of the deceased. If desired, brief tributes of the deceased's witness to the faith may be offered by friends or family, but these should be brief and few in number and, may be offered more appropriately during the service for Comforting the Bereaved (BCW 905–909) (discussed above, p. 235). Thanks for the particular gifts and characteristics of the deceased may be offered in the Prayers of Thanksgiving and Intercession (BCW 921–924).

Creed

It is appropriate that the Apostles' Creed be said (BCW 920) or sung (HL 139, 151). The Apostles' Creed originated as a baptismal confession of the faith. Using it in the funeral testifies to the faith into which we are baptized, and by which we live until our baptism is made complete in death.

The "We Praise You, O God," or Te Deum Laudamus (BCW 577), is appropriate as an affirmation of faith for use in this service and is provided as an alternate liturgical text (BCW 920, rubrics). The Te Deum proclaims Christ's redemptive work—"You overcame the sting of death, and opened the kingdom of heaven to all believers"—and ends with the petition "Bring us with your saints to glory everlasting" (PH 460; PS 170, 171).

As the rubric indicates, another scripturally based affirmation of faith (BCW 96, #2, or BCW 98, #5) also may be used.

Prayers of Thanksgiving, Supplication, and Intercession

Several prayer models are provided which the minister can use or modify (BCW 921–924; also 907–908). Free prayer is appropriate. Instead of delivering a eulogy at the place where a sermon should be preached, the minister may include particular thanksgivings for the characteristics and service of the person who has died. These prayers should be prepared carefully with sensitivity to the circumstances of the person's death. If the Lord's Supper is not included, the service proceeds directly to the commendation.

The Lord's Supper (BCW 928–935)

The celebration of the Sacrament of the Lord's Supper provides a rich opportunity to proclaim and enact the resurrection faith. The minister should consult with the family before the decision to include the Lord's Supper is made. The session must authorize the celebration of the Sacrament. To avoid a called meeting before every funeral, the session can adopt a policy authorizing the celebration of the Supper when given criteria are met.

The presiding minister should be hospitable to all who are present while exercising care not to compromise the Supper as the feast of the baptized. A statement such as the following may appear in the printed order of service and/or may be spoken by the minister: *The Sacrament of the Lord's Supper is open to all baptized Christians. All present are invited to take part in this service as fully as your conscience allows.*

Commendation, Blessing, and Procession

The minister commends to the Lord the person who has died, using the words provided (BCW 925). Since many present for the service will not be at the graveside or columbarium for the committal, the commendation is said while the people are still gathered. As the rubric indicates, the minister should face the body (or ashes), if present. The commendation is appropriate even for a memorial service, at which the body is not present. A congregational blessing (BCW 926) follows the commendation.

The procession then forms as the rubric directs (BCW 926), with the presiding minister preceding the body (or ashes). Ashes may be carried by a pallbearer (see p. 239 for the order of the procession). If a pall has been used, it is removed when the coffin arrives at the door out of the church.

The Committal Service (BCW 939–946)

As the rubric states, the committal service may take place before the general service (BCW 939).

If the committal takes place *before* a service at the church, family and friends, at the conclusion of the service, may go directly to a reception held elsewhere in the church building(s). A reception after the service has many advantages. It expresses Christian hospitality, provides a setting for the family to receive support, and is convenient for those who have come from a distance.

The committal service, whether held before or after the service, ought to be simple and brief. When the body has been cremated, the ashes in their appropriate container should be placed in the columbarium niche (or other final resting place) in full view of those present.

If the committal is separated from the service by a significant lapse of time or distance, Scripture lessons and very brief comments may be helpful. The service should close with a blessing. If the entire service is held at the place of committal, prayers such as those provided (BCW 921–924) may be used.

In the case of earth burial, the minister may touch the coffin while saying the words of committal (BCW 940). The minister or others may also cast earth upon the coffin. In many settings, this earth will have to be secured ahead of time because the gravesite usually is covered with carpet or artificial grass.

The rubrics call for an action to accompany the committal, for example, the body is lowered into the grave, dropped into the sea, moved into the crematory, or the ashes are placed in their resting place. In some areas of the country, it is the custom for the coffin to remain in place over the grave until the mourners have left the graveside. If the coffin is to be lowered during the committal service, the minister must make appropriate arrangements.

Sometimes ashes are scattered over water or land. Because ashes are light and can be easily blown, extreme care must be taken when handling them. The container of ashes should be held close to the ground or surface of the water, and the ashes poured with a single motion.

The disposition or committal of the ashes sometimes takes place days or even months after the funeral. If the minister does not preside at this service, he or she can assist the family to prepare Scripture lessons and prayers to be used.

Funeral Directors and Employees

If a funeral home is providing professional services to the family, the minister should provide clear instructions to agents of the funeral home regarding their roles, if any, in the funeral rites.

Suggestions for a Service of Witness to the Resurrection

To those who will make decisions for my Christian funeral or memorial service: I have given prayerful thought to the service of worship following my death. The following express my preferences. I realize that circumstances may apply which will make it impossible to fulfill every suggestion. I offer these preferences as a gift to those who will gather for worship following my death:

My full name and date of birth:

_____

_____

My will and other important documents are located:

_____

_____

If the pastor of my church is not available, I would like _____ to be asked to preside at the service.

In addition to the presiding minister, I would like the following to be asked to assist the presiding minister: _____

I would like the following to serve as readers:

_____

I would like the following Scripture passages to be read:

_____

_____

I would like the following hymns or psalms in *The Presbyterian Hymnal* to be sung by the congregation:

_____

I would like the service to take place:

❑ in my home church, which is:

_____

❑ at this funeral home:

_____

❑ I prefer that both the funeral and committal service take place at the graveside or burial site.

Regarding the service, I prefer:

❑ a **memorial service**, at which my body or ashes (cremains) are not present

❑ a **funeral service**, at which my body or ashes are present

Disposition of my body:

Providing that state law allows, I prefer that my body be:

❑ embalmed before earth burial or entombment

❑ embalmed before cremation

❑ cremated directly after my death, without embalmment

❑ donated to medical research, for which I have made the following arrangements:

_____

❑ donated to help others who might need my organs and/or tissues

I prefer that my body be:

❑ buried in the earth   ❑ entombed

Regarding my ashes after cremation, I prefer that my ashes be

❑ buried in the ground   ❑ committed to a columbarium

❑ scattered at this location:

_____

I prefer that the service for committal of my body take place:

❑ before the memorial service   ❑ after the memorial service or funeral

I have made arrangements with this funeral home:

_____

_____

I would like memorial contributions to be made to:

_____

_____

Here is other information I would like my family to have:

_____

_____

_____

Pastoral Liturgies

(BCW 965)

Convictions about Pastoral Liturgies

Christians offer pastoral care to one another in support of daily living, as well as during those moments of need or crisis that occur both personally and communally. Pastoral ministry mediates the care of God to any who are in distress of body, mind, or spirit. The need to be addressed by this ministry may be physical, emotional, or spiritual in nature. Pastoral care is to be offered especially to the sick, the troubled, to any in distress, and to the dying both within and beyond the Christian community. When any persons are in these circumstances, Christians respond with prayer, visits, and other acts that express the love of Christ and the support of the community for those who suffer, as well as their families, caregivers, and friends. Other situations that may require pastoral care include times of natural disaster or national crisis. Care may be offered to individuals, families, groups, or whole communities. The role of the church in this area is wide and its influence potentially profound.

God expects every Christian to provide pastoral care; all are called at baptism to carry on this ministry of discipleship. Any person who encounters another in need is capable of, and should bear God's grace to those who suffer. The Christian community is called to care for its members at all times and in all circumstances. Christians share one another's burdens, their joys and sorrows. When needed, mutual forgiveness and reconciliation is offered. Within the community of faith, particular individuals are called and equipped for pastoral ministry. Pastors are to pray with and for the congregation. Pastors, elders, and deacons are to visit, comfort, and care for those in need.

The Providence of God

"In life and in death we belong to God" (A Brief Statement of Faith). We are always within the embrace of God, never away from God's love. We may feel that God has turned away, but our conviction is that God does not abandon us. Our God is Immanuel—God with us. God is a God who weeps with those who weep, who mourns with those who mourn. Though rivers rage and mountains are toppled into the sea, the Lord of hosts is with us. God is present with us even in our darkest moments, even at the moment of mortal death itself. Immanuel, God is with us. Nothing can separate us from the love of God in Christ Jesus our Lord (Romans 8).

The Centrality of Christ in Pastoral Care

In Reformed understanding, Jesus Christ is central to faith and life. Salvation is exclusively the work of God in Christ. We must guard against putting anything in place of that salvation, whether it be psychological theory or pastoral technique. Justification by Christ alone means rejecting all forms of self-justification and turning to Jesus Christ alone for wholeness.

The Reformation insistence on the priority of grace radically alters and influences the church's approach to pastoral care. Jesus Christ has opened the way to God. We approach God solely through Christ. The focus rests on who Christ is and what Christ does. The ministry of pastoral care provides an avenue through which an individual comes into a caring and healing relationship with Jesus Christ. Ministers or pastoral caregivers cannot substitute their own personalities or skills for Christ's humanity and healing.

A Present Savior and the Ministry of Presence

The ministry of Jesus provides the primary example for all who offer pastoral care. All true ministry continues the ministry of Jesus which was so largely one of healing and forgiveness. His experience of suffering and death gives meaning to suffering and death. The Gospels tell of a God who is neither remote nor indifferent to human weakness and misery. The resurrection of Christ declares God's triumph over sin and death, pain and suffering.

To visit a home or a hospital where there is sickness is to enter a place where Christ is already present. The ministry of Jesus, the present Savior, is expressed in the simple presence of the pastoral caregiver. Yet the pastoral visitor has more to offer than mere presence. Each Christian comes to those who are sick with the faith that God's grace can make the broken whole and lift the fallen. Authentic pastoral care is incarnational. It grows out of both the brokenness that lies at the heart of the universal human condition and the wholeness that God everlastingly renews by grace. The Christian's experience of both brokenness and God's grace in Christ bears witness to a grace that neither sickness nor death can resist.

Distinguishing Wholeness from Cure

Illness, injury, and psychological and spiritual distress weave their threads through the daily lives of God's people. These unwelcome visitors bring pain, disorientation, and fear, frequently chronic in nature. "A Christian can become a 'man with a withered hand,' a 'woman who has been suffering hemorrhages for twelve years,' or a 'woman whose little daughter has an unclean spirit' (Mark 3:1; 5:25; 7:25). Christians yearn for the touch that will bring wholeness, or yearn to be able to offer this touch of wholeness to another who suffers."[1]

In a day and age when the concept of healing is delegated to doctors offices and hospitals, the church emphasizes that for Christians the practice of healing is much greater. The image for Christians is "not *cure* but *wholeness*."[2] Wholeness may be received even when a cure is not. Sickness, suffering, and dying are occasions not only for professional care but also for an openness to the meaning of divine grace and the assurance of forgiveness.

Sickness and dying are occasions to rehearse our baptism into Christ. They are occasions to experience the reality that Christ is "our only comfort in life and death" (Heidelberg Catechism, Question 1). Our faith reminds us that human suffering, illness, and even the process of dying are not meaningless and mechanistic events; rather they are focal points of divine action in ourselves and in our world.

The Scriptures reveal a God who desires shalom for God's people. God's shalom is well-being and wholeness. It is shalom that God offers to all who suffer. Shalom is offered through God's forgiving and healing love made known to us in God's Son. It is rooted in the life, death, and resurrection of Jesus Christ. In him, we have the assurance of final victory over sickness and death.

Ministry with the Sick

In sickness and in any prolonged process of dying, the body is subjected to invasive procedures from without and painful reactions from within. Among the sick, their family and their friends fear, anger, worry, helplessness, and frustration are evident. The sick and the dying desire release from their circumstances. They turn to Christ and his church for help. They look for assurance that Christ, the one who comforts and makes whole, is present with them. To the extent that the sick and those around them find that assurance, a renewal of trust, companionship, acceptance, and love appear.

Since God is present with the sick, they are witnesses to the grace and power of God to help in time of need. In this manner, the sick and the dying not only need to receive pastoral care but may become ministers to others by virtue of their receipt of God's action. Pastoral caregivers and the entire community of faith, therefore, often receive God's grace through the witness of those who suffer.

The person ill in body, mind, or spirit may receive care from a variety of professional practitioners, family members, and friends. Frequently the most important practitioner is the one who bears witness to the grace, mercy, healing, and peace offered by the risen Christ. The caregiver offers that grace through conversation, shared laughter and tears, the reading of Scripture, prayer (both spoken and enacted), the Sacrament of the Lord's Supper, and the rite of repentance and forgiveness. Through these concrete and tangible ways, Christ may be fully experienced as present.

Pastoral Visits

Conversation

Sincerity and communication that involves careful listening and mutual respect characterize the best conversation with the sick and dying. The patient will quickly sense whether the visit is one prompted by duty or by sincere regard and affection. The helpful visitor does not control the conversation but allows the patient to indicate where the talk will flow. A patient is in some sense a captive—to the illness, to the bed, to the routine of hospital or nursing home, and even to the well-wishers who come by. It is a caring act to engage the patient as an active subject in the give-and-take of true conversation and not to treat the patient as an object to be soothed or informed.

It is not helpful for the visitor to speak in clichés about God's will or about how God sends suffering as a test. The visitor may say, "I know how you feel," but that is patently untrue. Only the sufferer knows the quality and extent of his or her suffering. Feigned cheerfulness for the sake of the patient will simply provoke resistance, for it evades what is in the heart and soul of the patient. On the other side, sickness does not necessarily bestow either nobility or gracefulness on disagreeable or selfish persons. A sensitive pastoral visitor, however, can help the egocentric patient to grow in character and the ability to love others.

Difficulties other than illness may present themselves in the conversation. For example, patients sometimes express concern that the stay in the hospital prevents them from attending to daily responsibilities. When members of the congregation learn of these concerns, they are often willing to help the patient by taking on those responsibilities. A simple gesture such as bringing the church flowers or the bulletin well expresses the continuing bond between the congregation and the patient. A patient may be asked to participate in the pastoral care of another through prayer. Words can be spoken that lift the spirit, give joy, or strengthen faith. These words may be Bible verses, hymn stanzas, familiar psalms, or stories. However simple or plain in speech, the pastoral visitor also has a word that points to our ultimate hope: "God is our refuge and strength, a very present help in trouble" (Ps. 46:1).

Length of Visit

Privacy is rare for a patient. The considerate visitor respects the right of the sick person to receive medical attention, or even attend to personal needs without an outsider present. The best method to judge the right length of the visit is to take cues from the patient. After receiving pain medication, a patient may simply want to hold the visitor's hand and fall asleep. Generally five to ten minutes suffice, since the ill tend to tire quickly and may find it embarrassing to ask a visitor to leave.

Extended illness of a chronic rather than acute nature involves a different pattern in visitation. As the illness extends, so typically should the length of the visit. Regular visits over extended periods provide an opportunity for telling family stories, recalling common memories, and enlarging friendship. The very duration of extended illness can provide an opportunity for a patient to develop a pastoral relationship of a depth previously unexperienced.

When the Visit Is with a Child

The child who is in the hospital will take an interest in the facts of illness according to age and intellectual capacity. But at any age the implicit questions of a patient, and particularly a child, have to do with security. The illness itself, and the possible threat of death, will be alarming to a child only to the extent that parents or visitors convey fear, anxiety, or stress. A pastoral visitor not only remembers the child, but also the parents and his or her caregivers who are in great need of care and support.

Pastoral visitors can share in appropriate activities with the child, for example, watching television or playing games. The visitor could bring a bouquet of balloons from all the children of the church school. Prayer with children should be age appropriate. The use of simple words with a small child can communicate God's love, care, and presence: *Dear Jesus, please be with Missy. Help her to remember that you love her and are right here with her all of the time. Amen.*

Qualities Helpful in Pastoral Visits with the Sick and the Dying

1. *Realism.* Death is the end of mortal life. It is definite and final. It is no comfort for the one on the sickbed to hear words of false hope or a comfort that hides the truth. A word of promise is always appropriate: *We are buried with Christ; we are raised with Christ.*

2. *Hopefulness.* God never ceases to love us, so we are safely lodged with God wherever we are in life or in death. *"In life and in death we belong to God. Through the grace of our Lord Jesus Christ, the love of God, and the communion of the Holy Spirit, we trust in the one triune God, the Holy One of Israel, whom alone we worship and serve"* (A Brief Statement of Faith, BCW 94).

3. *Truthfulness and Conviction.* It is neither pastorally helpful nor philosophically possible to give a good answer to every question about suffering and death. The sensitive visitor of the sick or the dying does not need to know why the crisis has occurred, let alone what God is doing. What is necessary is to offer a loving presence with the conviction that God will never leave nor forsake us. "We are convinced that neither death, nor life, nor angels, nor rulers, nor things present, nor things to come, nor powers, nor height, nor depth, nor anything else in all creation, will be able to separate us from the love of God in Christ Jesus our Lord" (Rom. 8:38–39).

4. *Resourcefulness.* Dying and death are supremely inconvenient. They never come at the right time. People who are inconvenienced appreciate appropriate help. Good help is simple, immediate, and practical. Various people have their own ministry to offer in the hospital room, including the housekeepers. The good visitor allows each to perform the appropriate ministry.

5. *Sensitivity.* Like houseguests, visitors to the sick often outstay their welcome. The visitor watches for signs that the sick person is tiring or does not feel up to the visit. The thoughtful visitor does not arrive at a bedside with preconceived ideas of what needs to be done or said. The visitor who regards the visit merely as a routine to be performed will not be able to share in what can be a mutually enriching ministry.

6. *Perceptiveness.* Sickness and death call forth painful and unpleasant

feelings such as anger, bitterness, resentment, and despair. The accepting caregiver does not judge such feelings and will allow the sick person to express them without offering criticism or judgment. When such feelings are respected, the person may move beyond them. The Psalter demonstrates that all feelings are properly placed at the feet of God as in many of the psalms. The pastoral visitor can help the patient express his or her feelings to God.

7. *Attentiveness.* If possible, it is better for the visitor to sit so that the patient does not get the sense that the visitor is about to dash off. Even a busy doctor or nurse can avoid conveying a sense of being too busy or preoccupied, so also the pastoral visitor. The considerate visitor listens carefully not only to the words being spoken but also to the feeling behind the words. The patient may say that everything is well, but may also convey a quite different message by tone of voice or facial expression. A skilled caregiver will respond to nuances of tone.

8. *Listening Together to the Story of Our Salvation.* The word *salvation* is closely bound up with the idea of wholeness. The ministry of the caring pastoral visitor is to set forth in word and deed the gospel of salvation through Jesus Christ. Jesus shared our life, pain, and death. Jesus' death and resurrection are events that have transformed all things. Through the person and work of Christ, we are made whole. The risen Christ has promised that he will be with us always; we are never alone, ever. Prayer during ministry to the sick and dying can help raise the dying into the dimension of the resurrection. If a person wishes to confess sin to the pastor, he or she should be given this opportunity.

Ending the Visit—Tokens of Remembrance

By leaving a small gift or token, the visitor and the community of faith remain symbolically present after departure:

> Church calling card or "greeting card"
> Church directory
> Church newsletter
> Devotional or prayer booklet
> Prayer card or pamphlet—generated with a word processor; customized, using Scripture and Prayers for the Sick (BCW 967–993); could include prayers written by individuals from the congregation
> Text of a favorite hymn
> Small cross (perhaps a woodworker or someone who does needlepoint in the congregation could make these on a regular basis)
> Cards made by children of the church school
> Audio/video tape of the church service

Copy of the Sunday sermon
Flowers from the church service
Church bulletin
Photographs
Magazine
Book
Bookmark made by church school children or church members, customized
Floral bouquet or plant
Cream or lotion
Lap robe
Afghan or quilt

In accordance with dietary restrictions, a visitor could leave a meal, home-baked goods, soup, herbal tea, or candy.

Training for Pastoral Caregiver

For some, visitation is natural and easy. For others, this ministry is difficult and awkward. Basic training is essential for elders, deacons, and other lay members willing to serve in this ministry. A basic training course could be offered during the church school hour or a weekday evening. Training may include an introduction to pastoral care, guidelines for visits, elements of a pastoral call, and role-playing. Intentional, regular training opportunities within a congregation will provide more extensive pastoral care for its members.

Commentary on Pastoral Liturgies

Ministry with the Sick (BCW 967–993)

When possible, find out about the patient's situation. Who is present in the room? What are the relationships between those present? What is the status of the patient (for example, is he or she able to communicate, in pain, in distress, in a coma)? The pastoral visitor is a listener putting aside his or her agenda. What is the patient trying to say? What are his or her needs? hopes? fears? What about the needs of others present? Does this visit need to be brief? Does it require more time because the patient is lonely and/or frightened? Once an assessment of the situation is made, pastoral care may be offered and shared.

Worship is the central component of ministry with those who are sick even though the sickroom does not at first seem to provide a typical or easy setting. In worship, human suffering is given a voice; the ill hear anew the familiar words of comfort and hope, all gathered in the room experience the healing presence of Christ.

Components of Liturgy of Ministry with the Sick

Sentences of Scripture. The pastoral caregiver is privileged to bring the Word of God to the sick. Worship begins with the Word. The BCW includes twenty-four sentences of Scripture, (BCW 967–970), from both Testaments. The sentences are brief. Often the phrases are familiar. These first words set the tone for worship. They bring hope into the midst of illness, pain, and suffering.

Scripture Readings. In the reading and hearing of Scripture we are reminded of the story of God's saving acts, comforted by the promises of God, and renewed by God's presence. The *Book of Common Worship* offers a comprehensive list of Scripture citations appropriate for ministry with the sick (BCW 971–973). In addition, thirty-two passages are printed in full (BCW 974 - 987). It is appropriate to ask which texts are meaningful to those present in the room. A familiar Bible story may be told. The text of a particular passage or psalm could be printed ahead of time and read together. Passages could be read by different persons. Scripture may be sung. Following the reading of Scripture, a brief interpretation may follow.

Prayers. One of the most important ministries of care and worship that a pastoral visitor can offer is prayer, including prayer for the patient by name. Prayer through the Holy Spirit gives voice to the cries of human pain, need, and hope and to the depths of God's steadfast love and healing grace. Prayer may be spoken, offered in silence, or enacted.

Some are hesitant to offer prayer, not wanting to intrude on a patient's privacy or to risk embarrassing a patient who may be uncomfortable with public prayer. A wise caregiver will attend to the patient's needs, feelings, and desires regarding prayer. The pastoral visitor could ask, "May I pray with you now or would you like me to remember you later in my private prayers at home?" This question allows the patient to be in control of the situation and yet know he or she will receive prayer.

A selection of prayers suitable for various situations is found in BCW 830–833, 988–993. Several personalized prayers printed from the *Book of Common Worship* could be left with the patient. Extemporary prayer is also valuable in giving voice to specific needs and issues raised during conversation. One hospital chaplain told a group of clergy of a prayer offered on his behalf while he was in critical care, gravely ill. The pastoral visitor spoke a simple and brief prayer that was always remembered by the chaplain: *Gracious God, we know and trust that you love your child, Jim. We know that you are present here with him now. We ask for healing. Amen.* The chaplain knew that his need for healing was placed in God's hands. The visitor assured him of God's love and presence.

When prayer is offered at the time of the visit, touch can be as important as the words spoken. Human touch is a tangible way of communicating the presence of Christ. If others are present in the room, all may be invited to make a circle with the patient with all holding hands. If the patient is unable to hold hands, the one who prays may gently rest a hand on a shoulder. Sensitivity must be used in those cases where touch causes anxiety or pain in the patient.

Almost invariably, the prayers include the Lord's Prayer. Use of the Lord's Prayer allows those present to speak the familiar words of prayer taught by our Lord and repeated regularly by God's people corporately and individually. Even those whose memory is clouded may remember this prayer and speak it clearly. The final prayer offered by the pastoral visitor could be an affirmation of faith, such as the prayer of Ambrose of Milan (BCW 830):

> You are medicine for me when I am sick.
> You are my strength when I need help.
> You are life itself when I fear death.
> You are the way when I long for heaven.
> You are light when all is dark.
> You are my food when I need nourishment! Amen.

Guidelines for Prayer

> Prayer is for this person and his or her needs. Be specific.
> Affirm the life of the person. Affirm what is realistic for him or her.
> Do *not* offer false hope.
> Validate without judgment the pain and other needs of the person.
> Use comforting and simple images for God (for example, the Good Shepherd).
> Incorporate Scripture (for example, Ps. 46 or Ps. 121).
> Remember that the one offering prayer does so on behalf of the ill who may not have the strength on his or her own.
> Remember wholeness and perfect healing may not mean physical cure.

Holy Communion with Those Unable to Attend
Public Worship (BCW 994–1002)

To receive Communion is a spiritual comfort because Christ is uniquely present in the sharing of this meal. We eat and drink for health and strength. The tangible signs of bread and wine provide life-giving nourishment. Communion is also a sign of the unity of the Christian community. In the Lord's Supper all who love Christ are one—the sick and the well, the living and the dead.

Pastoral ministry provides a critical link between the sick person and the congregation. In receiving Holy Communion, the ill are reminded of the community of which they are a part, but from whom they are physically separated. Sharing in the bread and cup, the ill or homebound are reconnected with the community of faith.

In worship, the Word and the Meal are right and left hands. The Word read and proclaimed brings comfort and hope by the power of the Holy Spirit. In the Meal we are renewed, greatly empowered by the memory of Christ's life, death, resurrection and promised return. We are sustained by Christ's pledge of undying love and continuing presence with us. And we are sealed in God's covenant of grace through partaking of Christ's self-offering (W-2.4004).

The Lord's Supper may be observed in connection with the visitation of the sick and those isolated from public worship in two ways:

1. *Extended Serving.* When the Lord's Day service includes the Lord's Supper, the "elements may be extended by two or more ordained officers of the church." The pastor's presence is not necessary. Those participating in the extension of the service will be instructed by the session in the theology and pastoral foundation of this ministry and the liturgical resources for it. The elements cannot be separated from the Word proclaimed. This offer of the Meal is a direct extension of serving the gathered congregation. Unity of Word and Sacrament is maintained by the reading of Scripture and the offering of prayers. [The officers who take the elements to those unable to partake with the worshiping community could be commissioned during the Lord's Day service: *We ask for the blessing of God to be with (name of officer) and (name of officer) as they go forth to share this meal with (name of patient) on our behalf.*]

The Directory for Worship provides for extended serving to strengthen the connection between the homebound and the worshiping congregation and to include all at the table as a sign of the community's unity in Christ. When the *Book of Common Worship* was published, extended serving was not an option. An example of a Service of Extended Communion might look like this:

GREETING
Elders and deacons should identify themselves with these or similar words:

We are N and N from the N Church. We have come to share the communion of your church.

Elders and deacons should take time to visit with the communicant.
As you visit, listen for concerns and joys to remember in prayer.

When all are ready for communion, prepare the elements by uncovering the bread and pouring the cup. Elders and deacons may invite others present to join in the service.

Our help is in the name of the Lord,
the Maker of heaven and earth.

The elder or deacon continues with these or similar words:

When our congregation gathered this morning for the celebration of the
Lord's Supper, we heard again the story of God's mighty acts of love,
embodied in the death and resurrection of our Lord Jesus Christ. With
thanksgiving we remembered that "on the night he was betrayed, Jesus
took bread, and gave thanks, broke it, and gave it to his disciples saying,
'this is my body, given for you. Do this in remembrance of me.' Again,
after supper, he took the cup, gave thanks, and gave it to his disciples,
saying, 'This cup is the new covenant in my blood, shed for you and for
all people for the forgiveness of sin. Do this in remembrance of me.'"
We were also given assurance of the Lord's presence through the gift of
his Holy Spirit. Now we bring you this same bread of life and this same
cup of blessing, that you may be strengthened through our Communion
in the body of Christ.

CONFESSION
*When circumstances permit, a prayer of confession such as those found on
pp. 87–88 in the Book of Common Worship may be said.*

DECLARATION OF FORGIVENESS
See for example p. 56 in the Book of Common Worship.

SCRIPTURE
*The reading from Scripture upon which the morning sermon was based may
be read.*

INTERPRETATION OF THE WORD
*Pastors should supply the extended serving teams with a brief synopsis of
the morning sermon, or teams may offer their own recollection of the
proclamation of the Word.*

*The Opening Prayer or Prayer of the Day from the Lord's Day service may
be said, followed by the Lord's Prayer.*

COMMUNION
The bread and cup are given, saying:

The body of Christ, given for you.
The blood of Christ, given for you.

PRAYERS OF THANKSGIVING AND INTERCESSION
Join hands to offer the prayer, if the physical circumstances are favorable.

> *Specific prayers for the individual or the church may be added. Before leaving, identify the next date elders and deacons may return with communion. Normally, the visit should take between twenty to thirty minutes. Elders and deacons should be alert for signs of fatigue or discomfort in the communicant and should adapt the service accordingly.*[3]

A tape of the service or a copy of the sermon could be left.

2. *Special Occasions.* The Lord's Supper is to be understood as an act of the whole church even if only a few members of the congregation are present, as a means of extending the church's ministry. The church is represented by the minister (or one authorized by the presbytery to administer the Sacrament) and by one or more members of the congregation authorized by the session to represent the church. The Word is read and proclaimed along with the administration of the Sacrament. This service is an abbreviated, but complete celebration of the Supper. The following four components are always present: the receiving of the elements, the giving of thanks (Great Thanksgiving), the breaking of the bread, and the communion of the people.

Components of the Liturgy of Holy Communion for Those Unable to Attend Public Worship (BCW 994–1002)

The Setting. The room and the pastoral situation determine the manner in which the Sacrament is administered. The service may be simple or elaborate. Each mode has its virtues. The full liturgy will evoke memories of the congregation at worship, however, the room and stamina of the sick may suggest a simple celebration of the Supper using a minimum of the liturgy.

If the setting allows, make the Meal as special as possible. This is the joyful feast of the people of God. This is not take-out, leftovers, or fast food. Pouring juice out of a little can or serving the bread from a plastic bag does not suggest a joyful feast. Set a table using the hospital tray or a tray brought for the purpose. The tray may be covered with a clean linen; a small strip of cloth in the appropriate color of the liturgical season may be placed across the linen. A small votive candle representing the light of Christ who illumines our darkness may be lighted. A simple chalice and paten (plate used for bread) may be used. Much is communicated to the ill or homebound for such care to be taken in the presentation of the Meal. *You are special; a beloved child of the Host.*

Elements of the Liturgy. If a full liturgy is to be used, then a printed order of service may be provided. In this way all who are present are able to participate. Various parts may be assigned to those who are present: representatives from the congregation, family members or friends, and the person who is ill or homebound if he or she is able. The printed order may be left with the person and reread.

Call to Worship. The call to worship sets the tone for the celebration of the Supper. Several options are offered (BCW 995–996).

Doxology, Psalm, Hymn, or Spiritual. Music is a powerful means of communicating the love and peace of God in Christ. Sacred music offers comfort and healing to the deep places of our souls. The pastoral care team may include a musician who leads the worshipers in a familiar hymn, psalm, or spiritual song; or a solo may be sung. The hymn chosen might be a favorite of the person who is ill.

Confession and Pardon. Jesus came to heal and save sinners. He came to bring healing to the spirit as well as to the body. Following Jesus' lead, the church directs its ministry to the healing of both the body and the soul. When one is in the valley of illness or the shadow of death, deep personal reflection often takes place. Painful issues may surface. Past sins, failings, or broken relationships bring feelings of guilt. Reconciliation, the name given to the act of confession and pardon, is medicine for a sick soul. The caregiver should not hesitate to include it in this liturgy.

A Confession of Sin (BCW 997). Others are found in the BCW. Use a *confession* that is familiar to the individual. The *declaration of forgiveness* comes directly from Scripture. Several suggestions are listed (BCW 997–998). The declaration is good news for a weary soul. The words will linger and continue to offer promise and hope.

Scripture and Brief Sermon. The Sacrament of the Lord's Supper is a seal of the Word. If the Sacrament is brought from the regular Lord's Day service, then use of the same Scripture with a shortened sermon is appropriate. On special occasions, the visitor should choose Scripture appropriate for the day and the situation. The sermon enables the person to more fully understand the Scripture and appropriate it for his or her situation. It should offer hope, encouragement, and promise of God's love and care.

Psalm, Hymn, or Spiritual. While this is optional, a psalm, hymn, spiritual, or refrain allows time for the Word to permeate the listener and for the Sacrament to be prepared.

[*Laying On of Hands.* This part of the service is optional. For instructions see BCW 1019–1021 and p. 164 of this *Companion*.]

Invitation to the Lord's Table. Other Invitations (BCW 68–69, 125).

Great Thanksgiving. The Great Thanksgiving is the table grace offered at the Lord's Supper. The Great Thanksgiving, or eucharistic prayer, includes a thanksgiving for creation and redemption and an invocation of the Spirit. The prayer highlights the work of God in Christ through which we are saved. This prayer provides assurance and confidence in time of need. The prayer included in this liturgy is Prayer H (BCW 152). The prayer may be prayed responsively if it is printed out for all worshipers. It may include the reading or singing of the Sanctus ("Holy, holy, holy Lord, . . ."). The Sanctus reminds the worshipers that the church is universal, not bound by time and space.

Lord's Prayer. The visitor uses the form of the Lord's Prayer that is most familiar to the patient.

Breaking of the Bread. A small loaf or dinner roll is broken. Wine is poured into the chalice on the table.

Communion. The elements are those used commonly by the congregation. Communion is served by intinction (dipping a piece of bread into the wine), by common cup (individually consuming a piece of bread and then drinking from the common chalice), or by eating a piece of bread and drinking the wine from an individual cup. The words *the body of Christ, the blood of Christ* are spoken as the elements are offered. If a patient is unable to eat or drink, the spiritual communion binding those present includes the patient.

Prayer after Communion. This prayer is said by the minister or all together. Other options are found in BCW 76–77, 157–158.

Blessing. The blessing is spoken by the minister. A blessing may be sung. Other blessings are found in BCW 83, 161.

A Service for Wholeness for Use with a Congregation (BCW 1003–1015)

> *O God, sanctifier of this oil,*
> *as you give health to those who are anointed*
> *and receive that with which you anointed kings, priests and prophets,*
> *so may it give strength to all who taste it,*
> *and health to all who are anointed with it.*
>
> (Hippolytus, ca. 215 C.E.)

A Reformed Understanding for the Service for Wholeness

All healing comes from God. Sometimes miraculous healing occurs. Generally, God works through human skill, knowledge, and training to bring about healing. Highly trained medical professionals, technology, and medicine aid in the healing process. All are direct gifts from God.

Healing was an integral part of the ministry of Jesus. Jesus healed from a distance (Luke 7:1–10), but he more typically used touch in the process of healing (Matt. 9:18; Mark 16:18; Luke 4:40). In Jesus' day many who were ill had become social outcasts. He reached out and brought healing and wholeness to those isolated in illness. As Jesus acted, so must his church. The Service for Wholeness reaches out and touches those who need healing in body, mind, or spirit.

The Service for Wholeness may include the laying on of hands and the anointing with oil. This is mystical and mysterious, but not magic. No tricks, gimmicks, or magical incantations are used to invoke the Holy Spirit. In this service, the church acknowledges the constant and abiding presence of God. The Service for Wholeness affirms that even in the midst of bodily illness, pain and suffering, our relationship with God in Christ sustains us. The service also recognizes that confession, forgiveness, and reconciliation are essential to wholeness.

The centerpiece of the Service for Wholeness is prayer. Prayer may be spoken, sung, and enacted. Enacted prayer is words combined with specific actions: laying on hands, anointing with oil. Prayer begins with a thanksgiving for God's promise of wholeness, intercessions, and supplications. Time is granted for silent prayer. In the laying on of hands, an outward sign of the prayer is given through touch. The touch of human hands is able to convey the grace-filled touch of Christ in a unique and tangible manner. Anointing with oil may also be included in this service as a sign of God's grace and healing mercy. The anointing of the sick has been part of pastoral ministry since New Testament times (Mark 6:13; Jas. 5:14–15). It is to be understood in terms of its spiritual effect as an external sign of the presence of Christ, who continues his ministry of salvation and healing.

Why use oil? Oil is something tangible that engages the senses. It aids in the communication of God's loving care and compassion for the person in need of healing and wholeness. Olive oil was the medicine of the ancients, used to soften and clean wounds. Olive oil was used to anoint prophets and kings, thereby signifying the blessing and calling of God. Jesus is referred to as the anointed Messiah.

The specific oil used is traditionally the finest grade of olive oil or chrism that is available. Chrism is a mixture of olive and aromatic oils. These oils and the small vessels used to hold the oil during the service may be found at regional church supply stores. Chrism is etymologically related to the name of Christ, the anointed One or Messiah. Chrismation can be a helpful sign of the individual's life in Christ.

Expectations for the Service for Wholeness

Healing is a gift not a right. When Jesus prayed in the Garden of Gethsemane he prayed, "Not what I want but what you want" (Matt. 26:39). His most faithful prayer did not take away his suffering and death, but instead provided him with strength for the journey.

Prayer spoken and enacted cannot guarantee healing in the sense of cure. Cure may not come. Cancer may not go into remission. The divorce may take place. An alienated child may not return home. Nevertheless, God is sovereign.

We do not control God or God's action. By God's invitation, we pray trusting in God's mercy and grace to grant wholeness.

A relationship with Jesus Christ will be reestablished or deepened and strengthened. The service may breach the barrier between the person and Christ, that is, serve a reconciling function, and help the person to be open to Christ's healing, reconciling love. Healing is to be understood as the gift of God through the power of the Holy Spirit not as the result of the faith of the ones seeking healing nor the holiness, earnestness, or skill of those offering the prayers.

Guidelines for the Use of the Service for Wholeness

The church is called to continue the healing ministry of Jesus. Through services for wholeness, the church enacts in worship its ministry as a healing community. The Directory for Worship specifies appropriate times and places for the service for wholeness. It provides direction for the session and the pastor. The service for wholeness is open to all in need of healing. Careful instruction is given to the congregation in order to avoid misinterpretation and misunderstanding.

Preparing the Congregation

Begin with the session. Study the Scripture, the Reformed understanding of healing and wholeness, and the instructions in the Directory for Worship. Introduce the service to the congregation through newsletter articles and announcements in the bulletin over several weeks. Carefully explain what the service is and what it is not. If the groundwork is carefully laid, this liturgy will be accepted by the congregation. Training should be provided for those who will lay on hands and anoint with oil.

Components of the Service for Wholeness

The service for wholeness follows a traditional liturgical pattern.

The Setting. The service may stand alone or follow "The Service for the Lord's Day," with or without the Lord's Supper.

Opening Sentences. The opening sentences affirm that we find in the Lord our only hope in times of suffering and trial.

Psalm, Hymn, or Spiritual. The psalm, hymn, or spiritual sets the tone and establishes the focus for the service.

Confession of Sin and the Declaration of Forgiveness. An order for confession and pardon establishes integral groundwork for prayers for healing and wholeness. Personal and communal sin cause injury to the self, the community, and to others. The healing of broken relationships and the reestablishment of wholeness begin with confession and pardon.

Doxology, Psalm, Hymn, or Spiritual. The community rejoices that in Christ we are forgiven. Song expresses the joy of redemption.

Readings from Scripture and Sermon. Participants in services for healing and wholeness are particularly vulnerable and, therefore, more open to the spoken Word. The presider needs to pay special attention to the selection of texts and the message delivered.

Offering of Our Lives to God. An allotted time for silent meditation provides an opportunity for personal reflection and the chance to offer ourselves with renewed commitment for service.

Intercession for Healing. The congregation responds in prayer to what is heard in Scripture and sermon. Each service includes the opportunity to pray for the specific needs of any who are present or on behalf of those who are absent. Requests may be for physical, emotional, or spiritual healing. A request may be personal or communal in nature. Particular people, places, and situations for which prayers have been asked will be named. Each person and situation is known to God, not as a problem to be solved, but as a focus for God's acceptance and love.

The congregation offers intercession for healing and wholeness using the form on BCW 1009–1011. A time of silence provides opportunity for individual intercession. Specific names, places, and situations may be spoken aloud. These intercessions take time; they need not be hurried or rushed. The petitions conclude with the words: "Lord, in your mercy, **hear our prayer.**" This response unites the congregation. The concluding collect, "Into your hands, O God, we commend all for whom we pray . . . ," may be prayed in unison or by the person leading the prayer.

Laying On of Hands and Anointing with Oil—Enacted Prayer.

Thanksgiving and Invocation. Several options are given on BCW 1011–1012. Prayer A (BCW 1011) is used when all who come forward are to receive the laying on of hands and anointing.

Enacting the Prayer. All who wish to come forward may do so on their own behalf or on behalf of another unable to attend. Individuals come forward to a previously designated area in the front of the sanctuary. A place to kneel may be provided for those who wish to do so. A person comes forward and has the option of speaking the request aloud or not. Each may elect to kneel. If the person kneels, so does the one (or do those) laying on hands and anointing. An extemporaneous prayer may be offered if a specific request is given. Then the minister and/or elders place their hands on the person's head. One of four prayers may be used from those found on page 1013. The minister or elder then dips his or her thumb in the oil and makes the sign of the cross on the person's forehead with the words of option 1 or 2 (BCW 1013–1014). The person returns to the pew.

As individuals come forward for the laying on of hands and the anointing with oil, congregational singing may take place. The singing, especially if prayerful in nature, may be the congregation's way of sharing in the prayers. An adult or youth choir or a soloist may also offer prayerful songs on behalf of the congregation.

The Lord's Prayer or Prayer. The time of prayer concludes with the Lord's Prayer when the Eucharist is not celebrated. If the service includes the Lord's Supper, Prayer B (BCW 1014) is used.

Hymn. A hymn is sung as the table is prepared for Communion. The service then proceeds with the invitation to the Lord's Table (BCW 998).

Blessing. The concluding blessing may be spoken or sung.

A Service for Wholeness for Use with an Individual (BCW 1018–1022)

When the need arises, a minister, spiritual director, or another member of the Christian community may lead the service for wholeness with an individual. The service may take place in a sanctuary, chapel, office, home, hospital, or nursing home. If it is physically possible, a place to kneel should be provided for the individual and the minister at the time of the laying on of hands and anointing. The service for wholeness may be combined with the service of repentance and forgiveness, with the Lord's Supper or with both. Outlines for these are provided on BCW 1016–1017.

A Service of Repentance and Forgiveness for Use with a Penitent Individual (BCW 1023–1024)

The call to healing in pastoral care involves the recognition in each one's life of the reality of sin, which is the source of all human brokenness. The believing community announces the good news of God whose love gives people grace to confess their sin, to repent, to accept God's forgiveness, to forgive the other and accept the other's forgiveness, to work for reconciliation, and to trust the power of God to bring healing and peace.

Even persons who have heard God's general promise of mercy in the Gospel sometimes remain in doubt concerning the forgiveness of their sins. The sick and the dying, too, may need to be relieved of a burdened conscience. For some the weight and guilt of sin can become unbearable. In any of these situations, the service of repentance and forgiveness can provide healing.

Jesus Christ is the only Savior and our mediator with God. Nevertheless, each Christian hears and receives the forgiveness of sins in a variety of ways. It is a powerful assurance for the troubled in spirit to hear a minister of the gospel declare that God is gracious and forgives and welcomes the penitent. Christ's words of grace and forgiveness can be proclaimed by a minister looking directly into the eyes of the penitent. Here in a profound way, the penitent may receive and embrace God's good news for him or for her.

The recovery of a ritual that proclaims the good news of God's grace and forgiveness is not a denial of the Protestant heritage but a recovery of its core: God graciously accepts the returning sinner. To proclaim the gospel from the pulpit is one thing; to make that gospel personal in confession and the appropriation of God's forgiveness is an act of caring ministry. This service may be used at the discretion of the pastoral caregiver.

The penitent person and the minister may sit face-to-face in the church or in some other place. The traditional sign of forgiveness is either the laying on of hands or the extension of a hand over the penitent, with or without the sign of the cross.

Prayer at the Time of Death (BCW 1025–1030)

The pastoral care of the dying and their families and friends is a singularly important ministry of the church. When death comes, it comes as an enemy. Many have died repeating in their own fashion the words of Jesus on the cross: "My God, my God, why have you forsaken me?" The illusion that the right medical technology will put things right is challenged by a dying patient's question: "Why is getting old and dying so painful?" Whenever death occurs, the pastoral visitor will be careful to act in a manner appropriate to the occasion. In particular, the considerate visitor will respect the wishes of the dying person and the attending family members.

This is a time of great respect and humility; death and resurrection are mysteries which the living do not know. The only thing of which the church is certain is, "I am the resurrection and the life." The pastoral care of the dying is the ministry of the risen Jesus Christ through his body, the church. In its ministry of pastoral care the church testifies to its baptismal faith, the faith that through Christ we have passed from death into life.

The commendation of the dying may be a simple blessing from Scripture. Time and opportunity may also allow for the reading of longer familiar passages and for prayer. The time immediately before dying can provide opportunity for transforming the emotional attachments of the present life. It can also allow for good conversation, farewells, forgiveness, expressions of affection, or a reassurance that affairs have been put in order.

Book of Occasional Services

Special occasions and transitions in the life of a congregation and the lives of its members are appropriately recognized in worship. Many of these are ordinarily celebrated at particular points in "The Service for the Lord's Day." Others may be celebrated in "The Service for the Lord's Day" or in other regularly scheduled services or in a service especially appointed for the occasion.

The *Book of Occasional Services* (BOS) was prepared as a tool for ordering those services which occur only occasionally in the church. While celebrated only periodically, they are important for the faith, life, and witness of the church. The services are rooted in baptism which "is the basic Christian 'ordination'" (BOS1, Preface). In baptism, we are individually claimed as God's own beloved sons and daughters and grafted into the body of Christ—the community of faith—the church. In baptism, we are made disciples of Jesus Christ and called to serve others as if we were serving Christ himself. All of the services in the book "are ways the whole church witnesses to its common baptismal commitment and calling" (BOS2, Preface).

The book includes introductory material prior to each section. The introductions provide theological background and practical guidelines for implementing the services. It is helpful in planning to begin with the introduction. After reading the introduction, the worship planner is encouraged to read through the entire liturgy under consideration. By reading through the entire liturgy, the worship planner will see the theological purpose behind the various elements that make up the service as a whole.

I. Ordination and Installation (Based on "The Service for the Lord's Day," BOS 6–118)

Within the community of the church,
some are called to particular service as deacons, elders,
and as ministers of the Word and Sacrament.
Ordination is Christ's gift to the church,
assuring that his ministry continues among us,
providing ministries of caring and compassion in the world,
ordering the governance of the church,
and preaching the Word and administering the sacraments.

(BOS 19)

There are a variety of gifts of service in the church. All are necessary for the body of Christ to function properly (Romans 12). Within the church, some are gifted for specific leadership roles. The Presbyterian church sets apart persons to serve as presbyters (ministers of Word and Sacrament or elders) and a baptized member of the church is called through election for service as a presbyter. The office of elder, deacon, and minister of Word and Sacrament is perpetual. The purpose and pattern of leadership in the church in all its forms of ministry is to be understood in terms of service, not power. Jesus came as a servant; to serve rather than be served. The example he gave to his disciples and to us is a master who washes feet (John 13). We follow his example by practicing servant ministry.

Ordination is the act by which the church sets apart persons who have been called through election by the church to serve as presbyters with prayer and the laying on of hands. Installation is the act by which the church sets apart those previously ordained to the office and called anew to service to it with prayer. The services of ordination and installation are rooted in the baptismal covenant of the church. All participants in a service of ordination and/or installation are reminded of their own calls to discipleship in Jesus Christ.

The Setting for a Service of Ordination and/or Installation

A Service of Ordination or Installation may occur in either of two settings. The first option is for the service to take place during "The Service for the Lord's Day" as a response to the proclamation of the Word. The second option is for a special service of ordination and installation that focuses on Jesus Christ and the mission and ministry of the church. This special service will always include a proclamation of the Word (W-4.4002).

The Focus of the Service

The focus of the Service of Ordination and Installation is Jesus Christ and the joy and responsibility of serving him through the mission and ministry of the church.

Form and Order. The form and order for the Service of Ordination and Installation is determined by the Book of Order. The rite follows the proclamation of the Word. Specific details and instructions for the service are outlined in the Directory for Worship. These are carefully followed by the one planning and organizing the ordination and/or installation. The service provided in the BOS is long in length. It can be celebrated in its integrity even if it is shortened.

Components of the Service of Ordination and Installation

Gathering. The service begins with a presentation of those who are to be ordained and/or installed. The rubric suggests that after assembling at the entrance of the place of worship, those to be ordained and/or installed are brought before the congregation accompanied by the members of the session. Another possibility is that they are seated together within the congregation and are asked to stand at the time of the presentation.

The presentation is followed by the ordinary elements of "The Service for the Lord's Day": The Call to Worship, Prayer of the Day, Hymn of Praise, Confession and Pardon, The Peace, and a Canticle of Praise. It is important to include a rite of confession and pardon as preparation for ministry which is characterized by humble service.

The Word. The Readings from Scripture are typically those appointed for the day by the Revised Common Lectionary or specifically chosen for the occasion (BOS 113–116). The rubrics suggest that an elder read one or more of the readings and a deacon read the Gospel. A youth or a child could also read a lesson as a reminder that all are called in baptism—men, women, boys and girls. A child reading Scripture calls to mind Jesus' teaching that we are to have faith as a child.

The Sermon is appropriate for the occasion. It could incorporate the theological understanding of baptism as the foundation for all service in the church. The model of the servant ministry of Jesus could be uplifted as the primary example of leadership for the church. The entire congregation could be affirmed in their baptismal calling to discipleship and service.

The response to the sermon is the order for Ordination and Installation. Having heard the Word read and proclaimed, we respond in faith by offering ourselves in lives of service. The Sentences of Scripture are taken from 1 Corinthians 12:4–7, 27. They should be read responsively. They may be divided between liturgist and congregation or between two different groups within the congregation (for example, women, men).

The moderator then reads a Statement interpreting the ordination and/or installation for the congregation. The names of those who are to be ordained and installed are read. The individual(s) proceed forward and face the congregation.

The Reaffirmation of the Baptismal Covenant may follow (BOS 20, 53). The rite takes place next to the baptismal font. All baptized Christians present participate in this liturgy. It serves to remind the congregation that their common calling is grounded in the waters of baptism. All are given the opportunity to affirm their faith, to be renewed, and to have their commitment strengthened. If the reaffirmation is omitted, the Apostles' Creed is included directly after the sermon, and may be led from the font.

Those who are to be ordained and/or installed then move to the front of the place of worship for the questions. The Constitutional Questions (BOS 23, 57, 93) are mandated in the *Book of Order*. The moderator asks the current questions of the candidates. An elder asks the questions of the congregation. It is appropriate to educate the congregation on the purpose of the questions. The ministry of deacon, elder, and minister of the Word and Sacrament is not to be entered into lightly. The questions outline in detail the commitment required for service. The commitment requires a number of affirmative responses for both the candidates and the congregation.

The Prayer of Ordination and the Laying On of Hands by the session (BOS 25, 59, 96) follows the constitutional questions. The session may invite other elders and ministers of Word and Sacrament to participate in the laying on of hands. Those who are to be ordained kneel, facing the congregation with the presbyters behind. Those already ordained remain standing. Several options are given for the actual prayer. The rubric calls for the laying on of hands during one portion of the prayer. It is also appropriate to lay on hands for the entire prayer. Following the prayer the newly ordained rise and stand with those formerly ordained.

In the Declaration of Ordination (and Installation) (BOS 30, 66, 99), the moderator addresses them using a formula provided in the *Book of Order*. The presbyters are welcomed by the elders and ministers. A time of greeting by the congregation is appropriate after the service. A Charge may be given but is not required. Traditionally, charges have been minisermons or exhortations offered to the candidates. This form may be appropriate and meaningful. However, the *Book of Occasional Services* offers several scriptural charges (BOS 31, 66, 100). These words of charge have been given to disciples for centuries and are, therefore, most appropriate on this occasion.

At this point Symbols of Ministry may be presented (BOS 32, 68, 102). These symbols serve as visual reminders of the office of ministry. Appropriate symbols include: pectoral cross, Bible, *Book of Order, Book of Confessions, Book of Common Worship, Companion to the Book of Common Worship, BCW: Daily Prayer Edition,* shell (reminder of baptism), basin and towel. A minister of Word and Sacrament could be given Communion ware, a vessel for anointing with oil, preaching stole, robe, or a book to record baptisms, marriages, funerals, or other services at which the minister presides. Other symbols may be appropriate for particular ministry settings.

The Eucharist. The newly ordained and installed along with all of the baptized community of faith share in the meal where Christ himself is host of the table. In the Sacrament of the Lord's Supper, the Word is sealed and the worshiping community is renewed and strengthened for service. A liturgy for the Lord's Supper is included in the BOS (32, 70, 102) or another from the BCW may be used.

Sending. A deacon dismisses the congregation using the charge given in the BOS (42, 79, 111) or another from the BCW. The minister then gives God's blessing to the congregation. The newly ordained and installed exit the place of worship during the hymn ahead of the congregation so that they may be greeted.

II. Commissioning (BOS 120–129)

In the life of the Christian community God calls people to particular acts of discipleship to use their personal gifts for service in the church and in the world. These specific acts may be strengthened and confirmed by formal recognition in worship. Agreeing to serve as a church school teacher when called at home on a Monday evening is one thing; standing before the congregation and committing oneself to that service is quite another. The act of commissioning gives the church the opportunity to affirm those called to service as well as pledge the support, prayers, and encouragement of the community of faith. "It also establishes a relationship of responsibility and accountability between the congregation and the individual"(BOS 120). When an individual is asked to serve in a particular ministry, it is appropriate to give him or her a copy of the service of commissioning. It details the serious commitment required for service within the church and allows the person to carefully and prayerfully consider his or her willingness to commit to it.

The *Book of Occasional Services* includes three services of commissioning:

1. Commissioning to Ministry within a Congregation
2. Commissioning to Ministry outside a Congregation
3. Commissioning Delegates to a Governing Body

The three are easily adapted to all types of ministry within and outside a congregation as well as for delegates to particular governing bodies. As in the other services included in the BOS, the liturgy is grounded in the baptismal covenant. "The Great Ends of the Church" from the *Book of Order* are given a prominent place in the services "to celebrate the diverse gifts from God given to different people and woven into an intricate fabric of mission by the power of the Holy Spirit" (BOS 121).

Setting

The service of commissioning belongs as a response to the Word read and proclaimed, or as a bearing and following of the Word into the world during the Service for the Lord's Day. The Directory for Worship allows for commissioning to take place during services of worship provided for this purpose or in other appropriate services.

Ideas for the Services of Commissioning

The service may be led by a minister, elder, deacon, or other person affiliated with the ministry to which those being commissioned are called.

A representative from each area of ministry could be involved in the leadership of the service.

A group of children could recite together "The Great Ends of the Church."

Children from the church school may ask the questions of those being commissioned to teach.

Members of the youth group could give the charge to the youth leaders being commissioned.

As with the services of ordination and installation, symbols of ministry may be given to those commissioned (for example, a Bible to a church school teacher, a *Presbyterian Hymnal* to the director of a children's choir, a cross, a *Book of Order* or a *Book of Confessions*).

Components of the Services of Commissioning

Sentences of Scripture. The words are taken from Galatians and Ephesians. They call to mind the unity of the church found in "one body, one Spirit, one hope, one Lord, one faith, one baptism, one God and Father of all." Ministry within the church is shared among all the members. Those commissioned for service are part of the greater mission of the church. These words may be read responsively between liturgist and congregation or they may be divided among different groups within the congregation.

Psalm 133. This brief psalm again calls the church to unity. In unity the blessing of God is found. Other psalms may be substituted for Psalm 133 (for example, Pss. 40, 132, 135).

Call to Discipleship. The Call includes "The Great Ends of the Church" (G-1.0200). This links individual ministries into the mission of the entire church. Those to be commissioned are asked questions similar to those asked at an ordination. "Who is your Lord and Savior? Will you be Christ's faithful disciple . . .? Do you welcome the responsibility of this service . . .? Will you serve the people with energy, intelligence, imagination, and love . . . ?" Those who serve publicly confess their faith and their commitment to faithful discipleship under the lordship of Jesus Christ. The congregation confirms the call of those commissioned and commits themselves to the support and encouragement of those commissioned.

Commissioning Prayer. Prayer is offered on behalf of those commissioned and for the church. The congregation is reminded that as part of its support it is to pray regularly, corporately, and as individuals for those commissioned.

Charge and Blessing. The Charge is offered by a deacon using an appropriate verse from Scripture (BOS 66–68). The minister addresses those who are commissioned with a Blessing.

The service continues with a hymn, with the prayers of the people or with the celebration of the Lord's Supper.

III. Dedication (BOS 142–191)

Buildings and their furnishings are physical things useful in the service of Christ. Care is taken for their planning, building, and purchase; care must be taken for their public dedication. Proper dedication gives the community the opportunity to unite together in thanksgiving and commitment. "It is appropriate for the church to celebrate these gifts from God and to make a commitment that they will be put to use in a faithful manner to advance the mission of the church in the world" (BOS 142). The *Book of Occasional Services* offers liturgies to dedicate buildings and furnishings of a church, Christian home, health care facility, educational institution, and community service agency. These may be adapted for other things that could be dedicated in service to the church (for example, a church playground). The services are as follows:

Order for Groundbreaking
Order for Laying of a Cornerstone
Dedication of a Church Building and Furnishings
Dedication of a Christian Home
Dedication of a Health Care Facility
Dedication of an Educational Institution
Dedication of a Community Service Agency

Orders for Groundbreaking and Laying of a Cornerstone (BOS 144–155)

The Setting. If the congregation is breaking ground or laying a cornerstone for a new place of worship, then the dedication may begin at the current place of worship. A second option is for the congregation to gather at the site of the new worship place or building. The orders follow the Service for the Lord's Day or may be held independently of Sunday morning worship.

Ideas for Groundbreaking or the Laying of a Cornerstone

Each member of the congregation is given the opportunity to design and paint a rock that will be placed in the new foundation. Before the service, the rocks are placed over the foundation site in the shape of a cross. Pictures are taken of individual rocks and of the rock cross. The foundation is poured over it.

A poem or piece of sacred music may be commissioned for the occasion.

A mission statement for the new building site may be composed and included in the service.

Church school children and youth groups may make colorful banners for the procession to the site.

A time capsule may be put together including such things as a Sunday bulletin and church directory and placed in the foundation or in the cornerstone.

Leadership of the service may include representatives from the entire congregation: charter members, children, youth, adults, church school teachers, choir members, representatives from various ministries of the congregation.

The prayers may be written by the children, youth, or other representatives of the congregation.

Dedication of a Church Building and Furnishings (BOS 156–179)

The purpose of this service of dedication is to give thanks corporately to God for the gift(s) and to offer them in service to God and for God's glory. The dedication properly belongs within "The Service for the Lord's Day," the primary service of the church. Because all property held by or for a particular church is held in trust for the use and benefit of the Presbyterian Church (U.S.A) (G-8.0200), members of a presbytery commission participate in this service along with the congregation.

The actual dedication of a building or particular furnishings follows the Gathering in the order of service. The components of the dedication include: Call to Worship, Prayer, Hymn, Anthem, Psalm or Spiritual, and Prayers of Dedication. Various representatives from the congregation (for example, deacons, elders, children, youth, choir members) and members of the presbytery commission may provide leadership for this service.

The *Book of Occasional Services* includes specific prayers of dedication for the baptismal font or pool, the pulpit, the pulpit/lectern Bible, the table, the Communion vessels, the organ or other musical instruments, the sanctuary or chapel, an educational facility, a columbarium (BOS 160–166). These prayers may be adapted when other furnishings are dedicated such as vestments, choir robes, candle stands, or vases.

Ideas for the Dedication of a Church Building and Furnishings

> Form a worship team to plan the dedication. Include persons from all areas of the congregation.
> Invite representatives from neighboring congregations.
> Give tours following the service.
> Provide an outline of a map/layout for coloring by the children.
> Commission a piece of music, a poem, or a special banner for the occasion.
> For the bulletin, use a drawing of the new church for the cover art. Include the church's mission statement on the inside cover.
> Write a booklet detailing the church and its furnishings.

Dedication of a Christian Home (BOS 180–183)

The Christian home is the primary place of Christian training and nurture. The stories and traditions of the faith are handed down from parents to their children. In the home, children learn what it means to live out their baptismal callings daily, to be disciples of Jesus Christ. The dedication of a Christian home bears witness to this reality and offers the home and those who reside in it to God's service and for God's glory.

A Christian home is an appropriate place for daily worship. Daily worship sets the rhythm and tone for daily life. Seasons of the Christian year provide direction and content for household worship. The Directory for Worship offers suggestions for household worship which includes: table prayer, reading of Scripture, singing, morning and evening prayer, study, reflection and Scripture memorization, expressions of giving and sharing.

When children are in a home, the family may share and tell Bible stories along with family stories of faith. The catechism, *Belonging to God,* provides an opportunity for the entire family to learn the basics of the faith. Sharing and learning may occur in a variety of places within a home such as around the table, at bedtime, or in the family room. Children may be taught the elements of corporate worship such as the creeds or the Lord's Prayer. In regular prayer, children are taught to give thanks, confess, and bring petitions and supplications to God. Worshiping at home gives praise and honor to God and reminds the family that worship is appropriate at all times and in all places.

The dedication of a Christian home may be a new service for many in the congregation. Information about it could be presented at a session meeting, in a Sunday morning Bible class, in a newsletter or bulletin article. A pastor, elder, or deacon might approach a family who has recently moved into a new home.

Components of the Dedication of a Christian Home

> Greeting—The dedication begins as all gather near the entry door.
> Scriptures—Matthew 5:14–16
> Prayers—The prayers are offered in each room of the home.

Ideas for the Dedication of a Christian Home

> Invitations may be sent to family members, friends, members of the congregation.
> A luncheon or supper could follow a dedication.
> The children could prepare special artwork depicting Bible stories or Christian symbols to decorate the walls of the home.
> A family member could write a poem for the occasion.
> The family could write their own prayers for each room.
> The family could prepare a personal mission statement.
> An order of service could be printed. It could include cover art by a member of the family.
> A candle is lighted at the beginning of the dedication representing the light of Christ. A baptismal candle could serve this purpose. The candle could be passed to the person offering the prayer in a particular room. After the dedication, the candle could be put in a special place as a reminder of Christ's presence.
> Prayers may be offered by different people. A child may say the prayer for his or her own room.
> The children of the family could sing a special hymn, psalm, or spiritual song.

Dedication of a Health Care Facility (BOS 184–186)

Dedication of an Educational Institution (BOS 187–190)

Dedication of a Community Service Agency (BOS 191–193)

The Setting. These liturgies may be used as part of a public ceremony to inaugurate the use of a particular agency or to inaugurate the use of a church-related school, college, or seminary. In a larger service of dedication, the liturgy of dedication follows the proclamation of the Word.

Components of the Services of Dedication

> Announcement of Purpose
> Sentences of Scripture
> Scripture Reading
> Prayer of Dedication
> Blessing

IV. Marking Transitions in a Congregation (BOS 196–257)

> Constituting a Congregation
> Reception of New Members
> Recognition of Departing Members
> Recognition of Thanksgiving for Faithful Service
> Dissolution of a Pastoral Call
> Celebration of a Congregational Anniversary
> Uniting of a Congregation by a Presbytery
> Vacating of a Church Building (Including the Dissolution of a Church)

Change is common in the life of God's people both corporately and individually. Transitions are at times welcome and at others not. Feelings about them may be strong or ambivalent. By marking transitions in worship God's people are given the opportunity to give thanks, to celebrate, to grieve, or to say good-bye together in the presence of God. Publicly ignoring such times in the life of a congregation curtails the healthy process of working through change and moving forward to a new phase of ministry and common life.

The worship planner(s) must take care and anticipate the feelings that may be present for a particular service marking a transition. A service where a pastoral call is dissolved may be joyful and celebrate the years of shared ministry as well as be a time of sadness, grief, and fear of an unknown future. Vacating a church building in favor of a new and larger worship space may be an exciting time for a congregation, but it is accompanied by feelings of nostalgia and particular memories. Perhaps in the older sanctuary a child was baptized, a marriage was celebrated, or a funeral took place and it is therefore difficult to leave a worship space so full of memories. Sensitivity must be used as the entire service is planned. The service may need to be both joyful, full of expectation and yet reflective, and thankful for the past.

V. Marking Transitions in a Governing Body (BOS 265–281)

Installation of Governing Body Officers and Staff
Receiving a Candidate under Care
Recognition of a Certified Christian Educator
Commissioning of a Lay Pastor
Recognition of Honorable Retirement from the Ministry of Word and Sacrament

Services marking transitions in a governing body provide an opportunity for the church to celebrate particular ministries of the church as well as specific stages of the ministry of Word and Sacrament. The church in worship is able to give thanks, and offer prayers and support for particular individuals and their work.

VI. Interfaith Resources (BOS 285–288)

In a pluralistic society, Christians encounter people from a variety of faith traditions in the workplace, in schools, in neighborhoods, and in families. At times, different faith communities gather around particular community concerns (for example, disaster relief, social services, advocacy for justice, peace). Sometimes in these settings, opportunities for prayer and religious rites arise. At these moments, Christians are faced with a choice. The event is treated as either a secular occasion or a time to include the religious expressions of the representative faiths.

It is possible for a Christian to make the latter choice with integrity. Interfaith prayer or celebration is different from the act of Christian corporate worship. In Christian worship, the baptized community is joined together by its commitment to respond to God's grace offered to it in Jesus Christ. In interfaith celebrations, two or more faith communities gather around common concerns and values. At these, each religious community present recognizes the distinctive religious traditions and commitments of the other communities. Christians may practice respectful presence. Guidelines for interfaith celebration, prayer, and worship are provided in the (BOS 286–287). Further guidelines are offered by the Office of Ecumenical and Interfaith Relations, Presbyterian Church (U.S.A.), 100 Witherspoon Street, Louisville, Ky. 40202–1396. A sample prayer is given (BOS 287–288). Other resources are offered (BOS 288).

VII. Additional Prayers for Various Occasions (BOS 290–296)

These Additional Prayers supplement the Prayers for Various Occasions (BCW 785–837).

Glossary of Terms

(including some examples from BCW and BOS)

Acolyte (Greek, "one who follows"). One who carries a torch or a candle in a liturgical procession; now, more widely applied to persons who help prepare the liturgical space and assist the ministers of the service.

Advent (Latin, *advenire,* "to come"). A (four-week) season of hope, anticipating the future coming of Christ to judge and to establish his rule over all things; therefore, preparations are made for the coming of the Word, Jesus Christ, in whom God's saving purposes are realized. (BCW 165)

Affirmation/Confession of Faith or Creed. Written statements in which an ecclesiastical body describes its faith in doctrinal terms. (BCW 63)

Affusion. The pouring of water on the candidate at baptism. (BCW 441)

Agnus Dei (Latin, "Lamb of God, you take away the sin of the world"). The opening words of an ancient Eastern hymn to Christ, based on John 1:29, Isaiah 53:7; and Revelation 5:6ff., sung at the breaking of the bread (the "fraction") in the Eucharist (BCW 74), during the serving of the elements, during the Great Litany (BCW 787), or following the Confession of Sin (BCW 55).

Alb (Latin, *alba,* "white"). Long white tunic, close-fitting, narrow-sleeved, ankle-length, worn at services by liturgical leaders, ordained and unordained. Became a vestment of Christians in the fifth century.

Anamnesis (Greek, "remembrance," "recalling"). An act by which a person or event is made ritually present; for example, the part of the Great Thanksgiving that remembers the whole life and work of Christ, making those saving deeds a present experience. (BCW 71)

Anointing with Oil. Enacted prayer whereby oil is placed on the forehead of the newly baptized (BCW 413) or an individual seeking intercession (BCW 1019).

Antiphonal (Greek, "opposite voices"). Two voices or groups of voices alternating sung responses.

Ascension of the Lord. The final resurrection appearance of the risen Christ, on the fortieth day after Easter, and his reception and coronation in heaven. This exaltation of Christ looks both back to transfiguration and Easter and forward to Christ the King (or Reign of Christ). (BCW 332)

Assembly. The gathered community at worship.

Ashes. Traditionally, the palms from the previous Palm/Passion Sunday are burned and their ashes used for the imposition of ashes on Ash Wednesday. (BCW 227)

Ash Wednesday. The first day of the Lenten journey to Easter; signifies a time to turn around, to change directions, to repent and, therefore, centers on both human mortality and confession of sin before God. (BCW 221)

Benediction/Blessing (Latin, *benedicare*, "to bless"). Imparting God's blessing on God's people at the close of a service. (BCW 78)

"Blessed is the one who comes" (Latin, *Benedictus qui venit*). The opening words (Ps. 118:26) of the anthem sung after the *Sanctus* ("Holy, holy, holy"). (BCW 70)

Candidate. One for whom baptism is appropriate (for example, a child of a parent who is an active member of a Christian church; or, an adult who is preparing to make a profession of faith). (BCW 405)

Canticle (Latin, *canticulum*, "a little song"). A biblical song other than one of the psalms. (BCW 573)

Cantor (Latin, *cantare*, "singer"). A singer; particularly, one who guides the singing of the congregation.

Chalice (from Latin, *calix*, for "cup"). The cup that contains the wine used in the celebration of the Eucharist.

Chancel (Latin, *cancelli*, "lattice work," "screen"). Area of the worship space beyond the nave often containing the choir.

Choir. A group of singers who assist in rendering musically the services of the church.

Chrism. Oil used for anointing, often mixed with a delicate fragrance. Strictly speaking, chrism is a mixture of oil (usually olive oil) and fragrance (often balsam). (BCW 413, 1019)

Chrismation. Anointing with chrism.

Christmas (Incarnation) Cycle. Advent, Christmas, and Epiphany. Christmas–Epiphany is preceded by a time of preparation, Advent. The Christmas cycle focuses on preparing for and celebrating the coming of the Word, Jesus Christ, in whom God's saving purposes are realized.

Christmas Day. The celebration of incarnation—God in flesh. The Gospel According to John (1:14) announces that "the Word became flesh and lived among us, . . . full of grace and truth." Christmas acclaims the advent of the messianic salvation. Christ was sent among us *in order to save us*. (BCW 178)

Christological. With reference to Christ (for example, a theology focusing on Christ's identity).

Christ the King (Reign of Christ). Ends our marking of Ordinary Time after the Day of Pentecost, and moves us to the threshold of Advent. Centers us upon the crucified and risen Christ, whom God exalted to rule over the whole universe. The celebration of the lordship of Christ thus looks back to Ascension, Easter, and transfiguration, and points ahead to the appearing in glory of the King of kings and Lord of lords. (BCW 394)

Church Year/Liturgical Year. The cycle of the Christian calendar, beginning with Advent.

Cincture. White rope worn around waist of the alb.

Clinical Baptism (Greek, *kline*, "bed"). Death-bed or emergency baptism.

Collect. See Prayer of the Day/Collect.

Columbarium (Latin, *columb(e)*, "dove," and *arium*, "place" = "dovecote" or "pigeon house," a fairly large and often elaborate structure). Used in Etruscan and (pre-Christian) Roman history as a sepulchral building that contained numerous niches for the urns of human ashes. In recent decades, a large-scale revival of crematory burial has resulted in the construction of many kinds of columbaria, both inside the church building and outside in the churchyard. (BCW 941)

Commissioning. The act by which the church publicly affirms individuals called to service as well as pledges the support, prayers, and encouragement of the community of faith. (BOS 119)

Communion Table. See Lord's Table.

Confession of Sin. A regular opportunity for congregations to bow in humility before the God of grace. By transferring the prayer of the priest to the whole congregation, the Reformers made the statement that it was the congregation as a whole who celebrated the liturgy, and not the priest alone with the congregation as an audience. In the Prayer of Confession, we trust God's mercy enough to lay before God not only those sins which may belong to us individually and personally, but also the sins and brokenness of the congregation, the church universal, and the world (that is, the tragic brokenness of our human condition). (BCW 53)

Cremains. The ashes of a deceased person. (BCW 941)

Daily Prayer/Office (Latin, *officium*, "duty" or "service"). The daily public prayers of the church which from the fifth century included morning and evening prayer as well as other hours of each day. (BCW 489)

Declaration of Forgiveness/Pardon. A proclamation, in the words of Scriptures, of the good news that in Jesus Christ we are forgiven. For Calvin, repentance is not a prior condition for mercy but the appropriate response to mercy and also, of course, a work of God. The Declaration announces God's faithfulness in doing for us what we cannot do for ourselves. Our lives are redeemed by the saving grace of God. (BCW 56)

Dedication. The act by which the church publicly celebrates the gift of a building, its furnishings, or other objects, and commits that they will be put to use in a faithful manner to advance the mission of the church in the world. (BOS 142)

Directory for Worship. In seventeenth-century England, Puritanism gained a foothold, leading to Parliament deciding to reform the standards of the church, thus convened the Westminster Assembly, in 1643, to write a confessional document *and* a prayer book. The Assembly produced the Westminster Confession, but was unable to please all three factions (Presbyterian Puritans, Independents, and Scots) regarding the service book. The Assembly did agree, however, on a compromise measure: a Directory that prescribed how things should be done (that is, shape and content but not texts). The Directory became the predominant influence on the worship of the English-speaking body of Reformed churches for the next three hundred years. Since 1788, the Directory has served as American Presbyterians' constitutional basis for worship and, thereby, sets the standards and the norms for worship. (BCW 1)

Dismissal. See Sending.

Dominical. Having to do with the Lord.

Doxology; doxological. Referring to acts of praise and glorifying the triune God.

Easter (Resurrection) Cycle. Lent, Easter, and the Day of Pentecost. The Easter cycle celebrates the central event of the story of our salvation—the cross *and* the resurrection. Lent anticipates the resurrection, and Easter remembers the cost of the cross's life-giving victory. On the eschatological *pentecoste* ("fiftieth") day of celebrating Christ's resurrection, Christians celebrate God's gift of the Spirit to empower witnesses to the resurrection.

Ecumenical. Representing the whole church throughout the world, transcending confessional and denominational boundaries.

Eighth Day. As the first Christians (primarily Jews) recalled the creation stories of Genesis, they remembered the creational week: how God worked for six days and rested on the seventh. On the eighth day of creation ("the first day of the week," according to all four Gospels), God continued the work of creation by raising Christ from the dead. This eighth day of creation/first day of the week is what became commonly known as the Lord's Day (Rev. 1:10), the day of resurrection—what the *Epistle of Barnabas* calls "the beginning of a new world, because that was when Jesus rose from the dead."

Enacted Prayer. Prayer that combines words and specific actions, for example, the laying on of hands, anointing with oil.

Epiclesis (Greek, "invocation"). Prayer seeking the blessing or work of the Holy Spirit in the Great (Prayer of) Thanksgiving at the Lord's Supper (BCW 72), or in the thanksgiving over the water during the Sacrament of Baptism (BCW 412).

Epiphany (Greek, *epiphainein*, "to appear"). The annual celebration on January 6 of the manifestation of the divinity of Christ to the Gentiles represented by the magi—the showing forth of the true Light to the world. (BCW 191)

Eschatology (Greek, *eschatos*, "last," "farthest"). The study of the ultimate destiny or purpose of humankind and the world.

Eucharist (Lord's Supper, Holy Communion); eucharistic. From a New Testament Greek word meaning "thanksgiving," it refers to the Lord's Supper or Holy Communion. (BCW 67)

Evening Prayer. The principle office of prayer for twilight—as the daylight fades and darkness enshrouds.

Ewer. A pitcher used to carry water to the baptismal font. (BCW 403)

Extended Serving. The serving of the Lord's Supper to those unable to share in the meal with the gathered community. The Sacrament is taken to absent members as a direct extension of the Lord's Day service. (BCW 995)

Flagon (from Latin, *flasco*, for "bottle" or "flask"). A pitcher in which the wine is kept before being poured into the chalice or cup during the Eucharist. (BCW 74)

Font (Latin, *fons*, "spring," "fountain"). A basin or tank that holds water for administering the Sacrament of Baptism. (BCW 403)

Fraction. The breaking of the eucharistic bread for distribution. (BCW 74)

Funeral: Service of Witness to the Resurrection. A service conducted at the time of death. (BCW 911)

Gathering. The first act of public worship: responding to God's call to join with others in praising God. The people, thus, assemble in the name of the Lord. (BCW 48)

Gloria Patri (Latin, "Glory to the Father"). The opening words of an ascription of glory to the three Persons of the Trinity, often used as an attribution of praise to the promise of God's mercy and reconciliation, as well as appended to psalmody and canticles. (BCW 59)

Gloria in Excelsis (Latin, "Glory [to God] in the highest"). The opening words of a fourth-century hymn based on the song of the angels (Luke 2:14), usually sung during the twelve-day Christmas and fifty-day Easter seasons as well as during the Eucharist. (BCW 58)

Good Friday. Annual Holy Week commemoration of the crucifixion: the day's penitential service also celebrates the good news of the cross. (BCW 281)

Great Vigil of Easter. The concluding service of The Three Days (*Triduum*). The principal service of the year, since at least the second century, that celebrates on the night of nights the promise of new life, of forgiveness of sins, and of victory over death. (BCW 297)

Healing. To experience wholeness, God's shalom, through the transforming power of God's love made known in the person of Jesus Christ.

Inclusive Language. Language that is sensitive to the fact that there are two genders, female and male.

Installation. The act by which the church sets apart those previously ordained to the office and called anew to service to it with prayer. (BOS 5)

Intinction. In Communion, the act of dipping a morsel of bread into the cup. (BCW 75, 1001)

Kirk. A Scottish word for church.

Laying On of Hands. A form of enacted prayer whereby one or more members of the community pray over an individual with the specific action of hands placed on the head or shoulders. (BCW 413; BOS 26, 60)

lectio continua (Latin, "continuous reading"). A beeline approach: reading continuously through Scripture, verse by verse, beginning one Sunday (or day) where the reading ended the prior Sunday (or day). Probably derives from the custom of continuous reading of the entire Torah (Pentateuch) in Jewish synagogues on a weekly basis throughout the year. (BCW 1034)

lectio (s)electa (Latin, "select reading"). A leapfrog approach: selecting a biblical text according to its relation to time of year, first lesson, festival, theme, and so forth. The Jewish practice of selecting a second lesson called *haftarah*, a reading from the Prophets, demonstrates this ancient method of choosing a biblical text to coincide with time of year or the lesson from the Torah. (BCW 1034)

Lectionary. Technically speaking, the name of the book of lections (Scripture lessons or pericopes) to be read according to a prescribed schedule during either Sunday worship or daily prayer. Generally speaking, a table of readings providing for a systematic reading of the Scriptures; an orderly sequence of selections from Scripture to be read during worship. (BCW 1033)

Lector/Reader. The liturgical leader who reads a lection (Scripture lesson) during a service.

Lent. "Forty days and forty nights" of the way of the cross to Easter. Apparently evolved as a time for training, particularly as a time of final preparation of candidates for baptism at Easter, a time for the renewal of the faithful, and a time for the excommunicated to prepare to return to the community of faith. Thus, a period of study, prayer, and almsgiving, focusing on what it means to be a follower of Christ. (BCW 235)

Litany (Greek "supplication"). An ancient responsive form of prayer. (BCW 103–117, 787, 792)

Liturgical Year/Church Year. The cycle of the Christian calendar, beginning with Advent.

Liturgy. From two Greek words (*laos* and *ergon*) meaning "people's service or work." In a context of worship, refers to the actions of the assembly as the service of the people. Also, the *ordo*, or sequence of linked events that combine to form the service of worship.

"Lord, have mercy" (Greek, *Kyrie Eleison*). Usually follows the Prayer of Confession. The Kyrie is possibly based on Psalm 51:3 or Matthew 15:25, and is first evidenced as a response in the fourth-century churches of Jerusalem and Antioch. Both John Calvin and Martin Luther used the Kyrie as an act of contrition. Actually it is both an "action of contrition" and "an affirmation," an affirmation that the Lord *has* mercy! (BCW 55)

Lord's Day/Sunday. The day of the resurrection, the first day of the new creation; the day on which Christians assemble for their liturgy.

Lord's Table. The table that holds the bread and wine for the Lord's Supper, along with the necessary vessels. A visible symbol of Christ's presence in the assembly.

Lucernarium. The Service of Light, thanking God for the day, that opens Evening Prayer. A Jewish practice carried forward by Christians over the centuries. (BCW 505)

Manual Acts. Actions that occur at the Communion when the presiding minister breaks the bread and pours from the chalice. (BCW 74)

Marriage. Grounded in the doctrine of creation; thus, the gift of God to all humanity. Also, a dimension of discipleship in which couples seek to bring their marriage into accord with the will of God and to allow their relationship with Christ to form the pattern for the covenant of marriage (Eph. 5:21ff.). (BCW 839)

Mass. The Roman Catholic eucharistic service (from the Latin word *missa* used at the end of the service to dismiss the congregation).

Maundy Thursday. The opening service of the Triduum (three days). The day gets its name from the term *mandatum* (Latin, commandment), which was applied to the rite of the foot-washing on this day (John 13:14–17). The service combines both penitential and celebra-tory acts: restoration through the bold declaration of pardon, the act of footwashing connoting humility and intimacy, the celebration of the Lord's Supper embodying the mys-tery of Christ's enduring redemptive presence, and the concluding act of the stripping of the church (worship space) when the stark, bare environment reflects the tone of the con-cluding days and services of the Triduum in preparation for Easter. Maundy Thursday's acts provide the paradox of a celebratively somber and solemnly celebrative service. (BCW 269)

Metrical Psalmody. A collection of psalms in which the psalm text is paraphrased into poetic meter (usually rhyming) and sung to a hymn tune.

Midday Prayer. The principle office of prayer for the middle of the day.

Morning Prayer. The principal office of prayer for early morning,

Narthex. A waiting or gathering area outside the worship space proper.

Nave (Latin, *navis*, "ship"; Greek, *naos*, "ship," "the principal area of a temple"). The main or large portion of a church's liturgical space, located between the narthex and the choir or crossing (the intersection of the nave, chancel, and transepts). The shiplike appearance of the nave is often related to the church's calling as the ark of salvation.

O Antiphons. Verses traditionally sung before and after the Magnificat during Evening Prayer on the seven days preceding Christmas Eve (December 17–23). (BCW 166)

Occasional Services. Liturgical acts observed infrequently, such as ordination, installation, commissioning, dedication, transitions (for example, reception of members, recognition of departing members, celebration of a congregational anniversary), services conducted in a governing body (for example, receiving a candidate under care, recognition of honorable retirement), and interfaith celebrations. (BOS)

Offering (Latin, *offere*, "to carry up"). The presentation of oneself and one's gifts for the ser-vice of God (cf. Rom. 12:1); the presentation of the gifts of bread and wine for the service of God. Because the offering is rooted in the people's offerings of bread and wine, it has a profound relation to the church's Eucharist. Reformed churches of the 1500s notably linked the church's calling to serve the poor and, therefore, scheduled the "collection" at the *end* of the service, as the people *departed*, because they believed *their meeting with Christ at the Table* was to be *continued in the world* where Christ awaited discovery in the guise of the neighbor in need. (BCW 67)

Orans (Latin, "praying"). Slowly raising hands on either side, palms up, in a lifting motion, used particularly during the eucharistic prayer. (BCW 69)

Ordinary Time. The periods between Epiphany and Lent, and between Pentecost and Advent, when the focus is on the Lord's (resurrection) Day which unfolds that which is becoming all of creation's ordinary time. (BCW 205, 354)

Ordination. The act by which the church sets apart persons who have been called through elec-tion by the church to serve as presbyters with the laying on of hands. (BOS 11, 45)

Ordo (Latin, "order," "structure," "shape," "pattern"). The sequence of events that developed historically as the shape of the Christian service of worship; particularly, the combination of Word and Sacrament that resulted when the synagogue service and the shared Meal (Lord's Supper) were combined in a single service. (BCW 33–47)

Ostinato. A response sung repetitively.

Paschal (Easter) Cycle. Having to do with Pascha, or Easter (related to the Greek word for Passover). See Easter (Resurrection) Cycle.

Passion/Palm Sunday. Combines the joyful entry of the palm processional and the somberness of the passion, the focus of Holy Week. The triumphal entry serves as a gateway to the week. Christ's suffering and death for all is then proclaimed through the passion narratives in Matthew, Mark, or Luke. (BCW 252)

Pastoral Liturgies. Services with the sick, the troubled, those in distress, the dying both within and beyond the Christian community, and those unable to attend public worship; services for wholeness; and services of repentance and forgiveness for use with a penitent individual. (BCW 965)

Paten (Latin, *patina*, "main dish"). A plate or shallow dish that holds the bread used in Holy Communion.

Penitent. An individual seeking forgiveness.

Pew. Thirteenth-century Western innovation: wooden benches for the congregation. Previously, standing or kneeling was the customary posture, except for the infirm for whom stone ledges were provided around the church walls.

Piety. Love for God manifested in the believer's heart and in specific Christian disciplines or practices.

Prayer for Illumination. Asks God by the Holy Spirit to open our minds and hearts to the Word so that we may not only hear but understand and believe and enact. A tradition cherished by the Reformed churches, expressing the conviction that the words of Scripture of themselves have no power apart from God's power. (BCW 60, 90)

Prayer of the Day/Collect. A brief prayer consisting of an opening address, petition, and closing doxology. (BCW 50)

Preaching. See Sermon.

Presider. The one who takes the leading role in worship; particularly, the one who offers the Great Thanksgiving at the Lord's Table.

Reformation. A reform movement in the church, particularly associated with the sixteenth-century reforms initiated by Martin Luther, and supported and further developed by Huldrych Zwingli, Martin Bucer, John Calvin, and by English reformers such as Thomas Cranmer. On the left wing of the Reformation, Anabaptists took a more radical approach.

Reformed. That stream of Protestantism stemming particularly from the Swiss Reformation, particularly influenced by Zwingli and more profoundly by John Calvin. Reformed churches are variously named. The most common in English-speaking countries is Presbyterian or Congregational; in Europe, the most common name is "Reformed." However, the Reformed tradition has had a broader influence than those churches. For example, early Anglicans espoused Reformed theology.

Responsorial Psalmody. An art in which a person (called a cantor) or a choir sings the stanzas of the psalm, and the congregation sings a refrain after each verse or group of verses.

Revised Common Lectionary. Provides for a three-year cycle of three Scripture readings, following the basic calendar of the Western church. The 1992 revised edition and its earlier edition of 1983 continue the pattern of the Roman *Lectionary for Mass* of 1969.

Rubrics. Directions for the conduct of the service; received name from the red (Latin, *ruber*) ink in which they usually were printed in liturgical books.

Sabbath. Saturday, the seventh day, kept by Jews as holy to the Lord in honor of the creation.

Sacrament. A classic definition is "an outward and visible sign of an inward and spiritual grace." Certain actions accompanied by prayer with the intention of laying claim to God's promises, most especially for Protestants, baptism and the Lord's Supper.

Sanctus (Latin, "Holy"). A doxology sung during the Great Thanksgiving, drawn from Isaiah 6 and Psalm 118. The doxology begins "Holy, holy, holy Lord . . ." (BCW 70)

Seekers' Service. An assembly designed to attract and convert persons who have made no spiritual commitment, but are curious about the possibilities.

Sending. Dismissal of the people with God's blessing to serve. (BCW 77)

Sermon (from Latin *sermo*, "conversation" or "discourse"). Exposition of a scriptural text addressed by a preacher to an assembly, connecting the proclamation of the Bible with contemporary experience and situations so that by the Holy Spirit, Jesus Christ may be present to the assembly, both offering grace and calling for our obedient response. (BCW 62)

Sursum corda (Latin for "Lift up your hearts"). Part of the opening dialogue of the Great Thanksgiving. (BCW 69)

Symbols of Ministry. Objects that serve as visual reminders of the office of ministry presented at the time of ordination and/or installation.

Thanksgiving. Pertains to gratitude for what God has done for you in Christ (for example, Col. 3:12–17).

Third Use. Calvin's understanding that the Torah, or Law of God (particularly the moral law as expressed in the Ten Commandments) is useful to Christians not as a means to their salvation, but as a guide in the living of a devout, righteous, and just life. The "first use" is to use the careful keeping of the Law as a claim on God's favor; the "second use" is to understand the Law as beyond the capacity of human beings to keep, and therefore, God's rightful accusation against us, driving us to God's free grace as the only remedy for our condition.

Tokens of Remembrance. A gift or small token left by a pastoral visitor as a reminder of the faith community's love and support.

Transfiguration of the Lord. Commemoration of the transfiguration (a change in form) of Christ (cf. Matt. 17:1–8; Mark 9:2–8; Luke 9:28–36). As the event marking the transition in Jesus' ministry in which he "set his face to go to Jerusalem" (Luke 9:51), where he would die, the transfiguration is observed on the Sunday immediately prior to Ash Wednesday. Thus ends our marking of Ordinary Time after Epiphany, and moves us to the threshold of Lent. (BCW 214)

Trinity Sunday. Celebration of the unfathomable mystery of God's being as Holy Trinity. A day of adoration and praise of the one, eternal, incomprehensible God who has taken flesh and dwelt among us in Jesus Christ, and in the Holy Spirit has become our Sanctifier, Guide, and Teacher. (BCW 348)

Trisagion (Greek, "Holy God . . . have mercy upon us"). A common hymn in the liturgies of Eastern churches which sing it three times. (BCW 55)

Westminster Directory. Adopted by an English Puritan assembly in 1644; later, became part of the constitution of the Church of Scotland and many Presbyterian churches, including those in America. The Directory was a set of rubrics, giving general directions about the conduct of worship without providing particular texts except for a few instances. The Westminster Directory was one of several documents produced by the Assembly, including the Westminster Confession of Faith and the Shorter and Larger Catechisms. American Presbyterian Directories for Worship are contemporary heirs of the tradition established by the Westminster Directory. (BCW 1)

Appendix B

For Further Reading

GENERAL TEXTS

Allen, Horace T. "Book of Common Worship (1993): The Presbyterian Church (U.S.A.), 'Origins and Anticipations.'" In *To Glorify God: Essays on Modern Reformed Liturgy*, ed. Bryan D. Spinks and Iain R. Torrance, 13–29. Edinburgh: T. & T. Clark, 1999.

———. "The Function and Authority of Liturgical Books in the Presbyterian Church (U.S.A.)." *Reformed Liturgy & Music* 27, no. 1 (1993): 11–14.

Anderson, Fred R. "Book of Common Worship (1993): A Pastoral Overview." *The Princeton Seminary Bulletin* 16, no. 2 (New Series 1995): 121–137.

Bower, Peter C. "Free Church and Prayer Book Church." *Reformed Liturgy & Music* 27, no. 1 (1993): 6–7.

Bradshaw, Paul. *Early Christian Worship: A Basic Introduction to Ideas and Practices*. Collegeville, Minn.: Liturgical Press, 2000.

Byars, Ronald P. *Christian Worship: Glorifying and Enjoying God*. Louisville, Ky.: Geneva Press, 2000.

Campbell, Cynthia M., and J. Frederick Holper. *Praying in Common*. Theology and Worship Occasional Paper No. 6. Presbyterian Church (U.S.A.), Christian Faith and Life, Congregational Ministries Division, n.d.

Daniels, Harold M. "The Book of Common Worship," *Vanguard* 30, no. 3 (July 1993): 3–7.

———. "The Making of the Book of Common Worship (1993)." In *To Glorify God: Essays on Modern Reformed Liturgy*, ed. Bryan D. Spinks and Iain R. Torrance, 31–53. Edinburgh: T. & T. Clark, 1999.

———. "Presbyterian Worship: Directories and Service Books," *Reformed Liturgy & Worship* 23, no. 4 (1989): 169–72.

———. *To God Alone Be Glory: The Story and Sources of the Book of Common Worship*. Louisville, Ky.: Geneva Press, 2003.

Davies, J. G., ed. *The New Westminster Dictionary of Liturgy and Worship*. Philadelphia: Westminster Press, 1986.

Dawn, Marva J. *Reaching Out without Dumbing Down*. Grand Rapids: Wm. B. Eerdmans Publishing Co., 1995.

Dix, Dom Gregory. *The Shape of the Liturgy*. Additional notes by Paul V. Marshall. New York: Seabury Press, 1982.

Duba, Arlo D. "The Book of Common Worship—The Book of Common Order: What do they say and what do they assume about Christ?" In *To Glorify God: Essays on Modern*

287

Reformed Liturgy, ed. Bryan D. Spinks and Iain R. Torrance, 115–41. Edinburgh: T. & T. Clark, 1999.

Erickson, Craig Douglas. *Participating in Worship: History, Theory, and Practice*. Louisville, Ky.: Westminster/John Knox Press, 1989.

Hageman, Howard G. *Pulpit and Table*. Richmond: John Knox Press, 1962.

Hoon, Paul W. *The Integrity of Worship*. Nashville: Abingdon Press, 1971.

Jones, Cheslyn, G. Wainwright, E. Yarnold, P. Bradshaw. *The Study of Liturgy*. London: Oxford University Press, 1992.

Lathrop, Gordon W. *Holy People: A Liturgical Ecclesiology*. Minneapolis: Fortress Press, 1999.

_____. *Holy Things: A Liturgical Theology*. Minneapolis: Fortress Press, 1993.

_____. *What Are the Essentials of Christian Worship?* Open Questions in Worship. Minneapolis: Augsburg/Fortress Press, 1994.

Maxwell, William D. *An Outline of Christian Worship: Its Development and Forms*. London: Oxford University Press, 1960.

Meeks, Blair Gilmer. *The Landscape of Praise: Readings in Liturgical Renewal*. Valley Forge, Pa.: Trinity Press International, 1996.

Pfatteicher, Philip H. *Liturgical Spirituality*. Valley Forge, Pa.: Trinity Press International, 1997.

Rice, Howard L., and J. C. Huffstutler. *Reformed Worship*. Louisville, Ky.: Geneva Press, 2001.

Saliers, Don E. *The Soul in Paraphrase: Prayer and the Religious Affections*. Akron: OSL Publications, 1991.

_____. *Worship Come to Its Senses*. Nashville: Abingdon Press, 1996.

_____. *Worship as Spirituality*, 2d ed. Akron: OSL Publications, 1996.

_____. *Worship as Theology: A Foretaste of Glory Divine*. Nashville: Abingdon Press, 1994.

Senn, Frank C. *Christian Liturgy: Catholic and Evangelical*. Minneapolis: Fortress Press, 1997.

Stake, Donald Wilson. *The ABCs of Worship: A Concise Dictionary*. Louisville, Ky.: Westminster/John Knox Press, 1992.

Thompson, Bard. *Liturgies of the Western Church*. Philadelphia: Fortress Press, 1961.

von Allmen, J. J. *Worship: Its Theology and Practice*. New York: Oxford University Press, 1965.

White, James F. *Introduction to Christian Worship*. 3d ed. Nashville: Abingdon Press, 2000.

BAPTISM

Baptism, Eucharist, and Ministry. Faith and Order Paper, no. 111. Geneva: World Council of Churches, 1982.

Benedict, Daniel. *Come to the Waters*. Nashville: Discipleship Resources, 1996.

Collins, A. "The Origin of Christian Baptism." *Studia Liturgica* 19, no. 1 (1989): 28–46.

Holper, J. Frederick. "'Choose This Day Whom You Will Serve'—The Significance of Renunciations in the Sacrament of Baptism." *Reformed Liturgy & Music* 29, no. 2 (1995): 74–77.

Johnson, Maxwell E. *The Rites of Christian Initiation: Their Evolution and Interpretation*. Collegeville, Minn.: Liturgical Press, 1999.

Johnson, Maxwell E., ed. *Living Water, Sealing Spirit: Readings on Christian Initiation*. Collegeville, Minn.: Liturgical Press, 1995.

Kavanagh, Aidan. *Confirmation: Origins and Reform*. New York: Pueblo Publishing Co., 1988.

Old, Hughes Oliphant. *The Shaping of the Reformed Baptismal Rite in the Sixteenth Century*. Grand Rapids: Wm. B. Eerdmans Publishing Co., 1992.

Stauffer, S. Anita. *On Baptismal Fonts: Ancient and Modern*. Alcuin/GROW Liturgical Study 29–30. Bramcote, Nottingham: Grove Books, 1994.

Stookey, Laurence Hull. *Baptism: Christ's Act in the Church*. Nashville: Abingdon Press, 1982.

Turner, Paul. *Confirmation: The Baby in Solomon's Court*. New York: Paulist Press, 1993.

Wasserman, Marney Ault. "Giving Thanks over the Water." *Reformed Liturgy & Music* 29, no. 2 (1995): 95–99.

Whitaker, Edward Charles. *The Baptismal Liturgy*. 2d ed. London: SPCK, 1981.

White, James F. *The Sacraments in Protestant Practice and Faith*. Nashville: Abingdon Press, 1999.

CATECHUMENATE

Dujarier, Michel. *A History of the Catechumenate*. New York: Sadlier, 1979.

Harmless, William. *Augustine and the Catechumenate*. Collegeville, Minn.: Liturgical Press, 1995.

CHRISTMAS CYCLE

Buttrick, David G. "The Christmas Cycle." *Reformed Liturgy & Music* 21, no. 3 (summer 1987): 178–80.

Erickson, Craig Douglas. "Epiphany: Christmas Finale or *Postscriptum*?" *Reformed Liturgy & Music* 22, no. 3 (summer 1988): 149–52.

Hickman, Hoyt L., Don E. Saliers, Laurence Hull Stookey, and James F. White. "From Hope to Joy: Advent and Christmas/Epiphany." *Handbook of the Christian Year*, 51–104. Nashville: Abingdon Press, 1986.

Jounel, Pierre. "The Christmas Season." In *The Liturgy and Time*, trans. Matthew J. O'Connell, 77–96. Vol. 4 of *The Church at Prayer: An Introduction to the Liturgy*. Collegeville, Minn.: Liturgical Press, 1986.

O'Gorman, Thomas J., ed. Tom Goddard (artist). *An Advent Sourcebook*. Chicago: Liturgy Training Publications, 1988.

Reformed Liturgy & Music 22, no. 3 (summer 1988). Theme: Christmas Cycle.

Simcoe, Mary Ann, ed. *A Christmas Sourcebook*. Chicago: Liturgy Training Publications, 1984

DAILY PRAYER

Anderson, Fred R. "A Case Study of Daily Prayer in a Downtown Presbyterian Church," *Reformed Liturgy & Music* 31, no. 4 (fall 1987): 224–27.

Bower, Peter C. "Morning and Evening Praise and Prayer: A Model for Congregational Use." *Reformed Liturgy & Music* 25, no. 2 (spring 1981): 94–101.

Bradshaw, Paul E.. "Cathedral vs. Monastery: The Only Alternatives for the Liturgy of the Hours?" *Time and Community*, 123–36. Washington, D.C.: Pastoral Press, 1990.

_____. *Daily Prayer in the Early Church*. Alcuin Club Collection 63. New York: Oxford University Press, 1982.

_____. "Whatever Happened to Daily Prayer?" *Worship* 64, no. 1 (January 1990): 10–23.

Butcher, Robert E. "Occasions for Daily Prayer." *Reformed Liturgy & Music* 21, no. 4 (fall 1987): 221–23.

Crichton, James D. *Christian Celebration: The Prayer of the Church*. London: Geoffrey Chapman, 1978. (Esp. Chapter 3, "An Historical Sketch of the Divine Office," 29–61.)

Davies, Horton. "Worship at Taizé: A Protestant Monastic Servant Community." *Worship* 49, no. 1 (January 1975): 23–34.

Erickson, Craig Douglas. "Reformed Theology and the Sanctoral Cycle." *Reformed Liturgy & Music* 21, no. 4 (fall 1987): 228–32.

Foley, Edward. "The Cantor in Historical Perspective." *Worship* 56, no. 3 (May 1982): 194–213.

Gallen, John, ed. *Christians at Prayer*. Notre Dame, Ind.: University of Notre Dame Press, 1977.

Gonzalez, Catherine Gunsalus. "Daily Prayer through the Centuries." *Reformed Liturgy & Music* 21, no. 4 (fall 1987): 199–201.

Grisbrooke, W. J. "A Contemporary Liturgical Problem: The Divine Office and Public Worship." *Studia Liturgica* 8 (1971–72): 129–68; 9 (1973): 3–18, 81–106.

Jungmann, Josef A. *Christian Prayer through the Centuries*. New York: Paulist Press, 1978.

Kline, C. Benton. "Individual Prayer and Corporate Prayer." *Reformed Liturgy & Music* 21, no. 4 (fall 1987): 202–4.

Old, Hughes Oliphant. "Daily Prayer." *Guides to the Reformed Tradition: Worship That Is Reformed According to Scripture*. Atlanta: John Knox Press, 1984.

_____. "Daily Prayer in the Reformed Church of Strasbourg, 1525–1530." *Worship* 52, no. 2 (March 1978): 121–38.

Saliers, Don E. "The Daily Offices as Sung Prayer." *Reformed Liturgy & Music* 21, no. 4 (fall 1987): 208–11.

Schulz-Widmar, Russell. "Hymns for Community Prayer at Morning and Evening," *Reformed Liturgy & Music* 21, no. 4 (fall 1987): 212–16.

Sloyan, Gerard S. "On Leadership in Prayer." *Worship* 73, no. 3 (May 1999): 246–303.

Stake, Donald Wilson. "Reclaiming Daily Prayer—A New Book" *Reformed Liturgy & Music* 21, no. 4 (fall 1987): 205–7.

Storey, William G. "The Liturgy of the Hours: Principles and Practice." *Worship* 46, no. 4 (July 1972): 194–203.

Taft, Robert. *The Liturgy of the Hours in East and West: The Origins of the Divine Office and Its Meaning for Today*. Collegeville, Minn.: Liturgical Press, 1986.

Task Force on Daily Prayer. "A Calendar of Commemorations." *Reformed Liturgy & Music* 21, no. 4 (fall 1987): 233–45.

Tripp, Diane Karay. "Daily Prayer in the Reformed Tradition: An Initial Survey." *Studia Liturgica* 21, no. 1 (1991): 76–107.

_____. "Daily Prayer in the Reformed Tradition: An Initial Survey (Part 2)." *Studia Liturgica* 21, no. 2 (1991): 190–219.

Winn, Albert C. "Daily Prayer in Contemporary Life." *Reformed Liturgy & Music* 21, no. 4 (fall 1987): 217–20.

EUCHARIST/LORD'S SUPPER/HOLY COMMUNION

Baptism, Eucharist, and Ministry. Faith and Order Paper, no 111. Geneva: World Council of Churches, 1982.

Bouyer, Louis. *Eucharist: Theology and Spirituality of the Eucharistic Prayer*. Translated by Charles Underhill Quinn. Notre Dame, Ind.: University of Notre Dame Press, 1968.

Crockett, William R. *Eucharist: Symbol of Transformation*. New York: Pueblo Publishing Co., 1989.

Foley, Edward. *From Age to Age: How Christians Celebrated the Eucharist*. Chicago: Liturgy Training Publications, 1991.

Gerrish, Brian A. *Grace and Gratitude: The Eucharistic Theology of John Calvin*. Minneapolis: Fortress Press, 1993.

Hellwig, Monika. *The Eucharist and the Hunger of the World*. New York: Paulist Press, 1976.

Jasper, R. C. D., and Geoffrey J. Cuming, eds. *Prayers of the Eucharist: Early and Reformed*. 3d ed., rev. and enl. New York: Oxford University Press, 1987.

McDonnell, Killian. *John Calvin, the Church, and the Eucharist*. Princeton, N.J.: Princeton University Press, 1975.

Procter-Smith, Marjorie. *In Her Own Rite*, Chapter 6. Nashville: Abingdon Press, 1990.

Reuman, John. *The Supper of the Lord: The New Testament, Ecumenical Dialogues, and Faith and Order on Eucharist*. Philadelphia: Fortress Press, 1985.

Rordorf, Willy, et al. *The Eucharist of the Early Christians*. New York: Pueblo Publishing Co., 1978.

Seasoltz, R. Kevin. *Living Bread, Saving Cup: Readings on the Eucharist*. Collegeville, Minn.: Liturgical Press, 1982.

Stookey, Laurence Hull. *Eucharist: Christ's Feast with the Church*. Nashville: Abingdon Press, 1993.

Wainwright, Geoffrey. *Eucharist and Eschatology*. London: Epworth Press, 1971.

Wasserman, Marney Ault. "The Shape of Eucharistic Thanksgiving." *Reformed Liturgy & Music* 29, no. 3 (1995): 139–45.

White, James F. *Sacraments as God's Self Giving*, Chapter 6. Nashville: Abingdon Press, 1983.

_____. *The Sacraments in Protestant Practice and Faith*. Nashville: Abingdon Press, 1999.

FUNERAL: SERVICE OF WITNESS TO THE RESURRECTION

Ariès, Philippe. *The Hour of Our Death*. New York: Alfred A. Knopf, 1981.

Rutherford, Richard. *The Death of a Christian: The Order of Christian Funerals*. Rev. Ed. Collegeville, Minn.: Liturgical Press, 1990.

HISTORY AND ESCHATOLOGY

Taft, Robert. "Historicism Revisited." In *Liturgical Time,* ed. Wiebe Vos and Geoffrey Wainwright, 97–109. Rotterdam: Liturgical Ecumenical Center Trust, 1982.

Talley, Thomas J. "History and Eschatology in the Primitive Pascha." *Worship* 47 (1973): 212–21.

HYMNAL/SUNG LITURGY

Bower, Peter C. "Singing Our Way through the Book of Common Worship (1993)." *Reformed Liturgy & Music* 27, no. 1 (1993): 37–43.

McKim, LindoJo H., ed. *The Presbyterian Hymnal Companion*. Louisville, Ky.: Westminster/John Knox Press, 1993.

LITURGICAL ARTS

Apostolos-Cappadona, Diane. *Dictionary of Christian Art*. New York: Continuum Publishing Co., 1995.

Biedermann, Hans. *Dictionary of Symbolism: Cultural Icons and the Meanings Behind Them*. Translated by James Hulbert. New York: Facts On File, 1990.

Davies, Horton, and Hugh Davies. *Sacred Art in a Secular Century*. Collegeville, Minn.: Liturgical Press, 1978.

Dillenberger, John. *A Theology of Artistic Sensibilities: The Visual Arts and the Church*. New York: Crossroad, 1986.

White, Susan J. *Art, Architecture, and Liturgical Reform*. New York: Pueblo Publishing Co., 1990.

LITURGICAL LANGUAGE

Ramshaw, Gail. *Liturgical Language: Keeping It Metaphoric, Making It Inclusive*. Collegeville, Minn.: Liturgical Press, 1996.

_____. *Reviving Sacred Speech: The Meaning of Liturgical Language*. Akron: OSL Publications, 1999.
_____. *Words That Sing*. Chicago: Liturgy Training Publications, 1992.

LITURGICAL YEAR

Adam, Adolf. *The Liturgical Year.* New York: Pueblo Publishing Co., 1981 (English translation).

Bosch, Paul. *Church Year Guide*. Minneapolis: Augsburg Publishing House, 1987.

Cobb, Peter G. "The History of the Christian Year." In *The Study of Liturgy*, ed. Cheslyn Jones, Geoffrey Wainwright, and Edward Yarnold, 403–19. New York: Oxford University Press, 1978.

Martimort, Aime Georges, Irenée Henri Dalmais, and Pierre Jounel. *The Liturgy and Time.* Translated by Matthew J. O'Connell. Vol. 4 of *The Church at Prayer: An Introduction to the Liturgy*. Collegeville, Minn.: Liturgical Press, 1986.

Reformed Liturgy & Music 25, no. 1 (winter 1991). Theme: Liturgical Calendar.

Stookey, Laurence Hull. *Calendar: Christ's Time for the Church*. Nashville: Abingdon Press, 1996.

Talley, Thomas J. *The Origins of the Liturgical Year*. New York: Pueblo Publishing Co., 1986.

Wegman, Herman A. "Festivals and Celebrations throughout the Year." In *Christian Worship in East and West: A Study Guide to Liturgical History,* translated by Gordon W. Lathrop, 25–34, 98–107, 172–77, 225, 277–85. New York: Pueblo Publishing Co., 1985.

LORD'S DAY: SUNDAY

Allen, Horace T., Jr. "Lord's Day–Lord's Supper." *Reformed Liturgy & Music* 18, no. 4 (fall 1984): 162–66.

Burkhart, John E. "The Lord's Day." In *Worship: A Searching Examination of the Liturgical Experience*, 53–70. Philadelphia: Westminster Press, 1982.

_____. "Why Sunday?" *Reformed Liturgy & Music* 18, no. 4 (fall 1984): 159–61.

Maertens, Thierry. "Sabbath and Sunday." In *A Feast in Honor of Yahweh*, 152–92. Notre Dame, Ind.: Fides Publishers, 1965.

Porter, H. Boone. *The Day of Light—The Biblical and Liturgical Meaning of Sunday*. Greenwich, Conn.: Seabury Press, 1960.

Rordorf, Willi. *Sunday: The History of the Day of Rest and Worship in the Earliest Centuries of the Christian Church*. Philadelphia: Westminster Press, 1968.

MARRIAGE

Dominian, Jack. *Marriage, Faith, and Love*. London: Darton, Longman & Todd, 1981.

Stevenson, Kenneth W. *To Join Together: The Rite of Marriage*. New York: Pueblo Publishing Co. 1987.

PASCHAL (EASTER) CYCLE

Allen, Horace T., Jr. "Celebrating the Sunday before the Holy Week According to the New Calendar." *Reformed Liturgy & Music* 11, no. 4 (fall 1977): 7–17.

_____. "Proclaiming the Pascha." *Reformed Liturgy & Music* 21, no. 4 (fall 1987): 246–47.

Baker, J. Robert, Evelyn Kaehler, and Peter Mazar, eds. Suzanne M. Novak (artist). *A Lenten Sourcebook: The Forty Days*. 2 vols. Chicago: Liturgy Training Publications, 1990.

Berger, Rupert, and Hans Hollerweger, eds. *Celebrating the Easter Vigil*. Translated by Matthew J. O'Connell. New York: Pueblo Publishing Co., 1983.

Crichton, J. D. *The Liturgy of Holy Week*. Dublin: Veritas, 1983.

Davies, J. Gordon. *Holy Week: A Short History*. Richmond: John Knox Press, 1963.

Gunstone, John. *The Feast of Pentecost*. London: Faith Press, 1967.

Hickman, Hoyt L., Don E. Saliers, Laurence Hull Stookey, and James F. White. "Passion/Palm Sunday." *Handbook of the Christian Year*, 125–52. Nashville: Abingdon Press, 1986.

_____. "Holy Thursday Evening." *Handbook of the Christian Year*, 160–70. Nashville: Abingdon Press, 1986.

_____. "Good Friday." *Handbook of the Christian Year*, 179–90. Nashville: Abingdon Press, 1986.

_____. "Proclaiming the Paschal Mystery: An Introduction to the Seasons of Lent and Easter." *Handbook of the Christian Year*, 105–10. Nashville: Abingdon Press, 1986.

Huck, Gabe. *The Three Days: Parish Prayer in the Paschal Triduum*. Chicago: Liturgy Training Publications, 1981.

Huck, Gabe, Gail Ramshaw, and Gordon Lathrop, eds. Barbara Schmich (artist). *An Easter Sourcebook: The Fifty Days*. Chicago: Liturgy Training Publications, 1988.

Huck, Gabe, and Mary Ann Simcoe, eds. *A Triduum Sourcebook*. Chicago: Liturgy Training Publications, 1983.

Maertens, Thierry. "The Feast of the First Sheaf of Wheat or The Feast of Pentecost." In *A Feast in Honor of Yahweh*, 98–151. Notre Dame, Ind.: Fides Publishers, 1965.

Reformed Liturgy & Music 24, no. 1 (winter 1990). Theme: Easter Cycle.

Schmemann, Alexander. "Introduction: Lent: Journey to Pascha." In *Great Lent*, 11–15. Tuckahoe, N.Y.: St. Vladimir's Seminary Press, 1974.

Stevenson, Kenneth. *Jerusalem Revisited: The Liturgical Meaning of Holy Week*. Washington, D.C.: Pastoral Press, 1988.

_____. "On Keeping Holy Week." *Theology* 89 (1986): 32–38.

PASTORAL LITURGIES

Association of Brethren Caregivers. *Deacons Manual for Caring Ministries*. Elgin: ABC, 1998.

Bass, Dorothy C., ed. *Practicing Our Faith: A Way of Life for a Searching People*. San Francisco: Jossey-Bass, 1997.

Wasserman, Marney. "Extended Serving of the Communion of the Church." *Call to Worship* 35, no. 1 (2001): 17–21.

PRESIDING

Adams, William Seth. *Shaped by Images: One Who Presides*. New York: Church Hymnal Corp., 1995.

Hovda, Robert W. *Strong, Loving and Wise: Presiding in Liturgy*. Collegeville, Minn.: Liturgical Press, 1976.

Kavanagh, Aidan. *Elements of Rite: A Handbook of Liturgical Style*. Collegeville, Minn.: Liturgical Press, 1966, 1990.

PSALMS/PSALTER

Brueggemann, Walter. *The Message of the Psalms: A Theological Commentary*. Minneapolis: Augsburg Publishing House, 1984.

Hopson, Hal H. *Psalm Refrains and Tones for the Common Lectionary: With Inclusive Language for God and People*. Carol Stream, Ill.: Hope Publishing Co., 1992.

Marty, Martin E. *A Cry of Absence: Reflections for the Winter of the Heart*. San Francisco: Harper & Row, 1983.

Morgan, Michael. *Psalter for Christian Worship*. Louisville, Ky.: Witherspoon Press, 1999.

Routley, Erik. *Exploring the Psalms*. Philadelphia: Westminster Press, 1975.

Troeger, Thomas H. *Rage! Reflect. Rejoice! Praying with the Psalmists*. Philadelphia: Westminster Press, 1977.

Wahl, Thomas Peter. "Praying Israel's Psalms Responsibly as Christians: An Exercise in Hermeneutic." *Worship* 54, no. 5 (September 1980): 386–96.

RITUAL

Driver, Tom F. *The Magic of Ritual: Our Need for Liberating Rites That Transform Our Lives and Other Communities*. New York: HarperSanFrancisco, 1991.

Mitchell, Leonel. *The Meaning of Ritual*. New York: Paulist Press, 1977.

SCRIPTURE READINGS IN NARRATIVE FORM

Wangerin, Walter, Jr. *The Book of God: The Bible as Novel*. Grand Rapids: Zondervan Publishing House, 1996.

_____. *The Book of God for Children*. Grand Rapids: Zondervan Publishing House, 1981.

TIME

Bouyer, Louis. "Sacred Time." In *Rite and Man*, 189–205. Notre Dame, Ind.: Notre Dame Press, 1963.

Dix, Dom Gregory. "The Sanctification of Time." In *The Shape of the Liturgy*, 303–96. London: A. & C. Black, 1945.

Hatchett, Marion J. *Sanctifying Life, Time, and Space*. New York: Seabury Press, 1976. (Read portions relevant to the "sanctification of time.")

Johnson, Lawrence J., ed. *The Church Gives Thanks and Remembers: Essays on the Liturgical Year*. Collegeville, Minn.: Liturgical Press, 1984.

Micks, Marianne H. "Rhythm in the Calendar." In *The Future Present: The Phenomenon of Christian Worship*, 35–53. New York: Seabury Press, 1970.

Appendix C

Study Guide for the *Book of Common Worship* (1993)

> *"In order that all the People should take their part in the Public Worship of God, it is most earnestly recommended that, in those churches which choose to make use of the following Orders and Forms of Service, every member of the Congregation should be supplied with a copy of this Book; and, also, that the directions which precede each part of the different services should be studied beforehand both by Minister and People, so that confusion or uncertainty in the conduct of Worship may be avoided."*
>
> *(BCW 1906 vii)*

This study guide is intended for worship committees, musicians, pastors, educators, church officers, adult education groups, and all others who wish to study the *Book of Common Worship*. The two main purposes of this study guide are:

1. To introduce people to the arrangement and contents of the *Book of Common Worship*
2. To engender conversation concerning the use of the BCW in the life of congregations

Contents

1. Introduction

This edition of the *Book of Common Worship* may be new to you, but in this century it is the fifth edition. Previous editions were published in 1906, 1932, 1946, and 1970.

> *Question:* What is a book of common worship? Any hunches? Anybody have any prior experience with a previous book of common worship? (HINT: *The Worshipbook*, published in 1970, is also a book of common worship, but was called by a different name.) So, again, what do you think a book of common worship is?

Now, sit closely together, especially if you have only one copy of the *Book of Common Worship* (1993) to share among you. For the next gathering, you are encouraged to bring your own copy to these study sessions. (In fact, next to the Bible and the Directory for Worship, the most important book to us is a book of common worship (see p. xii). You may want to brood over that statement throughout the study.)

Our point of entry to this *Book of Common Worship* will be page 504, which displays an outline (an order) for a service. So, open your book to that page only, scan it, and respond to the following:

1. What looks familiar? Be specific.

2. What looks *un*familiar? Be specific.

NOTE: This outline presents *two* basic patterns for Evening Prayer. One starts in the upper left, and the other starts in the upper right, but both merge at the psalm, and then follow the same order from there. In effect, the structure of the first one-third of the service has two possibilities, and the structure of the final two-thirds of the service is always the same.

Suppose you are responsible for leading the Prayers of Thanksgiving and Intercession for an evening prayer service. What to do? No need to panic. (*You know what to do, but you may need some help* locating *what you are to do.*) Several *models* of Prayers of Thanksgiving and Intercession are provided on BCW 516–520. So, flip to those pages and peruse them.

If today were Monday, then ordinarily you would select the prayers beginning on the bottom of page 517. Then you can be creative:

1. You could pray the texts as printed.
2. You could edit the texts by adding, subtracting, or altering (for example,

for bidding prayers, invite personalizing by naming persons or people, events, or issues).
3. You decide how best to appropriate the texts.

Some occasions on which you or your congregation could use this centuries-old tradition of evening prayer might be midweek evening services, meetings of boards or governing bodies, choir rehearsals, youth groups, potluck supper-programs, retreats, at home, while traveling, or (*add your own*).

Who could lead such evening prayer?

"Leadership in worship is assigned to those with gifts, training, and authorization." (W-3.1003)

"It is appropriate to encourage members and ordained officers with such abilities to assist in leading worship." (W-1.4003)

Browse through BCW 504–523 only, and see what else you can find or learn. The BCW offers *models*, carefully prepared *theological models*. They are not to be dispensed with easily; nevertheless, they are *models* to be expanded or abbreviated or even used as is. To most effectively use the BCW, planners of worship will need to learn to do three fundamental things with this book: how to (1) appropriate; (2) appropriate; (3) appropriate.

2. Praying for Others

Often, we are tempted to approach our prayers of intercession as a time to pray for our own needs, a time to focus our own "self" entirely on God. But in the intercessions (by definition), we are called to offer God the needs and concerns of others. "Supplications, prayers, intercessions, and thanksgivings should be made for everyone" (1 Tim. 2:1). Such prayer for others enlarges our worldview, expands our horizons to see others around us. "Commending one another in their prayers," John Calvin wrote, "serves to foster love among them, while they, as it were, share one another's needs and bear their burdens naturally" (*Institutes* 3.20.24).

As we pray for the needs of our sisters and brothers in Christ in our particular community of faith and in the whole church around God's world, our union with the body of Christ broadens and deepens. The BCW structures this both geographically (Morning Prayer, BCW 496– 499) and by various traditions of the church (Evening Prayer, BCW 518–520).

Examine the prayers of thanksgiving and intercession for Morning Prayer (BCW 496–499). Note that the final intercession on each day is for Christians according to **geography** (space): church of Jesus Christ in every land . . . , in Europe . . . , in Africa . . . , in Asia and the Middle East . . . , in the Pacific region . . . , in Latin America . . . , in North America . . . .

Scan the prayers of thanksgiving and intercession for Evening Prayer (BCW 518–520). Note that each day's last intercession is for Christians according to **church tradition**: Roman Catholics . . . , Orthodox and Coptic . . . , Episcopal and Methodist . . . , Baptist, Disciples of Christ, and other free churches . . . , Reformed, Presbyterian, and Lutheran churches . . . , ecumenical councils and church agencies . . . .

> *Question:* What could be some possible *effects* of praying regularly for sisters and brothers in Christ in all places and according to all traditions?

Time is also a crucial aspect, expressed by BCW's emphases on various days of the week:

> Friday centers on the crucifixion, Christ's sacrifice on the cross, Christ's self-giving love (read BCW 499, 519; midday prayer, BCW 548).
> Saturday is reflective of Holy Saturday (read BCW 499, 520).
> Sunday focuses on resurrection (read BCW 496, 517).

Daily cycles are integrated with the annual cycles of time marked by the church: distinctive texts are provided for Advent, Christmas–Epiphany, Lent, and Easter–Pentecost (BCW 510–511).

Our prayers can never be merely private, individualized, much less self-centered pleadings, for we are connected in our praying with others in the church and in the whole world. Note the range of **individual** and **social situations** (see BCW 496–499, and BCW 518–520):

- occupations: health care, entertainers, teachers, ministries of comfort, night shift workers
- people holding positions of authority: political leaders, lawmakers
- the outcast, refugees, persecuted, victims of violence, the hungry, poor, imprisoned
- separated families, enemies, students, unemployed
- sickness, nursing homes, dying, bereaved

Any other patterns you can discern?

These prayers extend us beyond ourselves and our known world. We are bound with all people of the world *and* the whole of God's creation as we offer intercession for those in authority and those in need. Our faith must be lived in the world of power and conflicting passions, joy and anguish, abundance and poverty. The BCW strives to free us to pray for others in all places, all times, and in all circumstances. In what ways does it succeed?

3. Relationship between the Directory for Worship and a BCW

1. The constitutional document ordering the worship of the Presbyterian Church (U.S.A.) is the D __ __ __ __ __ __ ry for Worship, which describes the theology that underlies Reformed worship, sets standards, and presents norms for the conduct of worship in the life of the church. (DW Preface)

2. True or False: A Directory for Worship has the authority of church law. (BCW 2; DW Preface)

3. True or False: Since 1970 every candidate for ordination as a minister of the Word and Sacrament in the Presbyterian Church (U.S.A.) *must* pass an exam on the Directory. (see G-14.0310d)

4. The Directory for Worship is mandatory for Presbyterians and, therefore, our worship (a. must, b. could, c. when convenient, d. when in our self-interest) be directed by the Directory.

5. *Actual orders for worship, collections of prayers, texts, and rituals* are contained within the Presbyterian Church's *Book of C __ __ __ __ __ Worship* (BCW) and *must* be in harmony with the "legal, theological, and pastoral mandates" of the Directory. (BCW 2)

6. What does a church risk by using an out-of-date edition of the BCW, or no BCW?

7. What will result when a congregation's orders for worship conflict with the Presbyterian Church's "legal, theological, and pastoral book" on worship (the Directory for Worship)?

8. True or False: To encourage the participation of its people in worship, the session should (*"strongly recommended"*) provide all church members with education in Christian worship. (W-1.4007)

9. The session (a. shall/must, b. should, c. may choose to) provide for the *regular* study of the Directory for Worship in the education of church officers. (W-1.4007; G-10.0102)

10. True or False: The session has the responsibility in a particular church to provide for the worship of the people of God *in keeping with the principles in the Directory for Worship*. (G-10.0102)

11. Those responsible for worship are to be guided by the Holy Spirit speaking in (*Check correct ones*):

    A. Scripture
    B. the historic experience of the church universal
    C. the Reformed tradition
    D. the *Book of Confessions*
    E. the needs and particular circumstances of the worshiping community

F. provisions of the Form of Government

G. provisions of the Directory for Worship (W-1.4001)

12. "To ensure that the guiding principles [in #11 above] are being followed, those responsible on behalf of presbytery for the oversight and review of the ministry of particular worshiping congregations should [*"strongly recommended"*] discuss with those sessions the

[a] quality of worship,

[b] the standards governing it, and

[c] the fruit it is bearing in the life of God's people as they proclaim the gospel and communicate its joy and justice." (W-1.4002)

Question: How often has such discussion occurred between your session and presbytery?

Question: The results?

13. Which, if any, of the above answers surprised you? Why?

14. If you sense any disparity between your congregation's corporate worship and the Directory for Worship, what do you intend to do about it?

4. A Story and a Meal

For nearly 2,000 years, Christ's church has employed two foundational services:

1. Service for the L __ __ d's D __ __ (the day of resurrection; Sunday)
2. Service for Daily Prayer (for example, morning prayer, evening prayer)

Open your BCW to page 46, which displays an outline (an order) for a Service for the Lord's Day. Scan only that page, and respond to the following:

1. What looks familiar about the order? Be specific.

2. What looks *un*familiar about the order? Be specific.

Observe that the service has not one but two centers: Word and Sacrament. They are two parts of *one action*. The two centers of the one action are the story and the Meal. The **one action of Word and Sacrament** is introduced by the rite of "Gathering," and concluded by the rite of "Sending."

- **Gathering**: Call to Worship, Prayer of the Day, Hymn, Confession and Pardon, and so on.
- **Word**: Prayer for Illumination, Readings, Sermon, Affirmation of Faith, Prayers of the People

and

- **Sacrament**: The Eucharist
- **Sending**: Hymn, Charge, Blessing

Far more than a Presbyterian order for worship, this Lord's Day service of Word and Sacrament has been the Christian church's basic order for worship for nearly 2,000 years. (*Now that's tradition!*) Far more than an order for worship that conforms to a Presbyterian Directory for Worship, this order for worship conforms to the one, holy, catholic, and apostolic church of all times and places into which each of us has been baptized in the name of the triune God. (*Now that's heritage!*)

1. "**Word and Sacrament have an integral relationship**" (W-2.4008): the story *and* the Meal comprise the *one action* of our corporate worship on the Lord's Day. "From its beginning, the Christian community has gathered on the first day of the week to **hear the scriptures read and proclaimed,** *and* to **celebrate the Lord's Supper**" (BCW 34). The normative structure for the

Lord's Day service is the *one action* of Word *and* Sacrament. *Hearing* the Word of God *leads to doing* the Word. Conversely, the Lord's Supper "shows" the end of the sermon. Preaching the Word of God leads to celebrating at the Lord's Table where the community receives the sustaining presence of Christ and pledges their obedience anew (W-1.3033). From Word to Table is *one action*. To what extent do you think most congregations experience *the story and the meal*—Word and Sacrament—as comprising the *one action* of the Lord's Day service? How so or why not?

2. On the Lord's Day, **we celebrate Christ's resurrection**, looking ahead to a final "fulfillment." "Gathered on the Lord's Day, [we] **celebrate the age to come**, which was revealed in the risen Christ, by remembering the words and deeds of Jesus and celebrating the presence of the risen Christ among [us] in the Word proclaimed and in the bread and cup of the Eucharist" (BCW 34).

> "In this meal the church celebrates the joyful feast of the people of God, and anticipates the great banquet and marriage supper of the Lamb." (W-2.4007)

In the **Eucharist**, the church joyfully, ecstatically, thankfully celebrates the promised presence of the Lord, for the **Lord's Supper** is the actualization of **Holy Communion** with the Lord and with one another. In what ways has your experience of celebrating the Lord's Supper been a foretaste of the great banquet, the age to come? If not, then what do you perceive to be some obstacles to experiencing the church's definitive celebration and experience of the resurrection of the Lord?

3. "It is appropriate to celebrate the Lord's Supper as often as each Lord's Day. It is to be [i.e., *'must be'*] celebrated regularly and frequently enough to be recognized as *integral* to the Service for the Lord's Day" (W-2.4009, emphasis added). "Integral" means essential, indispensable, or necessary. Does your congregation celebrate the Lord's Supper "regularly and frequently enough to be recognized as *integral* to the Service for the Lord's Day"? If not, then how do you address this issue?

4. Is this the time? In what ways is the BCW (1993) our opportunity to recover our tradition and link with other Christians of all times and places?

NOTE: Turn to BCW 33–45 for an explication of the whole Service for the Lord's Day.

5. Offering Our Thanks before the Meal

Following the invitation to the Lord's Table, all stand for the Great Thanks-giving or Eucharistic Prayer. All Great Prayers of Thanksgiving follow the same basic structure. The prayer—addressed to the first person of the Trinity—takes a Trinitarian form in which:

- the first part thankfully attests to the work of the first person of the Trinity,
- the second thankfully recalls the saving work of Christ, and
- the third emphasizes the empowering and sustaining mission of the Holy Spirit.

Sound familiar?

Turn to BCW 929, and look at **the opening section** of the Great Thanks-giving for a funeral (*which may also be used for the All Saints' Day service*). Since at least the early third century, eucharistic prayers have opened with this **dialogue** between the presiding minister and the congregation. (*Tradition!*) This dialogue calls the community to acknowledge God as God, *and* to thank God for all that God has done for it. Some congregations *sing* the Sursum Corda ("Lift up your hearts"). Could it also serve as an introduction to other table prayers of thanks?

1. The "preface" or "pre-sanctus" ("it is truly right and . . ."), begins with **thankful praise of God for**:

- God's work in creation and providence and in covenant history
- the witness of the prophets
- God's constant love in spite of human failure
- and the ultimate gift of sending Jesus Christ among us

For what specifically does this first section on BCW 929 ("It is truly right and our greatest joy . . .") offer thanks?

This first section then peaks (BCW 930, top) in its affirmation that the praise of this community on earth is joined to the praise of the church triumphant—the **saints** who have preceded us in death. It then concludes—as does each of the three major sections of the prayer—with an acclamation sung by the congrega-tion, here an acclamation of praise: the Sanctus ("Holy, holy, holy").

2. **A thankful recalling of God's salvific acts accomplished for us in Jesus Christ**: his birth, life, and ministry; his death and resurrection; his

present intercession for us, the promise of his coming again, and the gift of the Sacrament. This section reaches its apex (BCW 931, middle) in the words called the *anamnesis-oblation* ("remembrance-offering"). Our *remembrance*, our experience, of Christ present in this Sacrament, becomes the occasion for *offering* ourselves as a living and holy sacrifice dedicated to serving God's reign in the world. This section then concludes with a (sung) congregational acclamation, here a remembrance—"the memorial acclamation." Note the variety of acclamations on BCW 931–932, each with its own "cue line" so the congregation knows which response to use.

3. **The empowering and sustaining** (BCW 932) **work of the Holy Spirit** is called upon to:

- make the breaking of the bread and sharing of the cup a communion of the body and blood of Christ
- unite us with the living Christ *and* with all who are baptized in his name—the **saints**
- nourish us with the body of Christ so we may mature into the fullness of Christ
- keep us faithful as Christ's body, representing Christ in ministry in the world

This section builds to its crescendo ("until the promised day . . .") with an anticipation of the messianic banquet when we will feast with all God's **saints** in the joy of God's eternal realm, and then moves to a Trinitarian doxology ("Through Christ . . ."), which summarizes the work of the triune God. It concludes with a (sung) acclamation of assent ("Amen") to all that has occurred prior to our thanks.

Finally, the whole community is invited to pray the **Lord's Prayer**—the summary of all prayer—which has concluded the church's eucharistic prayer for centuries. This is how Christians have always offered their thanks before the meal. Can we offer any less?

6. Advent Hope for the Second Coming

1. The church's most traditional prayer—offering our thanks before the meal—is commonly known as "The Great Tha _ _ _ _ _ _ ing" or "Eu _ _ a _ i _ _ ic Prayer." Remember, *all* **eucharistic prayers** are Trinitarian in form, and are addressed to the (a. first?, b. second?, or c. third?) person of the Trinity. Look at the model on BCW 168–171 and note the basis for "Advent Hope for the Second Coming" that appears in each major section of the prayer:

The first part (BCW 168) *thankfully praises the work of the first person of the Trinity*:

> you spoke to us through prophets who look for that day
> when justice shall triumph
> and peace shall reign.

The second part (BCW 169) *thankfully recalls the saving work of Christ*, who was sent:

> to satisfy the longings of your people for a Savior,
> to bring freedom to the captives of sin,
> to establish justice for the oppressed.

The third part (BCW 171) *emphasizes the empowering and sustaining mission of the Holy Spirit* to strengthen us:

> to bring good news to the poor
> and lift blind eyes to sight,
> to loose the chains that bind.

> *Question:* In what ways do the three major sections of this eucharistic prayer interweave with one another?

2. Turn to BCW 165–166. Review the biblical images used during the lighting of the Advent candles. Why are these **biblical texts** lifted up during Advent? HINT: Reread the above eucharistic prayer.

3. On BCW 166–167 is the Litany for Advent—**O Antiphons**. You know these from singing "O Come, O Come, Emmanuel" (PH 9)—a ninth-century text set to the twelfth-century tune VENI EMMANUEL. Traditionally, a different stanza was sung each day during evening prayer from December 17 through 23. Note particularly the plea at the end of each stanza: "Come . . ."

Question: What do this eucharistic prayer, the biblical images used during the lighting of the Advent candles, and the O Antiphons share in common? In other words, why are these biblical texts accented during Advent?

HERE'S A LITTLE HELP: In liturgies, ever since the first century, Christians have exclaimed *Maranatha*! Often translated as "Our Lord, come!", *maranatha* is a Greek transliteration from the Aramaic in 1 Corinthians 16:22, and usually printed in Greek New Testaments as one continuous word—*maranatha*. Aramaic, however, splits *maranatha* into two words, offering diverging translations:

1. *marana tha* is an imperative form oriented toward the future, translated as: "**Come, our Lord!**"
2. *maran atha* is the perfect form expressing a completed event in the past, translated as: "**Our Lord has come**."

These paradoxical meanings are crucial for our Advent liturgies of *the expectation of the coming of the Christ*. In Advent *we expectantly wait for the One who has already come*. We are longing for the beating of swords into plowshares, *yet* we rejoice that the Prince of Peace has come. We are anticipating the land where lions and lambs live in harmony, *yet* we acclaim the child who has led us into the promised land. We are yearning for the barren deserts of our inner cities to flourish, *yet* we laud the desert Rose that has bloomed. Christ has come! Christ is risen! Christ will come again! In Advent, we are living between the first and the second coming of the Lord. How shall we wait for the One who has already come?

- We are anticipating the promised justice of God's New World, yet we celebrate God's raising of the "righteous branch" who rules with justice and righteousness.
- We are hoping for the restoration of the afflicted, the tormented, and the grieving, yet we delight in healing that has come in Christ.

The dialectical tension of *maranatha*—straddling us between memory and hope—strengthens our Advent liturgies. *Maranatha*! Come, Lord Jesus! *Maranatha*! Our Lord has come!

7. Christmas Joy at the Coming of the Savior

From the beginning of time *God's saving purpose has been at work*. God has raised up the seed of Abraham, including Moses and Gideon and Samson and John the Baptist. Through all these generations, God has been faithfully at work raising this person and that person. For what purpose? *To bring us* the Davidic Messiah, the Messianic King, the Son of the Most High who will ascend the throne of David. Through all of human history, God has been bringing forth Jesus Christ, "who will save his people from their sins" (Matt. 1:21).

Now through the birth of the Savior, God's purpose will be fulfilled. God has acted to save God's people. The Christ child is born for the saving of the world. Therefore, we shout for joy! Sing a new song! Rejoice! Dance!

What Christmas pays homage to is that the ultimate fulfillment of God's saving purpose commences with the birth of Jesus—the Messianic Savior. **God's only Son is born among us in order to save the world is the message of Christmas**. Note how the Bible's "sending formula" ("God sent Christ in order to . . .") reveals Christ's saving purpose:

I must proclaim the good news of the kingdom of God to the other cities also; for *I was sent* for this purpose. (Luke 4:43)

For *God* did not *send the Son* into the world to condemn the world, but in order that the world might be saved through him. (John 3:17)

In this is love, not that we loved God but that *God loved us and sent his Son* to be the atoning sacrifice for our sins. (1 John 4:10)

And we have seen and do testify that *the Father has sent his Son* as the Savior of the world. (1 John 4:14)

Underline, circle, or restate in your own words "Christ's saving purpose" in each of the above biblical texts.

Moreover, the sending formula (including its salvific purpose) is combined with reference to the birth of Christ:

But when the fullness of time had come, *God sent his Son*, born of a woman, born under the law, in order to redeem those who were under the law, so that we might receive adoption as children. (Gal. 4:4–5).

Christmas celebrates far more than a birthday; Christmas proclaims the advent of the messianic salvation. God in flesh (Immanuel) has come "to save us from our sins."

In the Christmas "propers" (BCW 178f.), find at least four examples of the sending formula—*the purpose of sending Christ to dwell among us*. To save you some time, here are four clues:

- Prayer of Adoration (BCW 178)
- Great Thanksgiving (eucharistic prayer) (BCW 180)
- Prayer of Thanksgiving 2 (BCW 184)
- Prayer of the Day (Year ABC) (BCW 185)

With the birth of Christ, Christmas, the beginning of the ultimate fulfillment of God's saving purpose commences. A decisive new phase in the history of *God's hunger for human companions* has begun.

Joy to the world! the Lord is come. Joy to the world! the Savior reigns.

(Isaac Watts, 1719)

8. Epiphany: Showing Forth the True Light to the Whole World

Throughout the twelve days of Christmas we extol the advent of Jesus, the messianic Savior, for:

> The grace of God has appeared (*epephane*) bringing salvation to all, . . . the manifestation (*epephaneia*) of the glory of our great God and Savior, Jesus Christ. (Titus 2:11, 13)

During Christmas, we celebrate the "coming down" of the true Light *into* the world, and on Epiphany the "showing forth" of the true Light *to* the world.

The dominant natural symbol of the Epiphany is **light** (*a day for candles, candles, and more candles*). Skim BCW 191–197, which contain the Epiphany "propers," and observe how the "Epiphany vocabulary" is used both denotatively (dictionary meaning) and connotatively (figurative meaning):

> nouns: light, glory, brightness, star, splendor, radiance, dawn, (*Add your own*)
> verbs: shine, rising, dawned, illumine, (*Add your own*)

Now examine how the above Epiphany vocabulary is incorporated into the twin themes of Epiphany:

1. *Manifestation to all, or radical inclusiveness of the incarnation.* Jesus is the light to *all* nations, races, classes, peoples—the *whole* world. Epiphany's revelation of Christ to the "Gentile world" (symbolized in the magi story, Matt. 2:1–12) meant God's covenant with Israel was now extended to people of *every* place and time. *All* are invited to the gathering of the New Israel in the New Jerusalem. Jesus is the light to *all* people. The hope and promise of Immanuel's (God with us) advent shine in Christ's coming into the world for *all* people, to the ends of the earth.

2. *Show and tell, or "outreach dimensions" of the incarnation.* Epiphany *not only discloses* the Savior to the world but also calls us to *show forth* Christ, to be *witnesses* of God's true Light. The timeless mystery of the incarnation, God in flesh, sends us forth to *show and tell* about Christ as God's gift of grace and salvation for *all* persons. "Go therefore and *make* disciples of *all* nations" (Matt. 28:19a). The spiritual charges us: "Go, *tell* it on the mountain" (PH 29).

These two themes of Epiphany shimmer in the texts for the Prayer of the Day, Litany for Epiphany, Prayer of Confession, and Prayer of Thanksgiving. For example:

> Guide the nations of the earth by your light,
> that the whole world may see your glory. (BCW 192, #2)

let your gospel shine in every place
where the Word of life is not yet received. (BCW 192, bottom)

extend your church to every place.
Make it a place of welcome for people of every race and tongue. (BCW 193, top)

God of all nations (BCW 197, bottom)

Now look for more examples, especially use of figurative language, in the eucharistic prayer (Great Thanksgiving) for Epiphany (BCW 194–197).

Christmas and Epiphany rejoice in Jesus' cross-shaped advent, descending and spreading among us. Christmas joy is marked by our celebration of the improbability of the nativity moment: because new possibilities and hopes are given to us by the sheer grace of God, we rejoice. On Epiphany, the "coming down" of the Savior is manifested to the world. "Go, *tell* it on the mountain."

9. The First Day of Our Lenten Trek to the Cross: Ash Wednesday

On Ash Wednesday, we commence our Lenten journey of "forty days and forty nights" to the cross. A painful irony of our Lenten journey, however, is that its four starting blocks are also its stumbling blocks. The primary barriers to our completing the Lenten journey are ironically grounded in the initial Ash Wednesday steps of our pilgrimage to the cross.

1. Time to face our mortality, individually and corporately. To acknowledge our finiteness. To remember we are but temporary creatures poised to collapse back into dust from which we came and to which we shall return. To face the repugnant reality of death, the end, the final obliteration of who we are. To admit we live in a dust and ashes world, in a finite, broken world. In what ways do your Ash Wednesday/Lenten liturgies help you face your mortality?

2. Time to turn around, change directions, repent. Our Lenten journey is one of *metanoia* (turning around)—changing directions from our self-serving lives toward the self-giving way of the cross. This entails confessing our sins of striving for self-fulfillment, self-sufficiency, self-assertion, self-autonomy, and turning to seek the self-giving life in Christ via the way of the cross. In what ways do your Ash Wednesday/Lenten liturgies help you confess your sin and turn around ("repent")?

3. Time to surrender, to give up one's "self," to die. Unless we are willing to die to our old (selfish) selves, we cannot be raised to new life with Christ. The church's peculiar Lenten claim is that in dying we live. The way of the cross, the way to Easter, is through death of "self." As with Paul, we must "die every day" (1 Cor. 15:31)—parting with our self-preoccupations. New life requires a daily dying of self—surrendering the old life, letting go of the present order—so we may embrace the new humanity. In what ways do your Ash Wednesday/Lenten liturgies help you to "die every day"?

4. Time to bear the cross, which will be most difficult if not repulsive, for humans instinctively do anything possible to avoid bearing the cross. In our triumphalist culture, hell-bent on being number one, achieving self-sufficient independence, *cross-bearing* is especially an unacceptable goal. Bear the cross, however, of self-giving and self-sacrifice. In what ways do your Ash Wednesday/Lenten liturgies help you bear the cross?

For many traditions, these four starting blocks of our Lenten journey are symbolized through the imposition of ashes—**bearing a cross of ashes** on one's forehead on the first day of Lent—Ash Wednesday. (*Can you imagine a palmless Palm Sunday, or an ashless Ash Wednesday?*) The ashes represent **the dust and broken debris of our lives** as well as **the reality that each of**

us will die—will cease breathing, thinking, and feeling. Seeing the ashes on someone else's forehead is a sign to you—a mirror image of your human self and **a reminder of your mortality**, your finite creatureliness. Haunting words repeated during the imposition of ashes: "You are dust, and to dust you shall return" (Gen. 3:19) will echo in your ears for "forty days and forty nights."

Trusting in the "accomplished fact" of Christ's resurrection, however, we listen for the Word of God in the time-honored stories of the church's Lenten journey. We follow Jesus into the wilderness, resist temptation, fast, and proceed "on the way" to Jerusalem, and the cross.

The challenge of the liturgy for Ash Wednesday and the subsequent "forty days and forty nights" of Lent is to resist the temptation to stumble over these four starting blocks that direct us to resurrected life in Christ. Turn to BCW 221–234, and ponder these texts meditatively, open-mindedly, searchingly. The Lenten "way of the cross" to resurrected life in Christ will be easy to discern but difficult to undertake. So, look for these four starting blocks in the liturgies of Ash Wednesday; then employ them as guideposts rather than allowing them to become stumbling blocks that detour you. None of these four we may *want* to do, but we are *called* to do in the name of Christ.

10. The Easter Vigil

The early church's "annual calendar" began each year with the celebration of P _ sch_ (Easter). *Pascha* is the English transliteration of both the Greek and Hebrew words for "Passover," the central festival for Jews. Each year, Jews annually retell, in the context of a communal meal, the exodus story about God redeeming them from bondage. The Haggadah (narrative story) for the Seder (order of service) at Pesach (Passover) is an all-encompassing, identity-shaping, direction-giving story of how God liberates from slavery. By telling their children year after year the story of the exodus—affliction, suffering, sorrow, and struggle—Jews articulate an alternative world that forms the heart of their people. The more they relive the story, the more it becomes a part of their present and future lives.

Without the exodus story there is no people called Israel.

Likewise, the Easter Vigil shapes the people called Christians. Each year, on the annual celebration of the death and resurrection of Christ, the early Christians appropriated *Pascha* (Passover) because it signified the great deliverance accomplished in the Lord's new Passover. This annual liturgy of liberation (from sin, fear, self-centeredness, death, [*Add your own*]) for Christians is the Easter (Paschal) Vigil. The great saving acts of the Lord not only recorded in Scripture but read, contemplated, proclaimed, and lived over and over again provide a reality that lies at the heart of Christ's church. Open to BCW 296, which displays an outline of the Easter Vigil. Observe the shape of the Vigil, particularly, the four services that comprise the Vigil.

1. Light: As the principal service of the year, the Paschal (Easter) Vigil celebrates the promise of new life, of forgiveness of sins, and of death swallowed up in victory. Christ's passing through darkness to light is symbolized in the lighting of the fire and the paschal candle, followed by the singing of the *Exsultet* (the hymn in praise of the redemption). Examine the Service of Light (BCW 297–303). What rituals or symbols do you recall or could you anticipate during this part of the Vigil?

2. Word: On the final night of our Lenten journey, we pause in vigil at which time we remember stories about who we have been and are now becoming. As the community of faith, we recount our centuries-long pilgrimage culminating in the reaffirmation of baptismal promises. The Easter Vigil is akin to sitting around a campfire while listening to stories of generations past and future. Browse through the traditional stories told in the Service of Readings (BCW 304–309). What do you recollect or project about any of these stories as they were told or could be told during Easter Vigils?

On this night of nights, stories are recalled—of creation, of Israel passing through the waters from oppression to liberation, of God preparing the world for the coming of Christ, and of Christ's bursting the bonds of death and rising victorious from the grave.

3. Water: On this night of nights, new converts to the faith (in Paul's words),

> who have been baptized into Christ Jesus were baptized into his death. Therefore, we have been buried with Christ by baptism into death, so that, just as Christ was raised from the dead by the glory of the Father, so we too might walk in newness of life. (Rom. 6:3–4)

Turn to BCW 464–471, and scan the Reaffirmation of the Baptismal Covenant for a Congregation, which is traditionally used during the Easter Vigil. (NOTE: If the Sacrament of Baptism is celebrated, then you would *not* use the "Reaffirmation . . ." since such *reaffirmation always occurs* during the celebration of the Sacrament of Baptism. But, you knew that, right?)

4. Bread and Wine: As the concluding act of the Paschal (Easter) Vigil, the community of faith gathers at the table of the Lord to celebrate the Lord's Supper. Pascha is the central event, the time of transformation, becoming resurrected people, God's new people. Pascha transforms us, making us new people, which is why it is the principal service of the year.

> *Question:* Reread the opening paragraph about Jews annually retelling their identity-shaping story. To be a Jew is to retell the Haggadah. In what ways do we (continue to) reclaim the ancient tradition of passing on to our children the gift of the identity-shaping Easter Vigil that it may become part of their bloodstream as Christians?

11. Day of Pentecost

A key to the empowering and sustaining work of the Holy Spirit celebrated on this day is disclosed in the verbs throughout the texts. For example:

Litany for Pentecost: A (BCW 340) **Litany for Pentecost: C** (BCW 342)

breathed life into creation	**teach** us to value the highest gifts
inspired prophets	**show** us all things in the light of eternity
gave voice to Jesus' disciples	**guide** us along the straight and narrow path to . . .
created us children of God	**strengthen** us against every evil spirit and interest
gave gifts of the Spirit	**stir up** our minds and hearts

List some other empowering and sustaining verbs in "the propers" for Pentecost (BCW 338—347):

The predominant images employed throughout the Pentecostal texts are two in nature:

1. *Invisible forces of wind or breath.* The gift of the Holy Spirit is "unseen," as the wind. The Old Testament calls it *ruach YHWH*, "the wind or breath of God" (cf. John 3:8). The Spirit is the "unseenness of God" working among us. The invisible Holy Spirit works unseen among us to re-create the goodness of creation, and to conform us to Christ (for example, Prayer of Thanksgiving, BCW 347).
2. *The unrestrained power of fire*, signified by verbs such as ignite, enflame, empower, kindle, blaze, energize. The people of God are set on fire as witnesses to the crucified and risen Christ (for example, Prayer of the Day 3, BCW 339, or Prayer of Confession, BCW 343).

Scan the Litany for Pentecost: B (BCW 341), locating the images of fire and wind, breath and flames—the primary natural symbols of Pentecost.

What this *ruach* will do according to Joel 2:28–29 is to *open* everybody to God's future. People young and old will dream and will have visions of hope; they will be able to *turn loose* of the way things are now arranged, because God is establishing a whole new economy of creation. The Holy Spirit *breaks us out* of our preoccupation with ourselves and *frees us* to serve neighbors, *loosens* our grasp on possessions, and *sets us free* to love people. *New creation* is what Joel is talking about. Pentecost is new creation.

Newness may be a free gift of God, but it comes at a staggering cost: *breaking with* the status quo of our world. The dilemma for all of us, as with Christians in all times and places, is that we are enmeshed in our socioeconomic, political order, yet the biblical texts require that we *disengage*. A conversation that the Pentecost spirit strives to ignite among us is, Where are the points of disengagement from the present order so that we may welcome the new age? Allow the Spirit to open you to embracing biblical images and metaphors sprinkled throughout the propers for Pentecost. For example, the second part of the eucharistic prayer (BCW 344, bottom), which thankfully recalls the saving work of Christ, evokes a similar faithful response on our part, yes?

The same Spirit that prompted Jesus to preach the good news is the same Spirit that exhorted Christians throughout the ages to preach the gospel. The same Spirit that empowered Jesus to love enemies is the same Spirit that enabled Christians throughout the ages to love their antagonists. What makes possible the church's witness to the resurrection of Christ is the Spirit of God.

Without the gift of the Spirit, Christ's church shrivels up and withers away, and we are left with only our broken selves. A spirit-filled community of faith opens eyes to needs in the world and sees its mission as God's new people. The Day of Pentecost climactically closes the Great Fifty Days of Easter by celebrating the gift of the Spirit to the body of Christ—the church.

12. The Sacrament of Baptism (Part I)

Open BCW 402, the Outline of the Service for the Lord's Day. Note in the service the sequenced location of the Sacrament of Baptism. This placement of the Sacrament of Baptism *after* the proclamation of the Word is because (*Circle two of the following*):

1. It allows sufficient time to tidy up the candidate for baptism during the sermon.
2. Baptism fits nicely in the middle of the service, between two hymns.
3. This is a misprint: Baptism should be completed within the first ten minutes of the service (*especially so that fidgety, crying babies may then be removed from the sanctuary*).
4. Hearing the Word of God evokes faith responses such as a request for baptism.
5. Baptism is a response to hearing the Word of God proclaimed.

Note also the seven-act movement from Presentation (of the Candidate) to The Peace.

The First Three Actions of the Sacrament of Baptism

1. The **Presentation** commences with recalling the scriptural warrant for baptism recorded in the Great Commission (Matt. 28:18–20) *and* "one or more" New Testament texts (BCW 403–404). These have served, over the centuries, as foundational texts for the church's understanding of baptism.

SUGGESTION: When (a committee of) the session meets with a candidate for baptism or the parents presenting a child for baptism, the session is to instruct and discuss the meaning and responsibilities of baptism (W-2.3012). Often, one is unsure who experiences more anxiety before the meeting: the candidate for baptism *or* the session members. Fear not, now you know where to go for five biblical texts that will provide you cornerstones for the meeting. Read all five, study them, ponder them, brood over them, pray about them, and you will be well prepared.

"*An elder presents each candidate for baptism,*" (BCW 405) because this

A. provides an elder something to do in the church other than attend meetings, *or*
B. derives from the session's responsibility in the Reformed tradition to ensure that the sacraments are rightly administered.

Question: May ministers of the Word and Sacrament baptize someone on their own authority? *Anyone who gets this wrong must memorize W-2.3011 for public recitation.*

2. The **Profession of Faith** (BCW 406–410) consists of two actions: (a) renunciation (BCW 407) *and* (b) profession (BCW 408). The principle invoked here is that anyone desiring to *turn to* a new way of life, must first renounce (reject, repudiate) the old way. For instance, people who engage in the January 1 ritual of New Year's resolutions both renounce old ways and profess new commitments. They *turn from* an old way and *turn to* a new way of life. Likewise, baptismal candidates *turn from* ("renounce") the lordship of sin and *turn to* ("profess") the lordship of Jesus Christ and thereby join with the whole congregation in confessing the faith of the church catholic ("universal"), embodied in the ancient baptismal creed: the Apostles' Creed (BCW 408–409).

3. The prayer of **Thanksgiving Over the Water** (BCW 410) functions both:

A. *Experientially*: the common element of water is saturated with symbolic meanings that are both
death-dealing, such as floods, drowning, and (*Add your own*) *and* life-giving, such as amniotic fluids, baths, liquid refreshments, and (*Add your own*).

B. *Theologically*: water evokes for us many stories of the faith journey of the people of God: the creation, the flood, exodus, entrance into the promised land, Jesus' baptism, our dying and rising with Christ. Find these experiential *and* theological images of water within the prayer. (*This prayer also provides sessions with more foundational material for their meeting with candidates for baptism.*)

Now that you know how crucial *water* is to our faith, you can understand why the rubric on BCW 410 says, "*Water* is *poured visibly and audibly into the font.*" Water *must be* seen *and* heard. Why?

13. The Sacrament of Baptism (Part II)

The Concluding Four Actions of the Sacrament of Baptism

Center stage now are gestures, motions, actions, and words.

4. The *central action* of the Sacrament—**The Baptism** (BCW 413)—consists of water *and* words. Note the rubric that permits *three* methods of applying the water, which is in accordance with the Directory for Worship: "The water used for Baptism . . . shall be applied by pouring, sprinkling, or immersion. By whatever mode, the water should be applied visibly and generously" (W-3.3605). Which mode prevails in the life of your congregation? Describe the ways the water is applied visibly and generously.

Another rubric directs the minister to call: "*each candidate by his or her Christian (given) name or names only*" (BCW 413), *not* the family name. In the act of baptizing, *only* the Christian (given) name is used. In the life-and-death-event of baptism, we are given new identity and new relationships. We are made new, reborn, incorporated into *the larger family of the people of God*. Parents present their sons or daughters for baptism, and receive them back as sisters and brothers in Christ. Baptismal identity in Christ is indeed radically life-changing. Baptism is a calling and a new identity as sister or brother in Christ into which we grow for the rest of our life.

To what extent do we (a) truly recognize *every* member of the church—the body of Christ—as a sister or brother in Christ, and (b) call each other by our Christian (given) name rather than family name, much less any cultural title such as Mr., Mrs., Ms., Dr., Rev., or Honorable?

5. The **Laying On of Hands** (BCW 413) includes both action *and* words (*that offer a prayer for the gifts of the Holy Spirit*). Note the following *permissive* rubric: "*The minister* may *mark the sign of a cross on the forehead of each of the newly baptized. . . . Oil prepared for this purpose* may *be used.*"

A. The **cross** is the most common sign to identify Christians, reminding us of the victory Christ won over evil, especially death. So, to indicate that one belongs to Christ and is enlisted in his service, a cross has been traced on the forehead of most Christians at the time of their baptism, since at least A.D. 100. In baptism, you receive a permanent mark of Christ's ownership—the cross. Is "signing the cross" currently practiced in your congregation? Why or why not? In what ways does/could this action serve as a powerful symbol that God has claimed the baptizand as part of the people of God?

B. The use of **oil** has some historical and theological antecedents. Most congregations use scented oil in signing the cross, because its fragrance lingers as a source of remembrance. When the oil is then employed at times such as commissioning, ordination, or sickness, the oil activates the sense of smell, recalling one's baptism and its good news concerning to whom one ultimately belongs.

6. The **Welcome** (BCW 414). The body of Christ is *not* a "blood family" gathering, but a "water and word family" gathering. Into this one, holy, catholic, apostolic church of all times and places, baptism incorporates baptizands, and reorders relationships between them and congregations of all times and places. Together, all now share a common identity and calling as sisters and brothers in Christ. In addition to words spoken (BCW 414), what customs does your congregation have of welcoming the newly baptized into Christ's church?

7. **The Peace** (BCW 415) is *not* social chitchat with a neighbor, but a profound act of reconciliation. "In sharing the peace, we express the reconciliation, unity, and love that come only from God" (BCW 36), which is why the early church extended the kiss of peace, as one of their first acts, to the newly baptized.

Baptism is a calling and a new identity into which to grow, for the rest of your life. Ordinarily, we adults have concentrated our energies on educating the young regarding the "meaning" of the sacraments. For instance, conducting classes for children and parents prior to the celebration of the Lord's Supper intend to prepare participants for proper "understanding" (theology) of the Sacrament, or explanation of the mystery.

> *Question:* In what ways have we underestimated the power of (the action of) the Sacrament of Baptism to shape faith, even "teach" the faith?

> *Question:* To what extent do we experience and reaffirm our baptism during each celebration of the Sacrament of Baptism? Do we only see a child being baptized? Do we merely observe somebody receiving something? Do we simply photograph for a family album? Are we distant, separate, apart from the action, or are we part of the action?

> *Question:* In what ways, during the celebration of the Sacrament of Baptism, do we find ourselves inexplicably (mysteriously?) reexperiencing (reaffirming?) our baptism so that we know and say (confess?), "Yes, I/we, too, am forgiven, accepted, justified by faith, marked as one of God's children"? In what ways is the Sacrament celebrated by the whole community of faith?

> *Question:* In what ways does our practice of the Sacrament of Baptism match and mismatch our theology of baptism?

14. The Psalms: The Church's Songbook and Prayer Book

List some psalms, by number if possible, that you can recall. You might be surprised at how many you know. 1._____ 2._____ 3._____ 4._____ 5._____ 6._____ 7._____.

Calvin called the Psalms the "anatomy of the soul." Psalm-singing has always been characteristic of Reformed worship. Over the centuries, in fact, a commonly used nickname for Calvinists/Presbyterians has been "psalm-singers." Perhaps some of you were nurtured in the faith by psalm-singing, or have heard church members from past generations speak of singing the psalms in public worship or family devotions.

The reason psalm-singing was considered an essential part of the prayer of the church is that the Reformers understood psalms as prayers of the Holy Spirit.

Since prayer is not human response to God, but the work of the Holy Spirit in the body of Christ to the glory of God, then worshipers could both

> *learn how to pray* from the psalms and
> *use* the psalms as their prayers.

For Calvinists/Presbyterians, psalm-singing/psalm-praying has always been an essential element in public worship or daily prayer.

Psalms are for singing, and psalms are for praying. The Psalms are both **the church's songbook** and **the church's prayer book**.

The BCW states, "It is preferable that the psalms be sung" (BCW 599), and the Directory for Worship agrees: "Psalms were created to be sung by the faithful as their response to God. . . . Their full power comes to expression when they are sung" (W-2.1003).

Some various ways of Singing the Psalms are described on BCW 599, and Instructions for Singing Psalm Tones are found on BCW 600. Two indispensable resources for psalm-singing are:

1. *The Presbyterian Hymnal: Hymns, Psalms, and Spiritual Songs* (Louisville, Ky.: Westminster/John Knox Press, 1990); or *El Himnario Presbiteriano* (Louisville, Ky.: Westminster John Knox Press, 1999); or *Come, Let Us Worship: The Korean-English Presbyterian Hymnal and Service Book* (Louisville, Ky.: Geneva Press, 2001)
2. *The Psalter: Psalms and Canticles for Singing* (Louisville, Ky.: Westminster/John Knox Press, 1993)

There are 150 psalms from which to choose. But, which psalm(s) do you select for situations of sickness, grief, praise, rage, fear, vengeance, or compassion?

Let's begin at the beginning. Turn to BCW 611 and examine Psalm 1. As with most poetry, pay close attention to the word pictures—the images portrayed—as well as the emotions expressed.

1. What do you see? (Circle the images.)

2. What feelings are evoked?

3. What is the essence of this sung prayer?

This is the best-known Torah ("Way of Life") Psalm. Some call it a teaching psalm. Its placement at the beginning, as a prologue, sets the tone for all 150 psalms. In sum, Psalm 1 announces: Our

(a. primary?, or b. secondary?) agenda is to conduct
(a. all?, b. some?, or c. none?) of life in accordance with
(a. God's?, or b. humanity's?) purposes and ordering of the creation.

"Happy are those [whose]. . . delight is in the law [Torah] of the LORD" (Ps. 1:1–2).

Question: What might be an appropriate occasion or event to sing/pray Psalm 1? Sickness? Funeral? Marriage Service? Evening Prayer? Morning Prayer? Baptism?
Question: Any particular seasons or days of the liturgical year that might seem especially appropriate to sing/pray Psalm 1? Epiphany? Lent? Ordinary Time?

Psalms are for singing, and psalms are for praying. The Psalms are both **the church's songbook and prayer book**. This BCW provides us an opportunity to recover our tradition as psalm-singers.

15. The Prayers of the People: "Praying of the Scriptures"

Open your BCW to page 46. Observe that within the section titled "The Word" are many elements—hymn, affirmation of faith, prayers, and so forth. Each of these elements is located within this section of the service because each relates to the Word. In fact, each of these elements *derive* from the Word. Thus, a fundamental principle of Christian worship, especially in the Reformed tradition:

> Just as the sermon derives from the Scripture readings for the day, so also the hymns, affirmations, and prayers derive from the Scripture readings for the day. Each element within the section "The Word" is, therefore, evoked by the Scriptures read and preached. Conversely, the Word of God proclaimed summons forth song, affirmations of faith, and prayers. (*Pause here, and make sure that everyone understands this fundamental principle of Christian worship*).

So, having heard the Word of God, we are now anxious to live the Word, to sing it, to pray it, to do it. In the (intercessory) prayers of the people, we do begin to do the Word.

Question: How shall we ensure that our prayers derive from the Word of God proclaimed?

A helpful section is titled "Prayers for Various Occasions" (BCW 785–837). Turn to that section. Here the BCW offers some *models* for the "Prayers of the People." The question for us is, Which of these models might be evoked by the reading and preaching of the Word of God for the day? In short, how to select from this collection?

1. Suppose that you heard Deuteronomy 18:15–20 read and preached. In this text Moses authorizes a series of leadership roles—judges, kings, priests, and prophets—to guide and guard Israel when it comes into the land, so the community of faith may maintain a faithful course as YHWH's people. Thus, the prophets are called to be speakers of God's own Word (v. 17), and they are warned (v. 20) to stick to witnessing to the covenant, commands, and promises of God's Word, and to resist temptation to tone down the Word, which is to compromise YHWH. If you heard that biblical text read and preached, would it faithfully evoke the following prayers for:

> courage in Christ's mission (BCW 807, #34)?
> ministers of the Word and Sacrament (BCW 808, #39)?
> teachers in the church (BCW 810, #45)?
> others?

2. Imagine that you heard Isaiah 40:21–31 read and preached. In this text Israel is in exile (weighed down, boxed in, dead-ended) and, therefore, perceives itself as abandoned by God (v. 27). This text, however, recalls all of God's glorious splendor and power as the creator and giver of life, forming and shaping the heavens, which exist only through God's enormous power. Moreover, God is tireless, never faint or weak, never lacking in energy or vitality. This tireless God gives life to a tired creation, providing hope for Israel in its dismay. If you heard that biblical text read and preached, would it faithfully evoke the following prayers for:

> creation (BCW 799, #14)?
> nature (BCW 802, #20)?
> the proclamation of the Gospel (BCW 803, #24)?
> the oppressed (BCW 834, #114)?
> others?

(COMMENT: *Pray these prayers enough, and you will find yourself using them not simply "as is," but modifying them, or even writing your own prayers based on these models.*)

Only as we are formed by the Word of God, do we know how to pray, and the Spirit guides us. Remember what Paul wrote to the Romans: "We do not know how to pray as we ought, but that very Spirit intercedes with sighs too deep for words" (8:26b). Listen, listen, listen each Sunday for prayers of the people evoked by the reading and preaching of the Word of God, for what we Reformed Christians call a praying of the Scriptures.

Further, we believe that the proclamation of Scripture in reading and preaching has the power to change us, to transform us—the people of God. Having heard the Word of God, we do grow in the faith. Thus, we are more prepared to pray these texts, these stories, however unfamiliar or strange the new life in Christ to which they call us.

16. Holy Communion with Those Unable to Attend Public Worship

BCW 965–1030 offer "Pastoral Liturgies" for worship settings such as:

- Ministry with the Sick (BCW 967–993)
- A Service of Repentance and Forgiveness (BCW 1023–1024)
- Services for Wholeness (BCW 1005–1022)
- Prayer at the Time of Death (BCW 1025–1030)

You will want to browse through these services now or later.

BCW 994–1002 provide a service of "Holy Communion with Those Unable to Attend Public Worship." People who are homebound, hospitalized, or reside in a nursing home offer a congregation an opportunity to take the church's worship to those unable to attend. Name *some other circumstances* in which your congregation could serve others in the name of Christ by extending the church's ministry to those isolated from public worship.

Note that the structure of the service (BCW 994) is the same as that of "The Service for the Lord's Day": a story and a meal—Word and Sacrament—preceded by a gathering, and concluded by a sending.

- **Gathering**: Call to Worship, and Confession and Pardon
- **Word**: Scripture Reading and Brief Sermon

  and

- **Sacrament**: Holy Communion
- **Sending**: Blessing

Why do you think this structure is the normative one for this service?

Note also the introductory words on BCW 995 whose tone we have encountered throughout the BCW: *"the service may be expanded or abbreviated."* Yes! To most effectively use the BCW, planners of worship need to learn how to (1) appropriate; (2) appropriate; (3) appropriate.

Observe the opening rubric: *"The minister shall* [i.e., *"must"*] *be accompanied by one or more members of the congregation authorized by the session to represent the church."* Why *must* members accompany clergy for this service?

Even though such a celebration may involve only a few members, nevertheless it is not to be understood as a private ceremony or devotional exercise, but as *an act of the whole Church*, which shall be represented not only by the minister or the one authorized by presbytery to administer the Sacrament, but also by one or more members of the congregation authorized by the session *to represent the church*. (W-2.4010)

The physical, mental, and emotional abilities of the person(s) with whom you are worshiping, as well as the senses of hearing, touch, sight, smell, and taste will play crucial roles in determining *what* and *how* to appropriate the various elements of this service. For instance, note the images and the mood of the five biblical texts suggested for the Call to Worship (BCW 995–996). Given the life of your congregation, which of these texts might be most suitable for some of the situations in which you envision celebrating this service?

You will face choices also with other elements: Declaration of Forgiveness (BCW 997), Lord's Prayer (BCW 1000), Communion (BCW 1001), and Blessing (BCW 1002), which you can examine now.

For example, concerning the Declaration of Forgiveness (BCW 997), which of the two suggested forms do you think would be best suited to a particular situation: homebound, hospitalized, nursing home, other?

The Prayer after Communion (BCW 1002) concludes with the words:

> So strengthen us in your service
> that our daily living may show our thanks,
> through Jesus Christ our Lord.

Question: What are some specific ways in which those who are homebound, hospitalized, or residing in nursing homes may show their thanks in their daily living?

Question: What are some specific ways in which those who plan and lead this service may show their thanks in their daily living?

17. The Inseparable Link between Story and Time

It all began with the proclamation of the Word, which shaped the faith of the church. Throughout the church's history, hearing the **stories** of what God had done in the past (time), freed people to believe what God promised to do in the future (time) and, therefore, to live faithfully in the present (time). "Faith comes from what is heard," writes Paul (Rom. 10:17). By continually hearing the stories of God's faithfulness in the past *and* God's promises for the future, people know to whom they belong and to what they are called in the present. God's unfinished story today inevitably moves toward God's promised future (time). From the very beginning, **story** and **time** have been inseparable.

Open to BCW 1031, to the section titled "Calendar and Lectionaries" (or we could say "Time and Stories"). (*You will find it beneficial to review periodically the background information on BCW 1033–1034, regarding lectionary use.*) On BCW 1034, note the first sentence of the third paragraph: "The purpose of a lectionary is to provide for a disciplined use of the *whole range of Scripture* in the church's worship" (emphasis added). To ensure the hearing of the *full scope of the Scriptures*, the church has engaged itself in the discipline of lectionaries, which are rooted in our Jewish ancestors who utilized lectionaries for centuries before the time of Christ's church.

In the BCW (1993), you will find two lectionaries:
1. Sundays and Festivals (BCW 1035–1048)
2. Daily Lectionary (BCW 1049–1095) for morning, midday, evening, or night (praise and) prayer

The "Sundays and Festivals" lectionary (BCW 1035ff.) lists three annual cycles, labeled:

> **Year A** (the year of Matthew)
> **Year B** (the year of Mark)
> **Year C** (the year of Luke)

Each "Year" begins with the "First Sunday of Advent" (BCW 1035), and concludes with "Christ the King" (BCW 1048). Try this simple exercise: In the table of readings, find (a) next Sunday, and (b) the year we are in. Voila! You have found the readings (stories) for the day (or time of year).

That Jewish and Christian worship have instinctively linked **story** and **time** is no surprise. For instance, without the exodus **story** at the **time** of each year's Passover, there is no people called Israel. Likewise, the stories told during the time of each year's Easter Vigil shapes the people called Christians.

From the very beginning, **story** and **time** have been inseparable. Skim through the "Sundays and Festivals" lectionary in recalling the following stories and times:

> A **story** heralding the birth of Christ is told at the **time** of:

> At the **time** of proclaiming the Epiphany of the Lord (BCW 1036), a **story** recalled is:

> A Gospel **story** told on the transfiguration of the Lord (BCW 1038) is:

> On the First Sunday of our "forty days and forty nights" of Lent (BCW 1039), as we make our trek to the cross, a Gospel **story** read is:

> A **story** narrated on Passion/Palm Sunday (BCW 1040) is:

> The **story** of the resurrection of Christ is told at the **time** of:

> The empowering **story** of the gift of the Spirit is proclaimed on the Day of:

> As these stories and many, many more are retold year after year, they shape the lives of Christians. In what ways do you now better understand how throughout your lifelong baptismal pilgrimage you have been experiencing the inseparability of **time** and **story**?

Notes

THE SERVICE FOR THE LORD'S DAY

1. Gordon Lathrop, "Worship in the Twenty-first Century: Contextually Relevant and Catholic," *Currents in Theology and Mission*, August 1999, 294.

2. Aidan Kavanagh, *Elements of Rite: A Handbook of Liturgical Style* (Collegeville, Minn.: Liturgical Press, 1966, 1990), 67.

3. Calvini Opera, *Corpus Reformatorum* 43:538.

4. C. S. Lewis, *Letters to Malcolm: Chiefly on Prayer* (New York: Harcourt, Brace & World, 1964), 6.

5. Frank C. Senn, *Christian Liturgy: Catholic and Evangelical* (Minneapolis: Fortress Press, 1997), 73.

6. Bard Thompson, *Liturgies of the Western Church* (Philadelphia: Fortress Press, 1961), 9.

7. Ibid., 8.

8. Calvin, *Institutes* 3.4.11.

9. Hughes Oliphant Old, *The Shaping of the Reformed Baptismal Rite in the Sixteenth Century* (Grand Rapids: Wm. B. Eerdmans Publishing Co., 1992), 244.

10. *Service for the Lord's Day and Lectionary for the Christian Year* (Philadelphia: Westminster Press, 1964), 21.

11. *The Worshipbook: Services* (Philadelphia: Westminster Press, 1970), 33.

12. Gordon Lathrop, "Preaching in the Dialogue of Worship with Culture," in *Baptism, Rites of Passage, and Culture*, ed. Anita Stauffer (Geneva: Lutheran World Federation Studies, 1999), 250.

13. Kavanagh, *Elements of Rite*, 68.

14. Lewis, *Letters to Malcolm*, 12.

15. Laurence Hull Stookey, *Eucharist: Christ's Feast with the Church* (Nashville: Abingdon Press, 1993), 28.

16. John Calvin, *Institutes of the Christian Religion* 4.17.11; Library of Christian Classics, ed. John T. McNeill, trans. Ford Lewis Battles (Philadelphia: Westminster Press, 1960), 2:1373.

17. William D. Maxwell, *The Liturgical Portions of the Genevan Service Book* (London: Faith Press, 1965), 49–50.

18. William Seth Adams, *Shaped by Images: One Who Presides* (New York: Church Hymnal Corp., 1995), 55.

19. Thompson, *Liturgies of the Western Church*, 208.

20. Kavanagh, *Elements of Rite,* 13.

21. Ibid., 51.

22. Sylvia Dunstan, *Sing! A New Creation* (Grand Rapids: Calvin Institute for Christian Worship).

23. Adams, *Shaped by Images*, 27.

24. C. Kirk Hadaway, "Denominational Defection: Recent Research on Disaffiliation in America," in *The Mainstream Protestant "Decline": The Presbyterian Pattern*, ed. Milton J. Coalter, John M. Mulder, and Louis B. Weeks (Louisville, Ky.: Westminster/John Knox Press, 1990).

25. Kavanagh, *Elements of Rite*, 10.

26. Lewis, *Letters to Malcolm,* 4.

RESOURCES FOR THE LITURGICAL YEAR

1. Peter C. Bower, *Handbook for the Common Lectionary* (Philadelphia: Westminster Press, 1987), 19–21.

2. Thomas J. Talley, *The Origins of the Liturgical Year* (New York: Pueblo Publishing Co., 1986), 231–38.

3. Peter C. Bower, "Editorial Introduction," *Reformed Liturgy & Music* 16, no. 4 (fall 1982): 146.

4. *Didache* 14:1; *Early Christian Fathers*, trans. Cyril C. Richardson, Library of Christian Classics, vol. 1 (Philadelphia: Westminster Press, 1963), 178.

5. *First Apology of Justin, the Martyr*, 67; Richardson, *Early Christian Fathers*, 287.

6. John E. Burkhart, "Why Sunday?" *Reformed Liturgy & Music* 18, no. 4 (fall 1984): 160–61.

7. Horace T. Allen Jr., "Lord's Day–Lord's Supper," *Reformed Liturgy & Music* 18, no. 4 (fall 1984): 165.

8. *The Epistle of Barnabas*, 15; *Early Christian Writings: The Apostolic Fathers* (Baltimore: Penguin Books, 1968), 215.

9. Talley, *Origins of the Liturgical Year*, 85–103.

10. From the hymn, "God Rest You Merry, Gentlemen," an eighteenth-century Christmas carol.

11. Adolf Adam, *The Liturgical Year* (New York: Pueblo Publishing Co., 1981), 144–46.

12. These were examined closely by Bernard Botte in "Maranatha," *Noël, Epiphanie: retour du Christ, Lex Orandi* 40 (Paris, 1967), 25–42.

13. Since the beginning of the ultimate fulfillment of God's saving purpose commences with the birth of Christ, it is easy to understand why Christmas should be considered as the beginning of the liturgical year. Advent actually is the open-ended waiting, hoping, and pleading for the coming of Christ in glory which occurs in the last days (the eschaton). As such, Advent is the rightful way to end the liturgical year.

14. From the nineteenth-century carol "Away in a Manger."

15. Adrian Nocent, *The Liturgical Year, Volume One: Advent, Christmas, Epiphany* (Collegeville, Minn.: Liturgical Press, 1977), 163.

16. Other biblical or apocryphal allusions include the following: *O Wisdom*: Prov. 8:22–31; Sirach 24:3, 5; Wis. 8:1; Isa. 40:3–5. *O Adonai:* Exod. 3:1–15; 6:2, 3, 12, 13; 20:1–17; 3:2; 6:6. *O Root:* Isa. 11:1–10; Rom. 15:12; Isa. 5:15; Hab. 2:3; Heb. 10:37. *O Key:* Isa. 22:22 (cf. Rev. 3:7); Isa. 42:7; Ps. 107:14; Luke 1:79. *O Radiant Dawn:* Zech. 6:12; Luke 1:78; 2 Peter 1:19; Heb. 1:3; Mal. 4:2; Isa. 9:2; Luke 1:78, 79. *O Ruler:* Hag. 2:8; Pss. 2, 72,

110; Gen. 49:10; 2 Sam. 7; Isa. 28:16; Eph. 2:14; Gen. 2:7. *O Immanuel:* Isa. 7:14; 8:8; 33:22; Gen. 49:10.

17. The Episcopal hymnal, *The Hymnal 1982* (New York: Church Hymnal Corp., 1985), provides a stanza for each of the seven antiphons. Singing this hymn in the traditional sequence of the antiphons will require reordering the stanzas as they appear in the hymnal as follows: 2, 4, 5, 6, 7, 3, 1.

18. Easter Sunday is always the Sunday after the first full moon that occurs on or after the spring equinox on March 21. Therefore, Easter Sunday can occur no earlier than March 22 or later than April 25.

19. "Baptismal Homilies," in Edward Yarnold, *The Awe-Inspiring Rites of Initiations: Baptismal Homilies of the Fourth Century* (London: St. Paul's Publications, 1971).

20. William H. Willimon, "Letting Go Down Here," *The Christian Century*, March 5, 1986, 231–32.

21. Brian Heldge, in *A Triduum Sourcebook*, ed. Gabe Huck and Mary Ann Simcoe, (Chicago: Liturgy Training Publications, 1983), 77, 78.

22. Talley, *Origins of the Liturgical Year*, 57–61.

23. The Scots Confession in *The Constitution of the Presbyterian Church* (*U.S.A.*), Part I, *Book of Confessions* (Louisville, Ky.: The General Assembly of the Presbyterian Church (U.S.A.)), 3.13.

24. Jacques Berthier, *Music from Taizé,* vol. 1, vocal and instrumental editions (Chicago: G.I.A. Publications, 1978, 1980, 1981), vocal edition, p. 28, instrumental edition, p. 27.

25. See note above concerning Passion Narrative arrangements for choral reading, p. 133.

26. An alternative text for the Solemn Reproaches may be found in the Taizé Community's daily prayer book *Praise God* (New York: Oxford University Press, 1977), 151–52.

27. A table of readings used in various traditions and periods of history is provided in Huck and Simcoe, *A Triduum Sourcebook*, 80–81. (Order from Liturgy Training Publications, 1800 North Hermitage Avenue, Chicago, IL 60622–1101.)

28. The text may be found in Gabe Huck, *The Three Days: Parish Prayer in the Paschal Triduum* (Chicago: Liturgy Training Publications, 1981), 80, 81.

29. Consultation on Common Texts, *A Celebration of Baptism* (Nashville: Abingdon Press, 1988).

30. Joseph D. Small, III, "Practical Aids to Lectionary Use," *Reformed Liturgy & Music* 22, no. 1 (winter 1988): 37.

31. Harold M. Daniels, "Recent Changes in the Presbyterian Celebration of the Liturgical Year," *Reformed Liturgy & Music* 16, no. 4 (fall 1982): 155, 156.

BAPTISM AND THE REAFFIRMATION OF THE BAPTISMAL COVENANT

1. Harold M. Daniels, "Baptism," in *Worship in the Community of Faith: Liturgical Studies from the Perspective of the Contemporary Reformed Tradition*, ed. Harold Daniels (Louisville, Ky.: The Joint Office of Worship, 1982), 87.

DAILY PRAYER

1. John Calvin, Preface to *Commentary on the Psalms*.

2. For a thorough discussion of the history of daily prayer, see Robert Taft, *The Liturgy of the Hours in East and West: The Origins of the Divine Office and Its Meaning for Today* (Collegeville, Minn.: Liturgical Press, 1986). Other helpful accounts of the background of daily prayer are included in Marion J. Hatchett, *Sanctifying Life, Time, and Space* (New York:

Seabury Press, 1976); and idem, *Commentary on the American Prayer Book* (New York: Seabury Press, 1980), 89–153.

3. Hughes Oliphant Old, *Praying with the Bible* (Philadelphia: Geneva Press, 1980), 78.

4. Hughes Oliphant Old, "Daily Prayer in the Reformed Church of Strasbourg, 1525–1530," *Worship*, 52, no. 2 (March 1978): 121–38.

5. Old, *Praying with the Bible*, 126–27.

6. Ford Lewis Battles, ed., *The Piety of John Calvin* (Grand Rapids: Baker Book House, 1978), 137ff.

7. Calvin, *Institutes* 3.20.32.

8. Millar, ed., *The Scottish Collects from the Scottish Metrical Psalter of 1595* (Edinburgh: Church of Scotland Committee on Publications, n.d.), 3–8.

9. Ibid.

10. Two useful resources for such readings are John W. Doberstein, ed., *Minister's Prayer Book* (Philadelphia: Fortress Press, 1986), and Reuben P. Job and Norman Shawchuck, *A Guide to Prayer for Ministers and Other Servants* (Nashville: The Upper Room, 1983).

11. Philip H. Pfatteicher and Carlos R. Messerli, *Manual on the Liturgy: Lutheran Book of Worship* (Minneapolis: Augsburg Publishing House, 1979), 300.

12. *Lutheran Book of Worship* (Minneapolis: Augsburg Publishing House, 1978), 168–73.

13. *Lutheran Book of Worship: Ministers Desk Edition* (Minneapolis: Augsburg Publishing House, 1978), 86–91.

14. Familiarity with other resources for daily prayer will prove most helpful. For example, *Christian Prayer: The Liturgy of the Hours* (New York: Catholic Book Publishing Co., 1976); *Praise God: Common Prayer at Taizé* (New York, Oxford University Press, 1977); *Lutheran Book of Worship: Ministers Desk Edition* (Minneapolis: Augsburg Publishing House, 1978); *The Book of Common Prayer* (New York: Seabury Press, 1977). A useful edition of the Orthodox daily office is *A Prayerbook* (Cambridge, N.Y.: New Skete, 1976). Another daily office in the Eastern tradition is *Byzantine Daily Worship* (Allendale, N.J.: Alelua Press, 1969).

15. See *The Psalter: Psalms and Canticles for Singing* (Louisville, Ky.: Westminster/John Knox Press, 1993); *Psalter Hymnal* (Grand Rapids: Christian Reformed Church Publications, 1987); Hal H. Hopson, *Psalm Refrains and Tones for the Common Lectionary: With Inclusive Language for God and People* (Carol Stream, Ill.: Hope Publishing Co., 1992).

16. Calvin, *Institutes* 3.20.50.

17. A variety of incense resins and self-starting charcoal may be purchased from church supply houses.

18. *A Manual of Eastern Orthodox Prayers* (Crestwood, N.Y.: St. Vladimir's Seminary Press, 1983), 11.

THE PSALMS

1. Massey H. Shepherd Jr., *The Psalms in Christian Worship: A Practical Guide* (Minneapolis: Augsburg Publishing House, 1976), provides a helpful overview of the history of the use of psalms in Jewish and Christian worship.

2. Harold M. Daniels is to be credited for noting this potential confusion as well as its remedy.

3. John Folkening, *Handbells in the Liturgical Service* (St. Louis: Concordia Publishing House, 1984).

4. Psalmody among the Reformed on the Continent consisted of each psalm having its

own tune composed specifically for the particular psalm. In contrast, the Reformed in Scotland used the same tune for a number of psalms.

PRAYERS FOR VARIOUS OCCASIONS

1. Frank C. Senn, *Christian Liturgy: Catholic and Evangelical* (Minneapolis: Fortress Press, 1997), 279.

PASTORAL LITURGIES

1. Dorothy C. Bass, ed., *Practicing Our Faith: A Way of Life for a Searching People* (San Francisco: Jossey-Bass Publishers, 1997), 149.

2. Ibid.

3. Office of Theology and Worship, "A Service of Extended Communion," *Call to Worship* 35, no. 1 (2001): 22–23. Used by permission.

Acknowledgments

(BCW 1099–1106)

Sources

The liturgical texts and music in the *Book of Common Worship* have been gathered from many sources, some old and some new. As is the case with every piece of liturgical material in the *Book of Common Worship*, each has been identified with a small red number in brackets. The number provides a clue to its origin, using the section of the book titled "Acknowledgments" (BCW 1099–1106). For example, the first prayer, "For Peace" (BCW 795), identified with the red number 669 in brackets, is an altered version of one found in *The Book of Common Prayer*. One researching the prayer can find #669 in a list on BCW 1104. The search, however, is not always easy, because it is necessary to look under titles of sources.

Other prayers have been identified on the page where the prayer appears. For example, the second prayer for peace (BCW 795) comes from Brother Roger of Taizé. Others with similar on-page identifications indicate more general sources: "A Prayer of the Chippewa," (BCW 796, #6) or "A Prayer from Zaire" (BCW 797, #9). Some of the more interesting are a prayer based on text in the writings of Fyodor Dostoyevsky, the Russian novelist (BCW 802, #21); twentieth-century Japanese Christian Toyohiko Kagawa (BCW 807, #34); Reformation-era Lutheran Philip Melanchthon (BCW 809, #41); and a prayer for the nation by Presbyterian President Woodrow Wilson (BCW 816, #59). Another Presbyterian worthy is pastor and hymn writer Henry van Dyke (BCW 832, #107), who chaired the committee that produced the 1906 and 1932 *Books of Common Worship*. He also wrote many prayers in those editions of the *Book of Common Worship*, and also was elected once as a Moderator of the General Assembly. It is not surprising to find a prayer of Martin Luther King Jr. for social justice (BCW 819, #69). There are also prayers by Catholics from before and after the Reformation in the persons of Augustine

338

(BCW 828, #95); Teresa of Lisieux (BCW 828, #96); Thomas à Kempis (BCW 829, #97); Thomas Aquinas (BCW 829, #99); Ambrose of Milan (BCW 830, #103); and Mother Teresa (BCW 835, #116).

The definitive source of acknowledgments for these texts can be located in Harold M. Daniels, *To God Alone Be Glory: The Story and Sources of the Book of Common Worship* (Louisville, Ky.: Geneva Press, 2003), 171–257.

Index